Geometry to Go

A Mathematics Handbook

GREAT SOURCE
EDUCATION GROUP
A Houghton Mifflin Company

Acknowledgments

We gratefully acknowledge the following teachers and mathematics supervisors who helped make *Geometry to Go* a reality.

Dave Bradley
Mathematics Specialist
Granite School District
Salt Lake City, UT

Lauren L. Darling
Building Mathematics
  Facilitator
Beaverton School District
Beaverton, OR

Robert S. Fair
District Mathematics
  Coordinator
Cherry Creek School
  District
Greenwood Village, CO

Jo Anne Gerules
Mathematics Teacher
  (Retired)
Evanston Township High
  School, District 202
Evanston, IL

Julia Hernandez
Mathematics Teacher
La Mirada High School
La Mirada, CA

Leslie E. Hyatt
Middle School
  Mathematics
  Coordinator
District 8
Bronx, NY

Stephen J. Paterwic
Mathematics Teacher
High School of Science
  and Technology
Springfield, MA

Kelly A. Pelletier
Senior Administrator,
  Instructional Support
Orange County Public
  Schools
Orlando, FL

Patsy Westover
Mathematics Teacher
Booker High School
Sarasota, FL

Senior Consultant:
Laurie Boswell
Mathematics Teacher
Profile School District
Bethlehem, NH

Senior Consultant:
Dr. Marsha W. Lilly
Secondary Mathematics
  Coordinator
Alief ISD
Alief, TX

Senior Consultant:
Gloria Robinson
Adjunct Mathematics
  Instructor
University of New
  Hampshire
Manchester, NH

Writing: Edward Manfre; Marlys Mahajan, Ann Petroni-McMullen, Linda Van Hook Hall, Kane Publishing Services, Inc.
Editorial: Carol DeBold, Justine Dunn, Susan Rogalski; Amy Goodale, Randy Green, Marlys Mahajan, Kane Publishing Services, Inc.
Design Management: Richard Spencer
Production Management: Sandra Easton
Design and Production: Bill SMITH STUDIO
Marketing: Lisa Bingen
Illustration credits: see end of index

Printed in the United States of America

International Standard Book Number: [0-669-48130-0] (hardcover)
1 2 3 4 5 6 7 8 9 0 RRDC 05 04 03 02 01

International Standard Book Number: [0-669-48129-7] (softcover)
1 2 3 4 5 6 7 8 9 0 RRDC 07 06 05 04 03 02 01

Table of Contents

Measurement `168`

Similarity `212`

Congruence `255`

Transformations `273`

Circles `297`

Solids `320`

Problem Solving `339`

Non-Euclidean Geometry `363`

Almanac `369`

Yellow Pages `425`

Index `483`

How This Book Is Organized

Geometry to Go is a reference book. This means you're not ex-pected to read it cover to cover. Instead you'll want to keep it handy for those times when you're not clear about a math topic and need someplace to look up definitions, procedures, explana-tions, and rules.

Because this is a reference book and because there may be more than one entry on a page, we've given each topic an item number (003). When you are looking for an item, look for the numbered tab.

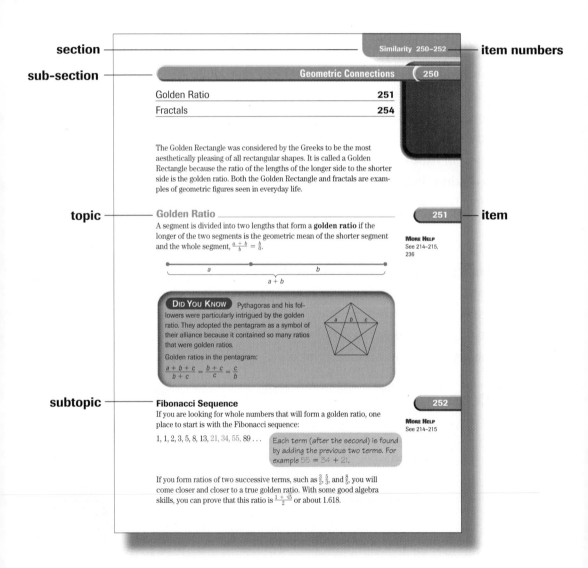

section ——— Similarity 250–252 ——— item numbers

sub-section ——— **Geometric Connections** (250)

| Golden Ratio | **251** |
| Fractals | **254** |

The Golden Rectangle was considered by the Greeks to be the most aesthetically pleasing of all rectangular shapes. It is called a Golden Rectangle because the ratio of the lengths of the longer side to the shorter side is the golden ratio. Both the Golden Rectangle and fractals are exam-ples of geometric figures seen in everyday life.

topic ——— **Golden Ratio** (251) ——— item

A segment is divided into two lengths that form a **golden ratio** if the longer of the two segments is the geometric mean of the shorter segment and the whole segment, $\frac{a+b}{b} = \frac{b}{a}$.

MORE HELP
See 214–215, 236

DID YOU KNOW Pythagoras and his fol-lowers were particularly intrigued by the golden ratio. They adopted the pentagram as a symbol of their alliance because it contained so many ratios that were golden ratios.

Golden ratios in the pentagram:
$$\frac{a+b+c}{b+c} = \frac{b+c}{c} = \frac{c}{b}$$

subtopic ——— **Fibonacci Sequence** (252)

If you are looking for whole numbers that will form a golden ratio, one place to start is with the Fibonacci sequence:

MORE HELP
See 214–215

1, 1, 2, 3, 5, 8, 13, 21, 34, 55, 89 . . .   Each term (after the second) is found by adding the previous two terms. For example 55 = 34 + 21.

If you form ratios of two successive terms, such as $\frac{3}{2}, \frac{5}{3}$, and $\frac{8}{5}$, you will come closer and closer to a true golden ratio. With some good algebra skills, you can prove that this ratio is $\frac{1+\sqrt{5}}{2}$ or about 1.618.

Because Geometry is such a highly structured discipline, and because we introduce the *Geometry to Go* style there, we recommend that you read the entire Logic and Proof Section.

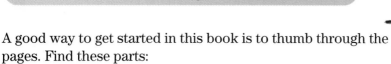

There are many ways to prove geometric statements. Some of these depend on what your teacher or textbook has already presented. When you refer to a proof in this handbook, make sure that the Theorems we use as reasons for making statements coincide with allowable reasoning in your course. If not, the Glossary of Theorems will give you an item number for the reasoning behind the Theorems.

A good way to get started in this book is to thumb through the pages. Find these parts:

■ **Table of Contents**
   This lists the major sections and sub-sections of the book.

■ **Sections and Sub-Sections**
   Each section of the handbook has a short table of contents so you know what is in the section. Sections have several sub-sections and each of these also has its own short table of contents. Notice the color bars across the tops of the pages. Each section has a different color to make it easy to find.

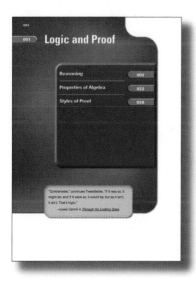

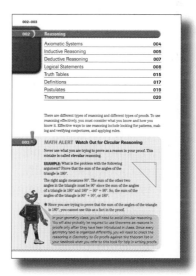

■ **Almanac**

This includes some very helpful tables and lists. It also has
hints on how to study, take a
test, and use geometry software and a graphing calculator. Check out all of the
almanac entries—you'll want
to refer to them often.

■ **Yellow Pages**

This part of the handbook has
five glossaries. The Glossary
of Mathematical Formulas is
the place to look if you forget
a formula. The Glossary of
Postulates and the Glossary of
Theorems list the postulates
and theorems we cover in this
book, cross-referenced to the
items in which they are introduced. In the Glossary of
Mathematical Terms, you will
find math terms that your
teacher, your parents, and
your textbook use. Finally,
there is a glossary of common
mathematical symbols.

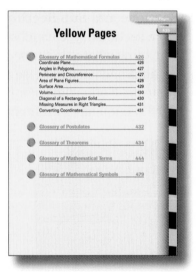

■ **Index**

This is at the very end of the book.

How to Use This Book

There are three ways to find information about a topic.

1 Look in the Index

We listed items in the index using any word we thought you might use to describe the topic. For example, you'll find degree of a node under both *degree* and *node*.

Degree(s)
    of angle measure, 062, 240
    of a node, 085
    and radians, 416
	Node(s), 083–085
	    degree of, 085
	    even, 085
	    odd, 085

Remember that you are being directed to item numbers, not page numbers. Use the item numbers located at the top of each page to help you find the topic you are looking for.

2 Look in the Glossaries

The Glossary of Mathematical Terms in this handbook is one of the most extensive high-school geometry glossaries around. Think of the Glossaries of Formulas, Postulates, and Theorems as your personal interpreter and turn to this part of the handbook whenever you see an unfamiliar word or want the full text of a formula, postulate, or theorem you find abbreviated in a proof.

topology: The branch of geometry that studies the properties of a figure that remain unchanged when the figure is distorted. **(083)**

Most glossary entries will give you an item number to refer to if you want more information about the topic.

T004	The distance between two parallel lines is constant.	059

3 Look in the Table of Contents

All the major topics covered in this book are listed in the Table of Contents. If you're looking for a general topic, like *Using the Coordinate Plane,* rather than a very specific one, like *Distance Between Two Points,* the Table of Contents is a quick way to find it. Notice that the color of each section's item number in the Table of Contents matches the color of the bar across the top of the pages for that section. This makes it easy to locate a section.

Logic and Proof

"Contrariwise," continues Tweedledee, "if it was so, it might be; and if it were so, it would be; but as it isn't, it ain't. That's logic."

—*Lewis Carroll in Through the Looking Glass*

How did you build that house of cards?

With geometry and flawless logic.

Rita felt there was no need to tell Carlos about the glue.

A friend says he saw you coming out of the movie theater Friday night at 9 o'clock. You say it must have been someone else and you can prove it. You were practicing with your band from 8 to 10 that night.

How does that prove it was someone else he saw and not you? Well, we share some basic notions about the world, such as the fact that a person can't be in two different places at the same time. We also share an understanding about some terms we use, such as time. We can use common notions and vocabulary along with some logic to show whether statements are true or untrue. Since you were with your band from 8 to 10, you could not have been at the movies at 9.

Geometry works with that kind of logical system, too. We have some basic notions about the world, called axioms or postulates, that we assume to be true even if we can't prove them. We have some terms so basic that we don't define them, and we have some terms we do define. We use these notions and terms to prove statements, called theorems.

Since we rely on geometry so much—to build movie theaters, for example—it's critical that we use flawless logic. After all, whether you really were at the movies Friday night may not be a matter of life and death, but whether the roof of the theater caves in certainly is.

002 Reasoning

There are different types of reasoning and different types of proofs. To use reasoning effectively, you must consider what you know and how you know it. Effective ways to use reasoning include looking for patterns, making and verifying conjectures, and applying rules.

003 MATH ALERT Watch Out for Circular Reasoning

Never use what you are trying to prove as a reason in your proof. This mistake is called **circular** reasoning.

EXAMPLE: What is the problem with the following argument? Prove that the sum of the angles of the triangle is 180°.

The right angle measures 90°. The sum of the other two angles in the triangle must be 90° since the sum of the angles of a triangle is 180° and 180° − 90° = 90°. So, the sum of the angles of the triangle is 90° + 90°, or 180°.

★ Since you are trying to prove that the sum of the angles of the triangle is 180°, you cannot use this as a fact in the proof.

In your geometry class, you will need to avoid circular reasoning. You will also probably be required to use theorems as reasons in proofs only after they have been introduced in class. Since every geometry text is organized differently, you will need to check the reasoning in *Geometry to Go* proofs against the theorem list in your textbook when you refer to this book for help in writing proofs.

Axiomatic Systems

An **axiomatic system** is a set of statements, some of which, **axioms** or **postulates**, we accept without proof. The other statements in an axiomatic system include theorems, which are truths that can be derived from the axioms. Mathematicians accept undefined terms and definitions as true so that they can build a consistent system.

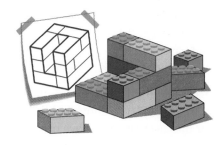

Like the pieces of a model which rest securely on others, the theorems of an axiomatic system rest on axioms and other theorems. If not placed with perfect logic, the whole system can come tumbling down.

Geometry, like all axiomatic systems, is tied together by logic. This logic is usually expressed in a convincing argument or **proof**. You can also use a proof to show that something is *not* true.

Inductive Reasoning

Have you ever done an experiment for a science project, using the scientific method to investigate a question? If so, then you have used inductive reasoning.

Consider a young scientist investigating oil and water. She mixes different amounts of oil and water and observes that the two liquids separate. She makes the following hypothesis: oil and water don't mix. The scientist is using inductive reasoning since she is making a generalization based on a pattern of observations.

Inductive reasoning is the process of observing and recording data, looking for patterns, and making generalizations from the observations.

MORE HELP
See 007, 058, 061, 141, 157, 164

Inductive reasoning is the basis of the scientific method. It is also important in mathematics. In science, you can use inductive reasoning to make and test a hypothesis. In mathematics, you can use inductive reasoning to investigate and make a conjecture. A **conjecture** is an unproven statement that is based on observations. It is like a hypothesis in the scientific method. Using the scientific method, you test the hypothesis. In mathematics, you try to prove the conjecture.

Reasoning in geometry often consists of the following three steps.

Step 1 Inductive Reasoning: Look for a pattern. Look at examples and try to discover a pattern. You can use tables and diagrams to help investigate the examples.

Step 2 Inductive Reasoning: Make a conjecture. Use the examples to make a generalization. This generalization is the conjecture. It is unproven and based upon your observations. If possible, discuss the conjecture with others and modify it if needed.

Step 3 Deductive Reasoning: Verify the conjecture. Use logical reasoning to try to show that the conjecture is true for all cases, not just for the cases that you have observed.

EXAMPLE 1: Use reasoning to find what figure is formed when the midpoints of the sides of a square are connected in order.

Step 1: Look for a pattern by investigating several cases.

The blue figure appears to be a square and the red figure does, as well.

Step 2: Make a conjecture.

The figure formed when the midpoints of the sides of a square are connected in order is another square.

Step 3: Verify the conjecture.

4. Since the diagonals of a square are congruent, each side of the figure formed is equal to half the measure of the diagonal. So, $\overline{EF}$, $\overline{FG}$, $\overline{GH}$, and $\overline{HE}$ are all congruent, making the figure either a rhombus or a square.

2. By the Midsegment Theorem, the segment connecting the midpoints of two sides of a triangle is parallel to the third side and half its length. So, $\overline{HE}$ is parallel to $\overline{DB}$ and $HE = \frac{1}{2}\, DB$.

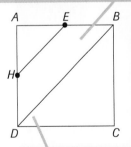

3. $\overline{HG}$ is parallel to $\overline{AC}$ by the Midsegment Theorem.

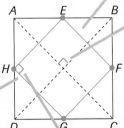

5. $\overline{DB}$ is perpendicular to $\overline{AC}$ because the diagonals of a square are perpendicular.

1. If you draw diagonal $\overline{DB}$ of the given square $ABCD$, $\triangle ABD$ is formed.

6. $\overline{HE}$ is perpendicular to $\overline{HG}$ since each is parallel to one of a pair of perpendicular segments.

Each pair of congruent adjacent sides of the quadrilateral forms an angle that measures 90°. Therefore, the figure formed when the midpoints of the sides of a square are connected in order is another square.

To prove that a conjecture is true, you must prove that it is true in all cases. However, to prove that a conjecture is false, you only need to find one case where it is not true. This case is a **counterexample**.

Not all conjectures can be shown to be true or false. These conjectures are called unproven or undecided. A famous unproven conjecture is the Goldbach Conjecture: *Every even number greater than two can be written as the sum of two primes.* For example, $12 = 5 + 7$ and $24 = 17 + 7$.

MATH ALERT Don't Leap to Conclusions About the Truth of a Conjecture

006

Remember, although something is true for several, or even many, cases, it may not be true for *all* cases.

EXAMPLE 1: Find a counterexample for the following conjecture: $n < n^2$.

n	n^2
10	100
7	49
3	9
2.9	8.41
1.1	1.21

You might jump to the conclusion that $n > n^2$. However, this is *not* true.

Notice that in the table, n and n^2 are greater than 1. Choose a value for n that is less than 1.

Counterexample: If n is 0.8, n^2 is 0.64. $0.8 > 0.64$.

★ If the length of a side of a square is 0.8 units, then the area is 0.64 square units. This is a counterexample to the conjecture that $n < n^2$.

EXAMPLE 2: You may think that any pair of lines that doesn't intersect must be parallel, but think about the edges of a box—some don't intersect and are also not parallel.

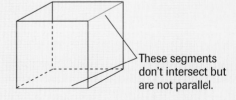

These segments don't intersect but are not parallel.

007

Deductive Reasoning _____

You use deductive reasoning when you verify a conjecture.

MORE HELP
See 005, 009

This is the type of reasoning that doctors often use to make a diagnosis. For example, a doctor might compare a list of your symptoms with the symptoms associated with a specific illness. The doctor may then draw blood and have it tested for antibodies that correspond to this illness. Based on the evidence and certain conditions being present, the doctor deduces that a given illness is present.

Deductive reasoning uses facts, definitions, and accepted properties in a logical order to present a convincing argument. A **logical argument** consists of a conjecture (or set of conjectures) and a conclusion. **Logicians** are mathematicians that specialize in logical arguments. They use symbols to represent statements and logical relationships. Look at 005 to see an example of the use of deductive reasoning to verify a conjecture.

008

Logical Statements _____

Suppose you are asked to draw a figure that is a triangle. Would you always draw a right triangle? Probably not. However, if you were asked to draw a triangle with one right angle, you would draw a right triangle. This is the idea behind necessary and sufficient conditions in mathematical statements.

MORE HELP
See 009–011

A **necessary condition** is required to be true in order for something else to be true. For example, it is necessary for at least three pairs of corresponding parts to be congruent to prove two triangles are congruent. If the necessary condition is false, then what it is a condition for is also false. If you don't have at least three pairs of congruent corresponding parts, then you can't possibly have congruent triangles. However, this condition may not be enough to assure that you have congruent triangles.

A **sufficient condition** is required to be true based upon the truth of a statement. For example, three pairs of congruent parts that assure congruent triangles are side-side-side, side-angle-side, or angle-side-angle.

The table below shows how basic statements are related to necessary and sufficient conditions:

Basic Statement	Conditions	Examples	
If p then q $p \longrightarrow q$	p only if q p is a sufficient condition for q	p = figure is a square q = figure is a quadrilateral If a figure is a square, then it is a quadrilateral.	**MORE HELP** See 009
If q then p $q \longrightarrow p$	q only if p p is a necessary condition for q	p = figure has two acute angles q = figure is a △ with obtuse ∠ If a figure is a triangle with an obtuse angle, then it has two acute angles.	**MORE HELP** See 009–010
p if and only if q $p \longleftrightarrow q$	p is a necessary and sufficient condition for q	p = equilateral △ q = equiangular △ A triangle is equilateral if and only if it is equiangular.	**MORE HELP** See 011

Conditional Statements

009

You have probably recognized how important it is to have precise meanings for words and figures in geometry. It is also very important to know the mathematical meanings of small words such as *and, if, then,* and *or,* and to understand the meanings of symbols such as $>$, $=$, and $<$.

MORE HELP
 See 007

A statement in the form *If . . ., then . . .* is called a **conditional statement**. A conditional statement has two parts, the hypothesis and the conclusion. The *if* part of the statement is the **hypothesis**. It is denoted by p. The *then* part of the statement is the **conclusion**. It is denoted by q.

When you translate conditional statements into symbolic form, you use letters such as p, q, r, *and* s to stand for simple statements. The statements are either true or false. Logical statements can be written symbolically.

Write	Say
$p \longrightarrow q$	if p then q or p implies q
$p \longleftrightarrow q$	p if and only if q
$\sim p$	not p

MORE ▶

EXAMPLE: Write the statement, *If today is Saturday, then I don't have school*, in symbolic form.

p: *today is Saturday*

q: *I don't have school.*

★ *p* ⟶ *q*: *If today is Saturday, then I don't have school*

Here is a summary of the different types of conditional statements.

Basic Statement	Symbolic Form	Example
Conditional	$p \longrightarrow q$	If both pairs of opposite sides of a quadrilateral are congruent, then it is a parallelogram.
Converse	$q \longrightarrow p$	If a quadrilateral is a parallelogram, then both pairs of opposite sides are congruent.
Negation	$\sim p$	Both pairs of opposite sides of a quadrilateral are not congruent.
Inverse	$\sim p \longrightarrow \sim q$	If both pairs of opposite sides of a quadrilateral are not congruent, then it is not a parallelogram.
Contrapositive	$\sim q \longrightarrow \sim p$	If a quadrilateral is not a parallelogram, then both pairs of opposite sides are not congruent.

MORE HELP
See 010

MORE HELP
See 012

MORE HELP
See 013

MORE HELP
See 014

010

Converse Statements

The **converse** of a conditional statement is formed by reversing the hypothesis and the conclusion, so the converse of the statement *if p then q* is *if q then p*. Or symbolically, if the statement is *p* ⟶ *q* then the converse is *q* ⟶ *p*. The converse of a statement may or may not be true.

EXAMPLE 1: Write the converse of the statement, *If an animal is a collie, then it is a dog.* Is the converse of this statement true?

Statement: If an animal is a collie, then it is a dog.

Reverse the hypothesis and the conclusion.

Converse: If an animal is a dog, then it is a collie.

You know, however, that while a dog could be a collie, it could instead be a poodle, or a hound, or some other breed.

★ The converse is: *If an animal is a dog, then it is a collie.* Since a dog may or may not be a collie, the converse is false.

EXAMPLE 2: Is the converse of this statement true?

MORE HELP
See 072

Statement: If two angles are vertical angles, then the angles are congruent.

Converse: If two angles are congruent, then they are vertical angles.

You know that two angles can be congruent without being vertical angles.

★ The statement is true but the converse is false. Congruent angles do not have to be vertical angles.

EXAMPLE 3: Is the converse of this statement true?

Statement: If two nonvertical lines are parallel, then they have the same slope.

Converse: If two nonvertical lines have the same slope, then they are parallel.

The converse is a true statement.

★ Both the statement and its converse are true.

MORE HELP
See 107

When a statement and its converse are both true, as in Example 3, they can be combined into a biconditional statement: *Two nonvertical parallel lines are parallel if and only if they have the same slope.*

If and only if is sometimes abbreviated as iff.

Biconditional Statements

011

When a statement and its converse are both true, we sometimes write them as a **biconditional statement**, *p if and only if q*. The statement is equivalent to $p \longrightarrow q$ and $q \longrightarrow p$.

Write: $p \longleftrightarrow q$

Say: *p if and only if q*

A good definition is biconditional. For example, congruent segments have equal measure. Although if and only if is not included in the definition, it is implied. This means that equivalent forms of the definition are: If two segments are congruent, then they have equal measure and if two segments have equal measure, then they are congruent.

012

Negations

Have you ever been joking with your friends and said something like, *I like sardines. NOT!* Such a statement is called a negation.

The **negation** of a statement p, called not-p, is a statement that is true when p is false and is false when p is true.

Write: $\sim p$

Say: *not p*

You can often write a negation by inserting the word *not* into the statement.

EXAMPLE 1: Write the negation of the statement.

Statement: *Natalie is training for the race.*

★ Negation: *Natalie is not training for the race.*

> If the statement is already negative, then the negation takes out the not in the statement.

EXAMPLE 2: Write the negation for p: The polygon is not a hexagon.

★ $\sim p$: The polygon is a hexagon.

013

Inverse Statements

The **inverse** of a statement is formed by negating both the hypothesis and the conclusion. The inverse of the statement, *if p then q* is *if not p then not q*. Symbolically, write the inverse of $p \longrightarrow q$ as $\sim p \longrightarrow \sim q$. The inverse of a statement may or may not be true.

EXAMPLE 1: Write the inverse of the statement.

Statement: *If two lines are parallel,* **then** *the distance between them is constant.*

★ Inverse: *If two lines are* **not** *parallel,* **then** *the distance between them is* **not** *constant.*

EXAMPLE 2: Write the inverse of this statement. Determine whether it is true.

Statement: *If a triangle is equilateral,* **then** *it has three acute angles.*

Inverse: *If a triangle is* **not** *equilateral,* **then** *it does* **not** *have three acute angles.*

Remember, you only need one counterexample to show that a statement is not true. Look at the diagram. The triangle is not equilateral, but it does have three acute angles.

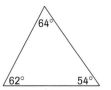

★ The statement is true, but the inverse is false.

EXAMPLE 3: Write the inverse of this statement. Determine whether it is true.

Statement: *If two angles are supplementary,* ***then*** *the sum of their measures is 180°.*

Inverse: *If two angles are* ***not*** *supplementary,* ***then*** *the sum of their measures is* ***not*** *180°.*

By definition, for two angles to be supplementary, they must have a sum of 180°. If two angles are not supplementary, then their sum cannot be 180°.

★ Both the statement and its inverse are true.

Contrapositive Statements

014

The **contrapositive** of a conditional statement is formed when both the hypothesis and the conclusion are reversed *and* negated. As a result, the contrapositive of the statement, *if p then q is if not q then not p.*

Write: $\sim q \longrightarrow \sim p$

Say: *if not q, then not p*

EXAMPLE: Write the contrapositive of this statement. Decide whether it is true.

Statement: *If a figure is a square,* ***then*** *it is a parallelogram.*

★ Contrapositive: *If a figure is* ***not*** *a parallelogram, then it is* ***not*** *a square.* The contrapositive is true.

Notice that in the example, the statement and its contrapositive are both true. It turns out that this is always the case. The **law of the contrapositive** says that a statement and its contrapositive are logically equivalent. You may replace one with the other.

Truth Tables

A statement can be true or false. The truth or falsity of a statement is called its **truth value**. A convenient way of tabulating the truth of a statement is with a **truth table**. A truth table is completed by considering the truth value of each part of a statement.

This truth table is for p and $\sim p$. Notice that when p is true (T), $\sim p$ is false (F) and vice versa.

To construct a truth table for the conditional statement $p \longrightarrow q$, consider all the possible combinations of true and false for p and q.

p	$\sim p$
T	F
F	T

p	q	$p \rightarrow q$
T	T	
T	F	
F	T	
F	F	

The only case in which $p \longrightarrow q$ is false is the case where p is true and q is false. You can't force a true statement to imply a false statement.

$$p \qquad\qquad\qquad q$$
If **it rains**, then **I will give you a ride home.**

p	q	$p \rightarrow q$	
T	T	T	It rains and I give you a ride home.
T	F	F	It rains and I don't give you a ride home. (I lied.)
F	T	T	It doesn't rain and I give you a ride home. (That's ok, I never said I'd *only* give you a ride if it rained.)
F	F	T	It doesn't rain and I don't give you a ride home.

The truth table shows that the conditional $p \longrightarrow q$ is considered false only if p is true and q is false.

EXAMPLE: Let p represent *the mystery state is the smallest state* and let q represent *the mystery state is in New England*. Find the truth value for $p \longrightarrow q$.

Write a complete sentence to show what $p \longrightarrow q$ represents: *If the mystery state is the smallest state, then it is in New England.*

★

p	q	$p \rightarrow q$	
T	T	T	If Rhode Island is the smallest state, then it is in New England.
T	F	F	If Rhode Island is the smallest state, then it is not in New England.
F	T	T	If Texas is the smallest state, then it is in New England.
F	F	T	If Texas is the smallest state, then it is not in New England.

MORE HELP
See 011

The biconditional statement $p \longleftrightarrow q$ is related to the conditional statement $p \longrightarrow q$. Here is a truth table for $p \longleftrightarrow q$.

p	q	$p \rightarrow q$	$q \rightarrow p$	$p \leftrightarrow q$
T	T	T	T	T
T	F	F	T	F
F	T	T	F	F
F	F	T	T	T

Notice in the truth table that a biconditional statement is true only if both p and q are true or if both p and q are false.

To construct the truth tables for the converse and the inverse of a conditional statement, use what you know about truth values for p, q, $\sim p$, and $\sim q$.

		Conditional	Converse			Inverse
p	q	$p \rightarrow q$	$q \rightarrow p$	$\sim p$	$\sim q$	$\sim p \rightarrow \sim q$
T	T	T	T	F	F	T
T	F	F	T	F	T	T
F	T	T	F	T	F	F
F	F	T	T	T	T	T

Notice that the truth tables for the converse and the inverse of a conditional statement are the same. This means that the statements are logically equivalent. Therefore, if the inverse of a conditional statement is true, the converse is also true. If the converse of a conditional statement is true, the inverse is also true. If the converse is false, the inverse is false, and if the inverse is false, the converse must be false.

From the law of the contrapositive, you know that a conditional statement is logically equivalent to its contrapositive. You can also use a truth table to show this.

		Conditional			Contrapositive
p	q	$p \rightarrow q$	$\sim p$	$\sim q$	$\sim q \rightarrow \sim p$
T	T	T	F	F	T
T	F	F	F	T	F
F	T	T	T	F	T
F	F	T	T	T	T

Law of Detachment and Law of Syllogism

Two patterns of logical reasoning that use conditional statements are the law of detachment and the law of syllogism. You might think of both laws as plain common sense and, in a way, that's what logic is.

The **law of detachment** says:

if $p \longrightarrow q$ is true
and p is true
then q is true

> The law of detachment is sometimes referred to by its Latin name, Modus Ponens.

EXAMPLE 1: Assume that, *if Allie goes to the mall, then she will have pizza* is true. Today, Allie goes to the mall. Will Allie have pizza? Why?

p: Allie goes to the mall
q: she will have pizza.
p $\longrightarrow$ q: If Allie goes to the mall, then she will have pizza.

Since $p \longrightarrow q$ is assumed to be true and p is also true, the law of detachment says that q, *Allie will have pizza*, will occur.

★ Allie will have pizza.

The **law of syllogism** says:

if $p \longrightarrow q$ is true
and $q \longrightarrow r$ is true
then $p \longrightarrow r$ is true

> The law of syllogism is sometimes called the Chain Rule.

EXAMPLE 2: If Clayton gets a job, then he will earn money. If Clayton earns money, then he will buy a mountain bike. If both statements are true, what can you conclude?

p: Clayton gets a job
q: he will earn money
r: he will buy a mountain bike

p $\longrightarrow$ q: if Clayton gets a job, then he will earn money
q $\longrightarrow$ r: if Clayton earns money, then he will buy a mountain bike
p $\longrightarrow$ r: if Clayton gets a job, then he will buy a mountain bike

Since $p \longrightarrow q$ and $q \longrightarrow r$ are both true, then $p \longrightarrow r$ must be true by the law of syllogism.

★ You can conclude: *if Clayton gets a job, then he will buy a mountain bike.*

Definitions

Definitions are important in geometry because we must have agreement on what terms mean if we are going to use them in a precise way. A definition itself must be precise.

Definitions in geometry are reversible (they are biconditional). Although *if an only if* is not included in the definition statement, in most definitions it is implied. They can be interpreted forward or backward. For example, either of the following two definitions is acceptable as the definition of a triangle. (1) A triangle is a polygon with exactly three sides. (2) A polygon with exactly three sides is a triangle.

MORE HELP
See 011, 444

MATH ALERT Don't Confuse Definitions with Properties

018

Here is a definition of rectangle.
rectangle: A parallelogram with four right angles.

MORE HELP
See 157, 162

This is *not* the same as saying a rectangle has four right angles; two pairs of congruent, parallel sides; perpendicular diagonals; and so on. This listing of properties is not the definition but a consequence of the definition.

Postulates

A deductive system like geometry is based on statements that are assumed to be true but are never proved. These statements are called **postulates**. We accept postulates without proof.

MORE HELP
See 432

Postulates are statements that often seem obvious to you. They should make sense and seem natural to you.

In general, postulates must be *consistent, complete,* and *independent.* **Consistent** means that proofs using all the same postulates cannot contradict each other. **Complete** means that all theorems in the system can be deduced from the same set of postulates. **Independent** means that no postulate is a consequence of another postulate.

You can build a whole mathematical system on one set of postulates. Once you have a set of postulates, together with undefined terms and definitions, you can develop new rules in the system (called theorems) that you can prove are true. If you change the postulates, you change the whole system.

For example, in this book and, most likely, in your geometry textbook, the Parallel Postulate says that if there is a line and a point not on the line, then there is exactly one line through the point parallel to the given line.

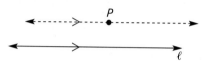

MORE HELP
See 364, 368

This postulate is essential to Euclidean Geometry. In fact, if your axiomatic system has a Parallel Postulate that says that more than one line through the point can be drawn parallel to the given line, a different form of geometry, called **hyperbolic geometry** arises.

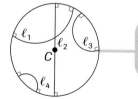

The hyperbolic plane is disc-shaped. The lines on this disc are arcs, and any number of arcs can intersect point C while never intersecting line ℓ_4.

If your parallel postulate says that through any point on the plane, there exists no line parallel to a given line, the geometry is **elliptic** or **spherical geometry**.

In spherical geometry, the *plane* can be visualized as a sphere and the *lines* on this sphere as great circles. Since every great circle of a sphere has the same center, every great circle will intersect every other one and no lines can be parallel.

Theorems

020

A **theorem** is a mathematical statement or proposition that is derived from previously accepted results. Theorems are based on postulates, definitions, or on other established theorems.

MORE HELP
See 434

Corollaries

021

A **corollary** is a theorem that follows easily from another theorem that has already been proved.

EXAMPLE: Show that a triangle is equilateral if and only if it is equiangular.

MORE HELP
See 145, 434

Proof

The Base Angles Theorem and its converse state that two sides of a triangle are congruent if and only if the angles opposite those sides are congruent. If all three sides of a triangle are congruent, then it follows that all three angles must be congruent. You can turn this argument around and say that if all three angles are congruent, then all three sides must be congruent.

★ A corollary to the Base Angles Theorem is: *A triangle is equilateral if and only if it is equiangular.*

Suppose you have a check for $72 and some cash that you want to deposit in your savings account. Because you are in a hurry, you do not count the cash before you make the deposit. The teller says that your total deposit is $105. Without realizing it, you may use one of the properties of algebra to check how much cash you had. If you let c represent the amount of cash you had, then you can think of the total deposit as $c + \$72$. Since you know the total deposit, the equation $c + \$72 = \$105$ represents the situation. If you subtract to solve the equation ($c = \$105 - \$72$), you are actually using the Subtraction Property of Equality when you conclude that you had $33 in cash.

MORE HELP
See 030

Some of the properties of numbers have become so familiar that you may use them without thinking about it. When you subtract to make change, it is precisely because these properties simplify the process so much that they are both useful and important.

023 **Properties of Real Numbers** _____

One of the nice things about numbers is that they always behave in the same predictable way. They will not surprise you by changing their behavior from day to day. This is because real numbers follow a set of rules called **properties**.

024 **Commutative Property**

To *commute* means to go back and forth. The word *commutative* is derived from the word *commute* and the commutative property works the same either backward or forward. Both addition and multiplication are commutative.

The **Commutative Property of Addition** says that the order of two addends can be changed without changing the sum. For all real numbers a and b, $a + b = b + a$.

Many students erroneously call this the commu**na**tive property. Be careful!

EXAMPLE 1: Add. $3x + 19 + 5x = $ ■

Use the Commutative Property to switch the order of 19 and $5x$. Then you can add like terms.

$3x + 19 + 5x = 3x + 5x + 19$	Commutative prop. of $+$
$= 8x + 19$	Simplify

★ $3x + 19 + 5x = 8x + 19$

The **Commutative Property of Multiplication** says that the order of two factors can be changed without changing the product. For all real numbers a and b, $ab = ba$.

EXAMPLE 2: Multiply. $50x \cdot 417y \cdot 2z = $ ■

Use the Commutative Property to switch the order of $417y$ and $2z$. Then use mental math to multiply.

$50x \cdot 417y \cdot 2z = 50x \cdot 2z \cdot 417y$	Commutative prop. of $\times$
$= 100xz \cdot 417y$	Simplify
$= 41{,}700xyz$	Simplify

★ $50x \cdot 417y \cdot 2z = 41{,}700xyz$

MATH ALERT Subtraction and Division Are Not Commutative

025

Does $8 - 4$ have the same value as $4 - 8$? Does $8 \div 4$ have the same value as $4 \div 8$? Of course not. You can, however, rewrite subtraction and division expressions to make them commutative by using inverses.

$8 - 4 \neq 4 - 8$

but $8 - 4 = 8 + {}^-4$

and $8 + {}^-4 = {}^-4 + 8$

This is the additive inverse of 4.

$8 \div 4 \neq 4 \div 8$

but $8 \div 4 = \dfrac{8}{4}$

$= 8 \times \dfrac{1}{4}$

This is the multiplicative inverse of 4.

and $8 \times \dfrac{1}{4} = \dfrac{1}{4} \times 8$

026

Associative Property

People associate together in groups. The word *associative* is derived from *associate* and the associative property is about how you can group addends and factors. Both addition and multiplication are associative.

The **Associative Property of Addition** says that when adding three numbers, you can begin by grouping the first two addends or by grouping the second two addends. For all real numbers a, b, and c, $(a + b) + c = a + (b + c)$.

EXAMPLE 1: Add. $38x + 16x + 24x = \blacksquare$

You would normally add the first two addends, then add the third, but $38 + 16$ is not as easy to add mentally as $16 + 24$. Use the Associative Property to change the grouping to help you add mentally.

$(38x + 16x) + 24x = 38x + (16x + 24x)$	Associative prop. of $+$
$= 38x + 40x$	Simplify
$= 78x$	Simplify

★ $38x + 16x + 24x = 78x$

The **Associative Property of Multiplication** says that when multiplying three numbers, you can begin by grouping the first two factors or by grouping the second two factors. For all real numbers a, b, and c, $(ab)c = a(bc)$.

EXAMPLE 2: Multiply. $10q \cdot \frac{1}{3}p \cdot 6r = \blacksquare$

You would normally multiply the first two factors, then multiply by the third, but $10 \cdot \frac{1}{3}$ is not as easy to multiply mentally as $\frac{1}{3} \cdot 6$. Use the Associative Property to change the grouping to help you multiply mentally.

$$\left(10q \cdot \tfrac{1}{3}p\right) \cdot 6r = 10q \cdot \left(\tfrac{1}{3}p \cdot 6r\right)$$
$$= 10q \cdot (2pr)$$
$$= 20pqr$$

★ $10q \cdot \frac{1}{3}p \cdot 6r = 20pqr$

027

Distributive Property

When you *distribute* construction tools in a geometry class, you make sure that each student has received a ruler, a protractor, and a compass. When you use the Distributive Property, you distribute a factor to several terms in an expression.

The **Distributive Property** states that for any real numbers a, b, and c, $a \cdot (b + c) = ab + ac$. You use this property often when you multiply in your head.

EXAMPLE 1: Multiply. $9(7m + 3n) = \blacksquare$

> Multiply both terms inside the parentheses by 9.

$9(7m + 3n) = (9 \cdot 7m) + (9 \cdot 3n)$	Distributive prop.
$= 63m + 27n$	Simplify

★ $9(7m + 3n) = 63m + 27n$

EXAMPLE 2: Write in factored form. $42a^2 + 7a = \blacksquare$

$42a^2 + 7a = (7 \cdot 6 \cdot a \cdot a) + 7a \cdot 1)$	Factor $42a^2$ and $7a$
$= (\mathbf{7a} \cdot 6a) + (\mathbf{7a} \cdot 1)$	Simplify
$= \mathbf{7a}(6a + 1)$	Distributive prop.

Algebraic Properties of Equality

028

Some important properties from algebra are about the equality of real numbers. These properties can be used to solve equations. Geometry has similar properties relating to congruence.

MORE HELP
See 256

Addition Property of Equality

029

Let a, b, and c be real numbers. The **Addition Property of Equality** says that if you add the same number to equal amounts, the sums will also be equal. If $a = b$, then $a + c = b + c$.

> The Addition Property of Equality also states that if you add equal amounts to equal amounts, the sums will also be equal. If $a = b$ and $c = d$, then $a + c = b + d$.

MORE ▶

MORE HELP
See 072

The algebraic properties can be used in a geometric context.

EXAMPLE: If $m\angle 3 = m\angle 1 + 15°$, what is $m\angle 4$?

> The little m before an angle symbol means the measure of.

Because $\angle 1$ and $\angle 2$ are vertical angles, their measures are equal. This means that $m\angle 1 = m\angle 2 = 30°$. Since both the angles are increased by the same number of degrees, the Addition Property of Equality gives the measures of $\angle 3$ and $\angle 4$, the new vertical angles.

★ Both $\angle 3$ and $\angle 4$ measure $45°$.

030

Subtraction Property of Equality

MORE HELP
See 256

Let a, b, and c be real numbers. The **Subtraction Property of Equality** says that if you subtract the same number from equal amounts, the differences will also be equal. If $a = b$, then $a - c = b - c$.

EXAMPLE: $\overline{RT} \cong \overline{SU}$. Is $\overline{RS} \cong \overline{TU}$? Explain.

$$R \quad S \quad T \quad U$$

★ Because segments RT and SU are congruent, they have the same length. You know from the Subtraction Property of Equality that if both lengths are decreased by the same amount, the new lengths will still be congruent. Since $RS + ST = RT$ and $ST + TU = SU$, then $RT - ST = SU - ST$, and $RS = TU$. This means that $\overline{RS} \cong \overline{TU}$.

> The Subtraction Property of Equality also states that if you subtract equal amounts from equal amounts, the differences will also be equal. If $a = b$ and $c = d$, then $a - c = b - d$.

031

Multiplication Property of Equality

Let a, b, and c be real numbers. The **Multiplication Property of Equality** says that if you multiply equal amounts by the same number or by equal amounts, the products will also be equal. If $a = b$, then $ac = bc$, and if $a = b$ and $c = d$, then $ac = bd$.

EXAMPLE: Look at $\overline{AB}$. What is the length of a segment that is twice as long?

You know from the Multiplication Property of Equality that if $AB = 4$, then $2AB = 2(4)$.

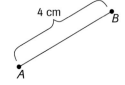

★ A segment that is twice as long as $\overline{AB}$ is 8 centimeters long.

Division Property of Equality

Let a, b, and c be real numbers. The **Division Property of Equality** says that if you divide equal amounts by the same number, except for 0, the quotients will be equal. If $a = b$ and $c \neq 0$, then $a \div c = b \div c$.

EXAMPLE 1: If $4(\text{m}\angle A) = 120°$, find the measure of $\angle A$.

Use the Division Property of Equality to find $\text{m}\angle A$. Let $a = 4(\text{m}\angle A)$, $b = 120$, and $c = 4$. Since four times the measure of $\angle A$ is 120°, divide each side of the equation by 4 to get one times the measure of $\angle A$.

$4(\text{m}\angle A) = 120$	Given
$\dfrac{4(\text{m}\angle A)}{4} = \dfrac{120}{4}$	$\div$ prop. of $=$
$\text{m}\angle A = 30$	Simplify

★ 30° is the measure of $\angle A$.

You can combine properties of equality to solve equations.

EXAMPLE 2: Solve $7x - 12 = 4x + 3$ and write a reason for each step.

$7x - 12 = 4x + 3$	Given
$7x - 4x - 12 = 4x - 4x + 3$	Subtraction prop. of $=$
$3x - 12 = 3$	$a = 7x - 12,\ b = 4x + 3,\ c = 4x$
$3x - 12 + 12 = 3 + 12$	$+$ prop. of $=$
$3x = 15$	$a = 3x - 12,\ b = 3,\ c = 12$
$3x \div 3 = 15 \div 3$	$\div$ prop. of $=$
$x = 5$	$a = 3x,\ b = 15,\ c = 3$

Geometric Properties of Equality

The algebraic properties of equality can be used in geometry. They are true for segment length and for angle measure which are, after all, numbers.

Reflexive Property

A relationship is reflexive if the object is equal to itself. The **Reflexive Property of Equality** says that $a = a$. When you're talking about segment length, this property means that for any line segment AB, $AB = AB$. When you are talking about angle measure, this property means that for any angle A, $\text{m}\angle A = \text{m}\angle A$. The Reflexive Property is also true for congruent segments and angles. $\overline{AB} \cong \overline{AB}$ and $\angle A \cong \angle A$.

MORE HELP
See 258

035

MORE HELP
See 258

Symmetric Property

The **Symmetric Property of Equality** says that if $a = b$, then $b = a$. A relationship is **symmetric** if, whenever a is related to b, it is also true that b is related to a in the same way. When you're talking about segment length, this property means that if $AB = CD$, then $CD = AB$. When you're talking about angle measure, this property means that if $m\angle A = m\angle B$, then $m\angle B = m\angle A$.

The Symmetric Property is also true for congruent segments and angles. If $\overline{AB} \cong \overline{CD}$, then $\overline{CD} \cong \overline{AB}$. If $\angle A \cong \angle B$, then $\angle B \cong \angle A$.

MORE HELP
See 024

Do NOT confuse the **Symmetric Property**, which deals with **both** sides of an equation, with the Commutative Property, which deals with **one** side of an equation.
If $a + b = c$, then $b + a = c$ is a commutative example.
If $a + b = c$, then $c = a + b$ is a symmetric example.

036

Transitive Property

The **Transitive Property of Equality** says that if $a = b$ and $b = c$, then $a = c$. When a relationship is **transitive,** if a and b have the same value, and b and c have the same value, it follows that a and c have the same value. When you're talking about segment length, this property means that if $AB = CD$ and $CD = EF$, then $AB = EF$. When you're talking about angle measure, this property means that if $m\angle 1 = m\angle 2$ and $m\angle 2 = m\angle 3$, then $m\angle 1 = m\angle 3$.

The Transitive Property is also true for congruent segments and angles. If $\overline{AB} \cong \overline{CD}$ and $\overline{CD} \cong \overline{EF}$, then $\overline{AB} \cong \overline{EF}$. If $\angle A \cong \angle B$ and $\angle B \cong \angle C$, then $\angle A \cong \angle C$.

EXAMPLE: $\ell \parallel m$ and $m\angle 1 = 65°$. Use the transitive property of equality to show that $m\angle 3 = 65°$.

MORE HELP
See 076, 258

★ Because $\ell \parallel m$, the corresponding angles have the same measure. $\angle 1$ and $\angle 2$ are corresponding angles, so $m\angle 1 = m\angle 2$. $\angle 2$ and $\angle 3$ have the same measure because they are vertical angles, which are congruent, $\angle 2 \cong \angle 3$, so $m\angle 2 = m\angle 3$. The transitive property of equality says that $m\angle 1 = m\angle 3$ and therefore, $m\angle 3 = 65°$.

Substitution Property of Equality

037

Let a and b be real numbers. The **Substitution Property of Equality** says that if $a = b$, then a can be substituted for b in any equation or expression. For example, suppose $MN + PQ = 15$ and $MN = 6$, then by the substitution property of equality, $6 + PQ = 15$.

MORE HELP
See 029, 034, 057

You can combine properties to show that a statement is true.

EXAMPLE: If $AB = CD$, show that $AC = BD$. Write a reason for each step.

$AB = CD$	Given
$BC = BC$	Reflexive prop. of =
$AB + BC = CD + BC$	+ prop. of =
$AB + BC = AC$	Seg. + postulate (P09)
$BC + CD = BD$	Seg. + postulate (P09)
$AC = BD$	Substitution prop. of =

It may be fine to just write *substitution* when you mean *substitution property of equality*. It may also be OK to write *reflexive* when you mean *reflexive property of equality*. Check with your teacher.

) **Styles of Proof**

A **proof** is a logical argument that convinces someone that a statement is true. In real life there are different ways to prove statements. For example, you can prove that you are a member of the library by showing your library card.

In mathematics, there are different *styles* of proof, but they're all based on logic. When you write a proof, you can use definitions, properties, postulates, and theorems. However, when you use a theorem to prove a new theorem, you can only use theorems that previously have been proved. In your geometry class, if you use a theorem that hasn't yet been introduced, your teacher is not likely to accept your proof. When you look up topics in this handbook, be prepared to investigate the theorems we use in proofs for two reasons:

1. they may be theorems your course hasn't yet discussed, and
2. they may be different from theorems used in your course.

There are *lots* of postulates and theorems in geometry, and while we've included as many as we could, we certainly missed some, combined others, and re-worded still others.

To prepare any proof, follow these steps:

1. Write the information you've been given as true.
2. Write what you need to prove.
3. Draw diagram and mark given information.
4. Plan how to get from the *given* to the *prove.*
5. Add to the diagram if needed.
6. Set out a logical sequence of statements and reasons beginning with what you know and ending with what you've been asked to prove.

Using Diagrams in Proofs _____

In geometry it is especially important to begin each proof with a diagram, regardless of the style of proof that you choose. If a diagram is not provided, you should draw your own diagram. Mark the information that is given. Also mark any information that can be deduced from the statement, such as whether angles are vertical angles, corresponding angles, and so on.

MORE HELP
See 066

EXAMPLE: Draw a diagram and label it with the given information.

Given: $\overleftrightarrow{AB}$ intersects $\overline{CD}$ at P
$\angle APC \cong \angle BPD$

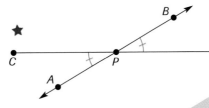

This is not the only way the diagram can be drawn. There are lots of other ways. Just make sure that the diagram has all the information. Notice how the congruent angles, the line, and the segment are marked on the drawing.

MATH ALERT Don't Make Figures Special Unless You Know They're Special

Don't draw your diagram with perpendicular, parallel, or congruent segments (or angles) unless those are given facts. If you do, you may mislead yourself when you use the diagram in a proof.

From this diagram, it may appear that the segments are perpendicular. It may also appear that $\overline{AB} \cong \overline{BC}$. Unless the angles are marked as right angles with a right-angle symbol, you should not assume that angles that look like right angles are right angles. Also, unless you're clearly given a reason to believe angles are right angles, don't draw or mark them as such. Similarly, unless segments are marked as congruent, you should not assume that they have the same length just because the lengths look the same in the diagram and be very careful when drawing a diagram not to imply any relationship you're not sure of.

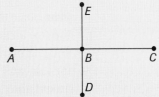

Two-Column Proof

A **two-column proof** is a sequence of statements, each with a corresponding reason, that starts with a given set of premises and leads to a conclusion which must be true. The steps are numbered to show a logical order in the argument.

To successfully complete a two-column proof, you must decide what is given and what needs to be proved. You can begin by drawing a diagram. Label all relevant information on the diagram. Then try to make a plan that outlines the steps you must follow to reach the conclusion logically. Sometimes, your plan will require you to make additions to the diagram. These additions are called **auxiliary lines**. It's probably a good idea to make your additions to the diagram in a different color. Acceptable additions include:

- extending segments,
- constructing parallel lines, perpendiculars, bisectors, etc., and
- connecting given points.

Sometimes the *given*, *prove*, and diagram are provided.

EXAMPLE 1:

Given: $\overrightarrow{PR}$ bisects $\angle SPQ$

Prove: $2(m\angle 1) = m\angle SPQ$

Diagram

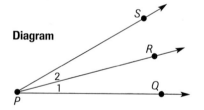

The most important part of your proof is the plan. Decide on a strategy to work through the proof. Then fill in the details of the proof. Your formal proof follows the plan with more detail and carefully spelled-out reasons.

Plan: Since the ray bisects the angle, the two angles must be congruent. You can mark the diagram to show this. Because the two angles are con-

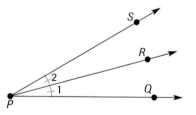

gruent, they must have the same measure. The two angles have the same measure, so you can substitute one for the other.

Now use your plan and the marked diagram to complete the proof. Record the statements in the left column and the reason for each statement in the right column. Usually you will want to begin the proof with the given information. Sometimes, to make the logic of your argument more obvious, you may write some of the given information later in the proof.

Proof

MORE HELP
See 073, 432

Acceptable statements are given information, additions to a diagram, and facts that fall out from statements you've already made.

Acceptable reasons are given, formulas, definitions, postulates, theorems, properties, substitution, and constructions.

In two-column proofs in this book, red abbreviations are for Postulates. The P-number tells you where to look in the Glossary of Postulates in the Almanac for the full postulate. Theorems are blue. Formulas are green.

Statements	Reasons
❶ $\overrightarrow{PR}$ bisects $\angle SPQ$	Given
❷ $\angle 1 \cong \angle 2$	Def. of $\angle$ bisector
❸ $m\angle 1 = m\angle 2$	Def. of $\cong$
❹ $m\angle 1 + \boxed{m\angle 2} = m\angle SPQ$	$\angle$ + Postulate (P13)
❺ $m\angle 1 + \boxed{m\angle 1} = m\angle SPQ$	Substitution
❻ $2(m\angle 1) = m\angle SPQ$	Distributive prop.

See steps 3 and 4.

The final statement should be the statement you were asked to prove.

EXAMPLE 2: Prove that if two sides of a triangle are congruent, then the angles opposite them are congruent. This is the Base Angles Theorem.

Proof

Given: $\overline{AB} \cong \overline{AC}$

Prove: $\angle B \cong \angle C$

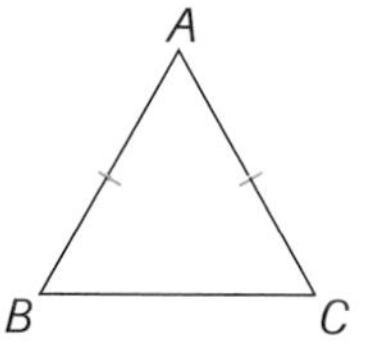

Plan: First draw the angle bisector of the vertex angle to form two triangles. Next show that the triangles are congruent by the SAS Congruence Postulate. You can then compare the two congruent triangles to help you conclude that the two base angles of $\triangle ABC$ are congruent. Your formal reason can be *CPCTC*, the abbreviation for *congruent parts of congruent triangles are congruent*.

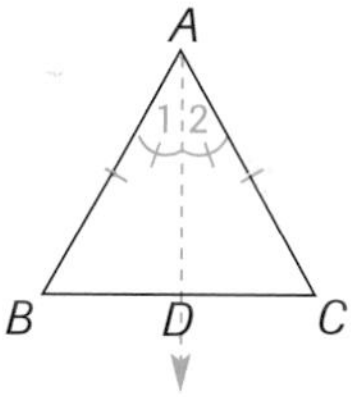

MORE HELP
See 145, 256, 260, 262, 374, 434

Given diagram   Annotated diagram

Statements	Reasons
❶ Construct $\overrightarrow{AD}$ to bisect $\angle A$	Construction
❷ $\angle 1 \cong \angle 2$	Def. of $\angle$ bisector Look back at step 1.
❸ $\overline{AB} \cong \overline{AC}$	Given
❹ $\overline{AD} \cong \overline{AD}$	Reflexive prop. of $\cong$ (T105)
❺ $\triangle BAD \cong \triangle CAD$	SAS $\cong$ Postulate (P23) Look back at steps 2, 3, and 4.
❻ $\angle B \cong \angle C$	CPCTC

Checking Your Proof

After you have completed a proof, you should look back at each statement and reason to make sure that your argument makes sense. A useful strategy for checking a proof is to work backward through each step. Start with the conclusion and make sure that the way you reached the conclusion was made possible by an earlier step. For example, if you used CPCTC, you should check that your proof includes the step that proves the triangles are congruent. If you used the definition of a midpoint, you should check that you were given a midpoint in the problem or that you were able to construct the midpoint.

EXAMPLE: Check the proof by working backward.

Proof

Given: $\overline{AB} \cong \overline{AC}$, D is the midpoint of $\overline{BC}$

Prove: $\angle 1 \cong \angle 2$

Diagram

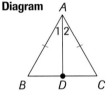

Statements	Reasons
❶ $\overline{AB} \cong \overline{AC}$	Given
❷ D is the midpoint of $\overline{BC}$	Given
❸ $\overline{BD} \cong \overline{DC}$	Def. of midpoint
❹ $\overline{AD} \cong \overline{AD}$	Reflexive prop. of $\cong$ (T105)
❺ $\triangle ADB \cong \triangle ADC$	SSS $\cong$ Postulate (P22)
❻ $\angle 1 \cong \angle 2$	CPCTC

MORE HELP
See 255

To check the proof, work backward.

■ In Step 6, CPCTC is used. This is OK since Step 5 shows the two triangles are congruent and that $\angle 1$ and $\angle 2$ *are* corresponding parts.

■ In Step 5, the SSS $\cong$ Postulate is used to show the triangles are congruent. Check that all three pairs of sides are really congruent. Steps 1, 3, and 4 establish that the sides are all congruent.

■ In Step 4, the reflexive property is used for the side that is shared by both triangles.

■ In Step 3, the definition of the midpoint is used to identify a pair of congruent sides. You can use the definition since the midpoint was given in Step 2.

■ In Steps 2 and 1, the *given* is stated.

The check shows that the proof makes sense.

Coordinate Proof

To use a **coordinate proof**, you must place a figure in the coordinate plane. Where you place the figure can make the proof easier. For example, placing a figure along one of the axes, with one vertex at the origin and using positive coordinates for the other vertices, will often simplify calculations. As long as all of the requirements of the *given* information are met, you are not skewing the results of your proof by placing the diagram in a convenient position.

You must also consider whether the proof involves numeric coordinates or variable coordinates. If you are trying to prove a specific case, you'll need to use the given coordinates. If you are trying to prove a general case, you may need to use variable coordinates.

EXAMPLE: Prove that the diagonals of a rectangle bisect each other.

Place the rectangle in the coordinate plane so that vertex O is at the origin, side $\overline{OA}$ is on the x-axis, side $\overline{OB}$ is on the y-axis and vertex C is in the first quadrant. Assign variable coordinates to each of the vertices.

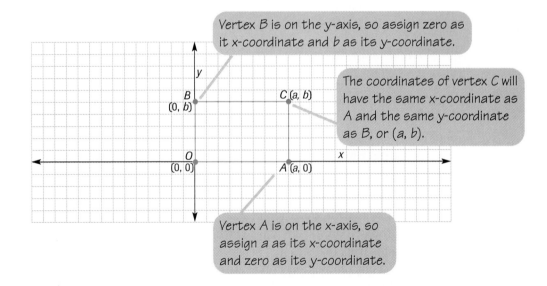

MORE HELP
See 089

Proof

Given: Rectangle $OACB$

Prove: $\overline{AB}$ and $\overline{OC}$ bisect each other

Plan: Draw the diagonals. Use the midpoint formula to find the midpoint of each diagonal. If the two midpoints are the same point, you know that the diagonals bisect each other.

$$\text{Midpoint } \overline{OC} = \left(\frac{x_1 + x_2}{2}, \frac{y_1 + y_2}{2}\right)$$

$$= \left(\frac{0 + a}{2}, \frac{0 + b}{2}\right)$$

$$= \left(\frac{a}{2}, \frac{b}{2}\right)$$

$$\text{Midpoint } \overline{AB} = \left(\frac{x_1 + x_2}{2}, \frac{y_1 + y_2}{2}\right)$$

$$= \left(\frac{a + 0}{2}, \frac{0 + b}{2}\right)$$

$$= \left(\frac{a}{2}, \frac{b}{2}\right)$$

Diagram

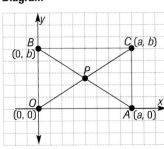

★ Since the midpoints are the same, $\overline{AB}$ and $\overline{OC}$ bisect each other.

044

Paragraph Proof

A **paragraph proof** is basically a two-column proof in paragraph form. It looks similar to a plan for a proof, but it contains more detail. You must state all of the reasons. You must explain why each statement follows from a previous one.

A paragraph proof usually begins with a diagram, just like other forms of proof. You should mark the diagram and then use the diagram to help you plan your proof. When you are finished with the proof, look back on your argument and check that it makes sense. Remember that working backward through any proof is a useful way to check whether any parts of the arguments are incomplete.

EXAMPLE:

Given: $\overline{AB} \parallel \overline{CD}$, $\overline{BC} \parallel \overline{AD}$

Prove: $\overline{AB} \cong \overline{CD}$

First use the diagram to help you plan the proof.

Diagram

Plan: Draw diagonal $\overline{BD}$. Show that $\triangle ABD \cong \triangle CDB$. Then use CPCTC to show that $\overline{AB} \cong \overline{CD}$. First mark the diagram with the information given.

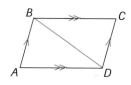

Then mark any information that you can deduce from the given information. Notice that $\overline{BD}$ is a transversal that intersects two parallel segments. This means that the alternate interior angles are congruent. Mark the congruent angles on the diagram. This should make it easy to decide which congruence postulate you should use in your proof.

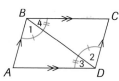

MORE HELP
See 077, 258

★ **ONE WAY** Use a paragraph proof.

Draw diagonal $\overline{BD}$. Because $\overline{AB}$ is parallel to $\overline{CD}$, it follows from the Alternate Interior Angles Theorem that $\angle 1 \cong \angle 2$. For the same reason, because $\overline{BC}$ is parallel to $\overline{DA}$, $\angle 3 \cong \angle 4$. The Reflexive Property of Congruence shows that $\overline{BD} \cong \overline{BD}$. From the ASA Congruence Theorem, you can tell that $\triangle ABD \cong \triangle CDB$. Finally, because corresponding parts of congruent triangles are congruent, $\overline{AB} \cong \overline{CD}$.

To check the proof, look back and make sure that everything needed to reach the conclusion was indeed shown in the proof. The conditions to use the ASA Congruence Theorem were all shown, so the proof makes sense.

ANOTHER WAY Use a two-column proof.

> Sometimes, for a long proof, it's easier to follow a two-column proof than a paragraph proof.

Statements	Reasons
❶ Draw diagonal BD	2 pts. determine a line (P05)
❷ $\overline{AB} \parallel \overline{CD}$, $\overline{BC} \parallel \overline{DA}$	Given
❸ $\angle 1 \cong \angle 2$, $\angle 3 \cong \angle 4$	Alt. Int. $\angle$s Theorem (T027)
❹ $\overline{BD} \cong \overline{BD}$	Reflexive prop. of $\cong$ (T105)
❺ $\triangle ABD \cong \triangle CDB$	ASA $\cong$ Theorem (T108)
❻ $\overline{AB} \cong \overline{CD}$	CPCTC

ANOTHER WAY If you can use theorems about parallelograms, this becomes a simple two-step proof. Show that $ABCD$ is a parallelogram, then use the definition to show $\overline{AB} \cong \overline{CD}$.

Flow Chart Proof

MORE HELP
See 069–070

A **flow chart** is a diagram that shows a step-by-step process. Boxes represent each step and arrows connect the boxes to show the flow of the reasoning. Computer programmers and software engineers often use flow charts to design programs and study computer systems.

A **flow chart proof** (or just a **flow proof**) uses a flow chart to show the flow of a logical argument. Flow charts can make it easier to map out the logic involved in a proof, both for the person writing the proof, and for the person following the argument presented in the proof.

In a flow chart proof, the statements are presented in boxes. The reason for each statement is written below the box containing the statement. The boxes are connected by arrows to show how statements are logically connected. As with other forms of proof, begin a flow chart proof by drawing a diagram. Mark on the diagram any information that is given or can be deduced.

EXAMPLE 1:

Given: $\angle 1$ and $\angle 2$ are a linear pair.

$\angle 2$ and $\angle 3$ are a linear pair.

Prove: $\angle 1 \cong \angle 3$

Plan: Use the fact that the angles are linear pairs to show that they are supplementary.

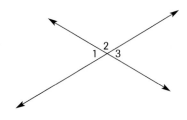

ONE WAY Use a flow chart proof.

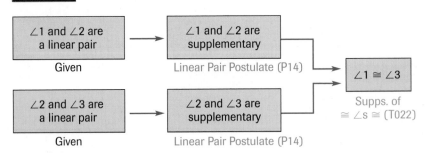

ANOTHER WAY Use a paragraph proof.

Because $\angle 1$ and $\angle 2$ are a linear pair, the Linear Pair Postulate says that $\angle 1$ and $\angle 2$ are supplementary. By the same reasoning, $\angle 2$ and $\angle 3$ are supplementary. Both $\angle 1$ and $\angle 3$ are supplementary to $\angle 2$, so they are congruent since supplements of the same angle are congruent. This means that $\angle 1 \cong \angle 3$.

ANOTHER WAY Use a two-column proof.

Proof

Statements	Reasons
❶ ∠1 and ∠2 are a linear pair ∠2 and ∠3 are a linear pair	Given
❷ ∠1 and ∠2 are supplementary ∠2 and ∠3 are supplementary	Linear Pair Postulate (P14)
❸ ∠1 ≅ ∠3	Supps. of ≅ ∠s ≅ (T022)

> Notice that three different methods were used to prove that ∠1 ≅ ∠3. All three methods used the same diagram, the same plan, and the same given and prove statements. The method of proof you choose often depends on your own preference.

Indirect Proof

046

In an **indirect proof**, you assume that what you are trying to prove is false. Then you show that this assumption leads you to a contradiction, so the statement you're trying to prove cannot be false; it must be true. Another name for this type of proof is **proof by contradiction**.

MORE HELP
See 145

To write an indirect proof:
1. Identify the statement that you want to prove is true.
2. Begin by assuming that the statement is false.
3. Use that assumption of falsehood to deduce other statements which contradict something you know is true. Sometimes it contradicts the *given*, other times it contradicts a Postulate, Theorem or definition.
4. Because the assumption that the original statement is false leads to a contradiction, the original statement must be true.

EXAMPLE: Use an indirect proof.

Given: In △ABC, $\overline{AB} \not\cong \overline{BC}$

Prove: ∠A ≇ ∠C

Plan: Begin by assuming that ∠A ≅ ∠C. Show that this leads to a contradiction of the given information.

Diagram

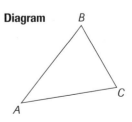

Assume ∠A ≅ ∠C. This would mean that △ABC is an isosceles triangle. According to the Converse of the Base Angles Theorem, this would make $\overline{AB} \cong \overline{BC}$. But this contradicts the *given*, that $\overline{AB} \not\cong \overline{BC}$. Then, the assumption that ∠A ≅ ∠C must be false. Therefore, ∠A ≇ ∠C.

Basic Elements of Geometry

"Let no one ignorant of geometry enter my door."

Plato, in *The Republic*

Think of geometry as a skyscraper. At its foundation are three basic terms: point, line, and plane. These terms are used to define other terms, like ray and line segment, which then can be used to define more terms, like angle and midpoint. All these defined terms are the steel beams of the skyscraper, built carefully upon one another and upon the foundation of the three basic, undefined terms.

How can the entire structure of geometry rest on undefined terms? Well, even though we say that point, line, and plane are undefined, they do have meaning. In fact, people agree so strongly about their meaning that these terms give geometry a very solid foundation.

But no matter how firm the foundation, a skyscraper won't stand unless its beams are carefully connected. In geometry, we connect geometric terms with relationships. Some of these relationships, called postulates, we know to be true but can't prove. Other relationships, called theorems, can be proved.

You may have worked with points, lines, and planes before. These are very real concepts that may be referred to as undefined.

A **point** is simply a location in space. You can describe its position by coordinates, but can't see it, because it has no length, width, or height. Since a line has length, but no width or thickness, and a plane has length and width, but no thickness, you can't see them either. These concepts start to feel real when they interact with other concepts to describe the geometric world. Once you've defined points and planes you can define lines and curves and other geometric figures and relationships.

A point is named by coordinates and/or by a capital letter, and its location may be indicated by a dot.

Write: *P*

Say: *Point P*

MORE HELP
See 017,
087–088

Collinear points are points that lie on the same line. **Coplanar points** are points that lie in the same plane.

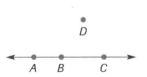

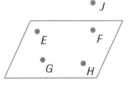

A, B, and *C* are collinear. *A, B,* and *D* are noncollinear (not collinear).

E, F, G, and *H* are coplanar. *E, F, G,* and *J* are noncoplanar (not coplanar).

Lines may also be coplanar.

While point, line, and plane are undefined terms, most other terms have precise definitions. A good definition is specific enough to identify everything with this property but not so specific that it screens out some things that belong. Consider some possible definitions of a dog.

It has four legs.
Not enough. Add some detail to the definition.

*It is a mammal
with four legs.*
Still not enough.
So, add more
detail.

It is a mammal with four legs that barks.
Dogs, and only dogs, meet these criteria.

If the detail included any more information, it might screen out perfectly
good members of the dog family. For example, *it is a mammal with four
legs that barks and is named Rover.*

Properties of Planes

049

A **plane** has length and width but no thickness. A wall is a model of a
plane but a plane extends forever in two dimensions. You can sketch a
plane in perspective by drawing a parallelogram. If you need to name a
plane, use a single capital letter.

MORE HELP
See 019, 051,157

Postulate	A plane contains at least three noncollinear points. Plane ⇒ 3 noncollinear pts. (P01)	**Diagram**

This postulate assures you that a plane is more than a line. Given any line
on a plane, the plane contains at least one point that is not on the line.

MORE ▶

MORE HELP
See 054

Postulate   If two distinct points lie in a plane, then the line containing them lies in the plane.

Points are said to lie on a line or in a plane.

Pts. A and B in plane $\Rightarrow$ $\overleftrightarrow{AB}$ in plane (P02)

Diagram

Distinct points means the points are not the same point. You can see that when mathematicians decide they need to be precise, they mean business!

In order for the line containing the two points to lie outside the plane, either the line would not be straight or the plane would not be flat!

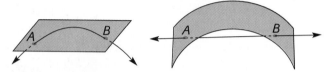

From this postulate you know that a plane and a line not in the plane can intersect in only one point. If the line intersected the plane in two points, then the whole line would lie in the plane.

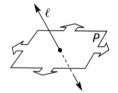

Postulate   If two distinct planes intersect, then their intersection is a line.
Plane $M \cap$ plane N is a line. (P03)

Diagram

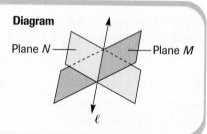

Plane N ———   ——— Plane M

ℓ

MORE HELP
See 058

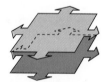

Not all planes intersect. Just as some lines may be parallel, some planes may be parallel. That is, they have no points in common.

A **half plane** is the part of a plane that is on one side of a line in that plane. The term *half plane* isn't really about size. It's just a way of identifying the part of the plane being discussed. The line ℓ is the boundary of each part of plane M. It is not part of either half plane.

050

MATH ALERT The Sketch of a Plane or a Line Includes Boundaries That Do Not Actually Exist

The boundaries you draw when sketching a plane are used to help visualize the plane but the plane itself extends infinitely in its two dimensions.

Lines are also unbounded. A line has infinite length and an infinite number of points on it. The arrowheads at each end of a sketch of a line indicate that it extends infinitely in either direction.

The line extends infinitely. It doesn't end at the arrowheads.

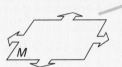

These boundaries don't exist. The plane extends infinitely.

Determining a Plane

051

One strange geometric term you will see often is *determined*. A figure is **determined** when there is one and only one such figure that meets a given set of conditions. For example, *Two points determine a line*. This means that if you take any two points, you can always draw exactly one line through the two points.

Postulate   Three noncollinear points determine a plane.
3 noncollinear pts. ⇒ unique plane (P04)

A line lies in an infinite number of planes, so you can't identify a plane simply by naming a line in it. However, if you name another point that's not on the line, then you've identified a plane. In short, a plane is determined by a line and any point not on the line.

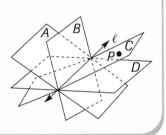

A plane can also be determined by two intersecting lines or by two parallel lines.

Two intersecting lines determine a plane.

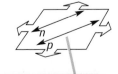

Two parallel lines determine a plane.

Line is undefined. It has no endpoints. You cannot measure its length. You can name a line using any two points on the line or by using a lower case letter. You *can* define parts of a line. A **line segment** has two endpoints. It contains these endpoints and all the points of the line between them. You can measure the length of a segment.

Write: $\overleftrightarrow{MN}$ or $\overleftrightarrow{NM}$ or ℓ
Say: *line M N or line N M or line ℓ*

Write: $\overline{JK}$ or $\overline{KJ}$
Say: *segment J K or segment K J*

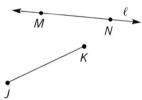

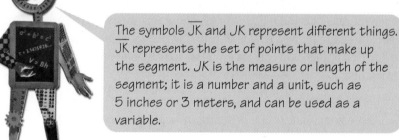

The symbols $\overline{JK}$ and JK represent different things. $\overline{JK}$ represents the set of points that make up the segment. JK is the measure or length of the segment; it is a number and a unit, such as 5 inches or 3 meters, and can be used as a variable.

A **ray** is a part of a line that has one endpoint and goes on infinitely in one direction. A pair of **opposite rays** form a line. You cannot measure the length of a ray because, while the zero-point of your ruler could line up with the ray's endpoint, there is no other endpoint to help you find the length on the ruler. To name a ray, write the letter for the endpoint first, then name any other point on the ray.

Write: $\overrightarrow{LM}$ or $\overrightarrow{LN}$
Say: *ray L M or ray L N*

Lines and segments can be related to each other in several ways.

MORE HELP
See 058, 061

Relationship	Diagram	Definition
Intersecting		Lines that meet at a point.
Concurrent		Three or more lines that meet at the same point.
Perpendicular		Lines that intersect to form a right angle.
Parallel		Lines in the same plane that don't intersect.
Skew		Lines not in the same plane that don't intersect.

The cube shows some of these relationships.

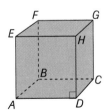

Write: $\overline{AD} \perp \overline{DH}$
Say: *Segment A D is perpendicular to segment D H.*

Write: $\overline{AD} \parallel \overline{EH}$
Say: *Segment A D is parallel to segment E H.*

Write: $\overline{AE}$ and $\overline{DC}$ are skew.
Say: *Segment A E and segment D C are skew.*

053

MATH ALERT $\overrightarrow{BA}$ Is Not the Same As $\overrightarrow{AB}$

A ray is named by using its endpoint first, so while $\overleftrightarrow{AB}$ is the same as $\overleftrightarrow{BA}$, $\overrightarrow{AB}$ is *not* the same as $\overrightarrow{BA}$.

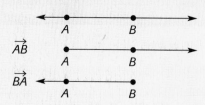

054

Lines and Segments

The next three postulates describe relationships among points and lines.

> **Postulate**　Through any two distinct points there exists exactly one line. 2 pts. determine a line. (P05)

A baseball field is an example of this postulate. The first base line is the line through the outer corners of home plate and first base.

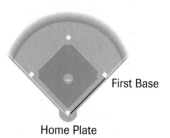

First Base

Home Plate

> **Postulate**　A line contains at least two points.
> Line contains at least 2 pts. (P06)

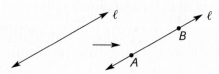

> **Postulate**　If two distinct lines intersect, then their intersection is exactly one point. 2 lines ∩ at a pt. (P07)

If distinct lines were allowed to intersect in two or more points, they would have to be curved!

Ruler Postulate

> **Postulate** The points on a line can be matched, one-to-one, with the set of real numbers. The **coordinate** of a point is the real number that corresponds to it. The distance between two points, A and B, equals $|a - b|$.
> Ruler Postulate (P08)

> On a number line, if A names a point, then we use a as the coordinate of that point.

Why is this postulate needed? It allows you to construct a number line on any line, and then tells you how to use the coordinates of two points to find the distance between them.

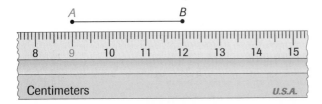

MORE HELP
See 087, 089

To find the length of the line segment, find the number on the ruler that corresponds to each endpoint. Remember, a ruler is just a physical number line. In this example, $AB = |9 - 12|$. $\overline{AB}$ is 3 centimeters long.

Bisectors—Midpoint, Perpendicular Bisector, Line of Symmetry

A **bisector** divides a figure into congruent halves. That is, one half must be exactly the same size *and shape* as the other half.

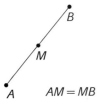

A point can bisect a segment.

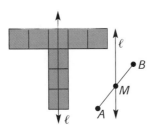

A line can bisect a segment or a two-dimensional figure.

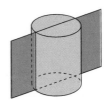

A plane can bisect a two- or three-dimensional figure.

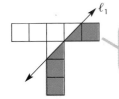

> Halves of a figure could be noncongruent. This figure could be divided in half as shown, but in this case, ℓ_1 is not a bisector of the figure.

MORE ▶

The bisector of a segment is its **midpoint**. Any line, segment, or ray containing this midpoint is considered a bisector.

A ————— M ————— C

Numbers can be equal, but only a set of points can be congruent.

Write: *AM = CM*
Say: *The length of segment A M equals the length of segment C M.*

Write: $\overline{AM} \cong \overline{CM}$
Say: *Segment A M is congruent to segment C M.*

EXAMPLE: Suppose you know the coordinates of points *A* and *C* on a number line. How can you find the coordinate of the midpoint?

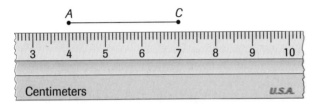

The distance between *A* and *C* is |4 cm − 7 cm|, or 3 cm. Since the midpoint is half the distance from *A* to *C*, it is 1.5 units from each point. Its coordinate is 7 cm − 1.5 cm or 4 cm + 1.5 cm.

★ The coordinate of the midpoint is 5.5 cm.

You can use this same method to find a formula that works for any two points on a number line.

Theorem　On a number line, the coordinate of the midpoint of the segment with endpoints *A* and *B* is $\frac{a + b}{2}$.
Endpt. coords. *a*, *b* ⇒ midpt. coord. $\frac{a + b}{2}$ (T001)

Proof

Given: endpoint coordinates *a* and *b*

Prove: the midpoint is $\frac{a + b}{2}$

Plan: If A is to the left of B on a number line, the distance between A and B is $b - a$. The midpoint is halfway between these two points: $\frac{b-a}{2}$.

Since $a < b$, add this distance to a, or subtract it from b, to get the coordinate of the midpoint. Simplify both expressions. They should be equivalent to $\frac{a+b}{2}$.

Diagram

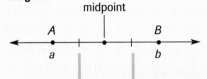

The tick marks show that the lengths of the segments are equal.

$$a + \frac{b-a}{2}$$

$$= \frac{2a}{2} + \frac{b-a}{2} \quad \text{Write equivalent fractions}$$

$$= \frac{2a+b-a}{2} \qquad\qquad \text{Add}$$

$$= \frac{a+b}{2} \qquad\qquad\quad \text{Simplify}$$

$$b - \frac{b-a}{2}$$

$$= \frac{2b}{2} - \frac{b-a}{2}$$

$$= \frac{2b-b+a}{2}$$

$$= \frac{b+a}{2} \quad \text{or} \quad \frac{a+b}{2}$$

You can think of a midpoint this way: the coordinate of the midpoint is the average (mean) of the coordinates of the endpoints.

MORE HELP
See 260, 276, 279, 432, 434

A **perpendicular bisector** is a line that is perpendicular to a segment at its midpoint.

Theorem   If a point is on the perpendicular bisector of a segment, then it is equidistant from the endpoints of the segment.
⊥ Bisector Theorem (T002)

Proof

Given: Line ℓ is the perpendicular bisector of $\overline{OP}$. Point X is on ℓ.

Prove: $OX = XP$

Plan: Divide the proof into two cases, one where X is on $\overline{OP}$ and the other where it is any other point on the perpendicular bisector. Use what you know about symmetry and corresponding points to show that $OX = XP$.

CASE 1 X is at the intersection of $\overline{OP}$ and ℓ.

Then $OX = XP$, because a perpendicular bisector passes through the midpoint of a segment. X is the midpoint of $\overline{OP}$.

Diagram

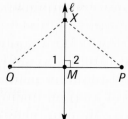

CASE 2 X is any other point on the perpendicular bisector of $\overline{OP}$.

MORE HELP
See 262

ONE WAY   The perpendicular bisector ℓ is a line of symmetry of $\overline{OP}$, so O and P are image points under a reflection across ℓ by definition of a reflection. X is its own image, again by the definition of reflection. By the Property of Isometries, $XO = XP$.

Diagram

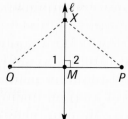

ANOTHER WAY   M is the midpoint of $\overline{OP}$ because it lies on the perpendicular bisector. This means that $OM = MP$ and therefore $\overline{OM} \cong \overline{MP}$. $\angle 1 \cong \angle 2$ because $\overline{XM}$ is perpendicular to $\overline{OP}$. $\overline{XM} \cong \overline{XM}$, so SAS tells us that $\triangle OMX \cong \triangle PMX$. $\overline{OX} \cong \overline{XP}$ because corresponding parts of congruent triangles are congruent, so $OX = XP$.

Diagram

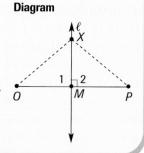

MORE HELP
See 061, 070,
256, 261, 432,
434

Theorem If a point is equidistant from the endpoints of a segment, then it is on the perpendicular bisector of the segment.

Converse of ⊥ Bisector Theorem (T003)

Proof

Given: $AC = BC$

Prove: C is on the perpendicular bisector of $\overline{AB}$

Plan: If you draw a line to connect C to the midpoint of $\overline{AB}$, you can show both that this line is perpendicular to $\overline{AB}$ and that it bisects $\overline{AB}$.

Diagram

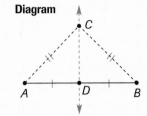

Statements	Reasons
❶ $AC = BC$	Given
❷ Mark D, the midpoint of $\overline{AB}$	Ruler Postulate (P08)
❸ Draw $\overleftrightarrow{CD}$	2 pts. determine a line. (P05)
❹ $AD = BD$ $\overline{AD} \cong \overline{BD}$	Def. of midpoint; def. of ≅
❺ $\overline{CD} \cong \overline{CD}$	Reflexive prop. of ≅ (T105)
❻ $\triangle CAD \cong \triangle CBD$	SSS Congruence Postulate (P22)
❼ $\angle CDA \cong \angle CDB$	CPCTC
❽ $\overleftrightarrow{CD} \perp \overline{AB}$	Lines form ≅ linear pair ⟹ ⊥ (T012)
❾ $\overleftrightarrow{CD}$ is ⊥ bisector of $\overline{AB}$	Def. of ⊥ bisector *See steps 4 and 8.*

Segment Addition Postulate

Postulate Point B lies between points A and C if and only if $AB + BC = AC$. Segment + Postulate (P09)

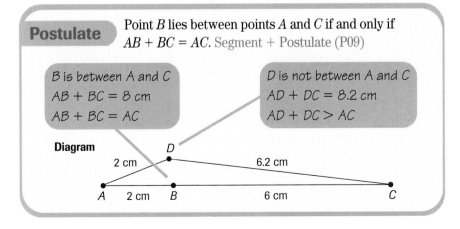

B is between A and C
$AB + BC = 8$ cm
$AB + BC = AC$

D is not between A and C
$AD + DC = 8.2$ cm
$AD + DC > AC$

Diagram

2 cm D

6.2 cm

A 2 cm B 6 cm C

058

Parallel Lines and Planes

Parallel lines are lines in the same plane that do not intersect.

Write: $\overleftrightarrow{DE} \parallel \overleftrightarrow{FG}$
Say: *Line D E is parallel to line F G.*

Parallel planes are planes that never intersect.

Imagine all the surfaces of the stairway represent planes. The treads (or top surfaces) of these steps are parallel. All the risers (vertical surfaces between the treads) are also parallel.

When sketching parallel planes, use dashed lines to indicate that part of a plane is behind the other. Begin by drawing the front edges as parallel lines to make your finished planes appear parallel.

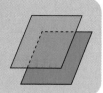

059

MORE HELP
See 162

Distance Between Two Parallel Lines

The **distance between two parallel lines** is the length of a perpendicular segment with endpoints on each line.

Theorem   The distance between two parallel lines is constant.
Dist. between ∥ lines constant (T004)

Proof

Given: $\ell \parallel m$; $\overline{AB}$ is perpendicular to ℓ at A and to m at B; $\overline{CD}$ is perpendicular to ℓ at C and to m at D

Prove: $AB = CD$

Since $ACDB$ is a quadrilateral with four right angles, it is a rectangle. Since opposite sides of a rectangle have the same length, $AB = CD$.

Diagram

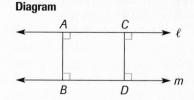

Properties of Parallel Lines and Planes

Theorem	If two parallel planes are cut by a third plane, then the lines of intersection are parallel. $2 \parallel$ planes cut by 3rd plane $\Rightarrow \parallel$ lines (T005)

MORE HELP
See 046, 058

Proof

Given: $R \parallel M$, N intersects R in $\overleftrightarrow{AB}$; N intersects M in $\overleftrightarrow{CD}$

Prove: $\overleftrightarrow{AB} \parallel \overleftrightarrow{CD}$

Diagram

Try an indirect proof. Suppose that $\overleftrightarrow{AB}$ and $\overleftrightarrow{CD}$ intersect. Then they would intersect at some point P. That means P would be in both plane R and plane M, because all the points of $\overleftrightarrow{AB}$ are in R and all the points of $\overleftrightarrow{CD}$ are in M. This makes P a point of intersection of planes R and M, which you know do not intersect. This means $\overleftrightarrow{AB}$ and $\overleftrightarrow{CD}$ cannot intersect. Since they don't intersect and are both in plane N, they must be parallel.

Theorem	If two or more lines are perpendicular to the same plane, then they are parallel. Lines $\perp$ same plane $\Rightarrow \parallel$ (T006)

MORE HELP
See 061, 081

Proof

Given: $\ell_1 \perp$ plane R at A; $\ell_2 \perp$ plane R at C

Prove: $\ell_1 \parallel \ell_2$

Plan: You need to prove first that the two lines are in the same plane, then that they are parallel.

Diagram

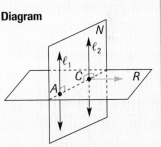

First, show that the two lines are in the same plane. Since two points determine a line and three points determine a plane, ℓ_1 and point C determine a plane, call it N. Planes N and R are perpendicular because if a line is perpendicular to a plane then any plane containing that line is also perpendicular to the given plane. At point C, you could construct a ray in plane N and a ray in plane R to form the plane angle of the dihedral angle formed by planes N and R. Since plane R is perpendicular to plane N, the measure of angle C is $90°$. There is exactly one line perpendicular to a plane at a point, so ℓ_2 contains the ray in Plane N. This means that ℓ_1 and ℓ_2 both lie in plane N.

MORE ▶

MORE HELP
See 046

Now, use an indirect proof to show the lines are parallel. Begin by assuming that ℓ_1 and ℓ_2 intersect at some point X. $\overline{AX}$ and $\overline{CX}$ would both be perpendicular to $\overline{AC}$ because if a line is perpendicular to a plane, it is perpendicular to every line in the plane passing through the point of intersection. That means that $\triangle CAX$ would have two right angles: one at A and one at C. Since a triangle can have at most one right angle, the assumption that the lines intersect is false. They must be parallel.

Diagram

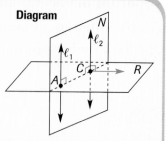

MORE HELP
See 061,
375–376

Theorem   If two planes are perpendicular to the same line, then they are parallel. 2 planes $\perp$ same line $\Rightarrow\ \|$ (T007)

Proof

Given: Plane R and plane S are both perpendicular to ℓ.

Prove: plane $R \parallel$ plane S

Construct lines in each of the planes that are perpendicular to ℓ and parallel to each other. They must lie in the same plane. If two coplanar lines are perpendicular to the same line, then they are parallel. Therefore, the planes that contain these lines must be parallel.

Diagram

MORE HELP
See 107, 363

DID YOU KNOW   Euclid, a mathematician in ancient Greece, organized all known geometry into postulates and theorems in his work *The Elements*. The Parallel Postulate was his fifth and most controversial postulate. Mathematicians for centuries thought it should be provable, and therefore not a postulate. It wasn't until the late 1800s that mathematicians found that by changing the parallel postulate whole new geometries could be created. At first these geometries seemed strange and useless. In the twentieth century, however, non-Euclidean geometry found a spectacular application in Einstein's Theory of Relativity. The following postulate is a foundation for Euclidean geometry.

Postulate If there is a line and a point not on the line, then there is exactly one line through the point and parallel to the given line. ‖ Postulate (P10)

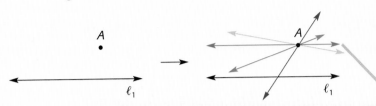

The red line through A is parallel to ℓ_1. Any other line through A will eventually intersect ℓ_1, and couldn't be parallel.

In algebra, the Transitive Property of Equality states that if $a = b$ and $b = c$, then $a = c$. There is also a Transitive Property of Parallel Lines.

Theorem If two lines are parallel to the same line, then they are parallel to each other. Transitive prop. of ‖ lines (T008)

This theorem needs to be broken into two cases, one in which all the lines are in the same plane, and one in which they are not, since the diagrams and methods of proof are not the same.

Proof

CASE 1 The three lines are coplanar.   **Diagram**

Given: $\ell \parallel m$ and $m \parallel n$

Prove: $\ell \parallel n$

Use an indirect proof. Assume that ℓ and n intersect at some point P. Then at P both ℓ and n would be parallel to m. The Parallel Postulate says that only one line through P and parallel to m is possible. This contradicts your assumption, so ℓ and n must be parallel.

CASE 2 The pairs of lines are in different planes.   **Diagram**

Given: $\ell \parallel m$ and $m \parallel n$

Prove: $\ell \parallel n$

The proof of this case is beyond the scope of this book. Look at this triangular prism to see why this theorem is true when the pairs of lines are in different planes.

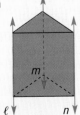

MORE ▶

MORE HELP
See 036,
074–075, 232

Theorem If three parallel lines intersect two transversals, then they divide the transversals proportionally. ∥ lines cut 2 transversals ⇒ transversal segs. proportional (T009)

Proof

Diagram

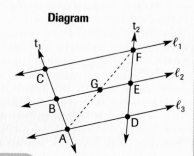

Given: $\ell_1 \parallel \ell_2 \parallel \ell_3$; cut by transversals t_1 and t_2

Prove: $\frac{AB}{BC} = \frac{DE}{EF}$

Plan: Draw a triangle and use the Triangle Proportionality Theorem. Then use the Transitive Property of Equality.

Statements	Reasons
❶ Draw $\overrightarrow{AF}$ intersecting l_2 at G	2 pts. determine a line. (P05)
❷ $\ell_1 \parallel \ell_2$	Given
❸ In $\triangle ACF$, $\dfrac{AB}{BC} = \dfrac{AG}{GF}$	△ Proportionality Theorem (T094)
❹ $\ell_2 \parallel \ell_3$	Given
❺ In $\triangle FAD$, $\dfrac{AG}{GF} = \dfrac{DE}{EF}$	△ Proportionality Theorem (T094)
❻ $\dfrac{AB}{BC} = \dfrac{DE}{EF}$	Transitive prop. of =

061

Perpendicular Lines and Planes

MORE HELP
See 052, 108

Two lines are **perpendicular** if they intersect to form a right angle. A **line is perpendicular to a plane** at point P if it is perpendicular to every line in the plane passing through P.

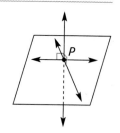

Is the transitive property true for perpendicular lines? Consider this example. On the football field, the sideline is perpendicular to the end line, and the uprights of the goal post are perpendicular to the end line. However, the sideline is not perpendicular to the goal post because the sideline and the goal post do not intersect; they lie in different planes. They are **skew** lines.

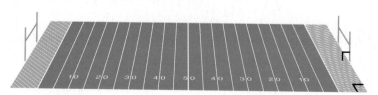

Postulate
If there is a line and a point not on the line, then there is exactly one line through the point and perpendicular to the given line. ⊥ Postulate (P11)

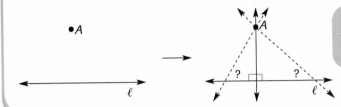

•A

If you draw any other line through A and ℓ, it will not meet ℓ at a right angle.

Theorem
If two coplanar lines are perpendicular to the same line, then they are parallel to each other. 2 lines in plane ⊥ 3rd line ⇒ ‖ (T010)

Diagram

Proof

Given: $\ell \perp n$ at A; $m \perp n$ at B; ℓ and m are coplanar

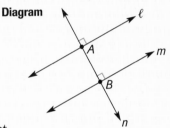

Prove: $\ell \parallel m$

Try to prove this theorem indirectly. First, assume that the theorem is not true. In that case ℓ and m would intersect at some point P. This would create an impossible triangle, PAB, with two right angles. Since the lines cannot intersect, and they lie in the same plane, they must be parallel.

MORE HELP
See 070, 072

Theorem
If two lines are perpendicular, then they intersect to form four right angles. ⊥ lines ⇒ 4 rt. ∠s (T011)

Proof

Diagram

Given: $\ell_1 \perp \ell_2$

Prove: m∠1 = m∠2 = m∠3 = m∠4 = 90°

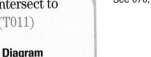

Angle 1: The lines are perpendicular, so they form a right angle. Call that angle 1. By definition, m∠1 = 90°.

Angle 4: Because vertical angles are congruent, ∠1 ≅ ∠4. Therefore, m∠4 = m∠1 = 90°.

Angle 2: ∠1 and ∠2 form a linear pair, so they are supplementary. Then, m∠1 + m∠2 = 180°. Since m∠1 = 90°, m∠2 = 90°.

Angle 3: ∠2 and ∠3 are vertical angles, so they must be congruent; m∠2 = m∠3. Since m∠2 = 90°, m∠3 = 90°.

MORE ▶

MORE HELP
See 070

Theorem If two lines intersect to form adjacent, congruent angles, then the lines are perpendicular. Lines form ≅ linear pair ⇒ ⊥ (T012)

Diagram

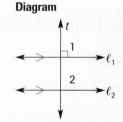

Proof

Given: $\angle 1 \cong \angle 2$, $\angle 1$ and $\angle 2$ are a linear pair

Prove: $\ell_1 \perp \ell_2$

Plan: Since the sum of the measures of a linear pair is 180°, you know that the measure of each angle must be 90°.

Statements	Reasons
➊ $\angle 1 \cong \angle 2$; $m\angle 1 = m\angle 2$	Given; def. of ≅ ∠s
➋ $\angle 1$ and $\angle 2$ are a linear pair	Given
➌ $m\angle 1 + m\angle 2 = 180°$	Linear Pair Postulate (P14)
➍ $m\angle 1 + m\angle 1 = 180°$	Substitution Look back at Step 1.
➎ $2(m\angle 1) = 180°$	Distributive prop.
➏ $m\angle 1 = 90°$; $\angle 1$ is a right angle	Division prop. of =; def. of rt. ∠
➐ $\ell_1 \perp \ell_2$	Def. of ⊥ lines

MORE HELP
See 076

Theorem If a transversal is perpendicular to one of two parallel lines, then it is perpendicular to the other. ⊥ Transversal Theorem (T013)

Proof

Diagram

Given: $\ell_1 \parallel \ell_2$, $t \perp \ell_1$

Prove: $t \perp \ell_2$

Plan: You can use the Corresponding Angles Postulate to show that $\angle 1 \cong \angle 2$. Then use the definition of perpendicular lines.

Statements	Reasons
➊ $\ell_1 \parallel \ell_2$; $t \perp \ell_1$	Given
➋ $\angle 1$ is a rt. ∠	Def. of ⊥ lines
➌ $\angle 1 \cong \angle 2$	Corresp. ∠s Postulate (P15)
➍ $\angle 2$ is a rt. ∠	Substitution
➎ $t \perp \ell_2$	Def. of ⊥ lines

A figure has **line symmetry** if a line divides it into congruent halves, each of which is the mirror image of the other.

Theorem

Every segment has exactly two symmetry lines: (1) its perpendicular bisector, and (2) the line containing the segment. Seg. symmetry: ⊥ bisector; line containing seg. (T014)

Diagram

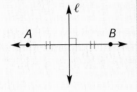

Proof

Given: line segment AB

Prove: the perpendicular bisector of $\overline{AB}$ is a line of symmetry of $\overline{AB}$; $\overleftrightarrow{AB}$ is a line of symmetry of $\overline{AB}$

MORE HELP
See 056, 279

CASE 1 The perpendicular bisector is a line of symmetry.

By definition of a reflection, A and B are reflections of each other about the perpendicular bisector, making it a line of symmetry for points A and B and all other pairs of corresponding points on $\overline{AB}$. This means that ℓ is a line of symmetry for $\overline{AB}$.

CASE 2 $\overleftrightarrow{AB}$ is a line of symmetry.

By definition of a reflection, all points on a line of symmetry are reflections of themselves, so A is a reflection of A about $\overleftrightarrow{AB}$ and B is a reflection of B. This is true of all points on $\overline{AB}$, so $\overleftrightarrow{AB}$ is a line of reflection for $\overline{AB}$.

Theorem

If a line is perpendicular to each of two intersecting lines at their point of intersection, then the line is perpendicular to the plane determined by these two intersecting lines. $\ell \perp \ell_1$ and ℓ_2 at $\ell_1 \cap \ell_2 \Rightarrow \ell \perp$ plane of ℓ_1 and ℓ_2 (T015)

Many statements like this are easier to follow if you picture them. For example, think of two lines that intersect. Now think about how you might place a toothpick so that it is perpendicular to both lines.

MORE ▶

MORE HELP
See 256, 261,
432, 434

Proof

Diagram

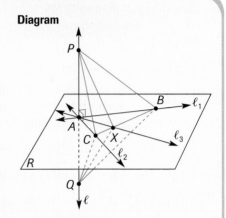

Given: $\ell \perp \ell_1$ at A; $\ell \perp \ell_2$ at A

Prove: $\ell \perp$ plane R

Plan: You need to prove that the line is perpendicular to *every* line in the plane through the point of intersection. By proving it for any generic line in the plane, your proof will apply to every line. Begin the proof by drawing any line in the plane through the point of intersection. Then, show that pairs of segments from points on that line to two specified points on ℓ are congruent.

Statements	Reasons
❶ $\ell \perp \ell_1$, $\ell \perp \ell_2$	Given
❷ Draw $\overline{BC}$ connecting point B on ℓ_1 and C on ℓ_2. Through A draw any other line ℓ_3 intersecting $\overline{BC}$ at X.	2 pts. determine a line (P05)
❸ Locate P and Q on ℓ so that $PA = QA$	Ruler Postulate (P08)
❹ ℓ_1 is a $\perp$ bisector of $\overline{PQ}$ ℓ_2 is a $\perp$ bisector of $\overline{PQ}$	Def. of $\perp$ bisector
❺ $PB = QB$; $PC = QC$	$\perp$ Bisector Theorem (T002)
❻ $\overline{BC} \cong \overline{BC}$	Reflexive prop. of $\cong$ (T105)
❼ $\triangle PCB \cong \triangle QCB$	SSS $\cong$ Postulate (P22)
❽ $\angle PCB \cong \angle QCB$	CPCTC
❾ $\overline{CX} \cong \overline{CX}$	Reflexive prop. of $\cong$ (T105)
❿ $\triangle PCX \cong \triangle QCX$	SAS $\cong$ Postulate (P23)
⓫ $\overline{PX} \cong \overline{QX}$	CPCTC
⓬ X lies on the $\perp$ bisector of $\overline{PQ}$	Converse of $\perp$ Bisector Theorem (T003)
⓭ $\ell \perp \overleftrightarrow{AX}$ (ℓ_3)	Def. of $\perp$
⓮ ℓ is perpendicular to every line in R through A, so $\ell \perp$ plane R	Def. of line $\perp$ plane

Theorem There is one and only one line perpendicular to a plane at a point in the plane. $1 \ell \perp$ plane at pt. (T016)

MORE HELP
See 046

Proof

Diagram

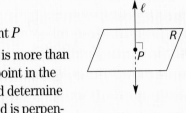

Given: $\ell \perp$ plane R at point P

Prove: ℓ is the only line $\perp$ plane R at point P

Use an indirect proof. Assume that there is more than one line perpendicular to the plane at a point in the plane. These two intersecting lines would determine a plane that intersects the given plane and is perpendicular to it at the line of intersection. However, if two coplanar lines are perpendicular to the same line, then they are *parallel* to each other. This is the contradiction you need to assert that the theorem is true.

Theorem There is one and only one line perpendicular to a plane from a point not in the plane. $1 \ell \perp$ plane from pt. not in plane (T017)

Diagram

Proof

Given: $\ell \perp$ plane R

Prove: ℓ is the only line $\perp$ to plane R from point P

Use an indirect proof. Assume that there are two lines perpendicular to the plane from P. Think about the triangle formed by the two lines and the segment between the two points of intersection. It would have two right angles! Since a triangle can have at most one right angle, this is the contradiction you need to assert that the theorem is true.

Proofs of the following two theorems are beyond the scope of this book. For each, there is more than one plane that fulfills the requirement.

Theorem All the perpendiculars to a line, at a point on the line, lie in a plane that is perpendicular to the line at that point. All $\perp \ell$ at pt. lie in plane $\perp \ell$ at same pt. (T018)

Theorem If a line is perpendicular to a plane, then every plane that contains the line is perpendicular to that plane. $\ell \perp$ plane $R \Rightarrow$ all planes with $\ell \perp$ plane R (T019)

Suppose you are piloting an airplane. How steep should your ascent be? How steep should your descent be? An angle can help you describe the path you want to follow to take off or land.

An **angle** is the union of two rays that share a common endpoint. This point is called the **vertex**. Angles are formed when lines, rays, or line segments intersect.

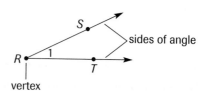

You can use three points to name an angle. The vertex must be the middle point in the name.

Write: ∠SRT or ∠TRS
Say: angle S R T or angle T R S

If there is no possibility of confusion, you can also use the vertex to name an angle: ∠R. Or, you can write a number inside the rays of the angle: ∠1.

MORE HELP
See 064, 281

Two angles that share a common ray, a common vertex, and no interior points are **adjacent angles.**

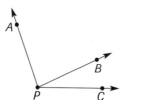

∠1 and ∠2 are not adjacent because they don't share a common vertex.

∠APB and ∠BPC are adjacent angles. ∠APB and ∠APC are not adjacent because they share interior points.

Angles are measured by the amount of rotation about the vertex needed for one side to overlap the other. Like rotations, angles are measured in units called degrees (°).

Write: m∠CAB = 85°
Say: *The measure of angle C A B is 85 degrees.*

$\overrightarrow{AC}$ is rotated counterclockwise 85° from $\overrightarrow{AB}$.

Two angles are **congruent angles** if they have the same measure.

∠Q ≅ ∠T because m∠Q = 48° and m∠T = 48°.

When you see this symbol, say *is congruent to.*

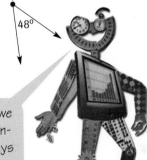

Angle measures are real numbers. When they are the same we say they are equal: m∠Q = m∠T. When we talk about the angles themselves we say they are congruent: ∠Q ≅ ∠T. Always distinguish *measures* which can be *equal or not equal* from *figures* which can be *congruent or not congruent.*

MATH ALERT Be Sure to Name Your Angles Carefully

063

When an angle is named using three letters, the letter representing the vertex *must* be the middle letter. You cannot always use a single letter to name an angle.

∠ACB is *not* the same as ∠ABC. It *is* the same as ∠3 or ∠BCA. You can rename ∠1 as ∠A, but you cannot rename ∠3 as ∠C because there are many angles with a vertex at C.

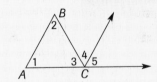

064

Protractor Postulate

The postulates for angles are similar to the postulates for segments. P12 tells you how to measure an angle, much as the Ruler Postulate (P08) told you how to measure a segment.

A **protractor** is a tool you can use to measure angles in degrees. As with any tool, the measure you read from the scale is approximate. Because this is always true, you do not need to say that a measured angle (or distance) is approximate.

MORE ▶

Postulate Rays from point O on $\overrightarrow{OA}$ to any point B can be matched one-to-one with the real numbers from 0 to 180. The measure of $\angle AOB$ is the absolute value of the difference between the numbers matched with $\overrightarrow{OA}$ and $\overrightarrow{OB}$.
Protractor Postulate (P12)

EXAMPLE: Look at the figure to help understand the Protractor Postulate. It shows you two ways to measure $\angle AOB$.

ONE WAY $\quad m\angle AOB = |0° - 105°|$
$= 105°$

ANOTHER WAY $\quad m\angle AOB = |140° - 35°|$
$= 105°$

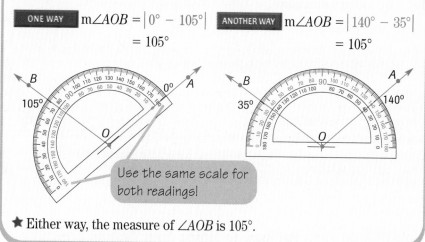

 Use the same scale for both readings!

★ Either way, the measure of $\angle AOB$ is 105°.

The next theorem is obvious, but it will be a convenient shortcut in many other proofs.

Theorem All right angles are congruent. All rt. $\angle$s $\cong$ (T020)

Proof

Given: $\angle 1$ and $\angle 2$ are right angles.

Prove: $\angle 1 \cong \angle 2$

Since $\angle 1$ and $\angle 2$ are both right angles, they both have a measure of 90°. Since angles with the same measure are congruent, $\angle 1 \cong \angle 2$.

Diagram

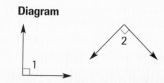

The ⌐ on a diagram tells you that the angle is a right angle.

Angle Addition Postulate _____

The Angle Addition Postulate is similar to the Segment Addition Postulate.
Angle measures can be added only if the angles don't overlap.

MORE HELP
See 057

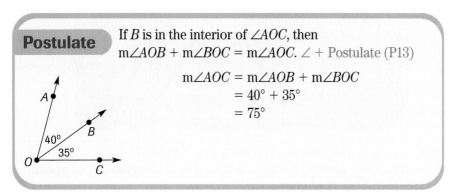

Postulate   If B is in the interior of $\angle AOC$, then
$\text{m}\angle AOB + \text{m}\angle BOC = \text{m}\angle AOC.$ $\angle$ + Postulate (P13)

$$\text{m}\angle AOC = \text{m}\angle AOB + \text{m}\angle BOC$$
$$= 40° + 35°$$
$$= 75°$$

Classification of Angles _____

Think of an angle with its two sides very close together. The measure of the
angle increases as one ray is rotated, like the hand of a clock.

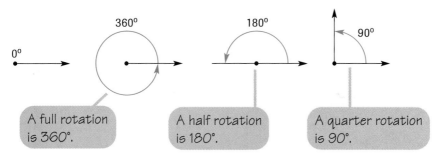

360°

180°

90°

0°

A full rotation
is 360°.

A half rotation
is 180°.

A quarter rotation
is 90°.

Angles are classified by their relationship to the benchmark angles of 0°,
90°, and 180°.

Figure	A	B	C	D
Name	Acute	Right	Obtuse	Straight
Measure	$0° < \text{m}\angle A < 90°$	$\text{m}\angle B = 90°$	$90° < \text{m}\angle C < 180°$	$\text{m}\angle D = 180°$

Special Pairs of Angles

If you look at the trusses of a bridge, you may notice many angle relationships. Some of these relationships have special names.

MORE HELP
See 256

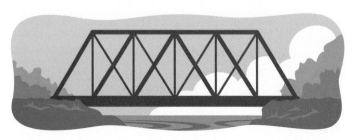

Angles with the same measure are **congruent angles**. In some cases, for angles formed by intersecting lines, you can tell that angles are congruent just by the way they are related in the diagram.

Complementary Angles

Two angles are **complementary** if the sum of their measures is 90°. Each angle is the **complement** of the other.

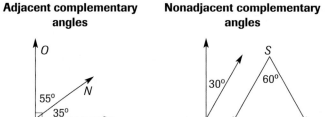

Adjacent complementary angles

Nonadjacent complementary angles

EXAMPLE: Two angles are complementary. If one angle has twice the measure of the other, find the measure of each angle.

Let $\angle J$ and $\angle K$ be complementary. This means $m\angle J + m\angle K = 90°$.
Let $m\angle K = x$. Then $m\angle J = 2x$.

$2x + x = 90°$

$3x = 90°$

$x = 30°$

$2x = 60°$

★ The measures of the two angles are 30° and 60°.

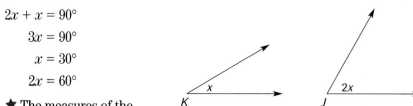

Theorem	If two angles are complements of the same angle or congruent angles, then the angles are congruent. Comps. of ≅ ∠s ≅ (T021)

Proof

Plan: There are two cases. In the first case, two sets of angles are involved and you are given that two out of the four angles are congruent. In the second case, two of the angles are complementary to the same angle.

CASE 1 If two angles are complements of congruent angles, then the angles are congruent.

Diagram

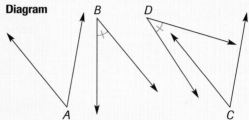

Given: ∠A and ∠B are complementary; ∠C and ∠D are complementary; ∠B ≅ ∠D

Prove: ∠A ≅ ∠C

MORE HELP
See 030, 036

Statements	Reasons
❶ ∠A and ∠B are complementary; ∠C and ∠D are complementary; ∠B ≅ ∠D	Given
❷ m∠A + m∠B = 90°; m∠C + m∠D = 90°	Def. of comp. ∠s
❸ m∠A + m∠B = m∠C + m∠D	Transitive prop. of =
❹ m∠B = m∠D	Def. of ≅
❺ m∠A + m∠B = m∠C + m∠B	Substitution
❻ m∠A = m∠C	Subtraction prop. of =
❼ ∠A ≅ ∠C	Def. of ≅

CASE 2 If two angles are complements of the same angle, then the angles are congruent.

Given: ∠A and ∠B are complementary; ∠C and ∠B are complementary

Diagram

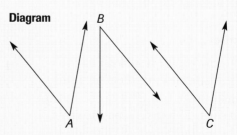

Prove: ∠A ≅ ∠C

Since ∠A and ∠B are complementary and ∠C and ∠B are also complementary, their sums are 90°. m∠A + m∠B = m∠C + m∠B. The Subtraction Property of Equality allows you to subtract m∠B from both sides of the equation: m∠A = m∠C, so ∠A ≅ ∠C.

Supplementary Angles

Two angles are **supplementary** if the sum of their measures is 180°. Each angle is the **supplement** of the other.

Adjacent supplementary angles

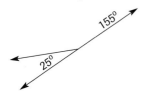

Nonadjacent supplementary angles

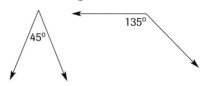

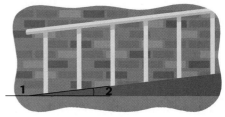

EXAMPLE: A handicapped access ramp is built at an incline of 6.5° from level ground. What is the measure of ∠1?

$$m\angle 1 = 180° - m\angle 2$$
$$= 180° - 6.5°$$
$$= 173.5°$$

★ The measure of ∠1 is 173.5°.

m∠2 = 6.5°

Theorem If two angles are supplements of the same angle or congruent angles, then the angles are congruent. Supps. of ≅ ∠s ≅ (T022)

The case for supplements of congruent angles is shown. Since an angle is congruent to itself, this case also applies to the case in which you have supplements of the same angle.

Proof

Diagram

Given: ∠A and ∠B are supplementary; ∠C and ∠D are supplementary; ∠B ≅ ∠D

Prove: ∠A ≅ ∠C

Since ∠A and ∠B, and ∠C and ∠D are supplementary, their sums are equal. m∠A + m∠B = m∠C + m∠D. Since m∠B = m∠D, you can substitute one for the other. This means m∠A + m∠B = m∠C + m∠B. The

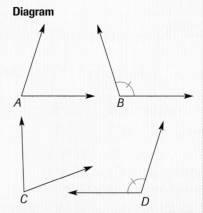

Subtraction Property of Equality will let you subtract m∠B from both sides of the equation, leaving m∠A = m∠C and ∠A ≅ ∠C.

Linear Pairs of Angles

Two adjacent angles share one side. If the two sides they don't share are
opposite rays, the angles are a **linear pair**.

Linear pairs: ∠1 and ∠2,
∠3 and ∠4, ∠4 and ∠5,
∠5 and ∠6, ∠6 and ∠3

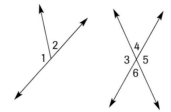

| **Postulate** | If two angles form a linear pair, then they are supplementary; the sum of their measures is 180°. Linear Pair Postulate (P14) |

$$m\angle 1 + m\angle 2 = 180°$$

**MATH ALERT Supplementary Angles Are Not
Always a Linear Pair**

A linear pair always forms supplementary angles but supplementary
angles do not always form a linear pair.

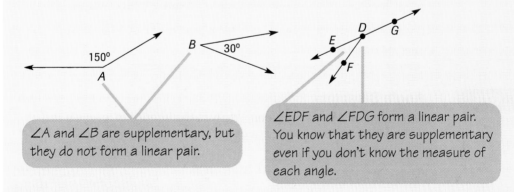

∠A and ∠B are supplementary, but
they do not form a linear pair.

∠EDF and ∠FDG form a linear pair.
You know that they are supplementary
even if you don't know the measure of
each angle.

072

Vertical Angles

Two angles are **vertical angles** if their sides form two pairs of opposite rays. They are the non-adjacent angles formed when two lines intersect.

∠1 and ∠3 are vertical angles.

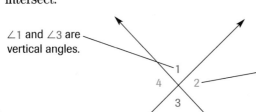

∠2 and ∠4 are vertical angles.

Vertical angles don't go straight up and down. The word *vertical* in this case is related to the word *vertex*. Vertical angles may also be called **opposite** angles.

Theorem Vertical angles are congruent. Vert. ∠s ≅ (T023)

Proof

Given: ∠1 and ∠3 are vertical angles.

Prove: ∠1 ≅ ∠3

Diagram

MORE HELP
See 070

Because ∠1 and ∠2 form a linear pair, the Linear Pair Postulate says that they must be supplementary. By the same reasoning, ∠2 and ∠3 are supplementary.

Because ∠1 and ∠3 are each supplementary to the same angle, ∠2, they must be congruent.

073

Angle Bisectors

An **angle bisector** is a segment or ray in the interior of an angle that divides it into two congruent angles.

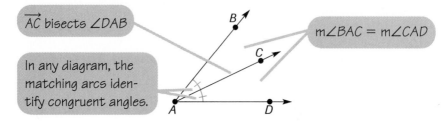

$\overrightarrow{AC}$ bisects ∠DAB

m∠BAC = m∠CAD

In any diagram, the matching arcs identify congruent angles.

The **distance from a point to a line** is the length of the perpendicular segment from the point to the line. This property is used to cut down the angle in sports. Suppose a soccer player is trying to make a goal from some point on the field. The goalkeeper may try to stay on the bisector of the angle formed by the player and the two sides of the goal line to make it easier to intercept the ball.

MORE HELP
See 256, 265, 375

Theorem

If a point is on the bisector of an angle, then it is equidistant from the sides of the angle.
∠ Bisector Theorem (T024)

Proof

Diagram

Given: D is on the bisector of $\angle BAC$

Prove: $DB = DC$

By the definition of an angle bisector, $\angle BAD \cong \angle CAD$. Construct $\overline{BD} \perp \overrightarrow{AB}$ and $\overline{CD} \perp \overrightarrow{AC}$. Because $\angle ABD$ and $\angle ACD$ are right angles, $\angle ABD \cong \angle ACD$. By the Reflexive Property of Congruence, $\overline{AD} \cong \overline{AD}$. Then $\triangle BAD \cong \triangle CAD$ by the AAS Congruence Theorem. Since corresponding parts of congruent triangles are congruent, you know that $\overline{DB} \cong \overline{DC}$, so their measures are equal.

To convince yourself that any point on the bisector is the same distance from each ray, try this experiment.

1. Draw an angle with vertex J. Fold the two sides of the angle so that the rays line up. The crease line bisects the angle.

3. This forms two congruent angles that are a linear pair, so each angle must measure 90°.

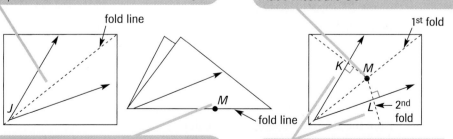

fold line

1st fold

fold line

2nd fold

2. Now label any point M on the bisector. With the angle still folded on its bisector, make a second fold that passes through M while each ray is folded over onto itself.

4. Label the points where the fold lines meet the rays as K and L. Now measure MK and ML.

MORE ▶

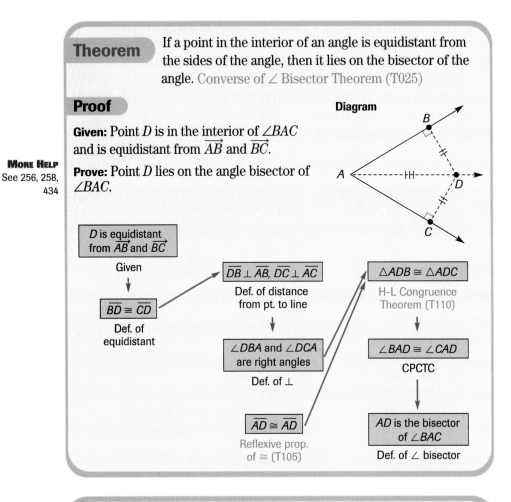

Theorem If a point in the interior of an angle is equidistant from the sides of the angle, then it lies on the bisector of the angle. Converse of ∠ Bisector Theorem (T025)

Proof

Given: Point D is in the interior of $\angle BAC$ and is equidistant from $\overrightarrow{AB}$ and $\overrightarrow{BC}$.

MORE HELP
See 256, 258, 434

Prove: Point D lies on the angle bisector of $\angle BAC$.

Diagram

D is equidistant from $\overrightarrow{AB}$ and $\overrightarrow{BC}$

Given

$\overline{BD} \cong \overline{CD}$

Def. of equidistant

$\overline{DB} \perp \overline{AB}, \overline{DC} \perp \overline{AC}$

Def. of distance from pt. to line

$\angle DBA$ and $\angle DCA$ are right angles

Def. of ⊥

$\overline{AD} \cong \overline{AD}$

Reflexive prop. of ≅ (T105)

$\triangle ADB \cong \triangle ADC$

H-L Congruence Theorem (T110)

$\angle BAD \cong \angle CAD$

CPCTC

AD is the bisector of $\angle BAC$

Def. of ∠ bisector

Theorem The line containing the bisector of an angle is a line of symmetry for the angle. ∠ Symmetry Theorem (T026)

Proof

MORE HELP
See 073, 279

Given: $\overrightarrow{BF}$ bisects $\angle ABC$

Prove: $\overleftrightarrow{BF}$ is a line of symmetry

Diagram

You know from the Angle Bisector Theorem that each point on the bisector is equidistant from the sides of the angle. The line of symmetry is also equidistant from the sides of the angle, so the line containing the bisector of an angle is a line of symmetry for the angle.

Angles Formed by Lines Cut by a Transversal

A **transversal** is a line that intersects two (or more) coplanar lines at two (or more) points. Pairs of angles with a vertex at each point of intersection are given special names. Look at lines ℓ and m with transversal t.

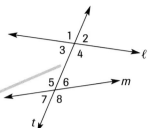

t is a transversal of lines ℓ and m.

Name	Angles	Description
Corresponding angles	∠1 and ∠5; ∠3 and ∠7; ∠2 and ∠6; ∠4 and ∠8	On the *same* side of the transversal and on the *same* side of the given lines
Alternate exterior angles	∠1 and ∠8; ∠2 and ∠7	On *opposite* sides of the transversal and on the *outside* of the given lines
Alternate interior angles	∠3 and ∠6; ∠4 and ∠5	On *opposite* sides of the transversal and on the *inside* of the given lines
Same-side interior angles	∠3 and ∠5; ∠4 and ∠6	On the *same* side of the transversal and on the *inside* of the given lines
Same-side exterior angles	∠1 and ∠7; ∠2 and ∠8	On the *same* side of the transversal and on the *outside* of the given lines

ℓ and m are the given lines.

Angles Formed by Parallel Lines Cut by a Transversal

075

When a transversal intersects two *parallel* lines, the angles formed by the transversal have special relationships.

Corresponding Angles

Postulate If two parallel lines are cut by a transversal, then the pairs of corresponding angles are congruent. Corresp. ∠s Postulate (P15)

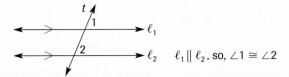

$\ell_1 \| \ell_2$, so, ∠1 ≅ ∠2

Postulate If two lines are cut by a transversal so that corresponding angles are congruent, then the lines are parallel. Converse of Corresp. ∠s Postulate (P16)

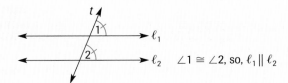

∠1 ≅ ∠2, so, $\ell_1 \| \ell_2$

Alternate Interior Angles

Theorem If two parallel lines are cut by a transversal, then the pairs of alternate interior angles are congruent. Alt. Int. ∠s Theorem (T027)

Diagram

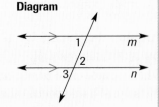

Proof

Given: $m \| n$

Prove: ∠1 ≅ ∠2

Plan: In a pair of corresponding angles, one is an exterior angle and one is an interior angle. The vertical angle of the exterior angle is an alternate interior angle of the interior angle. Use these relationships to prove the theorem.

Statements	Reasons
❶ $m \| n$	Given
❷ ∠1 ≅ ∠3	Corresp. ∠s Postulate (P15)
❸ ∠3 ≅ ∠2	Vert. ∠s ≅ (T023)
❹ ∠1 ≅ ∠2	Transitive prop. of ≅ (T107)

Remember, the converse of a theorem may or may not be true. If it can be proved, then you know it must be true.

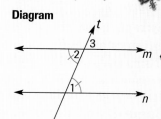

Theorem If, when two lines are cut by a transversal, alternate interior angles are congruent, then the lines are parallel. Converse of Alt. Int. ∠s Theorem (T028)

Given: $\angle 1 \cong \angle 2$

Prove: $m \parallel n$

Diagram

The proof of this theorem is the same as for the Alternate Interior Angles Theorem, except the reasoning is reversed.

Alternate Exterior Angles

The theorems about alternate exterior angles are similar to those for alternate interior angles. The only difference is in the choice of vertical angles to help with the proof.

Theorem If two parallel lines are cut by a transversal, then the pairs of alternate exterior angles are congruent. Alt. Ext. ∠s Theorem (T029)

Proof

Given: $p \parallel q$

Prove: $\angle 1 \cong \angle 2$

Diagram

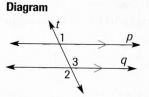

You know that $\angle 1 \cong \angle 3$ because they are corresponding angles. $\angle 2 \cong \angle 3$ because they are vertical angles. Use substitution to show that $\angle 1 \cong \angle 2$.

MORE ▶

> ### Theorem
> If, when two lines are cut by a transversal, alternate exterior angles are congruent, then the lines are parallel. Converse of Alt. Ext. ∠s Theorem (T030)
>
> #### Proof
>
> **Diagram**
>
>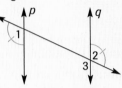
>
> **Given:** ∠1 ≅ ∠2
>
> **Prove:** $p \parallel q$
>
> You're given that ∠1 ≅ ∠2. ∠2 ≅ ∠3 because they are vertical angles. Substitute to show that ∠1 ≅ ∠3. This means $p \parallel q$ by the converse of the Corresponding Angles Postulate.

079 Same-Side Interior Angles

MORE HELP
See 069

> ### Theorem
> If two parallel lines are cut by a transversal, then the pairs of interior angles on the same side of the transversal are supplementary. Same Side Int. ∠s Theorem (T031)
>
> #### Proof
>
> **Diagram**
>
>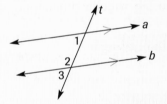
>
> **Given:** $a \parallel b$
>
> **Prove:** ∠1 and ∠2 are supplementary.
>
> ∠1 ≅ ∠3 because they are corresponding angles. Because ∠3 and ∠2 form a linear pair, they are supplementary. Then, through substitution, ∠1 and ∠2 must also be supplementary.

> ### Theorem
> If, when two lines are cut by a transversal, interior angles on the same side of the transversal are supplementary, then the lines are parallel. Converse of Same Side Int. ∠s Theorem (T032)
>
> #### Proof
>
> **Diagram**
>
>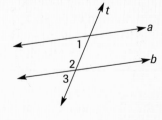
>
> **Given:** ∠1 and ∠2 are supplementary.
>
> **Prove:** $a \parallel b$
>
> ∠1 and ∠2 are supplementary. You know that ∠2 and ∠3 are supplementary because they are a linear pair. Substitute to show that ∠1 ≅ ∠3. Finally, $a \parallel b$ by the Converse of the Corresponding Angles Postulate.

Same-Side Exterior Angles

Theorem If two parallel lines are cut by a transversal, then the pairs of exterior angles on the same side of the transversal are supplementary. Same Side Ext. ∠s Theorem (T033)

MORE HELP
See 069

Proof

Given: $j \parallel k$

Prove: ∠1 and ∠2 are supplementary.

Diagram

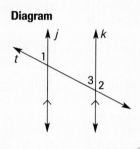

∠1 ≅ ∠3, because they are corresponding angles. Because ∠3 and ∠2 form a linear pair, they are supplementary. Then, through substitution, ∠1 and ∠2 must also be supplementary.

Theorem If, when two lines are cut by a transversal, exterior angles on the same side of the transversal are supplementary, then the lines are parallel. Converse of Same Side Ext. ∠s Theorem (T034)

Given: ∠1 and ∠2 are supplementary.

Prove: $j \parallel k$

Diagram

Prove this theorem by reversing the reasoning for the Same Side Exterior Angles Theorem.

Dihedral Angles

A **dihedral angle** is formed by two intersecting planes. The sides of a dihedral angle are half planes instead of rays, and instead of meeting at a vertex, the planes meet at a line.

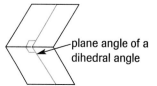

To measure a dihedral angle think about slicing the angle across the line of intersection. But this poses a problem. You can get many different measures for the same angle! To avoid this problem, mathematicians have agreed to slice the angle perpendicular to the line of intersection of the two planes. This is called the **plane angle** of the dihedral angle. Given this definition, postulates and theorems for angles that are formed by rays apply to angles that are formed by planes.

MORE HELP
See 062

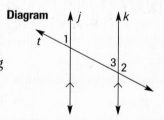

plane angle of a dihedral angle

Salespeople often take trips in which they make one stop in each of many places. How do they decide on the shortest route?

Salespeople, and others with similar problems to solve, can use networks to model and investigate efficient routes. Networks describe how a set of points, like a sales person's destinations, are connected. You don't need to specify distances between points for a network to be useful.

This branch of geometry is called **topology**. In topology, all figures can be twisted and stretched so that they change shape, without regard to lengths or angle measures, as long as no holes or tears are introduced. Networks are sets of points viewed topologically. Topology studies the properties of the figure that remain the same under these distortions.

083) ## Networks and Topology

Two figures are **topologically equivalent** if one of the figures can be bent, stretched, or compressed to form a figure that is congruent to the other figure. The figures cannot be cut apart or glued together when transforming one figure into the other.

In a plane, a circle and a triangle are topologically equivalent. Plane figures that are topologically equivalent divide the plane into the same number of regions. Both a circle and a triangle divide a plane into two regions: the inside of the figure and the outside. However, they are not topologically equivalent to the figure with the stacked triangles, which divides the plane into three regions.

Topologically Equivalent   **Not Topologically Equivalent**

In three-dimensional space, a sphere is topologically equivalent to a pyramid, but not topologically equivalent to the donut-shaped figure, called a **torus.** A torus has a hole while the sphere and the pyramid do not.

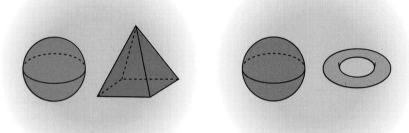

Topologically Equivalent   **Not Topologically Equivalent**

A **network**, or **graph**, is a collection of points, called **nodes** or **vertices** that may be connected by **edges**. Each edge connects two nodes or connects a node to itself. Nodes are not always connected by edges.

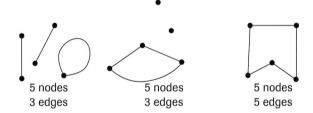

5 nodes   5 nodes   5 nodes
3 edges   3 edges   5 edges

Two networks are topologically equivalent if they have the same number of nodes and the same number of edges, and if it is possible to match the nodes of one network to the nodes of the other network so that the edges correspond. Having the same number of nodes and the same number of edges does not guarantee topological equivalence.

EXAMPLE: Are the two networks topologically equivalent?

By putting a sharp bend in the sides of the pentagon, it can be transformed into the star. This does not change the number of edges or the number of nodes.

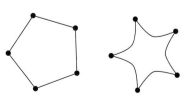

★ The two networks are topologically equivalent.

MORE ▶

A network is **connected**, or **closed**, if you can travel from one node to any other node by staying on the edges. You can draw a connected network without lifting your pencil from the paper. Points can be passed over more than once and edges may be traveled more than once to reach to all nodes.

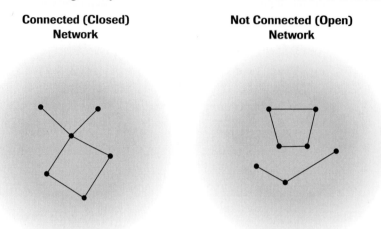

Connected (Closed) Network

Not Connected (Open) Network

084

Traceable Networks

A famous problem about networks concerns the seven bridges in the German town of Konigsburg. The problem is: How can you take a Sunday stroll so that you cross each of the seven bridges exactly once?

The problem was solved by Leonhard Euler (1701–1783), who used networks and founded topology in the process of solving the problem.

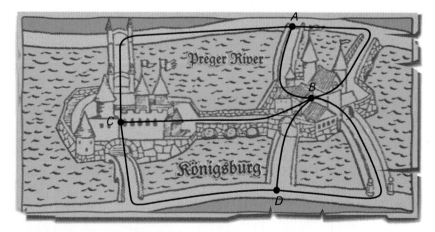

Euler began by describing a **traceable network** as one in which you can begin at one node and travel to all other nodes by traveling on each edge *exactly* once. A traceable network is connected and you can draw the network without lifting your pencil from the paper. However, deciding whether a network is traceable is often easier than tracing a route that works!

Testing for Traceable Networks

Euler's solution to the Konigsburg Bridge problem
depended on whether a node was **odd** or **even**. An
odd node is where an odd number of edges meet and
an even node is where an even number of edges meet.

Node A is an odd node because three edges meet
at point A. Node B is also an odd node because five
edges meet at point B. The **degree of a node** is the number of edges that
meet it. Euler discovered that the number of odd nodes was the key to
whether a network was traceable.

Theorem A network is traceable if and only if it is connected and
has at most two nodes of odd degree. Euler's Network
Theorem (T035)

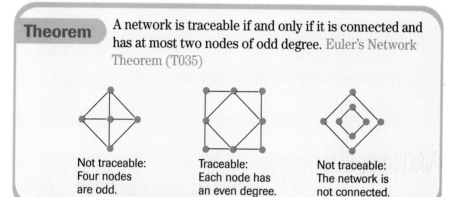

Not traceable:
Four nodes
are odd.

Traceable:
Each node has
an even degree.

Not traceable:
The network is
not connected.

The proof of this theorem is beyond the scope of this book, but read on to
learn more about Euler's discoveries about networks.

Euler made four general discoveries about networks.

- If a network is to be traveled in one journey, the number of odd nodes
  must always be even. This means you cannot travel a network with an
  odd number of odd nodes in one journey.

- If a network has all even nodes, it can be traveled in one journey. This
  means you can start from any node, travel a traceable network, and return to the starting node, as long as all the nodes are even.

- If a network contains exactly two odd nodes, it can be traveled in one
  journey. However, it is impossible to return to the starting point. You
  would have to start at one odd node and end at the other.

- If a network contains 4, 6, 8, or any higher even number of odd nodes,
  it is impossible to travel the network in one journey. In this case, the
  number of journeys needed is half the number of odd nodes. In the
  Konigsburg bridge problem, there are four odd nodes, so it will take
  $\frac{1}{2}$ of 4, exactly two, journeys to travel the compete network.

Coordinate Geometry

"Of all things, good sense is the most fairly distributed: everyone thinks he is so well supplied with it that even those who are the hardest to satisfy in every other respect never desire more of it than they already have."

—René Descartes in _Discours de la Methode_

f you weren't familiar with either town, would it be easier to find 348 East Third Street in Grid City or 348 Maple Street in Loopburg?

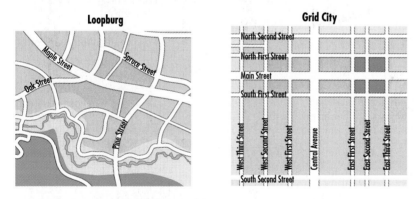

In some cities and towns, the roads form a grid. In others, the roads develop in a more haphazard fashion. Although curved, intertwining roads may be more charming, they don't make it easy to locate places. A grid system, though repetitive and predictable, offers convenience. Visitors know immediately that S. Sixth Street is between S. Fifth and S. Seventh, but won't know the order of Maple, Oak, and Spruce without a map.

Geometry, like navigation, uses location systems, such as the coordinate plane, that make it easy to talk about where things are located. A coordinate system is easy to use because it is based on patterns.

In this section, you'll see even more advantages of using systems such as the coordinate plane. If you study carefully, you may find that coordinate geometry is as easy to navigate as Grid City.

Are you familiar with this expression: *A picture is worth a thousand words*? In mathematics, the graph of an equation is just such a picture. With a graph, you can picture the solutions to an equation.

In the 17th century, a French mathematician and philosopher, Rene Descartes (day **cart**), was one of the first to show the solutions to an equation on a **coordinate grid**. The **Cartesian Plane** (also called the **co-ordinate plane**) is named in his honor. Such a plane is formed when two perpendicular number lines intersect. Usually, both number lines are drawn to the same scale. The two lines, one horizontal and one vertical, are called **coordinate axes**.

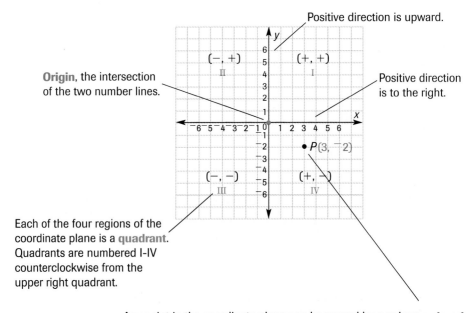

Positive direction is upward.

Origin, the intersection of the two number lines.

Positive direction is to the right.

Each of the four regions of the coordinate plane is a **quadrant**. Quadrants are numbered I-IV counterclockwise from the upper right quadrant.

Any point in the coordinate plane can be named by a unique **ordered pair**. The **x-coordinate** (or **abscissa**) is always the first number in this pair, and the **y-coordinate** (or **ordinate**) is always the second number. The point *P* has coordinates (3, ⁻2), which, like the address on the city map, name its location on the coordinate plane.

Ordered Pairs and Locating Points

A coordinate plane makes naming and locating points easy. To **plot a point** P with coordinates (x, y) means to locate the point in the coordinate plane. The point is represented by a dot. In this diagram, $(x, y) = (3, 4)$.

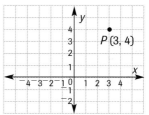

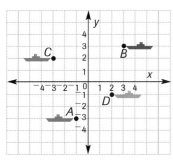

In a popular game, you place ships on a coordinate plane and your opponent tries to locate them. You can locate the bow of each ship in the plane using coordinates. Start at the origin and count x units along the x-axis (right if the number is positive and left if the number is negative). Then count y units up if the number is positive and down if the number is negative.

To locate Ship A, start at the origin. Count 1 unit left and 3 units down. The bow of Ship A is at the point with the coordinates ($^-$1, $^-$3).

Write: ($^-$1, $^-$3)
Say: *negative one, negative three*

> The coordinates of a point identify the quadrant in which the point is located.
>
> $x > 0$ and $y > 0 \Rightarrow$ Quadrant I
> $x < 0$ and $y > 0 \Rightarrow$ Quadrant II
> $x < 0$ and $y < 0 \Rightarrow$ Quadrant III
> $x > 0$ and $y < 0 \Rightarrow$ Quadrant IV
>
> Notice that the quadrants are named in order as you rotate counterclockwise, starting from the quadrant in which both x and y are positive.

Midpoint

Rest a 12-inch ruler across your index fingers. Move your fingers together while keeping the ruler balanced. Your hands will probably meet at the midpoint of the ruler. The **midpoint** of a line segment divides the segment into two congruent parts—in the case of the ruler, this is the balance point.

MORE ▶

MORE HELP
See 056,
375–376

Formula In the coordinate plane, the midpoint of the segment with endpoints (x_1, y_1) and (x_2, y_2) is $\left(\frac{x_1 + x_2}{2}, \frac{y_1 + y_2}{2}\right)$.
(F01)

(x_1, y_1) is a short way of writing (first value of x, first value of y). The little numbers below the line of type are called subscripts.

Write: x_1 **Say:** x one or x sub-one

Proof

Given: $P_1(x_1, y_1)$ and $P_2(x_2, y_2)$ are the endpoints of $\overline{P_1P_2}$

Prove: The coordinates of M are $\left(\frac{x_1 + x_2}{2}, \frac{y_1 + y_2}{2}\right)$

Plan: Construct a right triangle with hypotenuse P_1P_2, right angle at B, and legs parallel to the x and y axes. Find the midpoint of $\overline{P_1B}$ and label it A. Use similar triangles to show that a perpendicular segment through A also intersects P_1P_2 at the midpoint, then find the x- and y-coordinates of M separately.

Construct a perpendicular to $\overline{P_1B}$ at midpoint A. Let point M be the point where this line intersects $\overline{P_1P_2}$. $\angle P_1 \cong \angle P_1$ by the reflexive property of congruence and $\angle P_1AM \cong \angle P_1BP_2$ because all right angles are congruent. By the AA Postulate, $\triangle P_1AM$ and $\triangle P_1BP_2$ are similar. If A is the midpoint of $\overline{P_1B}$, then $P_1B = 2P_1A$. Since $\frac{P_1A}{P_1B} = \frac{P_1M}{P_1P_2} = \frac{1}{2}$, M must be the midpoint of $\overline{P_1P_2}$.

Since $\overline{P_1B}$ is parallel to the x-axis, the y coordinates of points P_1, A, and B are the same, y_1. If you think about $\overline{P_1B}$ as a number line, the coordinates of A are $\left(\frac{x_1 + x_2}{2}, y_1\right)$. $\overline{MA}$ is parallel to $\overline{P_2B}$ (two lines perpendicular to the same line are parallel). $\overline{P_2B}$ is parallel to the y-axis, so, by transitivity, $\overline{MA}$ is parallel to the

Diagram

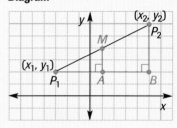

y-axis. This makes the x-coordinates of M and A the same so the x-coordinate of M is $\frac{x_1 + x_2}{2}$.

Use a similar argument and the midpoint of $\overline{P_2B}$ to show that the y-coordinate of M is $\frac{y_1 + y_2}{2}$. This means that the midpoint of $\overline{P_1P_2}$ is $\left(\frac{x_1 + x_2}{2}, \frac{y_1 + y_2}{2}\right)$.

EXAMPLE 1: Find the coordinates of the center of the square.

You can find the center of the square by finding the midpoint of either diagonal. Look at $\overline{PR}$.

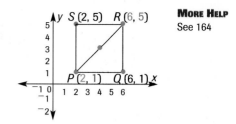

MORE HELP
See 164

$\dfrac{x_1 + x_2}{2}$	Midpt. formula (F01)	$\dfrac{y_1 + y_2}{2}$
$= \dfrac{2 + 6}{2}$	Substitution	$= \dfrac{1 + 5}{2}$
$= \dfrac{8}{2}$ or 4	Simplify	$= \dfrac{6}{2}$ or 3

★ The center of the square is at $(4, 3)$.

$\dfrac{x_1 + x_2}{2}$ gives you the average (mean) of the x-values. $\dfrac{y_1 + y_2}{2}$ gives you the mean of the y-values. This makes sense when you consider that the midpoint has the middle value.

EXAMPLE 2: The coordinates of one endpoint of $\overline{CD}$ are $(6, {}^-3)$ and the coordinates of the midpoint are $(4, {}^-2)$. Find the coordinates of the other endpoint.

MORE HELP
See 030–031

Use the midpoint formula and the coordinates of C $(6, {}^-3)$ for (x_1, y_1) use $(4, {}^-2)$ for the coordinates of the M. Solve for the coordinates of the other endpoint.

$\dfrac{x_1 + x_2}{2}$	Mid. Formula (F01)	$\dfrac{y_1 + y_2}{2}$
$\dfrac{6 + x_2}{2} = 4$	Substitution	$\dfrac{{}^-3 + y_2}{2} = {}^-2$
$6 + x_2 = 8$	× prop. of =	${}^-3 + y_2 = {}^-4$
$x_2 = 2$	Subtraction prop. of =	$y_2 = {}^-1$

★ The coordinates of the other endpoint are $(2, {}^-1)$.

Distance Between Two Points

You know the location in a coordinate plane of two trees in a park and want to find the straight-line distance between the points. You can use the Distance Formula to help.

Formula In the coordinate plane the distance between two points (x_1, y_1) and (x_2, y_2) is: $d = \sqrt{(x_2 - x_1)^2 + (y_2 - y_1)^2}$. (F02)

Proof

Given: Points $A(x_2, y_2)$ and $B(x_1, y_1)$ in the coordinate plane

Prove: $AB = \sqrt{(x_2 - x_1)^2 + (y_2 - y_1)^2}$

MORE HELP
See 055, 152

Plan: You can use the Ruler Postulate to find the distance between two points on the same vertical or horizontal line, so you can let $\overline{AB}$ be the hypotenuse of a right triangle whose two legs are vertical and horizontal segments. You can find the lengths of the legs by using the Ruler Postulate, and the length of the hypotenuse by using the Pythagorean Theorem.

Diagram

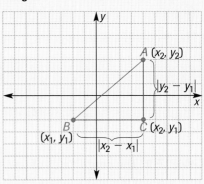

If $x_1 \neq x_2$ and $y_1 \neq y_2$, then $\triangle ABC$ is a right triangle with a right angle at C. Think of each axis as a number line. Then, from the Ruler Postulate, you know that $BC = |x_2 - x_1|$ and $AC = |y_2 - y_1|$.

Now use the Pythagorean Theorem to find the length of the hypotenuse, $\overline{AB}$. That length, AB, also is the distance between points (x_1, y_1) and (x_2, y_2). Let $a = |x_2 - x_1|$, $b = |y_2 - y_1|$, and $c = $ distance (d).

$$c^2 = a^2 + b^2$$
$$d^2 = |x_2 - x_1|^2 + |y_2 - y_1|^2$$
$$\sqrt{d^2} = \sqrt{|x_2 - x_1|^2 + |y_2 - y_1|^2}$$
$$\sqrt{d^2} = \sqrt{(x_2 - x_1)^2 + (y_2 - y_1)^2}$$
$$d = \sqrt{(x_2 - x_1)^2 + (y_2 - y_1)^2}$$

You can eliminate the absolute value symbol since squaring an absolute value always gives a positive result.

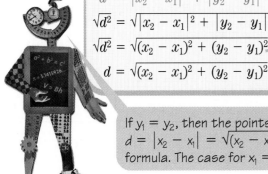

If $y_1 = y_2$, then the points lie on the same horizontal line and $d = |x_2 - x_1| = \sqrt{(x_2 - x_1)^2}$, a special case of the distance formula. The case for $x_1 = x_2$ (a vertical distance) is similar.

EXAMPLE: Find the distance between the two trees shown on the coordinate plane.

Use the coordinates of A for (x_1, y_1) and the coordinates of B for (x_2, y_2). Then use the formula to find the distance.

$(x_1, y_1) = (^-2, 3)$ $(x_2, y_2) = (4, ^-1)$

$d = \sqrt{(x_2 - x_1)^2 + (y_2 - y_1)^2}$

$ = \sqrt{(4 - ^-2)^2 + (^-1 - 3)^2}$

$ = \sqrt{(6)^2 + (^-4)^2}$

$ = \sqrt{36 + 16}$

$ = \sqrt{52}$, or about 7.21

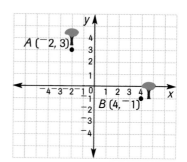

★ The distance between the trees is about 7.21 units.

MATH ALERT The Radical is a Grouping Symbol

091

Complete all of the calculations under the radical before simplifying a square root.

Consider this example.

$\sqrt{3^2 + 4^2} \overset{?}{=} \sqrt{3^2} + \sqrt{4^2}$

$\sqrt{9 + 16} \overset{?}{=} \sqrt{9} + \sqrt{16}$

$\sqrt{25} \overset{?}{=} 3 + 4$

$5 \neq 7$

Distance from a Point to a Line

MORE HELP
See 105, 108

The distance between a line and a point not on that line is the length of the perpendicular segment from the point to the line.

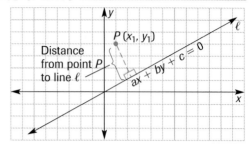

Distance from point P to line ℓ

$P(x_1, y_1)$

$ax + by + c = 0$

Formula — The distance between a line and a point not on that line is $d = \dfrac{|ax_1 + by_1 + c|}{\sqrt{a^2 + b^2}}$. (F03)

We won't give a proof for this formula, but you can see how it works in the following example.

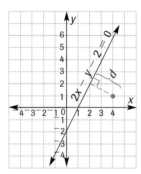

EXAMPLE: Find the distance between the line $2x - y - 2 = 0$ and the point at $(4, 1)$.

From the equation of the line, you know that $a = 2$, $b = {}^-1$, and $c = {}^-2$. From the coordinates of the point, you know that $x_1 = 4$ and $y_1 = 1$.

Substitute these values into the formula to find the distance.

$d = \dfrac{\left\|ax_1 + by_1 + c\right\|}{\sqrt{a^2 + b^2}}$	Formula (F03)
$= \dfrac{\left\|2(4) + {}^-1(1) + {}^-2\right\|}{\sqrt{2^2 + ({}^-1)^2}}$	Substitute
$= \dfrac{\left\|8 + {}^-1 + {}^-2\right\|}{\sqrt{4 + 1}}$	Simplify
$= \dfrac{5}{\sqrt{5}}$	Simplify
$= \dfrac{5 \cdot \sqrt{5}}{\sqrt{5} \cdot \sqrt{5}}$	$\times$ prop. of $=$
$= \sqrt{5}$	Simplify

★ The distance from point $(4, 1)$ to the line $2x - y - 2 = 0$ is $\sqrt{5}$, or about 2.24 units.

Distance Between Two Parallel Lines

Just as with the distance from a point to a line, the distance between two parallel lines is the length of the perpendicular segment from a point on one line to a point on the other.

If you know the equations of the parallel lines, you can find the distance between them. Just use the formula for the distance between a point and a line after picking a point on one of the lines. Remember to find the distance to the *other* line!

EXAMPLE: Line p, whose equation is $3x + y - 2 = 0$ and line q, whose equation is $3x + y - 5 = 0$ are parallel. Find the distance between the two lines.

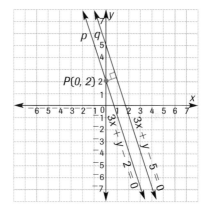

Find a point on line p. (You could use line q as well.) Substitute $x = 0$ into the equation for line p and solve for y. (You could choose any other value for x as well, but $x = 0$ is easy.)

$3(0) + y - 2 = 0$, so $y = 2$. The point $(0, 2)$ lies on line p.

Use the formula to find the distance from point $(0, 2)$ to line q. From the equation for line q, you know that $a = 3$, $b = 1$, and $c = {}^-5$.

From the point $(0, 2)$, you have $x_1 = 0$ and $y_1 = 2$.

Substitute these values into the formula to find the distance.

$d = \dfrac{\left| ax_1 + by_1 + c \right|}{\sqrt{a^2 + b^2}}$	Formula (F03)
$= \dfrac{\left| 3(0) + 1(2) + {}^-5 \right|}{\sqrt{3^2 + 1^2}}$	Substitute
$= \dfrac{\left| {}^-3 \right|}{\sqrt{10}}$	Simplify
$= \dfrac{3 \cdot \sqrt{10}}{\sqrt{10} \cdot \sqrt{10}}$	× prop. of =
$= 0.3\sqrt{10}$	Simplify

★ The distance between the two lines is $0.3\sqrt{10}$, or about 1 unit.

Straight Lines in the Coordinate Plane

The graph of a linear equation is the set of all points with coordinates (x, y) that satisfy the equation $ax + by + c = 0$.

095   ## Linear Equations

Linear relationships can be described with **linear equations**.

An equation that models the total cost of Internet use from one service provider is linear. As x, the number of minutes, increases, so does y, the total cost. An increase of $0.15 always buys another minute of service.

Number of minutes used each month

$$y = 0.15x + 14.95$$

Total cost per month   Per-minute rate   Monthly charge for service.

EXAMPLE: Graph the equation $2x + 3y - 6 = 0$ on a graphing calculator.

Check the WINDOW screen. Be sure the minimum and maximum values for x and y are appropriate. A calculator will only graph equations of the form $y = ax + b$, so rewrite the equation in this form.

$$2x + 3y - 6 = 0$$
$$3y = {}^{-}2x + 6$$
$$y = \frac{{}^{-}2x + 6}{3}$$

Y= ((–) 2 X,T,θ,n + 6) ÷ 3 ENTER GRAPH

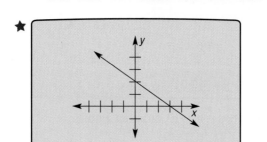

Linear Equations Using Ordered Pairs

You can make a table of values to graph a linear equation. Because two points define a line, you only need to find two ordered pairs to graph a linear equation. However, it is a good idea to try a third point as a check point and to help you sketch the line.

EXAMPLE: You want to furnish a U-shaped area including a 2-foot by 4-foot desk. Each running foot of countertop (which is two feet deep) costs $40. The total cost of your counter space can be modeled by $y = 40 \cdot (2 \cdot 4) + 40 \cdot 2x$ where x is the number of running feet of counter space on each side of the desk. Sketch the graph of the equation.

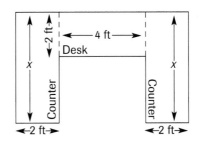

You will need to buy more than two feet of countertop for each side of the desk to create a U-shaped area. Substitute possible x-values into the equation to find corresponding y-values. The equation is $y = 8(40) + 40(2x)$. Make a table of values.

x	y
3	8(40) + 6(40) = 560
4	8(40) + 8(40) = 640
5	8(40) + 10(40) = 720

To sketch the graph, plot the ordered pairs (3, 560) and (4, 640). Use a straight edge to connect the points and extend the line. Use the point (5, 720) as a check point.

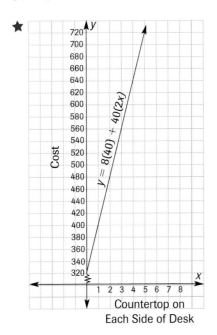

Because the scales of the x- and y-coordinates are so different, use a larger scale on the y-axis. Because you can't have a negative amount of countertop, the graph must be in the first quadrant.

Systems of Linear Equations

You can model the information given in some problems with two or more equations. This set of equations is a **system of equations**. The solution to a system of equations is the point or points common to the graphs of all of the equations.

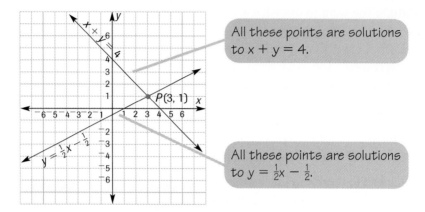

All these points are solutions to x + y = 4.

All these points are solutions to $y = \frac{1}{2}x - \frac{1}{2}$.

From the graph you can see that the intersection of the two lines is $(3, 1)$. This point is the solution of the system of equations, as this check shows.

Check

$x + y = 4 \qquad y = \frac{1}{2}x - \frac{1}{2}$

$3 + 1 \stackrel{?}{=} 4 \qquad 1 \stackrel{?}{=} \frac{1}{2}(3) - \frac{1}{2}$

$\quad 4 = 4 \qquad\quad 1 = 1$

EXAMPLE: The equations of the lines containing two sides of a triangle are $2x - y + 10 = 0$ and $3x - y + 5 = 0$. What are the coordinates of the common vertex of the two sides?

You need to find the coordinates of the point of intersection. Multiply the second equation by ⁻1, then add the second equation to the first. The sum of the y terms will be zero and you will be able to find a value for x.

$$2x - y + 10 = 0 \longrightarrow 2x - y + 10 = 0$$
$$^-1(3x - y + 5 = 0) \longrightarrow \underline{^-3x + y - \ 5 = 0}$$
$$^-x \quad\ + \ 5 = 0 \longrightarrow 5 = x$$

Substituting $x = 5$ into the first equation gives $2(5) - y + 10 = 0$, so $y = 20$.

★ The coordinate of the common vertex is (5, 20).

> Be sure to check the solution in the second equation also. This will help you catch any errors.
>
> $3(5) - 20 + 5 \stackrel{?}{=} 0$
>
> $15 - 20 + 5 \stackrel{?}{=} 0$
>
> $0 = 0$, so the solution is correct.

A system of linear equations can have no solutions (the lines are parallel), one solution (the lines intersect), or many solutions (the lines are collinear).

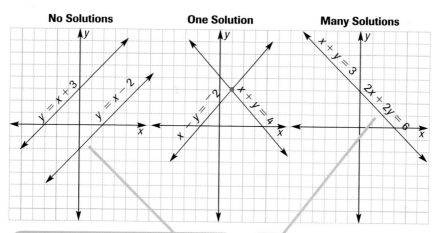

No Solutions　　　　**One Solution**　　　　**Many Solutions**

> The symbol ∅ describes this solution.
>
> **Write:** ∅
>
> **Say:** the empty set or the null set

> If you multiply both sides of the first equation by two you get the second equation. The two equations are the same. No wonder their graphs are the same line!

Slope

Have you ever seen a drawbridge being raised or lowered? The slope of the roadbed on the bridge changes from a horizontal, or level, position to a nearly vertical slope and then goes down again to a horizontal position. As the drawbridge rises, the roadbed gets steeper.

MORE ▶

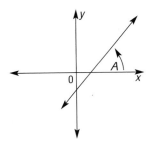

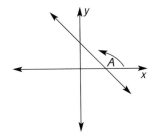

Angle *A* is acute.
The line is rising from
left to right.

Angle *A* is obtuse.
The line is falling from
left to right.

You can indicate the steepness of a line by using an angle. The part of a nonvertical line that is above the x-axis forms an angle with the positive x-axis. The measure of the angle is called the **inclination** of the line. For a line rising from left to right across the coordinate plane, $\angle A$ is acute. For a line falling from left to right, $\angle A$ is obtuse.

Another way to indicate steepness, which is common for lines on a graph, is to use a number, called slope. If the line rises as you move from left to right, its slope is a positive number; the steeper the rise, the larger the number. If the line falls from left to right, the slope is negative.

The **slope** of a line tells you how the y values of its points change as the corresponding x values change. The comparison of these values is a ratio. You can choose the coordinates of any two points on the line to write your ratio. It doesn't matter which point has coordinate x_1, as long as it is paired with the coordinate y_1.

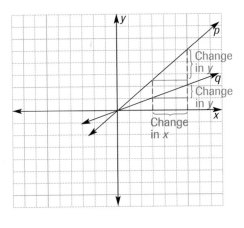

Look at the marked sections of lines p and q. For the same change in x-value, line p has a greater change in y-value. Therefore, the slope of line p is greater than the slope of line q.

Finding Slope Given Two Points

You can think of slope as the rate at which y changes with respect to a change in x. The slope tells how much y changes for every unit that x changes.

Formula The slope of a line containing points (x_1, y_1) and (x_2, y_2) is $m = \frac{y_2 - y_1}{x_2 - x_1}$. (F04)

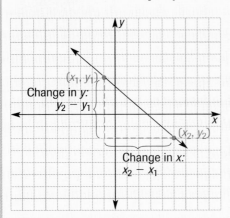

Change in y: $y_2 - y_1$

Change in x: $x_2 - x_1$

The change in y-values is sometimes called the **rise** because it indicates up or down change. The change in x-values is sometimes called the **run**. You can say that the slope is $\frac{rise}{run}$. Note that for carpenters the rise is positive, for mathematicians the rise can be negative as well.

EXAMPLE: An airplane is descending to an airport. When its altitude is 4 miles (or 21,120 ft), it is 200 miles from the airport. When its altitude is 2 miles (or 10,560 ft), it is 40 miles from the airport. What is the rate of descent of the airplane for these 160 miles? Should the plane continue to descend at this rate? Why or why not?

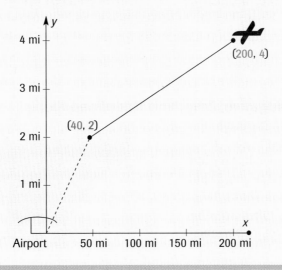

MORE ▶

The rate of descent is the slope of the line containing the points $(200, 4)$ and $(40, 2)$. To find the slope, use these coordinates in the slope formula.

$$m = \frac{y_2 - y_1}{x_2 - x_1}$$

$$= \frac{2 - 4}{40 - 200}$$

$$= \frac{{}^-2}{{}^-160}$$

$$= \frac{1}{80}$$

★ The slope is $\frac{1}{80}$. A descent of one mile per 80 land miles is 66 feet per mile, which means that the plane is descending at a rate of 66 feet for every mile closer to the airport it comes. If it continued on to the airport at this rate of descent, it would still be at 7920 feet when it reached the airport! The final approach will need to be at a much steeper rate of descent.

100 MATH ALERT The Vertical Change is Always the Numerator

When you compute the slope of a line, the *change in y* must be in the numerator. Note, too, that whichever point is used first in the numerator must also be used first in the denominator. You may use $y_1 - y_2$ in the numerator, but then you *must* use $x_1 - x_2$ in the denominator.

101 Positive, Negative, Zero, and Undefined Slope

The slope of a line can be positive, negative, zero, or undefined, depending on how the line lies in the coordinate plane. The table shows these relationships, taken from the cross section of a swimming pool.

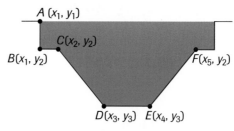

			Slope	
Segment	**Type**	**Relationship between Coordinates of Endpoints**	**Substitute Into** $m = \dfrac{y_2 - y_1}{x_2 - x_1}$	
$\overline{AB}$	Vertical	x-coordinates are the same	$\dfrac{y_2 - y_1}{x_1 - x_1} = \dfrac{y_2 - y_1}{0}$ The slope is undefined (no slope) because you can't divide by zero.	
A slope of 0 is not the same as no slope!				
$\overline{DE}$	Horizontal	y-coordinates are the same	$\dfrac{y_3 - y_3}{x_4 - x_3} = \dfrac{0}{x_4 - x_3}$ The slope is 0.	
$\overline{EF}$	Upward from left to right	$x_5 > x_4$ and $y_2 > y_3$ $x_5 - x_4 > 0;\ y_2 - y_3 > 0$	$\dfrac{y_2 - y_3}{x_5 - x_4} = \dfrac{+}{+}$ The slope is positive.	
$\overline{CD}$	Downward from left to right	$x_3 > x_2$ and $y_3 < y_2$ $x_3 - x_2 > 0;\ y_3 - y_2 < 0$	$\dfrac{y_3 - y_2}{x_3 - x_2} = \dfrac{-}{+}$ The slope is negative.	

Ask yourself if you can skate on the slope — you can skate on flat (0 slope), positive, or negative slopes, but vertical slopes are impossible to skate on.

Finding Slope from a Graph

If you know how to find the slope of a line from two points, then you can find the slope from a graph. Simply select any two points on the line to use in the slope formula.

MORE HELP
See 099

To make calculating easier, choose two points on the line with coordinates that are integers. As you move from the first point to the second, see how much y changes and how much x changes. Keep in mind the direction of the change — it's up/down then left/right.

EXAMPLE 1: Find the slope of the line.

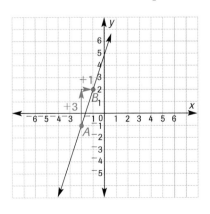

Choose points A and B on the graph. Count the number of units in the change in y. Then count the number of units in the change in x. Because the line rises from left to right, the slope is positive.

$$m = \frac{\text{change in } y\text{-value} \rightarrow \text{up 3 units}}{\text{change in } x\text{-value} \rightarrow \text{right 1 unit}}$$

$$= \frac{3}{1}$$

$$= 3$$

★ The slope of the line is 3.

MORE ▶

EXAMPLE 2: Find the slope of the line.

Choose points P and Q on the graph. Count units to find the change in y and the change in x. Because the line falls from left to right, the slope is negative.

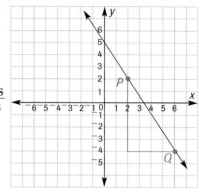

$$m = \frac{\text{change in } y\text{-value} \rightarrow \text{down 6 units}}{\text{change in } x\text{-value} \rightarrow \text{right 4 units}}$$

$$= \frac{^-6}{4}$$

$$= \frac{^-3}{2}$$

★ The slope of the line is $\frac{^-3}{2}$.

For a straight line, the slope doesn't change anywhere on the line. So, you can select any two points on the line for your calculations. For example, if you select the points (2, 2) and (4, ⁻1), then the change in y is ⁻3 and the change in x is 2, so the slope still comes out to be $\frac{^-3}{2}$.

103

Finding Slope Given the Equation of the Line

If you know the equation of a line, you can find its slope. If the equation is in **slope-intercept** form, $y = mx + b$, all you need to do is to look at m, because m is the slope and b is the y-intercept.

MORE HELP
See 106

EXAMPLE 1: What is the slope of the line $y = \frac{^-3}{8}x - 2.6$?

The line is in the form $y = mx + b$, with $m = \frac{^-3}{8}$ and $b = {}^-2.6$.

★ The slope of the line is $\frac{^-3}{8}$.

EXAMPLE 2: Suppose the equation $y = 0.35x + 19.95$ describes the cost of cellular telephone service from company A. If y is the total cost per month and x is the number of minutes used per month, find the rate per minute the cell phone company charges.

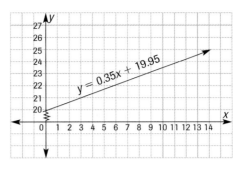

The slope represents the rate of change, which in this case is the rate at which the cost changes for every minute of use.

★ In the equation $y = 0.35x + 19.95$, the slope is 0.35 and the rate per minute is $0.35.

The equation of a line may not be in slope-intercept form. To find the slope of a line when you have its equation in the form $ax + by + c = 0$, you can rewrite it in slope-intercept form, $y = mx + b$; or you can use a formula.

Formula The slope of a line $ax + by + c = 0$ is $m = \frac{^-a}{b}$. (F05)

Given: line with equation $ax + by + c = 0$

Prove: $m = \dfrac{^-a}{b}$

Proof

Statements	Reasons
❶ $ax + by + c = 0$	Given
❷ $\quad by = {}^-c - ax$	Subtraction prop. of =
❸ $\quad \dfrac{by}{b} = \dfrac{^-c - ax}{b}$	÷ prop. of =
❹ $\quad y = \dfrac{^-c}{b} - \dfrac{a}{b}x$	Distributive prop.
❺ $\quad y = \dfrac{^-a}{b}x - \dfrac{c}{b}$	Commutative prop. of +

In this equation, slope m is $\frac{^-a}{b}$ and the y-intercept is $\frac{^-c}{b}$.

When an equation is written in slope-intercept form $y = mx + b$ and when it is written in standard form $ax + by + c = 0$, the b represents two different numbers. In the first equation it represents the y-intercept. In the second equation it is a placeholder for the coefficient of y.

MORE ▶

EXAMPLE 1: What is the slope of the line whose equation is $9x + 3y = 5$?

| ONE WAY | Rewrite the equation as $9x + 3y - 5 = 0$. Use the formula: $m = \frac{^-a}{b}$ with $a = 9$ and $b = 3$.

$$\text{slope} = \frac{^-a}{b}$$

$$= \frac{^-9}{3}$$

$$= {}^-3$$

| ANOTHER WAY | Rewrite the equation in slope-intercept form.

$$9x + 3y = 5$$
$$3y = 5 - 9x$$
$$\frac{3y}{3} = \frac{^-9x + 5}{3}$$
$$y = {}^-3x + \frac{5}{3}$$

★ Either way, the slope of the line whose equation is $9x + 3y = 5$ is ${}^-3$.

104

MATH ALERT The Coefficient of *x* Doesn't Always Equal the Slope

If the equation of a line is in the form $ax + by + c = 0$, the slope of the line is **not** a. The equation must be in the slope-intercept form $(y = mx + b)$, to read the coefficient of x as the slope.

105

Linear Equations Using Slope and a Point

If you know the slope of a line and the coordinates of a point on it, you can graph it and you can write an equation for it. The **point-slope** form of an equation is $(y - y_1) = m(x - x_1)$; m is the slope and (x_1, y_1) is a point on the line.

EXAMPLE 1: An airplane is on a flight path that can be modeled by the equation $y = \frac{3}{4}x + 2$. A second airplane, flying on a perpendicular flight path, passes through the coordinates $(4, 5)$ after the first airplane clears the path. Write the equation of the line that models the path of the second airplane in point-slope form.

MORE HELP
See 061, 108

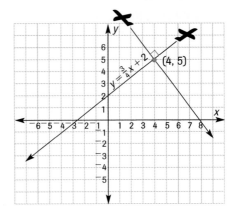

Since the flight paths are perpendicular, the slopes of the lines are negative reciprocals. The slope of the first airplane's path is $m = \frac{3}{4}$. The slope of the second airplane's path is $\frac{-4}{3}$.

Now use the formula and substitute.

$$y - y_1 = m(x - x_1)$$
$$y - 5 = \frac{-4}{3}(x - 4)$$

★ In point-slope form, the equation of the line that models the flight path of the second airplane is $y - 5 = \frac{-4}{3}(x - 4)$.

EXAMPLE 2: Draw a line through $(1, \,^-1)$ that is parallel to line q with slope 3.

Plot $(1, \,^-1)$. Use the definition of slope to find another point on the line you're looking for. For this line, $m = \frac{3}{1}$, so count 3 units in the positive y-direction and 1 unit in the positive x-direction from $(1, \,^-1)$. Connect the two points to draw the line.

MORE HELP
See 098, 105, 107

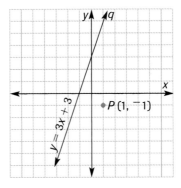

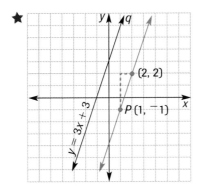

Linear Equations Using Slope and Intercepts

A quick way to sketch the graph of a linear equation is to find where the line crosses each axis. At these points, the non-zero coordinates are called the x- and y-intercepts. To find the **x-intercept**, let $y = 0$ and find the value of x. To find the **y-intercept**, let $x = 0$ and find the value of y.

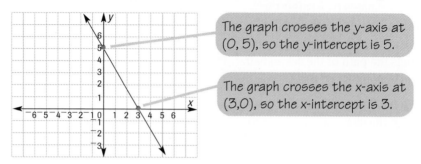

The graph crosses the y-axis at (0, 5), so the y-intercept is 5.

The graph crosses the x-axis at (3, 0), so the x-intercept is 3.

EXAMPLE 1: Find the x- and y-intercepts of $5x + 4y = 20$. Then graph.

First, find the intercepts.

x-intercept: let $y = 0$		y-intercept: let $x = 0$
$5x + 4y = 20$	Given	$5x + 4y = 20$
$5x + 4(0) = 20$	Substitution	$5(0) + 4y = 20$
$5x = 20$	Simplify	$4y = 20$
$x = 4$	÷ prop. of =	$y = 5$

★ The x-intercept is 4, so the point (4, 0) lies on the line. The y-intercept is 5, so the point (0, 5) lies on the line. Plot these points, and draw a line through them.

You can sketch a graph of a linear equation in many ways. The most efficient method depends on the form in which the equation is written. If an equation is in slope-intercept form, plotting the y-intercept and using the slope may work best. If an equation is in standard form, finding and plotting the intercepts may work best.

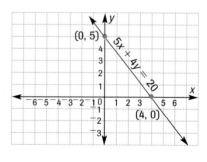

You can use the slope-intercept form of a linear equation to sketch its graph. The **slope-intercept** form of a linear equation is $y = mx + b$, where m represents the slope and b represents the y-intercept. The y-intercept is the value of y where the graph crosses the y-axis (that is, where $x = 0$).

EXAMPLE 2: Sketch the graph of $y = \frac{-1}{2}x + 3$.

Compare the linear equation to the slope-intercept form $y = mx + b$.

For $y = \frac{-1}{2}x + 3$, $m = \frac{-1}{2}$, and $b = 3$.

To sketch the graph, locate the y-intercept (3). Then use the definition of the slope to find another point.

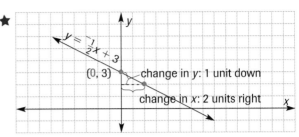

change in y: 1 unit down

change in x: 2 units right

You can check your graph by locating another point on the line. Substitute its coordinates into the equation to be sure it is also a solution.

For example, does (⁻2, 4) satisfy $y = \frac{-1}{2}x + 3$?

$4 \stackrel{?}{=} \frac{-1}{2}(^-2) + 3$

$4 \stackrel{?}{=} 1 + 3$

$4 = 4$

(⁻2, 4) is a solution to the equation, so the graph is correct.

EXAMPLE 3: Compare the graphs of $y = \frac{2}{3}x + 3$, $y = \frac{2}{3}x + 1$, and $y = \frac{2}{3}x - 1$.

Each graph has a slope of $\frac{2}{3}$, but each y-intercept is different. Locate each intercept and use the slope to find a second point on each line.

Locate (0, 3). Then count up 2 and right 3.

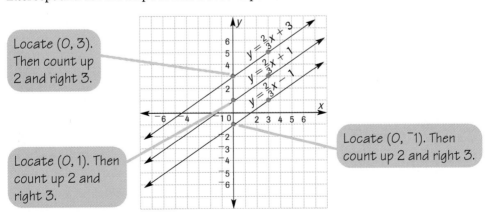

Locate (0, ⁻1). Then count up 2 and right 3.

Locate (0, 1). Then count up 2 and right 3.

MORE HELP
See 107

★ The three lines are parallel because parallel lines have equal slopes. The line with the greatest y-intercept falls above the other two. The line with the least y-intercept falls below the other two.

Slopes of Parallel Lines

It seems reasonable that lines that have the same steepness or slope would be parallel. This is proved in the next theorem.

> **Theorem** Two nonvertical lines are parallel if and only if they have the same slope. Nonvert. lines $\parallel \Leftrightarrow$ = slope (T036)

MORE HELP
See 376, 432, 434

Each part of the theorem needs to be proved separately.

CASE 1 If two lines are parallel, then they have the same slope.

Proof

Given: $\ell_1 \parallel \ell_2$

Prove: slope of ℓ_1 = slope of ℓ_2
($m_1 = m_2$)

Plan: Construct line t perpendicular to the x-axis forming right triangles CQD and APB. In the triangles, CQ and AP represent a change in y and DQ and BP represent a change in x. Show that the two triangles are similar, and that the ratios of the corresponding legs are proportional. The proportion shows that the slopes are equal.

Diagram

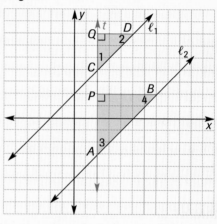

Statements	Reasons
❶ $\ell_1 \parallel \ell_2$	Given
❷ t is a transversal, $\overline{DQ} \perp t$, $\overline{BP} \perp t$	Construction
❸ $\angle 1 \cong \angle 3$	Corresp. $\angle$s Postulate (P15)
❹ $\angle CQD$ and $\angle APB$ are rt. $\angle$s	Def. of $\perp$
❺ $\angle Q \cong \angle P$	All rt. $\angle$s $\cong$ (T020)
❻ $\triangle CQD \sim \triangle APB$	AA $\sim$ Postulate (P21)
❼ $\dfrac{CQ}{QD} = \dfrac{AP}{PB}$	Def. of $\sim$ $\triangle$s
❽ $m_1 = m_2$	Def. of slope

CASE 2 If the slopes of two lines are equal, then the lines are parallel.

Given: slope of ℓ_1 = slope of ℓ_2
$(m_1 = m_2)$

Prove: $\ell_1 \parallel \ell_2$

The proof of Case 2 is similar to Case 1, except that you prove the triangles are similar by the SAS Similarity Theorem $\left(\frac{CQ}{QD} = \frac{AP}{PB}; \angle Q \cong \angle P\right)$.

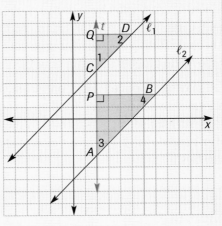

Then $\angle 1 \cong \angle 3$ because they are corresponding angles of the two triangles. Since $\angle 1$ and $\angle 3$ are corresponding angles formed by ℓ_1 and ℓ_2 and transversal t, the two lines are parallel.

EXAMPLE: Is $ABCD$ a parallelogram?

MORE HELP
See 157

To decide whether $ABCD$ is a parallelogram, you need to know whether the opposite sides are parallel. You can find the slope of each side, which will give you the answer you need.

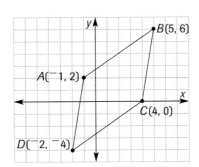

Slope of $\overline{AB} = \dfrac{y_2 - y_1}{x_2 - x_1}$

$\quad = \dfrac{6 - 2}{5 - {}^-1}$

$\quad = \dfrac{4}{6}$

Slope of $\overline{BC} = \dfrac{y_2 - y_1}{x_2 - x_1}$

$\quad = \dfrac{0 - 6}{4 - 5}$

$\quad = \dfrac{6}{1}$

Slope of $\overline{DC} = \dfrac{y_2 - y_1}{x_2 - x_1}$

$\quad = \dfrac{0 - {}^-4}{4 - {}^-2}$

$\quad = \dfrac{4}{6}$

Slope of $\overline{AD} = \dfrac{y_2 - y_1}{x_2 - x_1}$

$\quad = \dfrac{{}^-4 - 2}{{}^-2 - {}^-1}$

$\quad = \dfrac{6}{1}$

★ The slopes of $\overline{AB}$ and $\overline{DC}$ are equal, so these two segments are parallel. The slopes of $\overline{BC}$ and $\overline{AD}$ are equal, so these two segments are parallel. Since opposite sides of $ABCD$ are parallel, it is a parallelogram.

Slopes of Perpendicular Lines

MORE HELP
See 106

How are the slopes of perpendicular lines related? Perhaps you have used a geoboard in math class. Were you surprised to find that you could form perpendicular segments even if they didn't follow the rows of pegs?

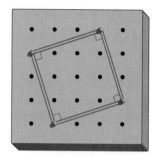

You may have noticed that if one segment is formed by moving over 3 and up 1, then a perpendicular segment is formed by moving over 1 and down 3. The next theorem shows why this is true.

Theorem   Two nonvertical lines are perpendicular if and only if the product of their slopes is $^-1$. Nonvert. lines $\perp \Leftrightarrow$ $m_1m_2 = {}^-1$ (T037)

This theorem needs to be proved in two parts. Both parts are about a pair of non-vertical lines that intersect. For simplicity, place the point of intersection of the two lines at the origin. Then the equations of the two lines are $y = m_1x$ and $y = m_2x$.

Proof

CASE 1 If two lines are perpendicular, then the product of their slopes is $^-1$.

Given: $\ell_1 \perp \ell_2$

Prove: $m_1m_2 = {}^-1$

Plan: Draw $\overleftrightarrow{AB}$ perpendicular to the x-axis. Use the Pythagorean Theorem in $\triangle AOB$ and the Distance Formula to show that the product of the slopes is $^-1$.

Diagram

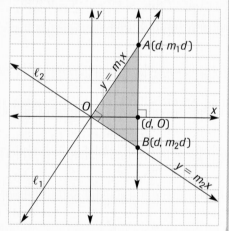

MORE HELP
See 055, 090,
152, 375

Statements	Reasons
❶ Construct $\overleftrightarrow{AB} \perp x$-axis at $(d, 0)$, intersecting ℓ_1 at (d, m_1d) and ℓ_2 at (d, m_2d)	Construction
❷ $\ell_1 \perp \ell_2$	Given
❸ $\angle AOB$ is a rt. $\angle$	$\perp$ lines $\Rightarrow$ 4 rt. $\angle$s (T011)
❹ $\triangle AOB$ is a rt. $\triangle$	Def. of rt. $\triangle$
❺ $(OA)^2 + (OB)^2 = (AB)^2$	Pythagorean Theorem (T059)
❻ $OA = \sqrt{(d-0)^2 + (m_1 d - 0)^2}$; $OB = \sqrt{(d-0)^2 + (m_2 d - 0)^2}$; $(OA)^2 = d^2 + (m_1d)^2$; $(OB)^2 = d^2 + (m_2d)^2$	Distance Formula (F02)
❼ $(AB)^2 = |m_2 d - m_1 d|^2$ $= (m_2d)^2 - 2m_1m_2d^2 + (m_1d)^2$	Ruler Postulate (P08)
❽ $d^2 + (m_1d)^2 + d^2 + (m_2d)^2$ $= (m_2d)^2 - 2m_1m_2d^2 + (m_1d)^2$	Substitution Look back at steps 5, 6, and 7.
❾ $2d^2 = {}^-2m_1m_2d^2$	Simplify; Subtraction prop. of =
❿ ${}^-1 = m_1m_2$	$\div$ prop. of =

CASE 2 If the product of the slopes is $^-1$, then the lines are perpendicular.

Given: ℓ_1 intersects ℓ_2 at O; $m_1m_2 = {}^-1$

Prove: $\ell_1 \perp \ell_2$

To prove this part, use the same diagram, but remember you don't know that the lines are perpendicular. The proof is the same as part 1, worked backward. Use the Converse of the Pythagorean Theorem to show that each of the triangles is a right triangle.

All vertical lines are parallel and any vertical line is perpendicular to any horizontal line.

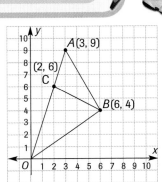

EXAMPLE: Is $\overline{BC}$ an altitude of $\triangle AOB$?

You need to find whether $\overline{OA} \perp \overline{BC}$

Slope of $\overline{OA} = \dfrac{9-0}{3-0}$ Slope of $\overline{BC} = \dfrac{6-4}{2-6}$

$= 3$ $= \dfrac{^-1}{2}$

★ Since $m_1m_2 \neq {}^-1$, $\overline{BC}$ is not an altitude of $\triangle AOB$.

Look at this sequence of rectangles. As the widths of the rectangles increase by one, the lengths increase by two. This is a linear relationship, because the lengths are increasing at a constant rate with a constant increase in width.

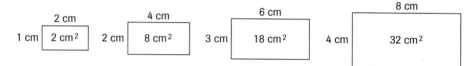

1 cm | 2 cm / 2 cm²   2 cm | 4 cm / 8 cm²   3 cm | 6 cm / 18 cm²   4 cm | 8 cm / 32 cm²

Now consider the areas of the rectangles. As the widths increase by 1, the areas increase by 6, 10, and 14. Since the area is not increasing at a constant rate, this relationship is not linear. The graph of this relationship is a curve.

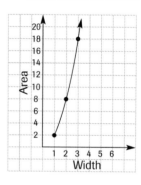

110) **Graphing Quadratic Equations** _____

Think of the path of a ball as you throw it (at an angle) up into the air and gravity curves its path back down to the ground. The path the ball traces is called a parabola.

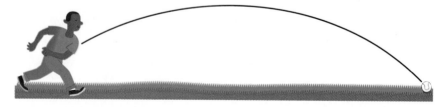

MORE HELP
See 112, 279

You can model a parabola with a **quadratic** equation, $y = ax^2 + bx + c$, where a, b, and c are real numbers. A **parabola** is a symmetric curve with a vertical line of symmetry. A parabola can open up or down. The direction depends on the value of a, the coefficient of x^2. The vertex and line of symmetry of a parabola can help you sketch its graph. Notice that the **vertex** (highest or lowest point) is on the line of symmetry.

$y = ax^2 + bx + c, a < 0$

$y = ax^2 + bx + c, a > 0$

Locating a Vertex

If a parabola opens upward, the y-coordinate of the vertex is the minimum y-value, or **lower bound,** of the curve. If a parabola opens downward, the y-coordinate of the vertex is the maximum y-value, or **upper bound**.

Formula	On the graph of an equation in the form $y = ax^2 + bx + c$, the x-coordinate of the vertex is $\frac{^-b}{2a}$. (F06)

To understand why, look at the equation in its factored form.

$y = ax^2 + bx + c$	Given
$y = a\left(x^2 + \frac{b}{a}x\right) + c$	Distributive prop.
$y = a\left(x^2 + \frac{b}{a}x + \frac{b^2}{4a^2}\right) + c - \frac{ab^2}{4a^2}$	Complete the square; Identity element
$y = a\left(x + \frac{b}{2a}\right)^2 + \left(c - \frac{b^2}{4a}\right)$	Simplify

The expression in the second term is a constant. Only the first term contains a variable. Since that term is squared, it will have its least possible value when $x + \frac{b}{2a} = 0$, or when $x = \frac{^-b}{2a}$. For any other value of x, $\left(x + \frac{b}{2a}\right)^2$ will be positive.

Since the line of symmetry of the parabola passes through the vertex, the line $x = \frac{^-b}{2a}$ is the equation of the line of symmetry. When $b = 0$, the equation of the parabola simplifies to $y = ax^2 + c$, and the line of symmetry is the line $x = 0$, the y-axis.

MORE ▶

The expression $a\left(x + \frac{b}{2a}\right)^2$ will have values that are positive or zero when $a > 0$. This means that y will have a minimum value when $x = \frac{-b}{2a}$, but no maximum value (that is, it will open upward). When $a < 0$, the expression $a\left(x + \frac{b}{2a}\right)^2$ will have values that are negative or zero, so y will have a maximum value at $x = \frac{-b}{2a}$ but no minimum value (it will open downward).

In either case, the x-coordinate of the vertex is $x = \frac{-b}{2a}$. For example, in the parabola $y = x^2$, $a = 1$ and $b = c = 0$. The x-coordinate of the vertex is 0, and the vertex of the parabola is $(0, 0)$.

The fraction $\frac{-b}{2a}$ will always be defined, because $a \neq 0$. If a did equal 0, the equation would be linear, not quadratic because the x² term would disappear.

EXAMPLE: Find the vertex and then sketch the graph of the parabola $y = x^2 + 4x + 7$.

To find the x-coordinate of the vertex, use the formula $x = \frac{-b}{2a}$. Then substitute the value of the x-coordinate into the equation of the parabola to find the value of the y-coordinate.

For $y = x^2 + 4x + 7$, $a = 1$ and $b = 4$.

Find the x-coordinate of the vertex.

$$x = \frac{-b}{2a}$$

$$= \frac{-(4)}{2(1)}$$

$$= {}^-2$$

Find the y-coordinate of the vertex.

$$y = x^2 + 4x + 7$$

$$= ({}^-2)^2 + 4({}^-2) + 7$$

$$= 3$$

Use the equation to find at least two other points. If $x = 0$, $y = 7$. If $x = {}^-4$, $y = 7$.

★ The vertex of the graph of $y = x^2 + 4x + 7$ is $({}^-2, 3)$.

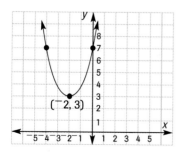

Finding the Line of Symmetry

Every parabola with an equation in the form $y = ax^2 + bx + c$ has a vertical **line of symmetry** through its vertex. This means that each point of the parabola has a mirror image across this line that is also on the parabola. Since the x-value of the vertex is $\frac{-b}{2a}$, the equation for the line of symmetry is $x = \frac{-b}{2a}$.

MORE HELP
See 279

You can use the line of symmetry to help you sketch the graph of a parabola. For example, as you find points on one side of the vertex, you can use the line of symmetry to find the corresponding points on the other side of the line. This can save you time!

EXAMPLE 1: Find the line of symmetry of the graph, $y = \frac{1}{2}x^2 - 2x + 1$. Identify the line of symmetry, two points on the graph, and their images. Then sketch the graph.

Find the line of symmetry.

$$x = \frac{-b}{2a}$$

$$= \frac{-(-2)}{2\left(\frac{1}{2}\right)}$$

$$= 2$$

> Remember, this is also the x-coordinate of the vertex.

Find the vertex.

$$y = \frac{1}{2}(2)^2 - 2(2) + 1$$

$$= {}^{-}1$$

The vertex is $(2, {}^{-}1)$.
Since $a > 0$, the parabola opens upward.

Make a table of values.

x	y
2	⁻1
0	1
4	1
⁻2	7
6	7

> This is the reflection of $(0, 1)$ across $x = 2$.

> This is the reflection of $({}^{-}2, 7)$ across $x = 2$.

★ The line of symmetry is $x = 2$, and the vertex is at $(2, {}^{-}1)$. Two points and their images are shown on the graph.

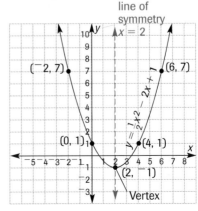

line of symmetry

MORE ▶

EXAMPLE 2: Sketch the graph of $y = {}^-x^2 - 8x - 13$.

In this equation, $a = {}^-1$ and $b = {}^-8$.

$${}^-x^2 = {}^-1(x \cdot x)$$

Find the x-coordinate of the vertex.

$$x = \frac{{}^-b}{2a}$$

$$= \frac{{}^-({}^-8)}{2({}^-1)}$$

$$= {}^-4$$

Find the y-coordinate of the vertex.

$$y = {}^-x^2 - 8x - 13$$

$$= {}^-({}^-4)^2 - 8({}^-4) - 13$$

$$= 3$$

MORE HELP
See 279

The vertex is $({}^-4, 3)$ and the line of symmetry is $x = {}^-4$. Plot the vertex and the line of symmetry on the graph. Since $a < 0$, the graph opens downward.

Next, make a table of values. Find two points on one side of the vertex and their images on the other side of the vertex so you can plot a total of five points.

x	y
${}^-2$	${}^-1$
${}^-6$	${}^-1$
0	${}^-13$
${}^-8$	${}^-13$

The reflection of $({}^-2, {}^-1)$ across $x = {}^-4$.

The reflection of $(0, {}^-13)$ across $x = {}^-4$.

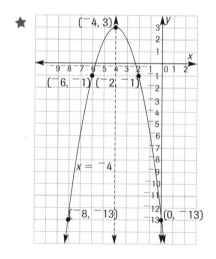

Graphing Circles

In one school district, students who live within a two-mile radius of school must walk to school. The boundary between the walkers and the bus riders is all the points that are 2 miles from the school. This is a circle whose radius is 2 miles.

MORE HELP
See 297

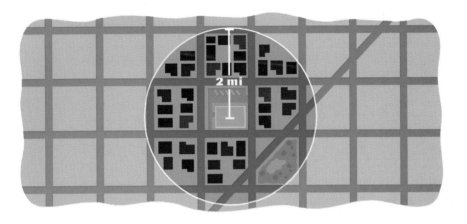

2 mi

Formula　The circle with center (h, k) and radius r is the set of points (x, y) satisfying the equation $(x - h)^2 + (y - k)^2 = r^2$. (F07)

Proof

Diagram

Given: Circle with center (h, k)

Prove: Its equation is
$(x - h)^2 + (y - k)^2 = r^2$

Plan: Suppose (x, y) is any point on the circle. To find the distance from this point to the center (h, k), you can use the distance formula. This distance is equal to r, the radius of the circle.

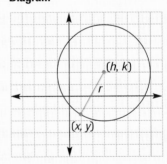

(h, k)

r

(x, y)

Statements	Reasons
❶ Circle with center (h, k)	Given
❷ The distance between any point (x, y) on the circle and (h, k) is r	Def. of circle
❸ $\sqrt{(x - h)^2 + (y - k)^2} = r$	Distance formula (F02)
❹ $(x - h)^2 + (y - k)^2 = r^2$	Simplify

MORE ▶

EXAMPLE: Sketch the circle with center ($^-$2, 3) and radius 4. Then write an equation for the circle.

To sketch the graph, locate the center and then use the radius to find four points on the circle. Count four units up, down, left, and right from the center to get the points (2, 3), ($^-$2, 7), ($^-$6, 3) and ($^-$2, $^-$1).

Remember that the center is not on the circle, so its coordinates will not satisfy the equation.

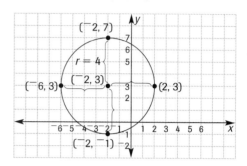

write the equation, use $r = 4$ and $(h, k) = ($$^-$$2, 3)$. Substitute these values into the general equation for a circle:

$$(x - h)^2 + (y - k)^2 = r^2 \longrightarrow (x - {}^-2)^2 + (y - 3)^2 = 4^2$$

★ The equation is $(x + 2)^2 + (y - 3)^2 = 16$.

To check, substitute (2, 3) for (x, y) in $(x + 2)^2 + (y - 3)^2 = 16$.

$$(2 + 2)^2 + (3 - 3)^2 \stackrel{?}{=} 16$$

$$16 + 0 \stackrel{?}{=} 16$$

$$16 = 16 \quad \text{The point (2, 3) checks.}$$

114

MATH ALERT Use Square Mode on Your Graphing Calculator

To use your graphing calculator, first put the equation for a circle into $y =$ form and set your calculator to *square mode*. *Square mode* is an option in the ZOOM menu that makes sure you are using a square grid, instead of rectangular, so that your circles don't turn into ovals!

The center of a circle is at $(-2, 3)$. Solve the equation for y.

$$(x + 2)^2 + (y - 3)^2 = 16$$

$$(y - 3)^2 = 16 - (x + 2)^2$$

$$y - 3 = \pm \sqrt{16 - (x + 2)^2}$$

$$y = 3 + \sqrt{16 - (x + 2)^2} \text{ and}$$

$$y = 3 - \sqrt{16 - (x + 2)^2}$$

You need to input both equations, since your calculator can only plot one value of y for each x value. The first equation will graph the top half of the circle and the second will graph the bottom half. You may have an incomplete graph due to your window setting and the number of pixels on your screen.

The Unit Circle

The circle with a radius of one unit and center at the origin is called the **unit circle.** The equation of the unit circle is $x^2 + y^2 = 1$.

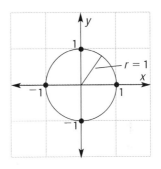

Notice that the points $(1, 0)$, $(0, 1)$, $(^-1, 0)$ and $(0, ^-1)$ all lie on the unit circle.

Functions

A **relation** consists of two sets of data and a way of pairing the items from one set with the items in the other. A **function** is a relation in which each first value of an ordered pair has one and only one second value. You can say that the second value *depends* on the first value that was selected.

MORE HELP
See 088

Relation

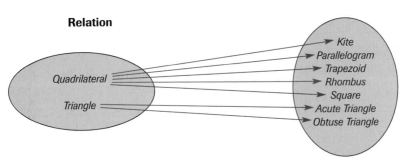

Function

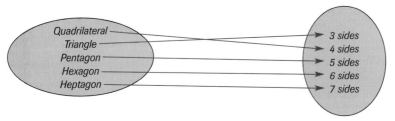

MORE ▶

If you live near an ocean, you may know that high tide occurs about every $12\frac{1}{4}$ hours. Nearly every day has two high tides; so the relation (date, time of high tide) is not a function, because usually there are two second values for each first value.

Now consider the relation (date, high temperature). Since every day can have only one high temperature, this relation is a function. A function is a relation that is *many-to-one* or *one-to-one*.

Here are some ways to think about y depending on x.

- The cost of a long distance telephone call depends on how long you talk.

- The amount of postage on a letter depends on the weight of the letter.

- The temperature of a cup of hot tea depends on how long it has been cooling.

- A turkey is taken out of a refrigerator and put into a heated oven. The temperature of the turkey depends on how long it has been in the oven.

CASE 1 In many-to-one functions each second value can have more than one first value.

To distinguish between a relation that is not a function and a many-to-one function think of the equations $y^2 = x$ and $y = x^2$.

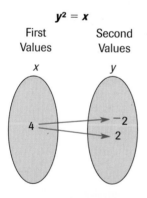

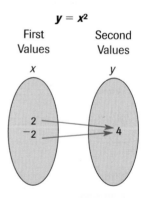

(4, 2) and (4, ⁻2) both belong to the relation. One x-value has two y-values. The relation $y^2 = x$ is not a function.

(2, 4) and (⁻2, 4) both belong to the relation. One x-value has only one y-value so the relation is a function. One y-value can be paired with two different x-values. The relation $y = x^2$ is a many-to-one function.

EXAMPLE 1: The relationship between the time since launch and the height of a model rocket can be modeled by a parabola with the equation $y = 64x - 16x^2$, where y is the height of the rocket and x is the number of seconds it has been in flight. The rocket can be at a height of, say, 48 feet, on the way up and again on the way down. This means that, except for the very top of the path, there are two x-values for every y-value, so it is a many-to-one function.

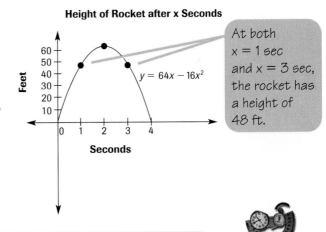

Height of Rocket after x Seconds

$y = 64x - 16x^2$

At both x = 1 sec and x = 3 sec, the rocket has a height of 48 ft.

Quadratic functions are many-to-one functions, unless x is restricted to all values greater than or equal to the x-coordinate of the vertex.

You can use a special notation to describe functions. For example, the height of the rocket at time x is modeled by $y = 64x - 16x^2$. Since the height of the rocket is y, you can say that y is a function of x.

To emphasize that one quantity is a function of the other, use $f(x)$. For the height of the rocket, you can write $f(x) = 64x - 16x^2$ instead of $y = 64x - 16x^2$.

Write: *f(x)*
Say: *f of x* or *function of x*

CASE 2 In one-to-one functions every second value can be paired with one and only one first value.

MORE HELP
See 095, 146, 239

Think about equilateral triangles. For each height there is one and only one equilateral triangle possible and it has one and only one perimeter. So each height is related to one and only one possible perimeter. You can say that the perimeter is a function of the height. You can use the 30°-60°-90° triangle relationships to find the perimeter that corresponds to each height.

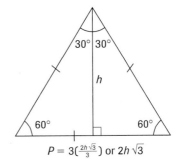

30° 30°

h

60°   60°

$P = 3(\frac{2h\sqrt{3}}{3})$ or $2h\sqrt{3}$

MORE ▶

Find the length of half a side.

$$h = \frac{s\sqrt{3}}{2}$$

$$\frac{2h}{\sqrt{3}} = s$$

$$\frac{2h \cdot \sqrt{3}}{\sqrt{3} \cdot \sqrt{3}} = s$$

$$\frac{2h\sqrt{3}}{3} = s$$

Find the perimeter.

$$\frac{2h\sqrt{3}}{3} = s$$

$$2h\sqrt{3} = 3s$$

$$2h\sqrt{3} = P$$

Half of a side of an equilateral triangle is the short leg of a 30°-60°-90° triangle.

The graph of $P(h) = 2h\sqrt{3}$ is a straight line through the origin. It is an example of a linear equation. A linear equation is always a one-to-one function.

You can tell from looking at a graph whether it is a function. Is there a place on the graph where an x-value has two or more y-values? If so, the graph does not represent a function.

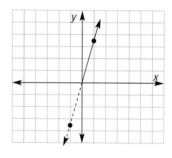

If (a, m) and (a, n) are both points on the graph of a relation, then one first value (a) has two second values (m and n). This means the relation isn't a function. This idea is summarized in the vertical line test.

If any vertical line intersects the graph of a relation in more than one point, then the relation is not a function.

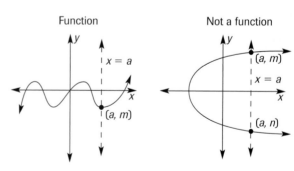

EXAMPLE 2: The graph shows $y = |x|$. Is y a function of x?

★ Any vertical line intersects the graph of $y = |x|$ at no more than one point, so y is a function of x.

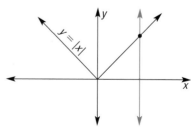

You need to use two numbers to locate a point in a plane. When the point is on a coordinate plane, you name it by giving two distances, one along the x-axis and one along the y-axis. However, on this map of the Northern Hemisphere, it is easier to name the line of longitude and a distance from the North Pole. Such a system of locating points is called a **polar coordinate system**.

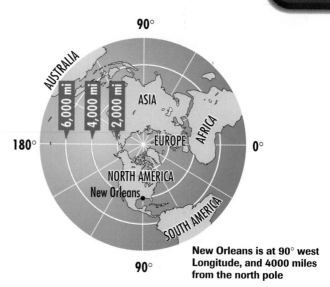

New Orleans is at 90° west Longitude, and 4000 miles from the north pole

In a system of polar coordinates, all points are measured from a fixed ray, called the **polar axis**, and its endpoint, called the **pole**. The polar axis corresponds to the positive x-axis in the rectangular system. For any point P in the plane (other than the pole O), r is the distance OP and θ is the angle between the polar axis and $\overrightarrow{OP}$. The coordinates of P are (r, θ) where r and θ are called **polar coordinates**.

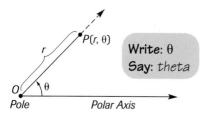

Write: θ
Say: *theta*

The angle θ is positive if the angle is generated by a counterclockwise rotation of a ray from the polar axis and negative if the rotation is clockwise.

Either degrees or radians may be used for the measure of θ. **Radians** are a way to measure angle rotation using real numbers instead of degrees. $180° = \pi$ radians, so one radian is equivalent to about $57°$.

MORE HELP
See 062, 416

Graphing Polar Coordinates

You can use polar graph paper to graph polar coordinates. When you graph polar coordinates on rectangular graph paper, you will have to estimate the length of r unless the angle lies on one of the axes.

EXAMPLE 1: Graph the points $A(4, 30°)$ and $B(5, 270°)$.

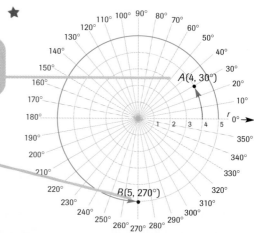

To graph point A, locate 4 on the polar axis. Then rotate 30° counterclockwise to plot the point (4, 30°).

To graph point B, locate 5 on the polar axis. Then rotate 270° counterclockwise to plot (5, 270°).

The polar coordinates of a point are not unique because the second coordinate is a rotation. For example, another point that is equivalent to the point A is the point (4, 390°). Another point that is equivalent to point B is the point (5, ⁻90°).

You can also use rectangular coordinates to graph polar coordinates. Then you usually use radian measure for θ. Since $180° = \pi$ radians, write radians as degrees by multiplying by $\frac{180°}{\pi}$. Here are the equivalent measures for some common angles.

MORE HELP
See 117, 416

$\frac{\pi}{2}$ radians $= 90°$ $\qquad$ $\frac{\pi}{3}$ radians $= 60°$

$\frac{\pi}{4}$ radians $= 45°$ $\qquad$ $\frac{\pi}{6}$ radians $= 30°$

EXAMPLE 2: Plot the points $C\left(3, \frac{\pi}{4}\right)$ and $D\left(⁻3, \frac{\pi}{4}\right)$.

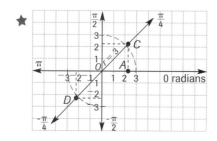

$\frac{\pi}{4}$ radians equal 45°, so $\overrightarrow{OC}$ bisects the angle formed by the two positive axes. $\overline{OC}$ is the hypotenuse of right triangle OCA. $\overline{OC}$ is 3 units long. A has coordinates (2.12, 0).

Converting Polar Coordinates to Rectangular Form

You can write polar coordinates in rectangular form and vice versa. To see why, consider the following diagram.

MORE HELP
See 152, 238, 241

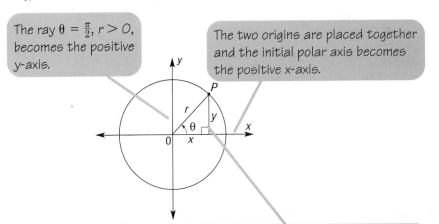

The ray $\theta = \frac{\pi}{2}$, $r > 0$, becomes the positive y-axis.

The two origins are placed together and the initial polar axis becomes the positive x-axis.

x, y, and r are the lengths of three sides of a right triangle. That means you can use the Pythagorean Theorem and trig. ratios to relate them.

$$x = r\cos\theta \quad y = r\sin\theta \quad x^2 + y^2 = r^2 \quad \tfrac{y}{x} = \tan\theta$$

To write polar coordinates in rectangular form, use the equations $x = r\cos\theta$ and $y = r\sin\theta$, so your coordinate point (x, y) becomes $(r\cos\theta, r\sin\theta)$.

EXAMPLE: Write the rectangular coordinates of the point $(\sqrt{2}, 45°)$.

You know from the polar coordinates that $r = \sqrt{2}$ and $\theta = 45°$.

Find x.

$x = r\cos\theta$

$x = \sqrt{2}\cos 45°$

$x = \sqrt{2}\left(\frac{\sqrt{2}}{2}\right)$

$x = \frac{2}{2}$ or 1

Find y.

$y = r\sin\theta$

$y = \sqrt{2}\sin 45°$

$y = \sqrt{2}\left(\frac{\sqrt{2}}{2}\right)$

$y = \frac{2}{2}$ or 1

★ The rectangular coordinates of the point are $(1, 1)$.

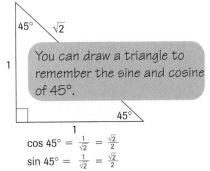

You can draw a triangle to remember the sine and cosine of 45°.

$\cos 45° = \frac{1}{\sqrt{2}} = \frac{\sqrt{2}}{2}$

$\sin 45° = \frac{1}{\sqrt{2}} = \frac{\sqrt{2}}{2}$

Converting Rectangular Coordinates to Polar Form

MORE HELP
See 152, 238, 241

To write rectangular coordinates in polar form, use the two equations:

$$x^2 + y^2 = r^2 \text{ and } \frac{y}{x} = \tan \theta.$$

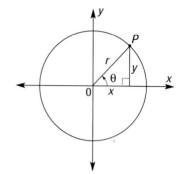

EXAMPLE: Find the polar coordinates of the point $(1, \sqrt{3})$.

From the rectangular coordinates, you know that $x = 1$ and $y = \sqrt{3}$.

Find r.

$$x^2 + y^2 = r^2$$

$$1^2 + \left(\sqrt{3}\right)^2 = r^2$$

$$4 = r^2$$

$$2 \text{ and } {}^-2 = r$$

Find θ.

$$\frac{y}{x} = \tan \theta$$

$$\frac{\sqrt{3}}{1} = \tan \theta$$

$$\theta = 60°$$

Think: What angle has a tangent of $\frac{\sqrt{3}}{1}$?

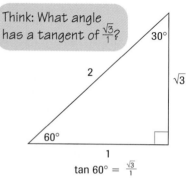

$$\tan 60° = \frac{\sqrt{3}}{1}$$

The original point $(1, \sqrt{3})$ has two positive coordinates, so it is in the first quadrant. Choose the positive value for r to keep the point in the first quadrant.

★ The polar coordinates are $(2, 60°)$.

When $\frac{y}{x}$ is not a common angle, use the $\tan^{-1}$ key on your calculator or a table of tangent values to find θ.

Graphing in Three Dimensions

Imagine a horizontal plane that slices through space. Every point in three-dimensional space not on the plane lies directly above or below a point in the plane. Since you can use two coordinates to describe any point in the plane, all you need to locate a point in space is a third coordinate that tells how far above or below the plane the point is located.

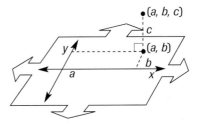

To locate points in three dimensions, use an **ordered triple** (x, y, z) in which x, y, and z are real numbers. Plot this ordered triple using three mutually perpendicular coordinate axes, called the x-, y-, and z-axes, with a common origin, called O. To visualize this, imagine that the x- and y-axes are the intersection of the floor with two adjacent walls and the z-axis is the junction of two walls.

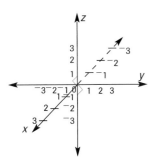

The coordinate plane determined by the x- and y-axes is called the **xy-plane**. Similarly, the coordinate plane determined by the y- and z-axes is called the **yz-plane** and the coordinate plane determined by the x- and z-axes is called the **xz-plane**. The origin of a three-dimensional grid is $(0,0,0)$.

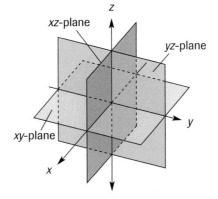

The three coordinate planes divide space into eight parts, called **octants**. The octant in which all the coordinates of an ordered triple (x, y, z) are positive is called the **first octant**.

Graphing Points and Coordinate Boxes _____

The coordinates (x, y, z) of a point P are the coordinates on the axes of the points where the planes through P perpendicular to the three axes cut the axes. To locate a point P you may want to construct a coordinate box for the point.

To locate a point $P(a, b, c)$, first locate the coordinates on each axis. Then construct a box to locate the point in space.

EXAMPLE: Plot the point $(2, 5, {}^-3)$ in three-dimensions.

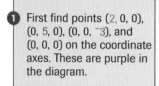

1 First find points $(2, 0, 0)$, $(0, 5, 0)$, $(0, 0, {}^-3)$, and $(0, 0, 0)$ on the coordinate axes. These are purple in the diagram.

2 Next find points $(2, 0, {}^-3)$, $(2, 5, 0)$ and $(0, 5, {}^-3)$ in the coordinate planes. These are open circles in the diagram.

3 The last vertex of the box is $(2, 5, {}^-3)$.

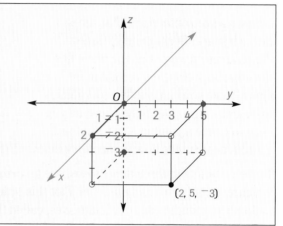

Distance Between Two Points in Three Dimensions

The formula for the distance between two points in three-dimensional space is similar to the one for points in a plane.

MORE HELP
See 090

> **Formula** The distance between two points (x_1, y_1, z_1) and (x_2, y_2, z_2) is $d = \sqrt{(x_2 - x_1)^2 + (y_2 - y_1)^2 + (z_2 - z_1)^2}$.
> (F08)
>
> The proof of the formula is omitted here, but it is similar to the proof of the distance formula in the plane and, in fact, uses that distance formula.

EXAMPLE: Two submarines are located on a grid laid out in nautical miles at $(3, {}^-2, {}^-1)$ and $({}^-2, 5, {}^-6)$ in a three-dimensional coordinate system. How far apart are the two submarines?

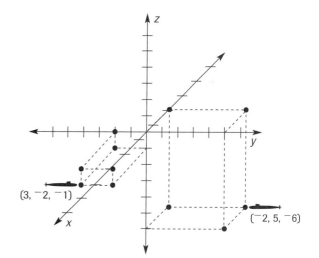

Let $(x_1, y_1, z_1) = (3, {}^-2, {}^-1)$ and let $(x_2, y_2, z_2) = ({}^-2, 5, {}^-6)$.
Use the three-dimensional distance formula.

$$d = \sqrt{(x_2 - x_1)^2 + (y_2 - y_1)^2 + (z_2 - z_1)^2}$$
$$= \sqrt{({}^-2 - 3)^2 + (5 - {}^-2)^2 + ({}^-6 - {}^-1)^2}$$
$$= \sqrt{({}^-5)^2 + 7^2 + ({}^-5)^2}$$
$$= \sqrt{25 + 49 + 25}$$
$$= \sqrt{99}$$

★ The two submarines are $\sqrt{99}$ or almost 10 nautical miles apart.

Midpoint of a Segment in Three Dimensions

You can find the midpoint of a line segment between two points in three dimensions using the three-dimensional midpoint formula.

MORE HELP
See 056

Formula The midpoint of the line segment with endpoints (x_1, y_1, z_1) and (x_2, y_2, z_2) is $\left(\frac{x_1 + x_2}{2}, \frac{y_1 + y_2}{2}, \frac{z_1 + z_2}{2}\right)$ (F09)

We won't give a proof for this formula, but you can see how it works by considering that it shows you that the x, y, and z values of the midpoint are each the mean (average) of the x, y, and z values of the endpoints. This is very similar to the midpoint of a segment in a plane, but now you have three coordinates to find, instead of just two.

EXAMPLE: Opposite vertices of a rectangular prism are located at $A(3, {}^-2, {}^-1)$ and $B({}^-2, 5, {}^-6)$. Find the center of the prism.

Let $(x_1, y_1, z_1) = (3, {}^-2, {}^-1)$ and let $(x_2, y_2, z_2) = ({}^-2, 5, {}^-6)$. Now use the formula.

$$\left(\frac{x_1 + x_2}{2}, \frac{y_1 + y_2}{2}, \frac{z_1 + z_2}{2}\right) = \left(\frac{3 + {}^-2}{2}, \frac{{}^-2 + 5}{2}, \frac{{}^-1 + {}^-6}{2}\right)$$

$$= \left(\frac{1}{2}, \frac{3}{2}, \frac{{}^-7}{2}\right)$$

★ The midpoint of $\overline{AB}$ is $\left(\frac{1}{2}, \frac{3}{2}, \frac{{}^-7}{2}\right)$.

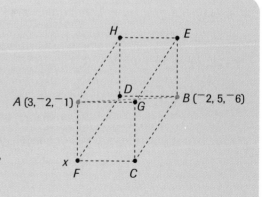

To find the other six vertices of the prism, list the points that have one coordinate from A and two from B, and then the points that have two coordinates from A and one from B.

$C(3, 5, {}^-6)$, $D({}^-2, {}^-2, {}^-6)$, $E({}^-2, 5, {}^-1)$ and $F(3, {}^-2, {}^-6)$, $G(3, 5, {}^-1)$, and $H({}^-2, {}^-2, {}^-1)$

$A (3, {}^-2, {}^-1)$

$B ({}^-2, 5, {}^-6)$

Equation of a Sphere

You can use the distance formula to write a general equation for a sphere.

MORE HELP
See 113, 332

Formula The sphere with center (h, j, k) and radius r is the set of points (x, y, z) satisfying the equation $(x - h)^2 + (y - j)^2 + (z - k)^2 = r^2$. (F10)

Given: Sphere with center (h, j, k) and radius r

Prove: Its equation is $(x - h)^2 + (y - j)^2 + (z - k)^2 = r^2$.

The proof is just like the proof for the equation of a circle, except that you use the distance formula for two points in space, rather than two points in a plane.

Diagram

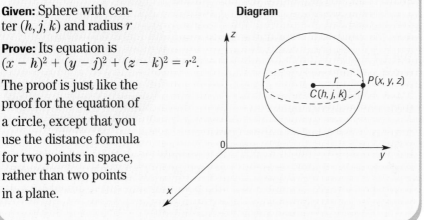

EXAMPLE: Write the equation of a sphere with center $(1, {}^-1, 4)$ and radius 6.

You know that $(h, j, k) = (1, {}^-1, 4)$ and $r = 6$. Substitute these values into the formula and simplify.

$(x - h)^2 + (y - j)^2 + (z - k)^2 = r^2$

$(x - 1)^2 + (y - {}^-1)^2 + (z - 4)^2 = 6^2$

$(x - 1)^2 + (y + 1)^2 + (z - 4)^2 = 36$

★ The equation of the sphere is $(x - 1)^2 + (y + 1)^2 + (z - 4)^2 = 36$.

Have you ever twirled a sparkler at night? If so, you know that you can form different shapes depending on how you hold your wrist and arm. If you keep both straight, you describe a circle, because every place the tip of the sparkler goes is the same distance from your shoulder joint.

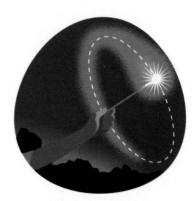

A **locus** is the set of all points that satisfy a given condition or a given set of conditions. A locus in a plane is often thought of as the path of an object moving in the plane. For example, the locus of a rolling billiard ball on a pool table is a line segment (until the ball hits the bumper). The locus of a swinging metronome is an arc.

Follow these steps to find a locus.
1. Draw any figures that are given.
2. Locate points that satisfy the given condition.
3. Draw and describe the locus.

EXAMPLE 1: Sketch and describe the locus of points in a plane that are 2 inches from a point P.

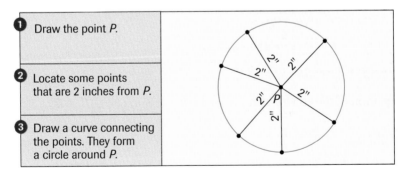

❶ Draw the point P.	
❷ Locate some points that are 2 inches from P.	
❸ Draw a curve connecting the points. They form a circle around P.	

★ The locus of points is a circle with a radius of two inches and center P.

EXAMPLE 2: A landscape designer for the Parks Department is designing a jogging path around a circular pond. All points on the path are between 820 and 850 feet from the center of the pond. Describe the jogging path. How wide is the path?

Let C represent the center of the circular pond.

★ The jogging path is a ring with an inner radius of 820 feet and an outer radius of 850 feet. The path is 30 feet wide.

You can also find the locus of points in three dimensions. The locus of all points that are three centimeters from a point in a plane is a circle, but the locus of all points that are three centimeters from a point in space is a sphere.

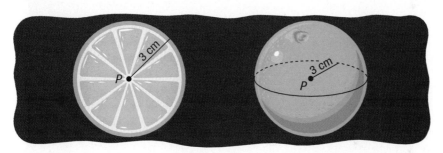

EXAMPLE 3: Have you ever been to a museum or a zoo where you drop a coin into a tube and watch the coin spin around until it falls through the hole in the center? Describe the locus of points of the coin as it goes down the tube.

The coin is dropped into the outer portion of the tube. It rotates around the center of the tube and rolls closer and closer to the hole at the center of the tube. On the outer part of the tube, the coin moves slowly. As it gets closer to the center, it moves more quickly. The coin traces out a spiral as it moves down the tube.

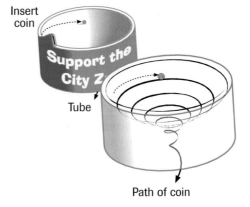

★ The locus of points is a spiral.

Polygons

"Whereas at the outset geometry is reported to have concerned itself with the measurement of muddy land, she now handles celestial as well as terrestrial problems. . . ."

—W. B. Frankland in _The Story of Euclid_

W hat do you see when you look at these pictures? Do you see what's actually drawn—groups of unconnected segments? Or do you see triangles, squares, rectangles, and other polygons?

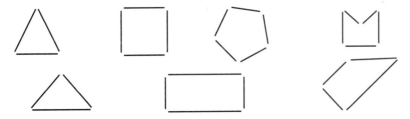

Polygons and other closed figures are so important to us that our brain sees them even when they're not really there. To understand why it's useful to perceive things this way, imagine a prehistoric hunter scanning the foliage for his dinner. Suddenly, among the trees and shrubs he sees parts of an outline visible here and there between the leaves. Instantly, his brain takes in the fragments and processes them. The hunter sees the outline of a familiar beast and knows whether to fight or flee.

Nowadays, we pay a lot of attention to closed figures for other reasons. Look at any bridge, stadium, school building, or space station, and you can see the triangles, rectangles, and other polygons that make these structures so strong and stable.

Attributes of Polygons

A **polygon** is a closed, plane figure formed by line segments that meet only at their endpoints. These segments are the **sides** of the polygon. Each side of a polygon intersects exactly two other sides. A point where two sides intersect is a **vertex** of the polygon.

More Help
See 054

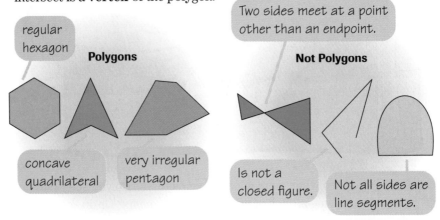

Two sides meet at a point other than an endpoint.

regular hexagon

Polygons

Not Polygons

concave quadrilateral

very irregular pentagon

Is not a closed figure.

Not all sides are line segments.

129) **Definitions and Hierarchy**

If a line that contains a side of a polygon also contains a point inside the polygon, the polygon is **concave** (or **non-convex**). Otherwise, the polygon is **convex**. Unless you are told otherwise, all polygons in this book are convex.

To name a polygon, write a capital letter at each vertex. Then list the vertices in consecutive order, either clockwise or counter clockwise: Pentagon *ABCDE* or hexagon *KJIHGF*.

Concave Polygons

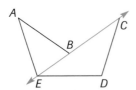

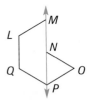

$\overleftrightarrow{BC}$, $\overleftrightarrow{HI}$, and $\overleftrightarrow{MN}$ all contain a side of their polygon as well as points inside it.

Convex Polygons

No lines containing the sides of these polygons contain points inside the polygon.

You can classify polygons by the number of sides they have. Since polygons come in many different shapes, you can classify them to simplify describing and working with them.

MORE HELP
See 256

Name	Number of Sides	Name	Number of Sides
Triangle	3	Octagon	8
Quadrilateral	4	Nonagon	9
Pentagon	5	Decagon	10
Hexagon	6	Dodecagon	12
Heptagon	7	n-gon	n

All the sides and all the angles of a **regular** polygon are congruent. If some of the sides or some of the angles of a polygon are not congruent, then the polygon is not regular (sometimes called **irregular**).

This is a polygon with any number of sides. This name is generally used when the number of sides is not known.

Regular   **Not Regular**

This polygon is equiangular but not equilateral.

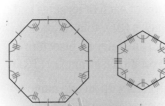

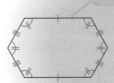

Tick marks are used to show sides or angles with the same measure.

MORE ▶

MORE HELP
See 056, 281

Theorem In any regular polygon, there is a point (its **center**) which is equidistant from all of its vertices. Regular polygon ⇒ center equidistant from vertices. (T038)

Given: $ABCDE$ is a regular polygon.

Prove: $AQ = BQ = CQ = DQ = EQ$

The proof for this theorem is complex and most geometry texts do not prove it. Here's a good way to convince yourself that it's true.

Diagram

Any regular polygon of n sides can be created as follows:

- Let $\triangle AQB$ be an isosceles triangle where the vertex angle, Q, has measure $\frac{360°}{n}$.

- Now, rotate the triangle counterclockwise about Q $n - 1$ times, using the measure of angle Q as your angle of rotation.
  The base, AB, and its images in the rotation will create a regular polygon with n sides.

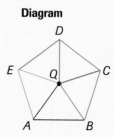

$\dfrac{360°}{n}$

For example, let $n = 3$. Then angle Q measures $\frac{360°}{3}$, or 120°. Rotate $\triangle AQB$, keeping Q fixed, 120°. Now rotate it again. You've created a regular (equilateral) triangle.

If $n = 4$, the measure of angle Q is 90° and three rotations of $\triangle AQB$ will create a regular quadrilateral (a square). If $n = 5$, the measure of angle Q is 72 degrees and four rotations of $\triangle AQB$ will create a regular pentagon. If $n = 10$, the measure of angle Q is 36° and nine rotations of $\triangle AQB$ will create a regular decagon.

MORE HELP
See 275, 281

Theorem Every regular n-gon has (1) n lines of symmetry, which are the perpendicular bisectors of each of its sides and the bisectors of each of its angles (2) n-fold rotational symmetry. n-gon ⇒ n lines of symmetry (⊥ bisectors of sides, bisectors of ∠s); n-fold rotational symmetry (T039)

We'll demonstrate this theorem for regular polygons with an odd number of sides. It also holds for regular polygons with an even number of sides, though each line of symmetry in that case bisects two angles or two sides instead of an angle and a side.

CASE 1 A figure has a line of symmetry if you can map the figure onto itself by a reflection in that line.

Diagram

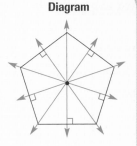

The regular pentagon has five sides and five lines of symmetry, each of which is a perpendicular bisector of a side and a bisector of an angle. You could check this by folding the pentagon on each line of symmetry.

CASE 2 A figure has rotational symmetry if it can be turned 180° or less to map onto itself.

Every time a regular pentagon is turned 72° about its center, it maps onto itself.

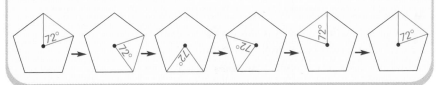

Angle Relationships in Polygons _____ 130

The fact that the angles of a triangle have a sum of 180° will help you prove these theorems about the angles of a polygon.

Interior Angles 131

An **interior angle** is formed by the sides of a polygon. A polygon has as many interior angles as it does sides. If you know the number of sides, you can find the sum of the measures of the interior angles of the polygon. If the polygon is regular, you can also find the measure of each interior angle.

MORE HELP
See 142

Formula The sum of the measures of the interior angles of an n-gon is $180°(n - 2)$. (F11)

Look at the figure. You can draw all the **diagonals** (segments that join non-adjacent vertices) that have an endpoint at A. These divide the polygon into $7 - 2$ triangles. Then the sum of all the angles of the heptagon equals the sum of the angles of the triangles: $5 \cdot 180° = 900°$.

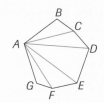

> **Formula**   The measure of each interior angle of a regular n-gon is $\frac{180°(n-2)}{n}$. (F12)
>
> **Proof**
>
> **Given:** A regular n-gon
>
> **Prove:** Each interior angle measures $\frac{180°(n-2)}{n}$
>
> By definition, a regular n-gon is a polygon that has n congruent angles. The formula for the sum of all the angles in a regular n-gon is $180°(n-2)$, so divide this number by n to find the measure of each of the n congruent angles. The measure of each angle is $\frac{180°(n-2)}{n}$.

132

Exterior Angles

An **exterior angle** is formed by a side and an extension of an adjacent side of a polygon. Two exterior angles, which are vertical angles because they're formed by intersecting lines, can be formed at each vertex.

MORE HELP
See 066

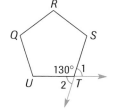

EXAMPLE: At vertex T, exterior angles 1 and 2 are formed by extending $\overline{UT}$ and $\overline{ST}$. Find m∠1 and m∠2.

m∠1 + m∠STU = 180°	Linear Pair Postulate (P14)
m∠1 + 130° = 180°	Substitution
m∠1 = 50°	Subtraction prop. of =
m∠1 = m∠2	Vertical ∠s ≅ (T023)
50° = m∠2	Substitution

★ Both ∠1 and ∠2 measure 50°.

When you count only one of the two congruent exterior angles at each vertex, they are related by this next formula.

MORE HELP
See 131

MORE HELP
See 069, 432, 434

Formula	The sum of the measures of the exterior angles of an n-gon, one at each vertex, is 360°. (F13)

Here is a paragraph proof for a hexagon. The proof for any other polygon is similar, except for the number of vertices used.

Diagram

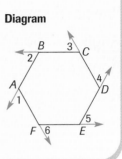

Proof

Given: Hexagon $ABCDEF$ with exterior angles 1, 2, 3, 4, 5, and 6

Prove:
$m\angle 1 + m\angle 2 + m\angle 3 + m\angle 4 + m\angle 5 + m\angle 6 = 360°$

Since the interior and exterior angle at each vertex form a linear pair, you know that the sum of each interior angle and its associated exterior angle is 180°. The Addition Property of Equality lets you add the six pairs of angles to get a sum of $180° \cdot 6$.

$$m\angle 1 + m\angle FAB + m\angle 2 + m\angle ABC + \ldots m\angle 6 + m\angle EFA = 180° \cdot 6$$

You already know that the sum of the interior angles is $180° \cdot 4$. Subtract that amount, and what you have left is the sum of the exterior angles.

$$\begin{aligned}
m\angle 1 + m\angle 2 + m\angle 3 + m\angle 4 + m\angle 5 + m\angle 6 &= (180° \cdot 6) - (180° \cdot 4) \\
&= 180° \cdot 2 \\
&= 360°
\end{aligned}$$

Formula	The measure of each exterior angle of a regular n-gon is $\frac{360°}{n}$. (F14)

You know that the interior and exterior angles at a vertex are supplementary. Since all the interior angles of a regular polygon are congruent, so must the exterior angles be congruent because supplements of congruent angles are congruent. Since the measures of all n angles have a sum of 360°, each angle must have a measure of $\frac{360°}{n}$.

EXAMPLE: $HIJKLMNO$ is a regular octagon. Find the measure of $\angle 1$.

Use the formula for $n = 8$.

$$m\angle 1 = \frac{360°}{8}$$
$$= 45°$$

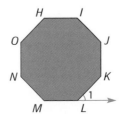

★ The measure of $\angle 1$ is 45°.

Triangles are the simplest polygons, having only three sides. You often see triangles in buildings, bridges, and furniture because they are rigid and, as a result, can support heavy loads.

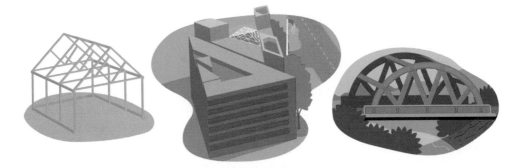

A triangular structure resists collapsing because it cannot change shape without falling apart, unlike other polygons. For example, if you press on a quadrilateral with hinges for vertices, the measures of its angles can change. Make a triangle and a quadrilateral from straws and try this yourself. The vertices of the quadrilateral stay connected but the structure collapses. The triangle will not collapse into a different triangle when you do this — it is rigid.

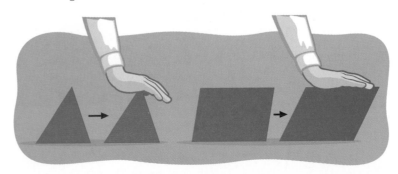

Classification of Triangles _____

CASE 1 You can classify triangles by side length.

MORE HELP
See 256

Name	Description	Example
Equilateral Triangle	all sides congruent	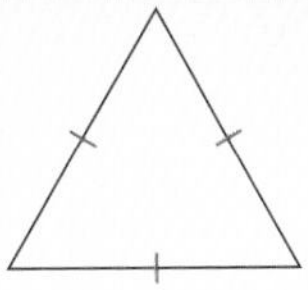
Isosceles Triangle	two sides congruent	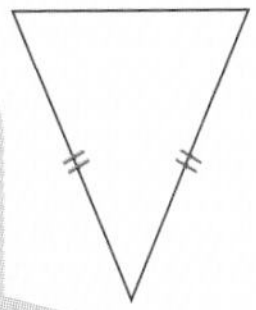
Scalene Triangle	no sides congruent	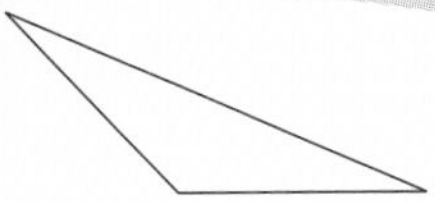

There is some disagreement about whether an isosceles triangle has *at least* two congruent sides or *exactly* two congruent sides. Ask your teacher what definition will be used in your class.

CASE 2 You can classify triangles by angle size.

Name	Description	Example
Acute Triangle	all interior angles measure less than 90°	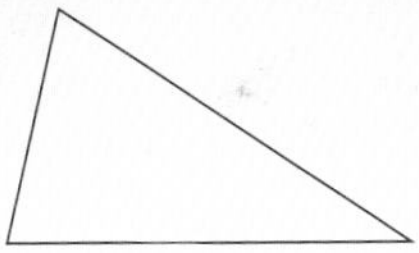
Equiangular Triangle	all interior angles are congruent; each measures exactly 60°	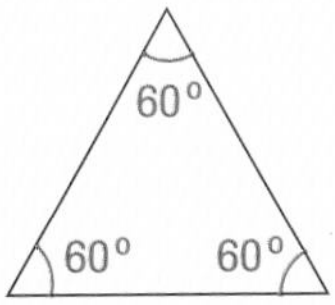 60° 60° 60°
Obtuse Triangle	exactly one interior angle measures more than 90°	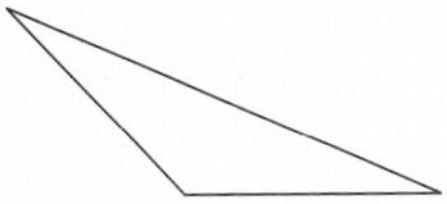
Right Triangle	exactly one interior angle measures 90°	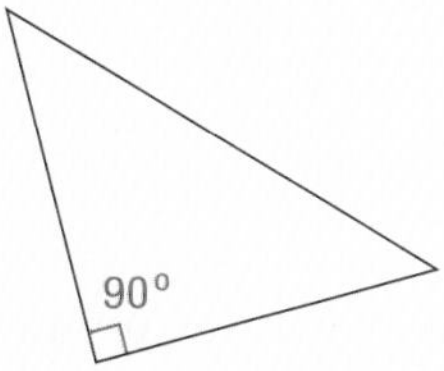 90°

MORE HELP
See 062

When you classify triangles, try to be as specific as you can.

EXAMPLE: Classify triangle *DEF* by its sides and angles.

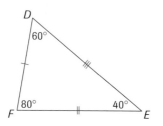

All interior angles are less than 90°, so it is acute. No sides are congruent, so the triangle is scalene.

★ Triangle *DEF* is an acute scalene triangle.

Special Segments in Triangles

The parts of an isosceles triangle have special relationships and names.

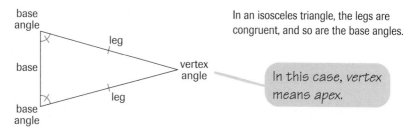

In an isosceles triangle, the legs are congruent, and so are the base angles.

In this case, vertex means apex.

Triangles contain segments that have special properties. To understand the properties, you need some vocabulary.

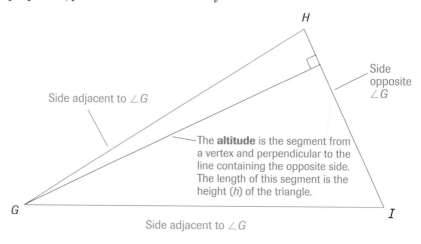

Side adjacent to ∠*G*

Side opposite ∠*G*

The **altitude** is the segment from a vertex and perpendicular to the line containing the opposite side. The length of this segment is the height (*h*) of the triangle.

Side adjacent to ∠*G*

Three or more lines intersecting at one point are concurrent. The point of intersection is the **point of concurrency**. Every triangle has special segments: medians, altitudes, perpendicular bisectors, and angle bisectors. Each set of segments has its own corresponding point of concurrency.

Median of a Triangle

A **median** of a triangle is a segment from a vertex to the midpoint of the opposite side. It differs from an altitude in that an altitude must be perpendicular to the opposite side, and so it may or may not bisect the side. Every triangle has three medians which are concurrent at a point called the **centroid.**

Concurrent lines or segments have one point in common.

Theorem	The medians of a triangle are concurrent. Their common point, the centroid, is two thirds of the distance from each vertex to the midpoint of the opposite side. Medians of △ concurrent, centroid $\frac{2}{3}$ the distance from vertex to opp. midpt. (T040)

MORE HELP
See 056

The proof of this theorem is beyond the scope of this book, though you might want to try a coordinate proof or one comparing areas. This experiment should convince you that the theorem is true. Cut a large triangle from a sheet of paper. Then label the vertices *A*, *B*, and *C*. Now fold each pair of vertices onto each other to find the midpoint of each side. Label these midpoints *D*, *E*, and *F* as shown in the figure. From each midpoint to the vertex opposite it, make a crease to show a median of the triangle. Now look at the three medians.

Diagram

The medians all meet at a point, call it *X*, within the triangle. Now measure these lengths: *AX* and *XD*, *BX* and *XE*, *CX* and *XF*. Although the medians may be of different lengths, the short segment of each median is half as long as the longer segment of the same median. So the centroid, *X*, is $\frac{2}{3}$ the distance from the vertex to the opposite side.

The centroid is also called the **center of gravity** or the **balancing point.** If you place the centroid of a cardboard triangle on the end of a pencil, the triangle will balance. Try it. Draw a scalene triangle on cardboard or stiff paper. Find the midpoint of each side and draw each median. Cut out the triangle and try balancing it at the centroid.

MORE HELP
See 061

Altitude of a Triangle

An **altitude** of a triangle is a segment from a vertex and perpendicular to the opposite side. Every triangle has three altitudes.

Theorem The lines containing the altitudes of a triangle are concurrent at the **orthocenter**. Altitudes of △ concurrent. (T041)

Proof

Given: △PQR and the lines containing the altitudes

Prove: The altitudes of △PQR are concurrent.

Diagram

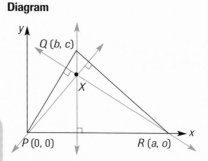

When the triangle is obtuse, two of the altitudes will be outside the triangle. In that case, the orthocenter will be outside the triangle.

MORE HELP
See 099, 105, 432, 434

Plan: Find the slopes of the sides of the triangle. Then find the slope of each altitude. (The slope of a line perpendicular to a given line is the opposite of the reciprocal of the slope of the given line.) Use the Point-Slope Formula to write an equation for each altitude. Solve the system of equations to find the intersection of the lines containing the altitudes. If you find a solution that works for all three equations, then you've found a point that lies on all three lines and the lines are concurrent. These steps are summarized in the table.

Side	Slope of Side	Slope of Altitude to Side	Equation of Line Containing Altitude
$\overline{PQ}$	$\dfrac{c-0}{b-0} = \dfrac{c}{b}$	$\dfrac{-b}{c}$	$y = \dfrac{-b}{c}x + \dfrac{ab}{c}$
$\overline{QR}$	$\dfrac{c-0}{b-a} = \dfrac{c}{b-a}$	$\dfrac{a-b}{c}$	$y = \left(\dfrac{a-b}{c}\right)x$
$\overline{PR}$	$\dfrac{0-0}{a-0} = 0$	undefined	$x = b$

Solve the first and third equations. $y = \frac{-b}{c}x + \frac{ab}{c}$ and $x = b$

$$y = \frac{-b}{c}b + \frac{ab}{c} \qquad X:\left(b, \frac{ab - b^2}{c}\right)$$

$$= \frac{ab - b^2}{c}$$

Check that this point is also a solution to the second equation. The x-coordinate is b, the y-coordinate is $\frac{ab - b^2}{c}$. Substitute these values into the second equation, $y = \left(\frac{a - b}{c}\right)x$.

Since $\frac{ab - b^2}{c} = \left(\frac{a - b}{c}\right)b$, $\left(b, \frac{ab - b^2}{c}\right)$ is the point of intersection of the altitudes. They are concurrent.

Perpendicular Bisector of a Triangle

138

A **perpendicular bisector** of a triangle is a line, segment, or ray that bisects one side and is perpendicular to it. Every triangle has three perpendicular bisectors.

MORE HELP
See 056

Theorem	The lines containing the perpendicular bisectors of a triangle are concurrent. Their common point, the **circumcenter**, is equidistant from the three vertices of the triangle. ⊥ bisectors of △ concurrent, circumcenter equidistant from vertices. (T042)

Proof

Diagram

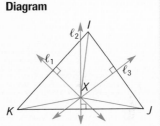

Given: Lines ℓ_1, ℓ_2, and ℓ_3 are ⊥ bisectors of $\triangle IJK$. X is the intersection of ℓ_1 and ℓ_2.

Prove: X is on ℓ_3, equidistant from I, J, and K.

Plan: Use the Perpendicular Bisector Theorem to show that endpoints of bisected segments are equidistant from any point on the bisector. Draw the segments from X to each vertex. This will help you show that X is equidistant from the vertices.

Because ℓ_1 is the perpendicular bisector of $\overline{IK}$ and X is on ℓ_1, $IX = KX$. Because ℓ_2 is the perpendicular bisector of $\overline{KJ}$ and X is on ℓ_2, $KX = JX$. The Transitive Property of Equality says that $IX = JX$ so X is equidistant from I and J, but every point that is equidistant from I and J is on ℓ_3 by the Converse of the Perpendicular Bisector Theorem. This means that X is the intersection of all three perpendicular bisectors and is equidistant from all three vertices.

MORE ▶

EXAMPLE: Circumscribe a circle about △*IJK*.

To **circumscribe** a circle about a triangle is to construct a circle that contains each of the vertices of the triangle.

MORE HELP
See 374

Locate the circumcenter *X* of △*IJK* by constructing the perpendicular bisectors of $\overline{IJ}$, $\overline{JK}$, and $\overline{IK}$. Since X is equidistant from the vertices of the triangle, $\overline{XI}$, $\overline{XJ}$, and $\overline{XK}$ can be radii of a circle with center *X* that intersects all three vertices. With *X* as the center of the circle, use a compass set to the length of *IX* to draw a circle.

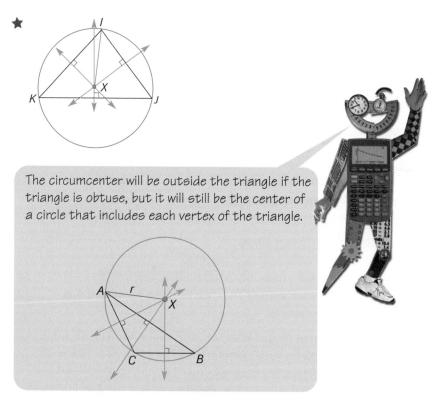

The circumcenter will be outside the triangle if the triangle is obtuse, but it will still be the center of a circle that includes each vertex of the triangle.

139

Angle Bisectors in Triangles

In a triangle the **angle bisectors** are lines, segments, or rays that bisect an angle of the triangle. Every triangle has three angle bisectors.

MORE HELP
See 073

Theorem	The angle bisectors of a triangle are concurrent. Their common point, the **incenter**, is equidistant from the three sides of the triangle. ∠ bisectors of △ concurrent, incenter equidistant from sides of △. (T043)

Proof

Given: Rays r_1, r_2, and r_3 bisect the angles of △LMN; X is the intersection of r_1, r_2.

Prove: X is on r_3 and is equidistant from $\overline{LM}$, $\overline{MN}$, and $\overline{LN}$

Plan: You know that two lines intersect at a point, so you can designate that intersection and prove it is also the point at

Diagram

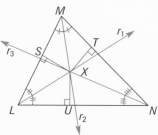

MORE HELP
See 374

which r_3 intersects the other two rays. Construct $\overline{TX}$, $\overline{UX}$, and $\overline{SX}$, each perpendicular to a side because you want to know whether distances are equal. Show that they are all congruent. Then X must be on r_3 because it is equidistant from the sides of ∠MNL.

Construct $\overline{TX}$, $\overline{UX}$, and $\overline{SX}$ from X, each perpendicular to a side of the triangle. Since X is on r_1, you know that $SX = UX$, by the Angle Bisector Theorem. Since X is on r_2, an angle bisector, you know that $SX = TX$. This means that $UX = TX$ by transitivity. Now you know that X is equidistant from sides $\overline{NL}$ and $\overline{MN}$. Since it is equidistant from both rays of ∠LNM, it is on r_3 from the Converse of the Angle Bisector Theorem, so X lies on all three rays and is equidistant from $\overline{LM}$, $\overline{MN}$, and $\overline{LN}$.

EXAMPLE: Inscribe a circle inside △LMN.

A circle **inscribed** in a polygon touches each side of the polygon at exactly one point.

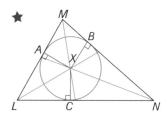

Locate incenter X of △LMN by constructing the bisectors of ∠L, ∠M, and ∠N and a segment perpendicular to $\overline{LM}$, $\overline{MN}$, or $\overline{LN}$ through X. With X as the center and $\overline{XA}$ as radius, use a compass set to the length of $\overline{XA}$ to draw a circle.

MORE ▶

In some triangles, a single line, segment, or ray can be more than one special element, just as one person can be a daughter, sister, and mother.

Theorem

In an isosceles triangle, the perpendicular bisector of the base, the bisector of the vertex angle, the altitude to the base, and the median to the base lie on the same line.

Isos. $\triangle \Rightarrow$ vertex $\angle$ bisector, $\perp$ bisector of base, altitude, median to base same line (T044)

Proof

Given: $\triangle EFG$ is an isosceles triangle with $\overline{EF} \cong \overline{GF}$; ℓ is the $\perp$ bisector of $\overline{EG}$

Prove: $\overline{FH}$ is the median, the altitude, and the angle bisector of $\angle EFG$

Plan: Use what you know about perpendicular bisectors and about isosceles triangles to tie together definitions of median, altitude, and angle bisector.

Diagram

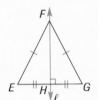

MORE HELP
See 145, 256, 260, 432, 434

ONE WAY

Statements	Reasons
❶ $\triangle EFG$ is an isosceles triangle with $\overline{EF} \cong \overline{GF}$; ℓ is the $\perp$ bisector of $\overline{EG}$	Given
❷ F is equidistant from E and G	Def. of $\cong$
❸ F is on the $\perp$ bisector of $\overline{EG}$	$\perp$ Bisector Theorem (T002)
❹ $\overline{EH} \cong \overline{HG}$	Def. of $\perp$ bisector
❺ $\overline{FH}$ is a median of $\triangle EFG$	Def. of median
❻ $\overline{FH} \perp \overline{EG}$	Def. of $\perp$ bisector
❼ $\overline{FH}$ is an altitude of $\triangle EFG$	Def. of altitude
❽ $\angle HEF \cong \angle HGF$	Base $\angle$s Theorem (T050)
❾ $\triangle EFH \cong \triangle GFH$	SAS $\cong$ Postulate (P23)
❿ $\angle EFH \cong \angle GFH$	CPCTC
⓫ $\overrightarrow{FH}$ is an $\angle$ bisector of $\angle EFG$	Def. of $\angle$ bisector

ANOTHER WAY Instead of using the SAS Congruence Postulate, you could use the SSS Congruence Postulate to prove the triangles congruent since $\overline{FH} \cong \overline{FH}$. Then use CPCTC as above.

MATH ALERT Angle Bisectors Don't Usually Bisect the Opposite Side

The bisector of a base angle of an isosceles triangle or of any angle of a scalene triangle does *not* bisect the opposite side.

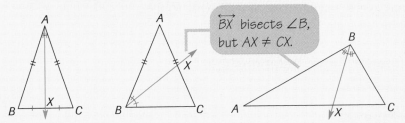

$\overrightarrow{BX}$ bisects $\angle B$, but $AX \neq CX$.

Midsegments

A **midsegment** connects the midpoints of two sides of a triangle.

Theorem

The segment connecting the midpoints of two sides of a triangle is parallel to the third side and half its length.
Midsegment Theorem (T045)

Proof

Given: C is the midpoint of $\overline{OP}$;
D is the midpoint of $\overline{PQ}$
Prove: $\overline{CD} \parallel \overline{OQ}$; $CD = \frac{OQ}{2}$

Plan: Place a coordinate system on the diagram to make the algebra less cumbersome. In this case, place the origin at one vertex and the positive x-axis along one side of the triangle. Use the formula for midpoint to find the coordinates of C and D.

Diagram

$$C: \left(\frac{2b + 0}{2}, \frac{2c + 0}{2}\right) = (b, c) \qquad D: \left(\frac{2b + 2a}{2}, \frac{2c + 0}{2}\right) = (a + b, c)$$

The slopes of $\overline{CD}$ and $\overline{OQ}$ are zero because the difference of the y-coordinates is zero. Therefore, $\overline{CD} \parallel \overline{OQ}$ because their slopes are equal.

Because $\overline{CD}$ and $\overline{OQ}$ are both horizontal, their lengths equal the absolute value of the difference of their x-coordinates.

$$CD = \left|b - (a + b)\right| \qquad OQ = \left|2a - 0\right| \qquad a = \frac{1}{2}(2a),$$
$$ = a \qquad = 2a \qquad \text{so } CD = \frac{OQ}{2}$$

MORE HELP
See 056,
089–090, 107,
426

MORE HELP
See 131–132

Angle Relationships in Triangles

Because triangles are polygons, they have interior and exterior angles. Since a triangle has three sides, it has three interior angles. At each of its three vertices, a triangle has two exterior angles. At vertex A, $\angle BAE$ and $\angle CAD$ are exterior angles. Since these angles are congruent, you usually work with one exterior angle.

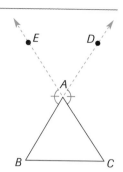

Interior Angle Relationships

| **Theorem** | The sum of the measures of the interior angles of a triangle is 180°. △ Sum Theorem (T046) |

Proof

MORE HELP
See 255, 376, 432, 434

Given: $\triangle XYZ$

Prove: $m\angle 4 + m\angle 2 + m\angle 5 = 180°$

Diagram

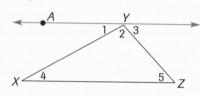

Plan: First, at one vertex construct a line parallel to the opposite side of the triangle. Then, show that the sum of the measures of the three angles of the triangle is the same as the sum of the measures of three angles at the vertex. Since the angles at the vertex form a straight angle which measures 180°, the sum of the measures of the angles of the triangle is 180°.

Statements	Reasons
❶ Construct $\overleftrightarrow{AY} \parallel \overline{XZ}$	Construction
❷ $m\angle 1 + m\angle 2 = m\angle AYZ$	∠ + Postulate (P13)
❸ $m\angle AYZ + m\angle 3 = 180°$	Linear Pair Postulate (P14)
❹ $m\angle 1 + m\angle 2 + m\angle 3 = 180°$	Substitution
❺ $\angle 1 \cong \angle 4$ $\angle 3 \cong \angle 5$	Alt. Int. ∠s Theorem (T027)
❻ $m\angle 1 = m\angle 4$ $m\angle 3 = m\angle 5$	Def. of ≅
❼ $m\angle 4 + m\angle 2 + m\angle 5 = 180°$	Substitution

Look back at steps 4 and 6.

You can use the Triangle Sum Theorem to prove the following theorems about the angles of triangles.

MORE HELP
See 255

Theorem If two angles of one triangle are congruent to two angles of a second triangle, then the third angles are also congruent. Third ∠s Theorem (T047)

Proof

Given: ∠A ≅ ∠D and ∠B ≅ ∠E

Prove: ∠C ≅ ∠F

Plan: You know that the sum of the measures of the angles in each triangle is 180°, and that two of the three addends are equal. This means that you can subtract the two equal addends for each triangle to show that the third addends must be equal.

Diagram

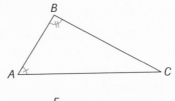

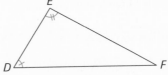

Statements	Reasons
❶ ∠A ≅ ∠D and ∠B ≅ ∠E	Given
❷ m∠A = m∠D and m∠B = m∠E	Def. of ≅
❸ m∠A + m∠B = m∠D + m∠E	+ prop. of =
❹ m∠A + m∠B + m∠C = 180° m∠D + m∠E + m∠F = 180°	△ Sum Theorem (T046)
❺ m∠A + m∠B + m∠C = m∠D + m∠E + m∠F	Transitive prop. of =
❻ m∠C = m∠F; ∠C ≅ ∠F	Subtraction prop. of =; def. of ≅

Since m∠B = m∠E, you can subtract these measures — you're subtracting the same amount from both sides of the equation. The same is true for the measures of angles A and D.

Exterior Angle Relationships

How are the exterior angles of a triangle related to the interior angles? The next two theorems explain these relationships.

144

MORE ▶

MORE HELP
See 070, 143,
432, 434

Theorem The measure of an exterior angle of a triangle is equal to the sum of the measures of the two nonadjacent interior angles. Exterior ∠ Theorem (T048)

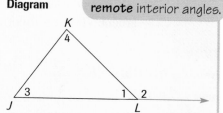

These are also called **remote** interior angles.

Proof

Diagram

Given: ∠2 is an exterior angle of △JKL

Prove: m∠2 = m∠3 + m∠4

Plan: The sum of the measures of the three angles of the triangle is 180°, and the sum of the measures of the two angles at L is also 180°. By subtracting the measure of ∠1 from each sum, you find that the other addends of each sum are equal.

Statements	Reasons
❶ ∠2 is an exterior angle of △JKL	Given
❷ m∠1 + m∠2 = 180°	Linear Pair Postulate (P14)
❸ m∠1 + m∠3 + m∠4 = 180°	△ Sum Theorem (T046)
❹ m∠1 + m∠2 = m∠1 + m∠3 + m∠4	Transitive prop. of =
❺ m∠2 = m∠3 + m∠4	Subtraction prop. of =

Recall from algebra the definition of $a > b$: $a > b$ *if and only if there is a positive number p such that* $a = b + p$. This will help explain the following theorem.

Theorem The measure of an exterior angle of a triangle is greater than the measure of either of the two nonadjacent interior angles. Exterior ∠ Inequality Theorem (T049)

Proof

Diagram

Given: ∠2 is an exterior angle of △JKL

Prove: m∠2 > m∠3 and m∠2 > m∠4

By the Exterior Angle Theorem, m∠2 = m∠3 + m∠4. Since angle measures are positive numbers, the definition of *greater than* proves that m∠2 > m∠3 and m∠2 > m∠4.

Relationships in Isosceles Triangles

Triangles with two congruent sides are **isosceles** triangles. The angles opposite the two congruent sides of an isosceles triangle are the **base angles**. The next theorem shows how these base angles are related.

Theorem If two sides of a triangle are congruent, then the angles opposite them are congruent. Base ∠s Theorem (T050)

Proof

Given: Isosceles △STU with $\overline{TS} \cong \overline{TU}$

Prove: ∠S ≅ ∠U

Plan: First, construct the angle bisector of the vertex angle to form two triangles. Show that the triangles are congruent by the SAS Congruence Postulate. Then you can compare the congruent triangles to show that the two base angles are congruent.

Diagram

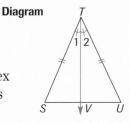

MORE HELP
See 134, 374

Statements	Reasons
❶ $\overline{TS} \cong \overline{TU}$	Given
❷ Construct $\overrightarrow{TV}$, the bisector of ∠STU	Construction
❸ ∠1 ≅ ∠2	Def. of ∠ bisector
❹ $\overline{TV} \cong \overline{TV}$	Reflexive prop. of ≅ (T105)
❺ △STV ≅ △UTV	SAS ≅ Postulate (P23)
❻ ∠S ≅ ∠U	CPCTC

Theorem If two angles of a triangle are congruent, then the sides opposite them are congruent. Converse of Base ∠s Theorem (T051)

Given: ∠M ≅ ∠Q

Prove: $\overline{PM} \cong \overline{PQ}$

Diagram

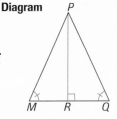

MORE HELP
See 056, 432

ONE WAY Use reasoning similar to that in the proof of the Base Angles Theorem, except construct the altitude to $\overline{MQ}$ and show that △MPR is congruent to △QPR using the AAS Congruence Postulate.

ANOTHER WAY Construct the angle bisector to show that △MPR is congruent to △QPR using the AAS Congruence Postulate.

Equilateral Triangle or Equiangular Triangle?

Triangles with all sides congruent are **equilateral**, and triangles with all angles congruent are **equiangular**. The corollaries to the Base Angles Theorem and its converse show that either term—equilateral or equiangular—can be used to classify the same triangle.

MORE HELP
See 134

> **Corollary** A triangle is equilateral if and only if it is also equiangular. Equilateral △⇔ equiangular △ (T052)
>
> To prove this theorem, you must prove two cases:
>
> 1. If a triangle is equilateral, then it is equiangular.
> 2. If a triangle is equiangular, then it is equilateral.
>
> **Proof**
>
> **CASE 1** If a triangle is equilateral, then it is equiangular.
>
> **Given:** Equilateral △*DEF*
>
> **Prove:** △*DEF* is equiangular.
>
> **Plan:** By applying the Base Angles Theorem twice to an equilateral triangle (which is after all, an isosceles triangle whose base happens to be the same length as its legs), you can prove that all of the angles are congruent, so the triangle is equiangular.
>
> **Diagram**
>
>
>
> | Statements | Reasons |
> |---|---|
> | ➊ Equilateral △*DEF* | Given |
> | ➋ $\overline{DF} \cong \overline{EF}$; $\overline{EF} \cong \overline{DE}$ | Def. of equilateral △ |
> | ➌ $\angle E \cong \angle D$, $\angle D \cong \angle F$ | Base ∠s Theorem (T050) |
> | ➍ $\angle E \cong \angle F$ | Transitive prop. of ≅ (T107) |
> | ➎ △*DEF* is equiangular | Def. of equiangular |

CASE 2 If a triangle is equiangular, then it is equilateral.

Given: Equiangular $\triangle DEF$

Prove: $\triangle DEF$ is equilateral.

Diagram

Equiangular $\triangle DEF$ has three congruent angles, which you can separate into pairs of congruent angles. The Converse of the Base Angles Theorem tells you that the sides opposite each pair of congruent angles are congruent. By the transitive property of congruence all three sides are congruent, so the triangle is equilateral.

Angle and Side Relationships in Triangles

In geometry you're often trying to show that segments or angles are congruent, just as in algebra you're often trying to find the solution to an equation. But some geometric relationships involve inequalities, just as in algebra you sometimes solve inequalities. The next few theorems will explore some of these relationships.

Relationships Among Sides and Angles in a Triangle

In these triangles, the longest side and the largest angle are labeled. Notice that in all of the triangles the largest angle is always opposite the longest side.

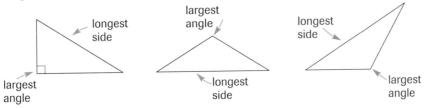

The next two theorems deal with inequalities in triangles. They are converses of each other.

Theorem

If one side of a triangle is longer than another side, then the angle opposite the longer side is larger than the angle opposite the shorter side. ∠ opp. longer side is larger (T053)

Diagram

Proof

MORE HELP
See 432, 434

Given: $TU > VU$

Prove: $m\angle 1 > m\angle 2$

Plan: First extend $\overline{UV}$ to W, so that $UW = TU$. Since $\overline{UV}$ is shorter than $\overline{TU}$, you know that W is really on the extended part of $\overline{UV}$. Draw $\overline{TW}$. Then show that $m\angle 1 > m\angle W$, $m\angle W = m\angle WTU$, and $m\angle WTU > m\angle 2$, so $m\angle 1 > m\angle 2$.

Statements	Reasons
❶ Construct $\overline{UW}$ so that $UW = UT$	Construction
❷ $m\angle WTU = m\angle W$	Base ∠s Theorem (T050)
❸ $m\angle 1 > m\angle W$	Ext. ∠ Inequality Theorem (T049)
❹ $m\angle 1 > m\angle WTU$	Substitution
❺ $m\angle WTU = m\angle 2 + m\angle 3$	∠ + Postulate (P13)
❻ $m\angle WTU > m\angle 2$	Def. of >
❼ $m\angle 1 > m\angle 2$	Transitive prop. of inequality

Theorem

If one angle of a triangle is larger than another angle, then the side opposite the larger angle is longer than the side opposite the smaller angle. Side opp. larger ∠ is longer (T054)

MORE HELP
See 046, 434

Diagram

Proof

Given: $m\angle R > m\angle Q$

Prove: $PQ > PR$

Use an indirect proof. Assume PQ is not greater than PR. If that were true, then either $PQ = PR$ or $PQ < PR$. If $PQ = PR$, then the Base Angles Theorem says that $m\angle R = m\angle Q$. This contradicts the given statement. If $PQ < PR$, then, since the angle opposite the longer side of triangle is larger, $m\angle R < m\angle Q$. This also contradicts the given statement. Since both possible alternatives to the statement you need to prove contradict the given statement, $PQ > PR$.

Theorem	The sum of the lengths of any two sides of a triangle is greater than the length of the third side. △ Inequality Theorem (T055)

Proof

Given: △WXY

Prove: $WY + YX > WX$

Plan: Extend side $\overline{XY}$ to Z so that $\overline{ZY} \cong \overline{WY}$. The theorem will be proved if you can show that $XZ > XW$. To do that, show $\angle XWZ > \angle 1$, which is congruent to $\angle Z$. In △WZX the side opposite the larger angle is longer, so $XZ > XW$.

Diagram

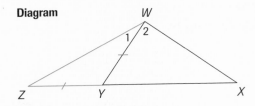

Statements	Reasons
❶ △WXY	Given
❷ Extend $\overline{XY}$ to Z so that $ZY = WY$	Ruler Postulate (P08)
❸ m$\angle XWZ$ = m$\angle 1$ + m$\angle 2$	$\angle$ + Postulate (P13)
❹ m$\angle XWZ$ > m$\angle 1$	Def. of >
❺ m$\angle 1$ = m$\angle Z$	Base $\angle$s Theorem (T050)
❻ m$\angle XWZ$ > m$\angle Z$	Substitution
❼ In △WZX, $ZX > WX$	Side opp. larger $\angle$ is longer (T054)
❽ $ZY + YX = ZX$	Seg. + Postulate (P09)
❾ $ZY + YX > WX$	Substitution
❿ $WY + YX > WX$	Substitution Look back at step 2.

Relationships Among Sides and Angles in Two Triangles

Imagine the blades of a scissors as two sides of a triangle. The tips of each blade and the hinge are the three vertices. As you open the scissors, the length of each blade stays the same. However, the angle formed by the blades increases and so does the distance between the tips. The Hinge Theorem and its converse describe this situation.

MORE ▶

149

Theorem If two sides of one triangle are congruent to two sides of another triangle, and the included angle of the first is larger than the included angle of the second, then the third side of the first is longer than the third side of the second. Hinge Theorem (T056)

Proof

Diagram

Given: $\overline{HI} \cong \overline{KL}$, $\overline{IJ} \cong \overline{LM}$, m∠$HIJ$ > m∠L

Prove: $HJ > KM$

Plan: Place a copy of △KLM inside △HIJ and construct some auxiliary segments to help you compare HJ to KM.

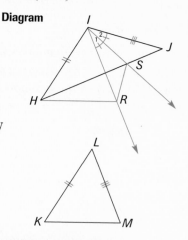

MORE HELP
See 373–374, 432, 434

Statements	Reasons
❶ $\overline{HI} \cong \overline{KL}$, $\overline{IJ} \cong \overline{LM}$, m∠$HIJ$ > m∠L	Given
❷ Construct $\overrightarrow{IR}$ so m∠HIR = m∠L	Construction
❸ Mark R so that $IR = LM$	Ruler Postulate (P08)
❹ △$HIR \cong$ △KLM	SAS ≅ Postulate (P23)
❺ $HR = KM$	CPCTC
❻ Construct $\overrightarrow{IS}$, the bisector of ∠JIR	Construction
❼ m∠1 = m∠2	Def. of ∠ bisector
❽ $IS = IS$	Reflexive prop. of =
❾ $IR = IJ$ *Look back at steps 1 and 3.*	Transitive prop. of =
❿ △$RIS \cong$ △JIS	SAS ≅ Postulate (P23)
⓫ $SR = SJ$	CPCTC
⓬ $HS + SR > HR$	△ Inequality Theorem (T055)
⓭ $HS + SJ > HR$	Substitution
⓮ $HS + SJ = HJ$	Seg. + Postulate (P09)
⓯ $HJ > HR$	Transitive prop. of inequality
⓰ $HJ > KM$	Substitution *Look back at steps 5 and 15.*

Now look at the converse and an application of the Hinge Theorem.

MORE HELP
See 432

Theorem — If two sides of one triangle are congruent to two sides of another triangle, and the third side of the first is longer than the third side of the second, then the included angle of the first is larger than the included angle of the second. Converse of Hinge Theorem (T057)

Proof

Given: $\overline{HI} \cong \overline{KL}$, $\overline{IJ} \cong \overline{LM}$, $HJ > KM$

Prove: $m\angle I > m\angle L$

Plan: Use an indirect proof. You need to see what would happen if $m\angle I$ is not greater than $m\angle L$. If this assumption leads to a contradiction, then you know that the assumption cannot be correct.

Diagram

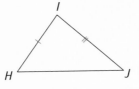

Assume that $m\angle I$ is not greater than $m\angle L$. If that were true, then either $m\angle I = m\angle L$ or $m\angle I < m\angle L$. If $m\angle I = m\angle L$, then $\triangle HIJ \cong \triangle KLM$ by the SAS Congruence Postulate and $HJ = KM$ by CPCTC. This contradicts the given information.

If $m\angle I < m\angle L$, then $HJ < KM$ by the Hinge Theorem. This also contradicts the given information.

Since both statements, $m\angle I = m\angle L$ and $m\angle I < m\angle L$, lead to a contradiction, it must be true that $m\angle I > m\angle L$.

EXAMPLE: The diagram shows the approaches that two airplanes are making to an airport. Which plane has the shorter flight path? Which plane is closer to the airport?

You can use the Hinge Theorem to find the plane that is closer to the airport. $\overline{ED} \cong \overline{AB}$, $\overline{DC} \cong \overline{BC}$, and $m\angle D > m\angle B$, so $EC > AC$.

★ The flight path of both planes is the same length, $40 + 90$, or 130 miles long. The plane approaching from the north is closer to the airport.

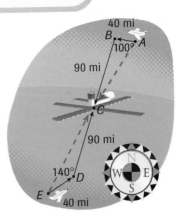

Right Triangles

Right triangles have one right angle. The side opposite the right angle is the **hypotenuse**, and the other two sides are the **legs**.

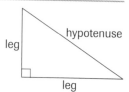

Angle Relationships in Right Triangles

Because one angle of a right triangle is special, it is reasonable to expect that the other two angles have a special relationship.

Theorem	The acute angles of a right triangle are complementary. Acute ∠s of a rt. △ comp. (T058)

Proof   **Diagram**

MORE HELP
See 068, 143

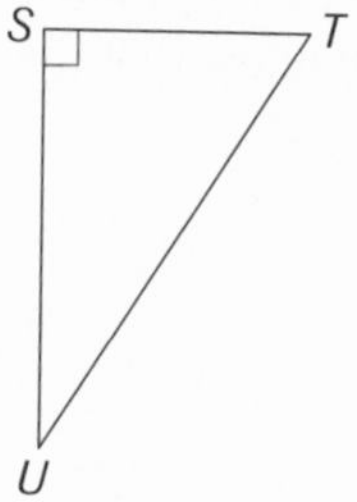

Given: △STU, ∠S is a right angle

Prove: ∠T and ∠U are complementary angles

Plan: The sum of the measures of the angles in a triangle is 180°, so since one angle has a measure of 90°, you can use this fact to prove the theorem.

Statements	Reasons
❶ ∠S is a right angle	Given
❷ $m\angle S = 90°$	Def. of rt. ∠
❸ $m\angle S + m\angle T + m\angle U = 180°$	△ Sum Theorem (T046)
❹ $90° + m\angle T + m\angle U = 180°$	Substitution
❺ $m\angle T + m\angle U = 90°$	Subtraction prop. of =
❻ ∠T and ∠U are complementary ∠s	Def. of comp. ∠s

Pythagorean Theorem

MORE HELP
See 236

One of the most famous theorems in geometry is the Pythagorean Theorem. It has been around for over a thousand years.

> **DID YOU KNOW**   In about 500 B.C., a group of Greek philosophers, mathematicians, and scientists, known as Pythagoreans, studied the 3-4-5 right triangle. They noticed a relationship that has become known as the Pythagorean Theorem. The theorem and one proof of it are shown here. Look in the Similarity section for another proof. Even James Garfield, who became president, developed a proof of this theorem.

MORE HELP
See 156,
180–181, 236

Theorem In a right triangle, the square of the length of the hypotenuse is equal to the sum of the squares of the lengths of the legs. Pythagorean Theorem (T059)

Proof

Given: a and b are the lengths of the legs of the right triangle ABC; c is the length of the hypotenuse

Prove: $c^2 = a^2 + b^2$

Plan: Begin by constructing a square with sides of length $a + b$. Then, draw segments inside your square so that you've carved off four right triangles with legs of lengths a and b. You can find the area of the small internal square you've created in two ways: by squaring the length of a side (c), or by finding the area of the large square and subtracting the areas of the four right triangles.

Diagram

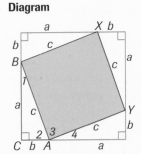

Construct a square with side lengths $a + b$ with one vertex at C. Mark points A, B, X, and Y that divide the sides into a ratio of $a:b$. Draw quadrilateral $ABXY$. All four triangles are congruent, because each is a right triangle with legs of lengths a and b. This makes $ABXY$ a rhombus because since corresponding parts of congruent triangles are congruent, its four sides are all congruent. Now m$\angle 1$ = m$\angle 4$ by CPCTC. Since $\angle 1$ and $\angle 2$ are complementary, $\angle 2$ and $\angle 4$ are also complementary. This means $\angle 3$ must be a right angle. So $ABXY$ is a rhombus with one right angle, making it a square.

The length of a side of the large square is $a + b$, so the area of the large square is $(a + b)^2$. The area of each of the four right triangles is $\frac{1}{2}ab$. Compute the area of the shaded square by subtracting the areas of the triangles from the area of the large square.

$$(a + b)^2 - 4\left(\tfrac{1}{2}ab\right) = a^2 + 2ab + b^2 - 2ab$$
$$= a^2 + b^2$$

Another way to find the area of the shaded square is to square the length of a side. Therefore, $c^2 = a^2 + b^2$.

MORE ▶

More Help
See 421

EXAMPLE 1: Find the length of the hypotenuse of the right triangle.

Use the Pythagorean Theorem.

$$c^2 = a^2 + b^2$$
$$c^2 = 8^2 + 15^2$$
$$c^2 = 64 + 225$$
$$c^2 = 289$$
$$c = 17$$

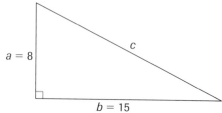

★ The hypotenuse is 17 units long.

To find the square root of 289, you may try several options. You can use guess-and-check to find a number whose square is 289. You may use the table of powers and roots in the Almanac, or you can use your calculator. If this key sequence doesn't work, look up square roots in your calculator manual.

EXAMPLE 2: The base of a 20-foot ladder is set 5 feet from a wall. How far up the wall will the ladder reach?

More Help
See 230

The ladder, wall, and ground form a right triangle, so use the Pythagorean Theorem.

$$c^2 = a^2 + b^2$$
$$20^2 = 5^2 + b^2$$
$$400 = 25 + b^2$$
$$375 = b^2$$
$$5\sqrt{15} = b$$

$\sqrt{375} = \sqrt{25 \cdot 15} = 5\sqrt{15}$

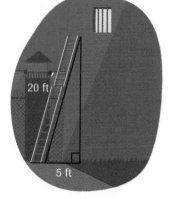

★ The ladder will reach $5\sqrt{15}$ feet, or about 19.4 feet up the wall.

153 Pythagorean Triples

Positive integers that make the statement $a^2 + b^2 = c^2$ true are called **Pythagorean Triples**. 8, 15, and 17 form a Pythagorean Triple. 5, $5\sqrt{15}$, and 20 do not form a Pythagorean Triple even though they work in the Pythagorean Theorem, because $5\sqrt{15}$ is not an integer.

More Help
See 230

Look up SSS Similarity for a third way to find Pythagorean Triples.

ONE WAY Choose two integers, m and n, such that $m > n$, and use these formulas to find Pythagorean Triples.

$$a = m^2 - n^2 \qquad b = 2\,mn \qquad c = m^2 + n^2$$

Suppose $m = 4$ and $n = 2$. Then,

$a = 4^2 - 2^2$	$b = 2(4)(2)$	$c = 4^2 + 2^2$
$= 12$	$= 16$	$= 20$

Check: $12^2 + 16^2 \stackrel{?}{=} 20^2$
$$144 + 256 \stackrel{?}{=} 400$$
$$400 = 400$$

Here's how this formula works.

❶ Find a^2, b^2, and c^2.	❷ Now find $a^2 + b^2$ and compare it to c^2.
$a = m^2 - n^2$	$a^2 + b^2 = m^4 - 2m^2n^2 + n^4 + 4m^2n^2$
$a^2 = (m^2 - n^2)(m^2 - n^2)$	$= m^4 + 2m^2n^2 + n^4$
$\quad = m^4 - 2m^2n^2 + n^4$	$= c^2$
$b = 2mn$	
$b^2 = (2mn)^2$	
$\quad = 4m^2n^2$	
$c = m^2 + n^2$	
$c^2 = (m^2 + n^2)(m^2 + n^2)$	
$\quad = m^4 + 2m^2n^2 + n^4$	

ANOTHER WAY Choose an integer n and use these formulas to find Pythagorean Triples.

$$a = 2n \qquad b = n^2 - 1 \qquad \boxed{c = n^2 + 1}$$

Suppose $n = 3$.

$a = 2(3)$	$b = 3^2 - 1$	$c = 3^2 + 1$
$= 6$	$= 8$	$= 10$

Check: $6^2 + 8^2 \stackrel{?}{=} 10^2$
$$36 + 64 = 100$$

To check that numbers from this formula will always work, compare $a^2 + b^2$ to c^2.

$a^2 + b^2 = (2n)^2 + (n^2 - 1)^2$	$c^2 = (n^2 + 1)^2$
$= 4n^2 + n^4 - 2n^2 + 1$	$= n^4 + 2n^2 + 1$
$= n^4 + 2n^2 + 1$	

Theorems Related to the Pythagorean Theorem

If you know that a triangle is a right triangle, then you can use the Pythagorean Theorem to tell you how the lengths of the sides are related. Other theorems work the other way: If you know how the side lengths are related, you can tell what kind of triangle you have.

Right Triangle

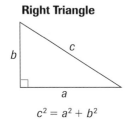

$$c^2 = a^2 + b^2$$

Acute Triangle

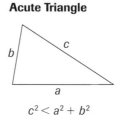

$$c^2 < a^2 + b^2$$

Obtuse Triangle

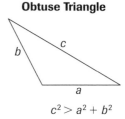

$$c^2 > a^2 + b^2$$

Theorem   If the square of the length of the longest side of a triangle is equal to the sum of the squares of the lengths of the two shorter sides, then the triangle is a right triangle.
Converse of Pythagorean Theorem (T060)

Proof

Given: $c^2 = a^2 + b^2$

Prove: $\triangle ABC$ is a right triangle

MORE HELP
See 373, 375, 432, 434

Plan: Construct right $\triangle GHI$ with legs of lengths a and b, and a right angle at I. Show that it is congruent to $\triangle ABC$ to prove the theorem.

Diagram

Statements	Reasons
❶ a and b are the lengths of the legs of right $\triangle GHI$, with rt. $\angle$ at I	Construction
❷ $d^2 = a^2 + b^2$	Pythagorean Theorem (T059)
❸ $c^2 = a^2 + b^2$	Given
❹ $d^2 = c^2$	Substitution
❺ $\sqrt{d^2} = \sqrt{c^2}$; $d = c$	Simplify
❻ $\triangle ABC \cong \triangle GHI$	SSS $\cong$ Postulate (P22)
❼ $\angle C \cong \angle I$	CPCTC
❽ $\angle C$ is a right angle	Substitution *Look back at step 1.*
❾ $\triangle ABC$ is a right triangle	Def. of rt. $\triangle$

The next two theorems extend the Converse of the Pythagorean Theorem.

Theorem If the square of the length of the longest side of a triangle is less than the sum of the squares of the lengths of the two shorter sides, then the triangle is acute.

$c^2 < a^2 + b^2 \Rightarrow$ acute $\triangle$ (T061)

Proof

Given: $c^2 < a^2 + b^2$; c is the length of the longest side

Prove: $\triangle XYZ$ is acute

Plan: Construct right $\triangle GHI$ with legs of lengths a and b. Then compare $\triangle GHI$ to $\triangle XYZ$.

Diagram

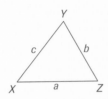
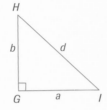

Statements	Reasons
❶ a and b are the lengths of the legs of $\triangle GHI$, with rt. $\angle$ at G	Construction
❷ $d^2 = a^2 + b^2$	Pythagorean Theorem (T059)
❸ $c^2 < a^2 + b^2$	Given
❹ $c^2 < d^2$	Substitution
❺ $\sqrt{c^2} < \sqrt{d^2}$; $c < d$	Simplify
❻ $m\angle X < m\angle G$	Converse of Hinge Theorem (T057)
❼ $m\angle G = 90°$	Def. of rt. $\angle$
❽ $m\angle X < 90°$	Substitution *Look back at step 6.*
❾ $\angle X$ is an acute angle	Def. of acute $\angle$
❿ c is the length of the longest side of $\triangle XYZ$	Given
⓫ $m\angle Z$ and $m\angle Y < m\angle X$	$\angle$ opp. longer side is larger (T053)
⓬ $\triangle XYZ$ is an acute triangle	Def. of acute $\triangle$

MORE HELP
See 134, 149, 373, 375

154–155

MORE HELP
See 134

Theorem	If the square of the length of the longest side of a triangle is greater than the sum of the squares of the lengths of the two shorter sides, then the triangle is obtuse.

$$c^2 > a^2 + b^2 \Rightarrow \text{obtuse } \triangle \text{ (T062)}$$

Given: $c^2 > a^2 + b^2$, c is the length of the longest side

Prove: $\triangle KLM$ is obtuse

Plan: The proof of this theorem follows reasoning similar to the proof of the previous theorem.

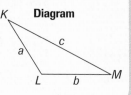

Diagram

EXAMPLE 1: A triangle has side lengths of 10, 11, and 12 units. Is the triangle right, acute, or obtuse?

Does $c^2 = a^2 + b^2$?

$$12^2 \overset{?}{=} 10^2 + 11^2$$
$$144 \overset{?}{=} 100 + 121$$
$$144 < 221$$

★ The triangle is acute.

155 Symmetry of Triangles

Isosceles and equilateral triangles can be folded in such a way that the elements on each side of the fold, or **line of symmetry**, match up exactly. If you wish to prove the relationships summarized in the following table, use what you know about the perpendicular bisector of the base of an isosceles triangle. Remember, a reflected point must be the same distance from the line of reflection as its preimage.

MORE HELP
See 285

Triangle	Symmetry	
Isosceles		One line of symmetry bisects the vertex angle and the base.
Equilateral		Three lines of symmetry bisect angles and opposite sides. Rotations of 120° map the triangle onto itself.

A **quadrilateral** is a four-sided polygon.

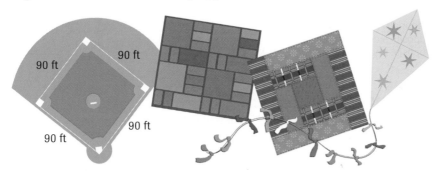

Quadrilaterals are classified by the characteristics of their sides and/or angles. Some quadrilaterals may be classified in more than one way. This diagram shows how some special types of quadrilaterals are related. The trapezoid category is shown here with no loops within it. This means that a trapezoid must have exactly one pair of parallel sides. This definition is not universal, however. Some mathematicians put all parallelograms within the trapezoid loop, considering all parallelograms to be a special type of trapezoid in which both pairs of opposite sides are parallel.

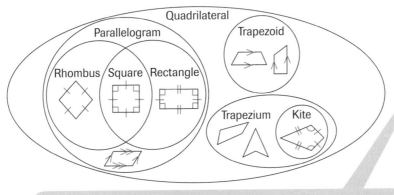

Square is within four of the loops in the diagram—rhombus, rectangle, parallelogram and quadrilateral—so it has all of the properties of these four quadrilaterals.

MORE ▶

A **diagonal** of a polygon is a line segment that connects two non-adjacent vertices. In an n-gon, you can connect any vertex to $n-1$ other vertices. Two of these segments will be sides of the polygon. The other $n-3$ segments will be diagonals. The **opposite sides** of a quadrilateral are sides that do not have a common endpoint. The **opposite angles** of a quadrilateral are pairs of interior angles with no common sides.

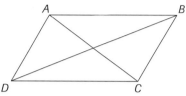

Diagonals: $\overline{AC}$ and $\overline{BD}$

Opposite sides: $\overline{AD}$ and $\overline{BC}$, $\overline{AB}$ and $\overline{DC}$

Opposite angles: $\angle DAB$ and $\angle DCB$

$\angle ABC$ and $\angle ADC$

Diagonals: $\overline{QT}$, $\overline{QS}$, $\overline{PR}$, $\overline{PS}$ and $\overline{RT}$

157

Parallelogram

A **parallelogram** is a quadrilateral in which both pairs of opposite sides are parallel. The properties of parallelograms are summarized in the chart.

MORE HELP
See 158–161

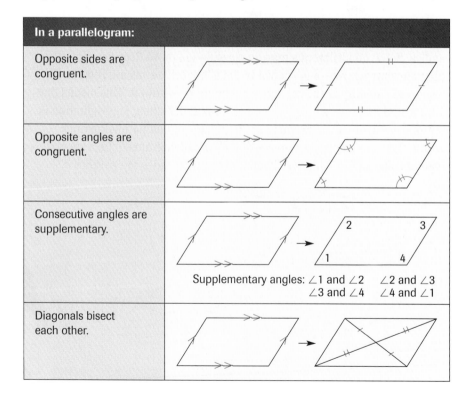

In a parallelogram:	
Opposite sides are congruent.	
Opposite angles are congruent.	
Consecutive angles are supplementary.	Supplementary angles: $\angle 1$ and $\angle 2$ $\angle 2$ and $\angle 3$ $\angle 3$ and $\angle 4$ $\angle 4$ and $\angle 1$
Diagonals bisect each other.	

Opposite Sides of a Parallelogram

Theorem If a quadrilateral is a parallelogram, then its opposite sides are congruent. Parallelogram ⇒ opp. sides ≅ (T063)

MORE HELP
See 263, 432, 434

Given: parallelogram $ABCD$

Prove: $\overline{AB} \cong \overline{CD}$, $\overline{AD} \cong \overline{CB}$

Diagram

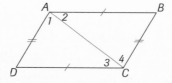

Plan: Draw diagonal $\overline{AC}$. Look for pairs of alternate interior angles. Then use the ASA Congruence Theorem to prove that $\triangle CBA \cong \triangle ADC$. The proof of the theorem will follow if you use CPCTC.

Statements	Reasons
❶ $ABCD$ is a parallelogram	Given
❷ Draw diagonal $\overline{AC}$	Def. of diagonal
❸ $\overline{AB} \parallel \overline{CD}$, $\overline{AD} \parallel \overline{CB}$	Def. of parallelogram
❹ $\angle 1 \cong \angle 4$, $\angle 2 \cong \angle 3$	Alt. Int. ∠s Theorem (T027)
❺ $\overline{AC} \cong \overline{AC}$	Reflexive prop. of ≅ (T105)
❻ $\triangle CBA \cong \triangle ADC$	ASA ≅ Theorem (T108)
❼ $\overline{AB} \cong \overline{CD}$, $\overline{AD} \cong \overline{CB}$	CPCTC

The converse of this theorem is also true.

Theorem If both pairs of opposite sides of a quadrilateral are congruent, then it is a parallelogram. Quadrilateral; opp. sides ≅ ⇒ parallelogram (T064)

Given: $\overline{AB} \cong \overline{CD}$, $\overline{AD} \cong \overline{CB}$

Prove: $ABCD$ is a parallelogram.

Diagram

The proof of this theorem uses reasoning similar to the previous proof. However, you need to reverse the steps and use the SSS Congruence Postulate, instead of ASA. Once you've shown that the triangles are congruent, use CPCTC to show $\angle 1 \cong \angle 4$, $\angle 2 \cong \angle 3$. This means that the opposite sides are parallel and proves you have a parallelogram.

MORE ▶

Theorem If one pair of opposite sides of a quadrilateral is parallel and congruent, then it is a parallelogram. Quadrilateral; opp. sides ∥ and ≅ ⇒ parallelogram (T065)

Proof

Diagram

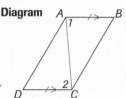

Given: $\overline{AB} \parallel \overline{DC}$, $\overline{AB} \cong \overline{DC}$

Prove: $ABCD$ is a parallelogram

Plan: Draw diagonal $\overline{AC}$ and show $\triangle CAB \cong \triangle ACD$. Use properties of parallelograms to prove the theorem.

Statements	Reasons
❶ $\overline{AB} \parallel \overline{DC}$, $\overline{AB} \cong \overline{DC}$	Given
❷ Draw diagonal $\overline{AC}$	Def. of diagonal; 2 pts. determine a line (P05)
❸ $\angle 1 \cong \angle 2$	Alt. Int. ∠s Theorem (T027)
❹ $\overline{AC} \cong \overline{CA}$	Reflexive prop. of ≅ (T105)
❺ $\triangle CAB \cong \triangle ACD$	SAS ≅ Postulate (P23)
❻ $\overline{AD} \cong \overline{CB}$	CPCTC
❼ $ABCD$ is a parallelogram	Quadrilateral; opp. sides ≅ ⇒ parallelogram (T064)

159 ## Opposite Angles of a Parallelogram

Theorem If a quadrilateral is a parallelogram, then its opposite angles are congruent. Parallelogram ⇒ opp. ∠s ≅ (T066)

Proof

Diagram

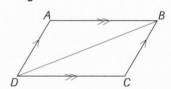

MORE HELP
See 069,
260–261

Given: parallelogram $ABCD$

Prove: $\angle A \cong \angle C$, $\angle ABC \cong \angle CDA$

Plan: Draw diagonal $\overline{DB}$, then compare congruent triangles to prove this theorem.

Because opposite sides of a parallelogram are congruent, $\overline{AB} \cong \overline{CD}$ and $\overline{AD} \cong \overline{CB}$. The Reflexive Property of Congruence says that $\overline{DB} \cong \overline{DB}$, so you can use the SSS Congruence Postulate to show $\triangle DAB \cong \triangle BCD$. $\angle A \cong \angle C$ by CPCTC. Think of $\overline{AD}$ and $\overline{BC}$ as transversals for parallel lines $\overleftrightarrow{AB}$ and $\overleftrightarrow{CD}$. Then, by the Same Side Interior Angles Theorem, $\angle A$ and $\angle CDA$ are supplementary, as are $\angle C$ and $\angle ABC$. Since supplements of congruent angles are congruent, $\angle ABC \cong \angle CDA$.

MORE HELP
See 069, 131,
427, 434

Theorem If both pairs of opposite angles of a quadrilateral are congruent, then it is a parallelogram. Quadrilateral; opp. ∠s ≅ ⇒ parallelogram (T067)

Proof

Given: $\angle A \cong \angle C$, $\angle B \cong \angle D$

Prove: $ABCD$ is a parallelogram

Diagram

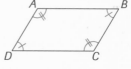

The sum of the measures of the interior angles of a quadrilateral is $(4 - 2)(180°)$, or 360°. Since you also know that $\angle A \cong \angle C$ and $\angle B \cong \angle D$, you have a lot of information about the angles of this quadrilateral.

$m\angle A + m\angle B + m\angle C + m\angle D = 360°$	Sum of the int. ∠s of a quad. (F11)
$m\angle A + m\angle B + m\angle A + m\angle B = 360°$	Substitution
$2(m\angle A + m\angle B) = 360°$	Distributive prop.
$m\angle A + m\angle B = 180°$	÷ prop. of =

This means that $\angle A$ and $\angle B$ are supplementary angles, and by the Converse of the Same Side Interior Angles Theorem, $\overline{AD}$ is parallel to $\overline{BC}$. Since $\angle C \cong \angle A$, $\angle C$ is also supplementary to $\angle B$, making $\overline{AB}$ parallel to $\overline{CD}$. Since opposite sides of the quadrilateral are parallel, $ABCD$ is a parallelogram.

Consecutive Angles of a Parallelogram

160

Theorem If a quadrilateral is a parallelogram, then its consecutive angles are supplementary. Parallelogram ⇒ consec. ∠s supp. (T068)

MORE HELP
See 079

Proof

Given: parallelogram $ABCD$

Prove: consecutive angles are supplementary

Diagram

Each pair of consecutive angles is also a pair of same-side interior angles. By the Same Side Interior Angles Theorem, each pair must be supplementary.

MORE ▶

Theorem
If an angle of a quadrilateral is supplementary to both of its consecutive angles, then the quadrilateral is a parallelogram. Quadrilateral; consecutive ∠s supp. ⇒ parallelogram (T069)

Proof

Diagram

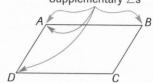

Supplementary ∠s

Given: ∠A is supplementary to ∠B and to ∠D.

Prove: ABCD is a parallelogram.

Since ∠A is supplementary to ∠B, $\overline{AD}$ is parallel to $\overline{BC}$ by the Converse of the Same Side Interior Angles Theorem. Similarly, because ∠A is supplementary to ∠D, $\overline{AB}$ is parallel to $\overline{CD}$. Thus, by definition, ABCD is a parallelogram.

161

Diagonals of a Parallelogram

Theorem
If a quadrilateral is a parallelogram, then its diagonals bisect each other. Diags. of parallelogram bisect (T070)

Proof

Diagram

Given: parallelogram ABCD

Prove: $\overline{AC}$ and $\overline{BD}$ bisect each other

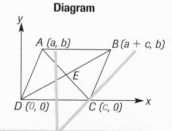

ONE WAY Place the parallelogram on a coordinate axis with one vertex at the origin and one side on the positive x-axis. You can now show that the coordinates of the midpoint of each diagonal are the same. This means they bisect each other.

MORE HELP
See 056, 089, 263

AB = DC, so the x-coordinate of A is a units to the right of x = 0, and the x-coordinate of point B is a units to the right of x = c.

The midpoint of $\overline{AC}$ is $\left(\frac{a + c}{2}, \frac{b + 0}{2}\right)$ or $\left(\frac{a + c}{2}, \frac{b}{2}\right)$. The midpoint of $\overline{BD}$ is $\left(\frac{a + c + 0}{2}, \frac{b + 0}{2}\right)$ or $\left(\frac{a + c}{2}, \frac{b}{2}\right)$. Since the midpoints of $\overline{AC}$ and $\overline{BD}$ have the same coordinates, they are the same point. This means that AE = CE and DE = BE, so you can say that $\overline{AC}$ and $\overline{BD}$ bisect each other.

ANOTHER WAY Think of $\overline{AC}$ and $\overline{BD}$ as transversals to help you find congruent angles. Then use the ASA Congruence Theorem to show that △AEB ≅ △CED. Then use what you know about corresponding parts of congruent triangles to show AE = CE and DE = BE.

Theorem If the diagonals of a quadrilateral bisect each other, then the quadrilateral is a parallelogram. Quadrilateral, diags. bisected ⇒ parallelogram (T071)

MORE HELP
See 098

Proof

Diagram

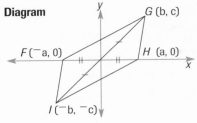

Given: $\overline{FH}$ and $\overline{GI}$ bisect each other

Prove: $FGHI$ is a parallelogram

Plan: Because $\overline{FH}$ and $\overline{GI}$ bisect each other, the coordinates of F and I are $(^-a, 0)$ and $(^-b, ^-c)$, respectively. Show that the slopes of opposite sides are equal, which means that they are parallel. Then $FGHI$ is a parallelogram.

Slope of $\overline{FG}$: $\dfrac{c - 0}{b - (^-a)} = \dfrac{c}{a + b}$ Slope of $\overline{IH}$: $\dfrac{0 - (^-c)}{a - (^-b)} = \dfrac{c}{a + b}$

Slope of $\overline{HG}$: $\dfrac{c - 0}{b - a} = \dfrac{c}{b - a}$ Slope of $\overline{IF}$: $\dfrac{0 - (^-c)}{^-a - (^-b)} = \dfrac{c}{b - a}$

Because the slopes of the opposite sides are equal, the opposite sides are parallel, and $FGHI$ is a parallelogram.

Rectangle

162

By definition, a **rectangle** is a parallelogram with four right angles, so all rectangles are also parallelograms and quadrilaterals. On the other hand, not all quadrilaterals and parallelograms are rectangles. The next theorems will help you to determine which parallelograms are rectangles.

Theorem If a parallelogram has one right angle, then it is a rectangle. Parallelogram; 1 rt. ∠ ⇒ rectangle (T072)

Diagram

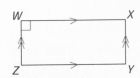

MORE HELP
See 011, 129

Proof

Given: parallelogram $WXYZ$, $\angle W$ is a right angle

Prove: $WXYZ$ is a rectangle.

Plan: Since you know that $WXYZ$ is a parallelogram, you just need to show that all four of its angles are right angles to prove that it is a rectangle.

The angle opposite the right angle must also be a right angle. The other angles must also be right angles because each is consecutive, and therefore supplementary, to a right angle. A parallelogram with four right angles is a rectangle.

MORE ▶

Theorem A parallelogram is a rectangle if and only if its diagonals are congruent. Rectangle ⇔ parallelogram with ≅ diags. (T073)

Proof

To prove this theorem, you must prove two cases.

CASE 1 If a parallelogram is a rectangle, then its diagonals are congruent.

MORE HELP
See 093

Given: *STUV* is a rectangle

Prove: $\overline{SU} \cong \overline{TV}$

Diagram

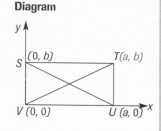

Because *STUV* is a rectangle, ∠*VST*, ∠*STU*, ∠*TUV*, and ∠*UVS* are right angles. This means that you can label the coordinates of *T* as (a, b). Now use the Distance Formula.

$$SU = \sqrt{(0 - a)^2 + (b - 0)^2} \quad VT = \sqrt{(a - 0)^2 + (b - 0)^2}$$

Since the lengths of $\overline{SU}$ and $\overline{VT}$ both simplify to $\sqrt{a^2 + b^2}$, $\overline{SU} \cong \overline{TV}$.

CASE 2 If the diagonals of a parallelogram are congruent, then it is a rectangle.

MORE HELP
See 131

Given: parallelogram *ABCD*, $\overline{AC} \cong \overline{BD}$

Prove: *ABCD* is a rectangle.

Plan: Show that $\triangle BAD \cong \triangle CDA$. Then show that ∠*BAD* and ∠*CDA* are supplementary congruent angles, so that each must be a right angle.

Diagram

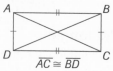

$\overline{AC} \cong \overline{BD}$

Statements	Reasons
❶ Parallelogram *ABCD*, $\overline{AC} \cong \overline{BD}$	Given
❷ $\overline{BA} \cong \overline{CD}$	Parallelogram ⇒ opp. sides ≅ (T063)
❸ $\overline{AD} \cong \overline{DA}$	Reflexive prop. of ≅ (T105)
❹ $\triangle BAD \cong \triangle CDA$	SSS ≅ Postulate (P22)
❺ ∠*BAD* ≅ ∠*CDA*; m∠*BAD* = m∠*CDA*	CPCTC; def. of ≅
❻ ∠*BAD* and ∠*CDA* are supplementary	Parallelogram ⇒ consec. ∠s supp. (T068)
❼ m∠*BAD* + m∠*CDA* = 180°	Def. of supp. ∠s
❽ 2(m∠*CDA*) = 180°	Substitution; distributive prop.
❾ m∠*CDA* = 90°; ∠*CDA* is a right angle	÷ prop. of =; def. of rt. ∠
❿ *ABCD* is a rectangle	Parallelogram; 1 rt. ∠ ⇒ rectangle (T072)

Rhombus

A **rhombus** is a parallelogram with four congruent sides. Here are some ways that you can tell that a parallelogram is a rhombus.

A parallelogram is a rhombus if:	
the diagonals are perpendicular.	
each diagonal bisects a pair of opposite angles.	

Theorem A parallelogram is a rhombus if and only if its diagonals are perpendicular. Parallelogram; rhombus ⇔ ⊥ diags. (T074)

MORE HELP
See 061

To prove this theorem you must show that:
1. If a parallelogram is a rhombus, then its diagonals are perpendicular.
2. If the diagonals of a parallelogram are perpendicular, then it is a rhombus.

Proof

CASE 1 If a parallelogram is a rhombus, then its diagonals are perpendicular.

Given: $DEFG$ is a rhombus.

Prove: $\overline{DF} \perp \overline{EG}$

Diagram

MORE HELP
See 056, 432, 434

Since all four sides of a rhombus are congruent, you know that $ED = EF$ and $GD = GF$. This means that E is equidistant from D and F, and G is equidistant from D and F. The Converse of the Perpendicular Bisector Theorem tells you that points E and G are both on the perpendicular bisector of $\overline{DF}$. Since E and G are both on the perpendicular bisector, $\overleftrightarrow{EG}$ is the perpendicular bisector of $\overline{DF}$. This means that $\overline{DF}$ is perpendicular to $\overline{EG}$.

MORE ▶

MORE HELP
See 073, 156

CASE 2 If the diagonals of a parallelogram are perpendicular, then the parallelogram is a rhombus

Given: parallelogram $IJKL$, $\overline{IK} \perp \overline{JL}$

Prove: $IJKL$ is a rhombus

Diagram

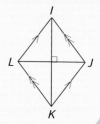

Since the diagonals of a parallelogram bisect each other, $\overline{IK}$ and $\overline{JL}$ bisect each other. You are given that IK and JL are perpendicular to each other. Then by the Perpendicular Bisector Theorem, $IJ = IL$, $JI = JK$, $KJ = KL$ and $LK = LI$. Therefore $IJKL$ is a rhombus by the definition of a rhombus.

Theorem   A parallelogram is a rhombus if and only if each diagonal bisects a pair of opposite angles. Parallelogram; diags. bisect opp. ∠s ⇔ rhombus (T075)

This theorem also needs to be broken into two cases:

1. If a parallelogram is a rhombus, then each diagonal bisects a pair of opposite angles.
2. If each diagonal of a parallelogram bisects a pair of opposite angles, the parallelogram is a rhombus.

Proof

CASE 1 If a parallelogram is a rhombus, each diagonal bisects a pair of opposite angles.

Given: $DEFG$ is a rhombus

Prove: $\overline{DF}$ bisects $\angle EDG$ and $\angle EFG$, $\overline{EG}$ bisects $\angle DEF$ and $\angle DGF$

Diagram

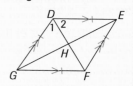

Plan: You can use SAS or SSS to find congruent triangles. Then use the congruent parts to help you prove the theorem.

Because, in a rhombus the diagonals bisect each other and all sides are congruent, $\triangle DHE \cong \triangle FHE \cong \triangle FHG \cong \triangle DHG$ by the SSS Congruence Postulate. By CPCTC, $\angle 1 \cong \angle 2$. Thus, by the definition of angle bisector, $\overline{DF}$ bisects $\angle EDG$. You can use the same reasoning to show that $\overline{DF}$ also bisects $\angle EFG$ and $\overline{EG}$ bisects both $\angle DEF$ and $\angle DGF$.

MORE HELP
See 265

CASE 2 If each diagonal of a parallelogram bisects a pair of opposite angles, it is a rhombus.

Given: parallelogram $DEFG$, $\overline{DF}$ bisects $\angle EDG$ and $\angle EFG$, $\overline{EG}$ bisects $\angle DEF$ and $\angle DGF$

Prove: $DEFG$ is a rhombus

Diagram

Because $\overline{DF}$ bisects $\angle EDG$, $\angle 1 \cong \angle 2$. Because $\overline{EG}$ bisects the congruent angles $\angle DEF$ and $\angle DGF$, $\angle 3 \cong \angle 4$. Add the fact that $\overline{DH} \cong \overline{DH}$ and you know that $\triangle DEH \cong \triangle DGH$ by the AAS Congruence Theorem. $\angle EHD \cong \angle DHG$ by CPCTC. Since $\angle EHD$ and $\angle DHG$ are congruent angles that form a linear pair, they are both right angles and $\overline{DF}$ is perpendicular to $\overline{EG}$. This means that $DEFG$ is a rhombus because a parallelogram is a rhombus if its diagonals are perpendicular.

Square

By one definition, a **square** is a rhombus with four right angles. You can also define a square as a rectangle with four congruent sides.

Here is just part of the diagram that shows how quadrilaterals are related. It shows that a square is a rhombus, a rectangle, and a parallelogram.

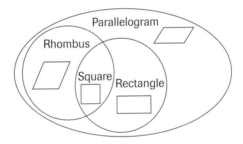

MORE HELP
See 156,
162–163

Squares have all of the properties of parallelograms, rhombuses, and rectangles.

For example, a square has two pairs of opposite sides parallel—a property of parallelograms. It also has four congruent sides—a property of rhombuses. It also has four right angles—a property of rectangles.

EXAMPLE: To assure that a frame is square, a carpenter will check that the diagonals of the frame intersect at their midpoints, are perpendicular, and are equal in length. How will making these checks assure that the frame is square?

Look for checks that will show the frame is both a rhombus and a rectangle. With these two qualifications, it must also be square.

★ Since the diagonals intersect at their midpoints and are perpendicular, they are perpendicular bisectors of each other. This assures you that the frame is a rhombus. Since the diagonals are equal in length, they are congruent. This assures you that the frame is a rectangle. Because the frame is a rhombus and a rectangle, it must be a square.

165 Trapezoid

A **trapezoid** is a quadrilateral with exactly one pair of parallel sides. The sides and angles of a trapezoid have special names. The parallel sides of a trapezoid are the **bases**.

> Sometimes a trapezoid is defined as a quadrilateral with *at least* one pair of parallel sides. Then a parallelogram becomes a special type of trapezoid. The bases are never the same length according to the first definition, but may be the same length according to the second. The rest of this discussion uses the first definition.

A pair of angles that have vertices at the endpoints of a base are a pair of **base angles**. The sides of a trapezoid that are not parallel are the **legs**. If the legs of a trapezoid are congruent, then the trapezoid is an **isosceles trapezoid**.

MORE HELP
See 058

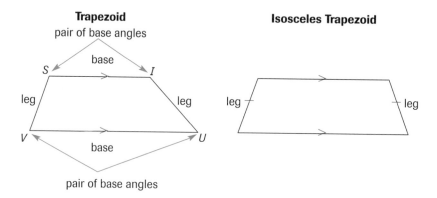

Trapezoid
pair of base angles
base
S — I
leg   leg
V — U
base
pair of base angles

Isosceles Trapezoid
leg   leg

MORE HELP
See 268, 375,
432, 434

Theorem	If a trapezoid is isosceles, then each pair of base angles is congruent. Trapezoid Base ∠s Theorem (T076)

Proof

Diagram

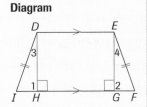

Given: isosceles trapezoid *DEFI* with $\overline{DI} \cong \overline{EF}$

Prove: $\angle I \cong \angle F$, $\angle IDE \cong \angle FED$

First construct altitudes $\overline{DH}$ and $\overline{EG}$. You know that $\overline{DH} \cong \overline{EG}$, because the distance between two parallel lines is always the same. Because $\overline{DH}$ and $\overline{EG}$ are perpendicular to $\overline{IF}$, $\angle 1$ and $\angle 2$ are right angles. Because *DEFI* is an isosceles trapezoid, $\overline{DI} \cong \overline{EF}$. Thus, by the H-L Congruence Theorem, $\triangle DHI \cong \triangle EGF$. Then you can use CPCTC to conclude that $\angle I \cong \angle F$.

Also by CPCTC, $\angle 3 \cong \angle 4$. $\overline{DH}$ and $\overline{EG}$ are perpendicular to the same line, making them parallel. A quadrilateral with opposite sides parallel and one right angle is a rectangle. This means that $\angle HDE$ and $\angle GED$ are right angles and congruent. The Angle Addition Postulate allows you to conclude $\angle IDE \cong \angle FED$.

Theorem	If a trapezoid is isosceles, then its diagonals are congruent. Trapezoid Diags. Theorem (T077)

MORE HELP
See 262

Proof

Diagram

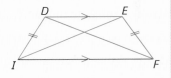

Given: isosceles trapezoid *DEFI*

Prove: $\overline{DF} \cong \overline{EI}$

ONE WAY Prove that $\triangle IDE \cong \triangle FED$, so $\overline{DF} \cong \overline{EI}$ by CPCTC.

Statements	**Reasons**
❶ *DEFI* is an isosceles trapezoid	Given
❷ $\overline{DI} \cong \overline{EF}$	Def. of isos. trapezoid
❸ $\angle IDE \cong \angle FED$	Trapezoid Base ∠s Theorem (T076)
❹ $\overline{DE} \cong \overline{ED}$	Reflexive Prop. of ≅ (T105)
❺ $\triangle IDE \cong \triangle FED$	SAS ≅ Postulate (P23)
❻ $\overline{DF} \cong \overline{EI}$	CPCTC

ANOTHER WAY You can get the same results by proving $\triangle FIE \cong \triangle IFD$.

Theorem

If the diagonals of a trapezoid are congruent, then it is an isosceles trapezoid. Converse of Trapezoid Diags. Theorem (T078)

Proof

Diagram

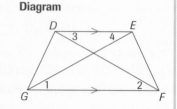

Given: trapezoid $DEFG$, $\overline{DF} \cong \overline{EG}$

Prove: $\overline{DG} \cong \overline{EF}$

Plan: You know that the lengths of $\overline{DG}$ and $\overline{EF}$ can be related in one of three ways: $DG > EF$, $DG < EF$, or $DG = EF$. Use an indirect proof. Begin by showing that both of the first two options lead to a contradiction, so the last one must be true.

You are given that $EG = DF$, and you know that $GF = GF$. Assume that $DG > EF$ and look for a contradiction.

By looking at $\triangle EFG$ and $\triangle DGF$ you can use the Converse to the Hinge Theorem to see that $m\angle 2$ would have to be greater than $m\angle 1$. By looking at $\triangle EDG$ and $\triangle DEF$ you would conclude that $m\angle 4 > m\angle 3$.

Diagram

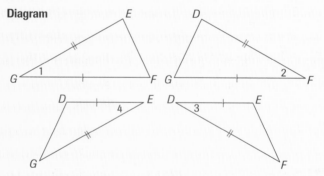

Because $\angle 1$ and $\angle 4$ are alternate interior angles, $m\angle 1 = m\angle 4$. Putting these equations and inequalities together you would find the following.

$$m\angle 2 > m\angle 1 \qquad m\angle 4 > m\angle 3 \qquad m\angle 1 = m\angle 4$$
$$\text{so } m\angle 2 > m\angle 4 \qquad \text{and } m\angle 2 > m\angle 3$$

However, $m\angle 2$ cannot be greater than $m\angle 3$, because they are alternate interior angles and must have the same measure. This contradiction shows that DG cannot be greater than EF.

If you assume $DG < EF$, you can make a similar argument and reach a similar contradiction. Then the only option left is that $DG = EF$ and trapezoid $DEFG$ is isosceles.

Theorem If a trapezoid has one pair of congruent base angles, then the trapezoid is isosceles. Trapezoid; 1 pair base ∠s ≅ ⇒ isos. (T079)

Proof

Given: trapezoid $DEFG$, $\angle D \cong \angle G$

Prove: $\overline{DE} \cong \overline{GF}$

Plan: Through E construct a line parallel to $\overline{GF}$, intersecting the line containing $\overline{DG}$ at H. H may or may not be between D and G. Consider these two cases separately.

1. H is between D and G.
2. H is not between D and G.

In both cases, you can prove that $EFGH$ is a parallelogram and DHE is an isosceles triangle. From these you can prove that $GF = EH = DE$, so that the trapezoid is isosceles.

CASE 1 H is between D and G.

Begin by constructing a line parallel to $\overline{FG}$ through E. It intersects $\overline{DG}$ at H.

You are given that $\angle D \cong \angle G$. Since $\angle G$ and $\angle 1$ are corresponding angles, they are also congruent. Now the Transitive Property of Congruence tells you that $\angle D \cong \angle 1$. This tells you that $\overline{DE} \cong \overline{HE}$ by the Base Angles Theorem. $HEFG$ is a parallelogram because both pairs of opposite sides are parallel, so you know that $\overline{HE} \cong \overline{GF}$ because they are opposite sides of parallelogram $HEFG$. Again by transitivity, $\overline{DE} \cong \overline{GF}$.

Diagram

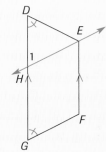

MORE HELP
See 260, 265, 376

CASE 2 H is not between D and G.

Again, you are given that $\angle D \cong \angle G$. Extend $\overline{DG}$. Construct a line parallel to $\overline{FG}$ through E. It intersects $\overleftrightarrow{DG}$ at H. Because $\angle G$ and $\angle 1$ are corresponding angles, $\angle G \cong \angle 1$, and the Transitive Property of Congruence makes $\angle GDE \cong \angle 1$. Now $\angle 2 \cong \angle 3$ because they are supplements of congruent angles. The rest of this argument continues in the same manner as Case 1.

Diagram

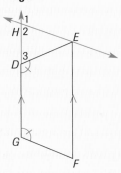

In either case, $\overline{DE} \cong \overline{GF}$, so the trapezoid is isosceles.

MORE ▶

MORE HELP
See 089, 141 The **midsegment** of a trapezoid joins the midpoints of the legs.

Theorem The midsegment of a trapezoid is parallel to each base and its length is half the sum of the lengths of the bases.
Midseg. Theorem for Trapezoids (T080)

The midsegment of a trapezoid is sometimes called the median.

Proof

Given: trapezoid $UVWX$, P is the midpoint of $\overline{UX}$, Q is the midpoint of $\overline{VW}$

Prove: $\overline{PQ} \parallel \overline{UV}$, $\overline{PQ} \parallel \overline{XW}$, $PQ = \frac{1}{2}(UV + XW)$

Plan: Place the trapezoid conveniently on a coordinate plane, with one vertex at $(0, 0)$ and one side along the positive x-axis. Use the midpoint formula to find the coordinates of P and Q. Then use the slope and distance formulas to complete the proof.

Diagram

Begin by finding the midpoints of $\overline{UX}$ and $\overline{VW}$.

P (midpoint of $\overline{UX}$): $\left(\frac{b + 0}{2}, \frac{d + 0}{2}\right)$ or $\left(\frac{b}{2}, \frac{d}{2}\right)$

Q (midpoint of $\overline{VW}$): $\left(\frac{a + c}{2}, \frac{0 + d}{2}\right)$ or $\left(\frac{a + c}{2}, \frac{d}{2}\right)$

Since $\overline{UV}$ and $\overline{XW}$ are horizontal lines, their slopes are 0. Since the y-coordinates of P and Q are equal, $\overline{PQ}$ is also a horizontal line, so it is parallel to both $\overline{UV}$ and $\overline{XW}$.

Now you need to find the lengths of the three horizontal segments. You can use the Ruler Postulate to find each distance by thinking of each line as if it were on the number line of the x-axis.

$UV = c - b$

$PQ = \dfrac{a + c}{2} - \dfrac{b}{2}$

$\quad = \dfrac{a - b + c}{2}$

$XW = a$

Substitute XW and UV into the equation for PQ.

$PQ = \dfrac{a - b + c}{2}$

$\quad = \dfrac{1}{2}(a + c - b)$

$\quad = \dfrac{1}{2}(XW + UV)$

MORE HELP
See 079

Theorem In a trapezoid, consecutive angles between a pair of parallel sides are supplementary. Trapezoid ⇒ consec. ∠s between ∥ are supp. (T081)

Proof

Given: trapezoid $PQRS$ with $\overline{PQ} \parallel \overline{SR}$

Prove: ∠P and ∠S are supplementary, ∠Q and ∠R are supplementary

Because $\overline{PQ} \parallel \overline{SR}$, ∠$P$ and ∠S are interior angles on the same side of transversal $\overleftrightarrow{PS}$ and are supplementary by the Same Side Interior Angles Theorem. Similarly, using transversal $\overleftrightarrow{QR}$, ∠Q and ∠R are supplementary.

Diagram

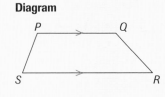

Kite

A **kite** is a quadrilateral with exactly two pairs of adjacent congruent sides. Opposite sides of a kite are not congruent. Notice that a kite has no pairs of parallel sides. All kites are trapeziums, but not all trapeziums are kites.

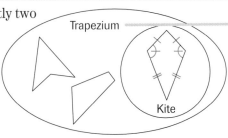

Trapezium

Kite

A **trapezium** is a quadrilateral with no parallel sides.

The next two theorems describe two properties of kites.

Theorem If a quadrilateral is a kite, then its diagonals are perpendicular. Kite ⇒ ⊥ diags. (T082)

Proof

Diagram

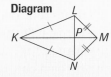

Given: Kite $KLMN$ with diagonals $\overline{KM}$ and $\overline{LN}$

Prove: $\overline{KM} \perp \overline{LN}$

Plan: Use the fact that if two points on a line are equidistant from a third point, the third point is on the perpendicular bisector.

MORE HELP
See 061, 255, 261–262

Statements	Reasons
❶ Kite $KLMN$	Given
❷ $\overline{KL} \cong \overline{KN}$, $\overline{ML} \cong \overline{MN}$	Def. of kite
❸ $KL = KN$, $LM = NM$	Def. of ≅ segments
❹ $\overline{MK}$ is the ⊥ bisector of $\overline{LN}$	Converse of ⊥ Bisector Theorem (T003)

Theorem If a quadrilateral is a kite, then exactly one pair of opposite angles is congruent. Kite ⟹ exactly one pair of opp. ≅ ∠s. (T083)

Proof

Diagram

Given: kite $KLMN$

Prove: $\angle KLM \cong \angle KNM$, $\angle LKN$ is not congruent to $\angle LMN$

Plan: Since the theorem says *exactly* one pair of opposite angles is congruent, the proof needs to show two things:
1. one pair of opposite angles is congruent, and
2. the other pair of opposite angles is not congruent.

MORE HELP
See 158–159

CASE 1 Prove $\angle KLM \cong \angle KNM$.

Because $KLMN$ is a kite, $\overline{KL} \cong \overline{KN}$ and $\overline{LM} \cong \overline{NM}$. You also know that $\overline{KM} \cong \overline{KM}$. This means that $\triangle KLM \cong \triangle KNM$ by the SSS Congruence Postulate. Then $\angle KLM \cong \angle KNM$ because corresponding parts of congruent triangles are congruent.

CASE 2 Prove $\angle LKN$ is not congruent to $\angle LMN$.

Use an indirect proof. Assume that $\angle LKN \cong \angle LMN$. This would make the opposite angles of this quadrilateral congruent, and $KLMN$ would be a parallelogram. If that were true, its opposite sides would be congruent. But opposite sides of a kite are not congruent. Therefore, $\angle LKN$ is not congruent to $\angle LMN$.

167

Symmetry of Quadrilaterals

MORE HELP
See 056, 073, 155

A figure has **line symmetry** if the part of the figure on one side of a line ℓ is the mirror reflection of the part of the figure on the other side of the line. The mirror reflection of any part of a figure is called its **reflected image**, or more commonly, just its **image**.

To prove that two points, A and A′, are reflections about line ℓ, you need to show that ℓ is the perpendicular bisector of $\overline{AA'}$.

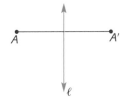

A figure has rotational symmetry if you can rotate it 180° (or less) about a point and have the rotated figure exactly match, or map onto, the original figure.

No Rotational Symmetry   **Rotational Symmetry**

Angle of rotation = 180°

If the angle of rotation is exactly 180°, the figure is sometimes said to have *point symmetry*. To show that two points, A and A′, have point symmetry about point P, you need to show that P is the midpoint of $\overline{AA'}$.

Some quadrilaterals have one or more lines of symmetry or a point of symmetry. These are identified in the table.

Figure	Diagram	Which type of symmetry?
Isosceles trapezoid		Line: The perpendicular bisector of the bases is the line of symmetry.
Kite		Line: The line passing through the vertices of the non congruent angles is the line of symmetry.
Parallelogram		Rotational: The midpoint of each diagonal is the center of symmetry, and the angle of rotation is 180°. Note: The diagonal is *not* a line of symmetry.
Rectangle		Line: The perpendicular bisector of each pair of parallel sides is a line of symmetry. Note: Because a rectangle is a parallelogram, it also has rotational symmetry.

Most textbooks do not include theorems about these relationships, but you can prove the relationships shown in the table by recalling that a perpendicular bisector is a line of symmetry of a line segment and that the only line of symmetry for an angle is the bisector of that angle.

Measurement

"When you can measure what you are speaking about, and express it in numbers, you know something about it; but when you cannot measure it, when you cannot express it in numbers, your knowledge is of a meagre and unsatisfactory kind. . . .

—*Lord Kelvin in Electrical Units of Measurement, a lecture delivered May 3, 1883*

Picture how ridiculous this would be: A surveyor measures the area of your state with a square meter of carpet, placing it down again and again to see how many squares it takes to cover the whole state. That may be extreme dedication, but it certainly isn't taking advantage of geometry. Even though geometry does come from the Greek words for *earth* and *measure* (and the surveyor is, after all, measuring the earth), such impractical methods are exactly what geometry helps you to avoid.

Geometry shows you how to find and use relationships among points, angles, line segments, and other basic elements. Instead of tediously measuring each and every square unit of a region, you can save time, and probably lots of mistakes, by simply measuring some distances and making calculations.

Geometry shows you how to create formulas for measuring simple figures, like polygons and circles, and how to use those to calculate perimeters, areas, and volumes of more complicated shapes.

The next time you need to figure how much paint you'll need to redo your room, or how much stuff you can fit into your trunk, or how far it is across town, don't forget the most efficient measurement tool of all—geometry.

MORE HELP
See 370
The **perimeter** of a figure is the distance around it. The perimeter of a circle is called its **circumference**. Perimeter is a one-dimensional measure and is measured in linear units such as inches, feet, yards, centimeters, and meters.

170

Perimeter of Polygons

The perimeter of a polygon is the sum of the lengths of the segments that make up the sides of the polygon. You can write this definition as a formula.

Formula If P represents the perimeter of an n-gon, and if $s_1, s_2, \ldots$ s_n represent the lengths of side 1, side 2, $\ldots$ side n, then $P = s_1 + s_2 + s_3 + \ldots + s_n$. (F15)

Rectangles and parallelograms have two pairs of congruent sides. This means you can simplify the perimeter formula for a polygon when you want to find the perimeters of rectangles and parallelograms.

Formula If ℓ and w represent the length and width of a rectangle or parallelogram, then its perimeter is $P = 2\ell + 2w$. (F16)

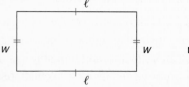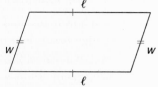

To show why this is true, use the definition of perimeter.

$$P = \ell + w + \ell + w \qquad \text{Def. of perimeter}$$
$$= \ell + \ell + w + w \qquad \text{Commutative prop. of } +$$
$$= 2\ell + 2w \qquad \text{Distributive prop.}$$

You can also find the perimeter of a square or rhombus by simplifying the polygon formula, because they both have four congruent sides.

> **Formula** If *s* represents the length of each side of a square or rhombus, then its perimeter is $P = 4s$. (F17)

To show why this is true, use the definition of perimeter and simplify the resulting expression.

$P = s + s + s + s$ Def. of perimeter
$\ \ = 4s$ Distributive prop.

In a regular polygon, all sides are congruent. This means you can simplify the expression for its perimeter into (number of sides) × (length of a side).

> **Formula** If *s* represents the length of each side of a regular *n*-gon, then its perimeter is $P = ns$. (F18)

To see why this is true, use the formula for perimeter and simplify it.

$P = s_1 + s_2 + s_3 \ldots + s_n$ — *n identical addends*
$\ \ = ns$

MATH ALERT Be Careful When Computing with Mixed Measures

171

A linear measurement may contain two or three different units, such as 3 yards 2 feet 5 inches. When you are computing with measurements like these, be sure to simplify your answers.

MORE HELP
See 134

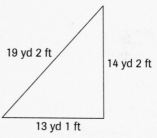

19 yd 2 ft

14 yd 2 ft

13 yd 1 ft

CASE 1 To add or subtract mixed measures, treat units separately.

EXAMPLE 1: Find the perimeter of the triangle.

Find the perimeter.

    13 yd 1 ft
    14 yd 2 ft
 + 19 yd 2 ft
    46 yd 5 ft

Simplify the answer since 5 ft > 1 yd.
  46 yd 5 ft = 46 yd + 3 ft + 2 ft
            = 46 yd + 1 yd + 2 ft
            = 47 yd + 2 ft

★ The perimeter of the triangle is 47 yards 2 feet.

EXAMPLE 2: Find the perimeter of this isosceles triangle.

25 cm | 4.6 m / 4.6 m

$$\begin{array}{r} 4.6 \text{ m} \\ 4.6 \text{ m} \\ + 0.25 \text{ m} \\ \hline 9.45 \text{ m} \end{array}$$

MORE HELP
See 419–420

Write 25 centimeters in meters before you add.

★ The perimeter of the triangle is 9.45 meters.

CASE 2 To multiply a measure by a number, multiply each unit of the measure separately.

EXAMPLE 3: Find the perimeter of the regular hexagon.

Use the formula for a regular n-gon: $P = ns$, where $n = 6$. Then simplify the answer.

$P = ns$
$\quad = 6(4 \text{ ft } 9 \text{ in.})$
$\quad = 6(4 \text{ ft } + 9 \text{ in.})$
$\quad = 24 \text{ ft } + \boxed{54 \text{ in.}}$
$\quad = 24 \text{ ft } + \boxed{48 \text{ in.} + 6 \text{ in.}}$
$\quad = \boxed{24 \text{ ft } + 4 \text{ ft}} + 6 \text{ in.}$
$\quad = \boxed{28 \text{ ft}} + 6 \text{ in.}$

4 ft 9 in.

★ The perimeter of the hexagon is 28 feet 6 inches or $28\frac{1}{2}$ feet.

MORE HELP
See 180

CASE 3 To multiply a measure by a measure, be sure all measures are in the same units before you begin multiplying.

8 ft 9 in.

EXAMPLE 4: Find the area of the square.

To find the area of the square, use the formula: $A = s^2$.

Multiply inches	or	**Multiply feet**	

$$\begin{array}{l} 8 \text{ ft } 9 \text{ in.} \longrightarrow \quad 105 \text{ in.} \\ \times 8 \text{ ft } 9 \text{ in.} \longrightarrow \underline{\times 105 \text{ in.}} \\ \hline \qquad\qquad\quad 11{,}025 \text{ in.}^2 \end{array}$$

$$8\frac{3}{4} \text{ ft} \times 8\frac{3}{4} \text{ ft} \quad \text{or}$$
$$= \frac{35}{4} \times \frac{35}{4}$$
$$= \frac{1225}{16}$$
$$= 76\frac{9}{16} \text{ ft}^2$$

$$\begin{array}{r} 8.75 \text{ ft} \\ \times 8.75 \text{ ft} \\ \hline 76.5625 \text{ ft}^2 \end{array}$$

Use the conversion factor 1 ft² = 144 in.² to write square inches as square feet.

★ Any way you choose to multiply, the area of the square is 11,025 square inches, or $76\frac{9}{16}$ square feet, or about 76.6 square feet.

Perimeter of a Regular Polygon in the Unit Circle

When a regular polygon is inscribed in the unit circle, you can calculate its perimeter by knowing only the number of sides.

MORE HELP
See 129, 241

Formula   The perimeter of a regular n-gon inscribed in a unit circle is $P = 2n \sin \left(\frac{180°}{n} \right)$. (F19)

To see why this is true, look at one triangle formed by a radius of the circle, an apothem, and half the length of a side of the polygon.

Diagram

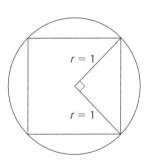

A **unit circle** has a radius of one unit, so this triangle is a right triangle with a hypotenuse of one unit. There are $2n$ of these triangles around the center of the circle, so the measure of each acute angle is $\frac{360°}{2n}$ or $\frac{180°}{n}$. Now use the sine ratio to find the length of the side of the polygon, and then the perimeter.

> The apothem is a perpendicular segment from the center to the midpoint of a side of a regular polygon.

Find the length of a side.

$$\sin \left(\frac{180°}{n} \right) = \frac{\frac{s}{2}}{1}$$

$$= \frac{s}{2}$$

$$2 \sin \left(\frac{180°}{n} \right) = s$$

Find the perimeter of the n-gon.

$$P = ns$$

$$= n \cdot 2 \sin \left(\frac{180°}{n} \right)$$

$$= 2n \sin \left(\frac{180°}{n} \right)$$

EXAMPLE 1: Find the perimeter of a square inscribed in the unit circle.

MORE HELP
See 238, 241

ONE WAY   Use the formula $P = 2n \sin \left(\frac{180°}{n} \right)$.

Because a square is a regular polygon with four sides, $n = 4$. Because the diagonals of a rhombus are perpendicular, the triangle formed by two radii of the unit circle and a side of the square is a $45°$-$45°$-$90°$ triangle.

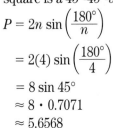

$$P = 2n \sin \left(\frac{180°}{n} \right)$$

$$= 2(4) \sin \left(\frac{180°}{4} \right)$$

$$= 8 \sin 45°$$

$$\approx 8 \cdot 0.7071$$

$$\approx 5.6568$$

MORE ▶

MORE HELP
See 238

ANOTHER WAY Use the formula $P = ns$.

A diagonal of the square is a diameter of the circle, so its length is 2 units. Since the triangle formed by two sides of a square and a diameter is an isosceles right triangle (45°-45°-90°), the length of each side of the square is $\sqrt{2}$. So, $n = 4$ and $s = \sqrt{2}$.

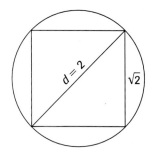

$P = ns$
$\quad = 4\sqrt{2}$
$\quad \approx 5.6569$

★ Either way, the perimeter of a square inscribed in a unit circle is about 5.7 units.

If the regular n-gon is inscribed in a circle with a radius other than one unit, you can modify the formula for perimeter by multiplying by the radius: $P = 2rn \sin\left(\frac{180°}{n}\right)$.

EXAMPLE 2: Find the perimeter of a regular hexagon inscribed in a circle of radius 2.

ONE WAY Each side forms an equilateral triangle with two radii. The radii tell you that the triangle is isosceles and $360° \div 6$ tells you that the vertex angle is $60°$. This means *all* the angles must be $60°$. Since the radius of the circle is 2 units, each side of the hexagon is also two units. Then the perimeter of the hexagon is $2 \cdot 6$ or 12 units long.

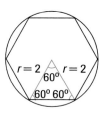

ANOTHER WAY Use the formula $P = 2rn \sin\left(\frac{180°}{n}\right)$.

$P = 2rn \sin\left(\dfrac{180°}{n}\right)$
$\quad = 2 \cdot 2 \cdot 6 \cdot \sin 30°$
$\quad = 24 \cdot \dfrac{1}{2}$
$\quad = 12$ units

★ Either way, the perimeter is 12 units.

Notice that you don't really need to inscribe the polygon in the circle to solve the problem. The radius of the circle is the same length as a segment to a vertex from the center of the regular polygon.

Perimeter of Similar Polygons

The perimeter of a 20-inch square tile is twice as long as that of a 10-inch square tile. That's because, as the next theorem shows, if you enlarge or reduce a polygon by a factor of k, the perimeter will also change by a factor of k.

Theorem	If two polygons are similar with corresponding sides in the ratio of $a{:}b$, then the ratio of their perimeters is $a{:}b$.

~ polygons, corresp. sides $a{:}b \Rightarrow$ perimeters $a{:}b$ (T084)

Proof

Diagram

 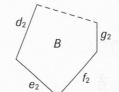

Given: Polygon A ~ Polygon B with ratio of side lengths $\frac{a}{b}$

Prove: $\frac{\text{perimeter of A}}{\text{perimeter of B}} = \frac{a}{b}$

Plan: First express each side of A in terms of the side lengths of B. Then write an expression for the ratios of the perimeters and simplify.

Statements	Reasons
❶ Polygon A with sides $d_1, e_1, f_1, \ldots$ ~Polygon B with sides $d_2, e_2, f_2, \ldots$	Given
❷ $\dfrac{d_1}{d_2} = \dfrac{a}{b}, \dfrac{e_1}{e_2} = \dfrac{a}{b}, \ldots$	Given
❸ $d_1 = \dfrac{d_2 \cdot a}{b}, e_1 = \dfrac{e_2 \cdot a}{b} \ldots$	$\times$ prop. of $=$
❹ Perimeter of A $= d_1 + e_1 + f_1 + \ldots$ Perimeter of B $= d_2 + e_2 + f_2 + \ldots$	Def. of perimeter
❺ Perimeter of $A = \dfrac{d_2 \cdot a}{b} + \dfrac{e_2 \cdot a}{b} + \ldots$	Substitution
❻ Perimeter of $A = \dfrac{(d_2 + e_2 + \ldots) \cdot a}{b}$	Distributive prop.
❼ $\dfrac{\text{perimeter of A}}{\text{perimeter of B}} = \dfrac{\frac{(d_2 + e_2 + \ldots) \cdot a}{b}}{d_2 + e_2 + f_2 \ldots}$	Substitution
❽ $\dfrac{\text{perimeter of A}}{\text{perimeter of B}} = \dfrac{\frac{a}{b}}{1}$	Identity prop. of $\times$
❾ $\dfrac{\text{perimeter of A}}{\text{perimeter of B}} = \dfrac{a}{b}$	$\times$ prop. of $=$

MORE ▶

EXAMPLE: You can make people in a movie appear to shrink by enlarging the props. How much wire is needed for the enlargement of this earring prop that has a scale of 1.5 cm : 2 mm?

8 mm

ONE WAY Use the scale factor after writing it using the same units. A scale factor of 1.5 cm : 2 mm is the same as 15 mm : 2 mm or 15:2.

P of enlarged earring in mm = P of original in mm · scale factor

$$P = (6 \cdot 8) \cdot \frac{15}{2}$$
$$= 360$$

ANOTHER WAY Use the scale with the units given.

P of enlarged earring = P of original · scale factor

$$P = (6 \cdot 8 \text{ mm}) \cdot \frac{1.5 \text{ cm}}{2 \text{ mm}}$$
$$= 36 \text{ cm}$$

★ To construct the prop earring, 360 mm (or 36 cm) of wire are needed.

174

Pi

The ratio of the circumference of a circle, C, to the diameter of the circle, d, is always the number called **pi**, or π. In fact, this is the definition of π.

$\pi = \frac{C}{d}$, where C is the circumference and d is the diameter of a circle.

Write: π or pi   **Say:** *Pie*

The number π is irrational. Its decimal approximation is known to more than a million decimal places. Here are the first 18.

$\pi = 3.141\ 592\ 653\ 589\ 793\ 238 \ldots$

Most scientific calculators have a key for π. They often give the first six or eight places of this decimal.

The most commonly used approximations for π are $\frac{22}{7}$, 3.14, and 3.1416. The value that you use for π depends on the problem you are solving.

■ If you need an exact answer, then you should leave π in the answer.

■ If you need an estimated answer, then use the most reasonable approximation for the given data.

Because π can be approximated to many decimal places, you can compute an answer to many decimal places. However, you do not want your answer to seem more precise than the actual data in a problem.

MORE HELP
See 176

EXAMPLE: Find the exact circumference of the circle.

For the exact answer, use the formula and leave π in the answer.

$C = \pi d$
$\quad = 14\pi$

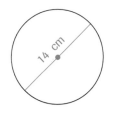

★ The exact circumference is 14π centimeters.

MATH ALERT π Is Not a Variable

175

Even though π is a ratio represented by a letter (of the Greek alphabet) and you can use many values to estimate the results of calculations involving π, it is *not* a variable. It occupies its own unique place on every number line. It cannot be expressed as an exact fraction or decimal, but that doesn't mean its value changes. Only your approximation of its value changes.

Circumference of Circles

176

When a car turns a corner, the tires on the right are actually sweeping out a section of a circle. The tires on the left are sweeping out a portion of a circle with a different radius. If the turn were to continue, the tires would sweep out the perimeters of complete circles. The shorter radius is called the **turning radius**.

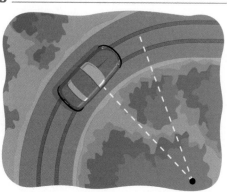

MORE HELP
See 174

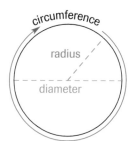

The **circumference** of a circle is the distance around it. It is always the same multiple (about 3.14) of the diameter of the circle.

MORE ▶

You can use the fact that π is, by definition, the ratio of the circumference to the diameter to write a formula for the circumference. This formula has two forms, one using the diameter and one using the radius of the circle.

Formula If a circle has circumference C, diameter d, and radius r, then $C = \pi d$ and $C = 2\pi r$. (F20)

Proof

Diagram

Given: Circle O of diameter d and radius r

Prove: $C = \pi d$ and $C = 2\pi r$

By definition, $\frac{C}{d} = \pi$. Multiplying both sides of the equation by d yields $C = \pi d$.
Since $2r = d$, $C = 2\pi r$ by substitution.

DID YOU KNOW In about 230 B.C., the Greek mathematician and geographer Eratosthenes determined the circumference of the earth.

On Midsummer's Day, he knew that the sun was directly overhead in Syene, Egypt. From where he was, near modern Aswan, Egypt, he measured the length of the shadow of a stick. He used similar triangles to show that the distance from Syene to Aswan was $\frac{1}{50}$ of Earth's diameter.

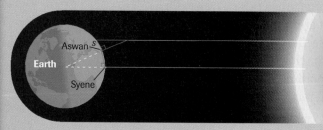

He then used the distance between these two cities, about 5000 stadia or 800 kilometers, to calculate the circumference of the earth.

$C = 50 \cdot 800 = 40{,}000$ km

His calculation was remarkably close to the actual circumference of 40,076 kilometers.

EXAMPLE: The tires of a bicycle have an 18.0-inch diameter. How many complete revolutions does each tire make on a one-mile trip?

Since you need to compare a distance in miles to one in inches, feet may be the most convenient unit to use. A mile is 5280 feet and the diameter of the tire is $\frac{18}{12}$ or 1.5 feet. Each revolution of a tire moves the bike forward a distance equal to the circumference of the tire. Write and solve an equation for the number of revolutions in a mile when C is the circumference of the tire in feet.

$$n = \frac{5280 \text{ feet}}{C}$$

$$n = \frac{5280}{\pi d}$$

> Since pi is an irrational number, you never compute with an exact value for pi. Use ≈ instead of = whenever you compute with an approximate value.

$$\approx \frac{5280}{3.14 \cdot 1.5}$$

$$\approx 1121.02$$

★ On a one-mile trip each tire makes about 1121 complete rotations.

Arc Length

An arc is a portion of a circle. You can find its length, called the **arc length**, if you know what portion of the whole circle it is.

MORE HELP
See 311

177

Formula

In a circle, the ratio of the length a of a given arc to the circumference is equal to the ratio of the measure of the arc to 360°; $\frac{a}{C} = \frac{m\widehat{AB}}{360°}$ and $a = \frac{m\widehat{AB}}{360°} \cdot 2\pi r$. (F21)

Diagram

length of arc
measure of arc

MORE ▶

EXAMPLE: The chain of a fixed-gear bicycle travels along the front and rear sprockets. How long is the chain to the nearest $\frac{1}{8}$ inch?

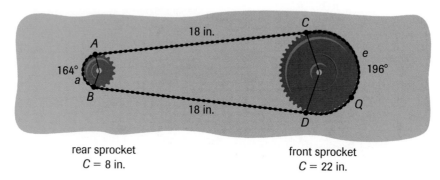

rear sprocket
C = 8 in.

front sprocket
C = 22 in.

For each sprocket, the chain goes around an arc whose measure equals its central angle. Because you know the circumference of each sprocket and the measure of the arc, you can find the arc length of each sprocket, which is the distance the chain will wrap around the sprocket. You know the circumference, not the radius of each sprocket. For the rear sprocket, use $C = 8$ in the formula and for the front sprocket, use $C = 22$ in the formula.

Find how much chain loops around the rear sprocket.

$$\frac{a}{C} = \frac{m\overset{\frown}{AB}}{360°}$$

$$\frac{a}{8} = \frac{164°}{360°}$$

$$a \approx 3.64$$

Find how much chain loops around the front sprocket.

$$\frac{e}{C} = \frac{m\overset{\frown}{CQD}}{360°}$$

$$\frac{e}{22} = \frac{196°}{360°}$$

$$e \approx 11.98$$

To find the total length of the chain, add.

Chain length $\approx 3.64 + 11.98 + 18 + 18$
≈ 51.62

> $\frac{62}{100}$ is between $\frac{50}{100}$ and $\frac{75}{100}$, so it's between $\frac{4}{8}$ and $\frac{6}{8}$.

★ The chain is $51\frac{5}{8}$ inches long to the nearest eighth of an inch.

Square Measurement in Polygons

Have you ever wished you could change something about your home? You might like to paint the walls, put in a new carpet, or even build a new patio. To do any of these projects, you would need to find or estimate an area.

The area of a plane figure is the number of square units that the figure covers. Area is measured in square units, such as square meters (m^2) or square feet (ft^2). For example, one square foot is the area of a square whose sides are each one foot long.

1 square foot · 1 foot · 1 foot

All of the formulas for areas of polygons are based on three postulates.

Postulate If two polygons are congruent, then they have the same area. Area ≅ Postulate (P17)

Postulate The area of a region is the sum of the areas of all of its non-overlapping parts. Area + Postulate (P18)

Formula The area of a square is the square of the length of its side; $A = s^2$. (F22)

MORE ▶

EXAMPLE: How does the area change when both dimensions of a square are doubled?

Compare the areas of the original squares with the areas of the new ones

$$\frac{\text{Area of square}_2}{\text{Area of square}_1} = \frac{2s \cdot 2s}{s \cdot s} = \frac{4s^2}{s^2} = 4$$

★ The area of the new figure is four times the area of the original square.

If only one dimension is doubled, the ratio of the areas of the two squares is $\frac{(s)(2s)}{s \cdot s} = \frac{2s^2}{s^2} = \frac{2}{1}$.

Square₁	Area₁	Double Two Dimensions	Area₂
	1 unit²		4 units²
	4 units²		16 units²
	16 units²		64 units²

---

179 **MATH ALERT A 4-Foot Square is not 4 ft²**

MORE HELP
See 186

A 4-foot square has sides four feet long. Its area is 16 ft².

The area of a 2-foot square is 4 ft².

---

180 **Area of a Rectangle** _____

Formula The area of a rectangle is the product of its length and width; $A = \ell w$. (F23)

Proof

Given: Rectangle with side lengths ℓ and w

Prove: $A(\text{rectangle}) = \ell w$

Plan: Construct a square with side lengths $s = \sqrt{\ell w}$. You know that its area is $\ell \cdot w$ by the Area of a Square Formula. If you can show that the area of the rectangle is equal to the area of the square, the formula will be proved. Show that the same-color pieces are congruent.

MORE HELP
See 220, 256, 271

Diagram

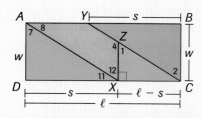
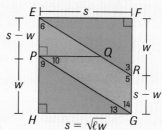

Part 1: All four large triangles are congruent.

Each triangle has a right angle, one side of length s and one side of length w, making them congruent by the SAS Congruence Postulate.

Part 2: The small triangles are congruent.

Statements	Reasons
❶ $\overline{ZX} \perp \overline{DC}$; $\overline{EP} \perp \overline{PQ}$	Construction
❷ $\overline{BC} \perp \overline{DC}$; $\overline{AD} \perp \overline{DC}$	Def. of rectangle
❸ $\overline{ZX} \parallel \overline{BC}$	2 lines in plane $\perp$ to 3rd line $\Rightarrow \parallel$ (T010)
❹ $\angle ZXC \cong \angle ADX \cong \angle EPQ$	All rt. $\angle$s $\cong$ (T020)
❺ $\overline{EH} \parallel \overline{FG}$	Def. of square
❻ $\angle 1 \cong \angle 2$, $\angle 3 \cong \angle 6$	Alt. Int. $\angle$s Theorem (T027)
❼ $\angle 2 \cong \angle 3$, $\angle 2 \cong \angle 7$	CPCTC Use $\triangle$s from Part 1.
❽ $\angle 1 \cong \angle 6$, $\angle 1 \cong \angle 7$	Transitive prop. of $\cong$ (T107)
❾ $\triangle CXZ \sim \triangle XDA$	AA $\sim$ Postulate (P21) Look back at steps 4 and 8.
❿ $\dfrac{w}{s} = \dfrac{XZ}{\ell - s}$	Def. of $\sim \triangle$s
⓫ $w(\ell - s) = XZ \cdot s$	Cross Product prop. (T091)
⓬ $XZ = \dfrac{\ell w - sw}{s}$	Distributive prop.; $\div$ prop. of $=$
⓭ $XZ = \dfrac{s^2 - sw}{s}$	Substitution Remember, you made $s = \sqrt{\ell w}$
⓮ $XZ = s - w$	Simplify
⓯ $XZ = EP$	Substitution Look back at the diagram.
⓰ $\triangle CXZ \cong \triangle QPE$	ASA $\cong$ Theorem (T108) See steps 4, 8, and 15.

Part 3: The two trapezoids are congruent.

Since $RG = s - w$, you know that $RG = XZ$ (see step 14 in part 2). $AX = PG$ by CPCTC using the congruent triangles ADX and PHG (part 1). Now $\angle 8 \cong \angle 10$, because they are both complements of the congruent angles $\angle 7$ and $\angle 9$. You also know that $\angle 12 \cong \angle 14$ because they are both complements of the congruent angles $\angle 11$ and $\angle 13$. And finally, $\angle 4 \cong \angle 5$, because they are both supplements of the congruent angles $\angle 1$ and $\angle 3$. This means that the two quadrilaterals are congruent by the ASASA $\cong$ Theorem.

The Area Congruence and Area Addition Postulates now allow you to conclude that the areas of the rectangle and square are the same, so the area of the rectangle is ℓw.

181

Area of a Triangle

You can find the area of a triangle by relating its area to the area of a rectangle. This can also help you find a formula for the area.

Formula The area of a triangle is half the product of a base and its corresponding height; $A = \frac{1}{2}bh$. (F24)

Plan: Since the altitude is involved in the formula, there are three cases of this theorem to consider.

■ The altitude is a side of the triangle.

■ The altitude lies inside the triangle.

■ The altitude lies outside the triangle.

CASE 1 The altitude is a side of the triangle.

Proof

Given: $\triangle LMN$ with height h and base b

Prove: $A(LMN) = \frac{1}{2}bh$

> $A(LMN)$ is a short way of saying Area of figure LMN.

Plan: First construct rectangle $LOMN$. Prove that $\triangle LMN \cong \triangle MLO$. Then the sum of the areas of the triangles must equal the area of the rectangle and the area of one triangle must be half the area of the rectangle.

Diagram

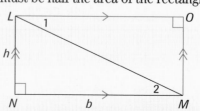

Statements	Reasons
❶ Construct rectangle *LOMN* with side-lengths *b* and *h*	Construction
❷ $\overline{LN} \cong \overline{OM}$, $\overline{LO} \cong \overline{NM}$	A rectangle is a parallelogram; parallelogram ⇒ opp. sides ≅ (T063)
❸ $LN = OM = h$; $LO = NM = b$	Def. of ≅ ; given
❹ $\overline{LM} \cong \overline{LM}$	Transitive prop. of ≅ (T107)
❺ $\triangle LMN \cong \triangle MLO$	SSS ≅ Postulate (P22)
❻ $A(LOMN) = A(LMN) + A(MLO)$	Area + Postulate (P18)
❼ $A(LOMN) = A(LMN) + A(LMN)$	Substitution
❽ $A(LOMN) = 2A(LMN)$	Distributive prop.
❾ $A(LOMN) = bh$	Area of rectangle formula (F23)
❿ $2A(LMN) = bh$	Substitution
⓫ $A(LMN) = \frac{1}{2}bh$	÷ prop. =

If the altitude is a side, then the triangle is a right triangle and you can also say that the area of a right triangle is half the product of the lengths of its legs.

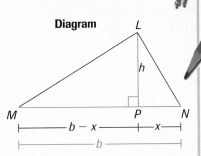

Diagram

CASE 2 The altitude lies inside the triangle.

Given: $\triangle LMN$ with height *h* and base *b*

Prove: $A(LMN) = \frac{1}{2}bh$

Plan: Begin by constructing the altitude to $\overline{MN}$, intersecting it at *P*. The area of $\triangle LMN$ is the sum of the areas of $\triangle LPM$ and $\triangle LPN$ by the Area Addition Postulate. Each of these triangles is a right triangle, so now you can use the results of Case 1 and the Distributive Property to complete Case 2.

MORE HELP
See 133, 180, 183, 375–376

CASE 3 The altitude lies outside the triangle.

Given: $\triangle LMN$ with height h and base b

Prove: $A(LMN) = \frac{1}{2}bh$

MORE HELP
See 241, 375

Diagram

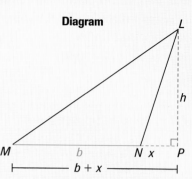

Plan: Begin by constructing the altitude to the line that contains $\overline{MN}$. Let P be the point where the altitude intersects $\overleftrightarrow{MN}$. Then the area of $\triangle LMN$ is the difference of the areas of the two right triangles, $\triangle LPM$ and $\triangle LPN$. Again you can use the results of Case 1 and the Distributive Property to complete the proof of Case 3.

Formula The area of a triangle is equal to half the product of any two sides and the sine of the included angle; $A = \frac{1}{2}ab \sin C.$ (F25)

Diagram

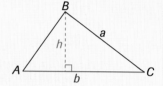

Proof

Given: $\triangle ABC$ with side lengths a and b, and m$\angle C$

Prove: $A(ABC) = \frac{1}{2}ab \sin C$

Plan: Since you know m$\angle C$, you can use a trigonometric ratio to find the height of the triangle. Construct the altitude to $\overline{AC}$ and use the sine ratio to find its length, h. Substitute that into the formula $A = \frac{1}{2}bh$.

Statements	Reasons
❶ $\triangle ABC$ with side lengths a and b	Given
❷ Construct the altitude to $\overline{AC}$	Construction
❸ $A(ABC) = \dfrac{1}{2}bh$	Area of a $\triangle$ formula (F24)
❹ $\sin C = \dfrac{h}{a}$	Def. of sine ratio
❺ $a \sin C = h$	$\times$ prop. of $=$
❻ $A(ABC) = \dfrac{1}{2}b \cdot a \sin C$	Substitution *See steps 3 and 5.*
❼ $A(ABC) = \dfrac{1}{2}ab \sin C$	Commutative prop. of $\times$

If you use this area formula with your calculator, be sure to use the degree mode when finding the sine of an angle given in degrees.

Hero's Formula

This formula was devised by the Greek mathematician, Hero, in the first century A.D. It uses the **semiperimeter** of a triangle with side lengths a, b, and c; $s = \frac{a + b + c}{2}$.

> **Formula**   The area of a triangle with side lengths a, b, and c, and semiperimeter s, is: $A = \sqrt{s(s - a)(s - b)(s - c)}$.
> Hero's Formula (F26)

EXAMPLE: Find the area of the scalene triangle.

ONE WAY You could use the Pythagorean Theorem to find h^2 in terms of x^2, then use the Pythagorean Theorem again to find x and again to find h. Then, you could use $A = \frac{1}{2}bh$ to find the area.

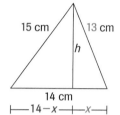

15 cm   13 cm
h
14 cm
$\longmapsto 14 - x \longmapsto x \longmapsto$

❶ Find h^2 in terms of x^2.	❷ Find x.	❸ Find h.
$h^2 + x^2 = 13^2$ $h^2 = 13^2 - x^2$ $= \boxed{169 - x^2}$	$h^2 + (14 - x)^2 = 15^2$ $\boxed{169 - x^2} + 196 - 28x + x^2 = 225$ $365 - 225 = 28x$ $140 = 28x$ $5 = x$	$h^2 + x^2 = 13^2$ $h^2 + 5^2 = 13^2$ $h^2 + 25 = 169$ $h^2 = 144$ $h = 12$

Now that you know $h = 12$, you can use the formula for the area of a triangle.

$$A = \frac{1}{2} bh$$
$$= \frac{1}{2} (14)(12)$$
$$= 84$$

ANOTHER WAY Use Hero's Formula. Let $a = 13$, $b = 14$, and $c = 15$.

Find the semiperimeter.

$$s = \frac{a + b + c}{2}$$
$$= \frac{13 + 14 + 15}{2}$$
$$= 21$$

Then find the area.

$$A = \sqrt{s(s - a)(s - b)(s - c)}$$
$$= \sqrt{21(21 - 13)(21 - 14)(21 - 15)}$$
$$= \sqrt{21(8)(7)(6)}$$
$$= \sqrt{7056}$$
$$= 84$$

★ Either way, the area of the triangle is 84 square centimeters.

Area of a Parallelogram

This diagram gives a convincing visual argument that the area of a parallelogram is equal to the area of a rectangle with the same base and height as the parallelogram.

Formula	The area of a parallelogram is the product of a base and its corresponding height; $A = bh$. (F27)

Proof

Diagram

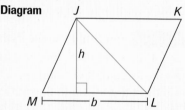

Given: Parallelogram $JKLM$

Prove: $A(JKLM) = bh$

Plan: The diagonal divides the parallelogram into congruent triangles, each with an area of $\frac{1}{2}bh$. Use the Area Addition Postulate to show that the area of the parallelogram is the sum of these two areas, or bh.

Statements	Reasons
❶ Parallelogram $JKLM$	Given
❷ Draw diagonal $\overline{JL}$	Two pts. determine a line (P05)
❸ $\overline{JM} \cong \overline{KL}$; $\overline{JK} \cong \overline{ML}$	Parallelogram $\Rightarrow$ opp. sides $\cong$ (T063)
❹ $\overline{JL} \cong \overline{JL}$	Transitive prop. of $\cong$ (T107)
❺ $\triangle JKL \cong \triangle LMJ$	SSS $\cong$ Postulate (P22)
❻ $A(LMJ) = \frac{1}{2}bh$	Area of a $\triangle$ formula (F24)
❼ $A(JKL) = A(LMJ) = \frac{1}{2}bh$	Area $\cong$ postulate (P17)
❽ $A(JKLM) = A(JKL) + A(LMJ)$	Area $+$ postulate (P18)
❾ $A(JKLM) = \frac{1}{2}bh + \frac{1}{2}bh$	Substitution
❿ $A(JKLM) = bh$	Distributive prop.

Any of the sides of a parallelogram can be used as the base. However, be sure the altitude is a segment perpendicular to that base.

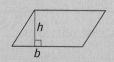
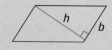

Area of a Regular Polygon

In a regular hexagon, all sides are congruent and all angles are congruent. Suppose you want to tile a floor with regular hexagonal tiles. You need to know the area that one tile covers to estimate the number of tiles you need to cover the floor. You can find this area if you know the length of one side of the hexagon and the length of the apothem. The **apothem** is the perpendicular segment from the center of a regular polygon to one of its sides.

MORE HELP
See 073, 129

Regular Pentagon

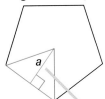

Regular Hexagon

Regular Octagon

The length of the apothem is the height of the triangle formed by a side and the two segments from the center to the endpoints of this side.

The side of the polygon is the base of the triangle.

Formula

The area of a regular polygon is half the product of the apothem, a, and the perimeter, P; $A = \frac{1}{2}aP$. (F28)

MORE HELP
See 129

Proof

Given: A regular polygon

Prove: $A = \frac{1}{2}aP$

Diagram

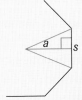

Plan: Remember that the area of a triangle is $\frac{1}{2}bh$, where b is length of the base of the triangle and h is height, and that a regular n-gon will be made up of n congruent triangles. Draw an apothem and segments from the center to two consecutive vertices of the n-gon. Use the fact that the perimeter of a regular polygon is $P = ns$ to simplify the formula.

$A = (\text{area of one congruent } \triangle) \cdot (\text{number of } \triangle s)$

$= \frac{1}{2}as \cdot n$

$= \frac{1}{2}a(ns)$

Note that an equivalent form of the formula is $A = \frac{1}{2}ans$, where a = length of apothem, n = number of sides, and s = length of one side.

$= \frac{1}{2}aP$

MORE ▶

MORE HELP
See 172, 181

EXAMPLE: Find the area of a regular pentagon with an apothem of 6 cm.

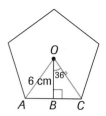

Begin by drawing a regular pentagon. Construct and label an apothem. Then draw the triangle containing the center and the two endpoints of the side that the apothem intersects.

To use the formula, you must find the length, s, of each side of the pentagon. You already know $a = 6$ and $n = 5$.

Because the pentagon is regular, you know that m$\angle AOC = \frac{360°}{5}$, or 72°. Then m$\angle BOC = \frac{1}{2}(72°)$, or 36°. Use the tangent ratio to estimate BC, and then double to find s.

Find $\overline{BC}$.

$$\tan 36° = \frac{BC}{6}$$

Since tan 36° is a rounded number, use ≈ to show that your answer is not exact.

$$0.7265 \approx \frac{BC}{6}$$

$$4.359 \approx BC$$

Find s.

$$s = 2BC$$
$$\approx 2(4.359)$$
$$\approx 8.718$$

Substitute a, n, and s into the area formula.

$$A = \frac{1}{2}ans$$

$$\approx \frac{1}{2}(6)(5)(8.718)$$

$$\approx 130.77$$

★ The area of this regular pentagon is about 131 square centimeters.

Area of an Equilateral Triangle

To find the area of an equilateral triangle, use the formula for the area of a regular polygon, the formula for the area of any triangle, or this formula.

Formula   The area of an equilateral triangle is one-fourth the square of the length of a side times $\sqrt{3}$; $A = \frac{s^2\sqrt{3}}{4}$. (F29)

Proof

Diagram

Given: $AB = BC = CA$.

Prove: $A(ABC) = \frac{s^2\sqrt{3}}{4}$

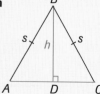

Plan: An equilateral triangle has two congruent sides so theorems for isosceles triangles apply to equilateral triangles. This means that altitude $\overline{BD}$ is also the perpendicular bisector of $\overline{AC}$. Use this fact and the Pythagorean Theorem to get an expression for h, then use that expression in the formula for the area of a triangle.

Statements	Reasons
❶ $AB = BC = CA$	Given
❷ Construct altitude from B to $\overline{AC}$	Construction
❸ $\overline{BD}$ is $\perp$ bisector of $\overline{AC}$	Isos. $\triangle \Rightarrow$ vertex $\angle$ bisector, $\perp$ bisector of base, altitude, median to base same line (T044)
❹ $DC = \dfrac{AC}{2} = \dfrac{s}{2}$	Def. of $\perp$ bisector
❺ $\left(\dfrac{s}{2}\right)^2 + h^2 = s^2$	Pythagorean Theorem (T059)
❻ $h^2 = s^2 - \dfrac{s^2}{4}$ $= \dfrac{3s^2}{4}$	Subtraction prop. of $=$
❼ $h = \dfrac{s\sqrt{3}}{2}$	Simplify
❽ $A(ABC) = \dfrac{1}{2}s \cdot \dfrac{s\sqrt{3}}{2}$	Area of a $\triangle$ formula (F24)
❾ $A(ABC) = \dfrac{s^2\sqrt{3}}{4}$	Simplify

MORE HELP
See 181, 184, 239, 375

EXAMPLE: Find the area of an equilateral triangle with sides of 6 meters.

Use $s = 6$ in the formula for the area of an equilateral triangle.

$$A = \dfrac{s^2\sqrt{3}}{4}$$
$$= \dfrac{(6^2)\sqrt{3}}{4}$$
$$= \dfrac{36\sqrt{3}}{4}$$
$$= 9\sqrt{3}$$
$$\approx 15.59$$

★ The area is about 15.6 square meters.

Area of Similar Polygons

If the scale factor of two similar polygons is k, then the ratio of their perimeters is $1:k$ and the ratio of their areas is $1:k^2$.

MORE HELP
See 173, 180

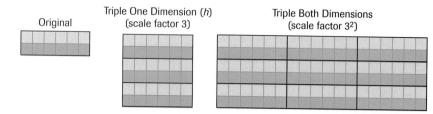

Original

Triple One Dimension (h)
(scale factor 3)

Triple Both Dimensions
(scale factor 3^2)

Theorem If two polygons are similar with corresponding sides in the ratio of $a:b$, then the ratio of their areas is $a^2:b^2$.

~ polygons, corresp. sides $a:b \Rightarrow$ areas $a^2:b^2$ (T085)

Proof

Read A(A)
as Area of
polygon A.

Given: Figure A ~ Figure B; ratio of corresponding sides $a:b$

Prove: $\dfrac{A(A)}{A(B)} = \dfrac{a^2}{b^2}$

Diagram

Plan: A proof using rectangles can be generalized to any two similar polygons. Draw two similar rectangles and compare the areas.

Statements	Reasons	
❶ $\dfrac{\ell_1}{\ell_2} = \dfrac{a}{b}, \dfrac{w_1}{w_2} = \dfrac{a}{b}$	Given	
❷ $\ell_1 b = \ell_2 a, w_1 b = w_2 a$	Cross Product prop. (T091)	
❸ $\ell_1 = \ell_2\left(\dfrac{a}{b}\right), w_1 = w_2\left(\dfrac{a}{b}\right)$	÷ prop. of =	
❹ $A(A) = \ell_1 w_1, A(B) = \ell_2 w_2$	Area of a rectangle formula (F23)	
❺ $A(A) = \ell_2\left(\dfrac{a}{b}\right) \cdot w_2\left(\dfrac{a}{b}\right)$	Substitution	Look back at steps 3 and 4.
❻ $A(A) = \ell_2 w_2\left(\dfrac{a^2}{b^2}\right)$	Simplify	
❼ $\dfrac{A(A)}{A(B)} = \dfrac{\ell_2 w_2\left(\frac{a^2}{b^2}\right)}{\ell_2 w_2}$	Substitution	Look back at steps 4 and 6.
❽ $\dfrac{A(A)}{A(B)} = \dfrac{a^2}{b^2}$	Simplify	

EXAMPLE: A friend sends you a digital photograph that you want to print in two sizes. Photographic paper is available in 4-inch by 6-inch sheets and 8-inch by 12-inch sheets. One sheet of the smaller size paper costs $0.15. If the cost of the paper is directly related to its area, what is the cost for the larger sized paper?

The ratio of the side-lengths of the two rectangular sheets of paper is 1:2. Both the length and the width are increased by the same scale factor. This means that the ratio of the areas of the sheets of paper is $1^2:2^2$ or 1:4. The cost of the larger sheet should be about four times the cost of the smaller sheet.

★ An 8-inch by 12-inch sheet of photographic paper should cost $0.60.

Area of a Quadrilateral with Perpendicular Diagonals

Sometimes you don't know the lengths of the base or the altitude of a quadrilateral. If the quadrilateral has perpendicular diagonals (as in rhombuses, kites, and squares), you can find the area using the diagonals.

MORE HELP
See 156

Formula | If the diagonals of a quadrilateral are perpendicular, then the area is half the product of the diagonals; $A = \frac{1}{2}d_1 d_2$ (F30)

Proof

Given: ⊥ diagonals of lengths d_1 and d_2 in quadrilateral $PQRS$

Prove: $A(PQRS) = \frac{1}{2}d_1d_2$

Plan: A diagonal divides the quadrilateral into two triangles with the same base. The two segments of the other diagonal are altitudes of the two triangles. The area of the quadrilateral is the sum of the areas of the two triangles, so use the formula for the area of a triangle to find the area of the whole quadrilateral.

Diagram

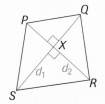

MORE ▶

MORE HELP
See 153

Statements	Reasons
❶ d_1 and d_2 are the lengths of the diagonals in $PQRS$	Given
❷ $\overline{QS} \perp \overline{PR}$	Given
❸ $\overline{PX}$ is an altitude of $\triangle PQS$; $\overline{RX}$ is an altitude of $\triangle QRS$	Def. of altitude
❹ $A(PQS) = \frac{1}{2}d_1 \cdot PX$ $A(QRS) = \frac{1}{2}d_1 \cdot RX$	Area of a $\triangle$ formula (F24)
❺ $A(PQRS) = A(PQS) + A(QRS)$	Area + postulate (P18)
❻ $A(PQRS) = \frac{1}{2}d_1 \cdot PX + \frac{1}{2}d_1 \cdot RX$	Substitution
❼ $A(PQRS) = \frac{1}{2}d_1(PX + RX)$	Distributive prop.
❽ $PX + RX = PR = d_2$	Seg. + postulate (P09)
❾ $A(PQRS) = \frac{1}{2}d_1 d_2$	Substitution

EXAMPLE: Find the area of the rhombus.

Given what you know, it is best to use the area formula that uses the lengths of the perpendicular diagonals. The Pythagorean Theorem tells you that each triangle within the rhombus is a 3-4-5 right triangle, so the diagonals have lengths 6 meters and 8 meters.

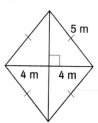

$A = \frac{1}{2}d_1 d_2$

$= \frac{1}{2} \cdot 6 \cdot 8$

$= 24$

★ The area of the rhombus is 24 square meters.

188 ## Area of a Trapezoid

Formula The area of a trapezoid is half the product of the height and the sum of the bases; $A = \frac{1}{2}h(b_1 + b_2)$. (F31)

$\frac{1}{2}(b_1 + b_2)$ is the mean of the two bases, so you might think of the formula as Area = mean of the bases × height.

Proof

Given: trapezoid $PQRS$, with height h and bases b_1 and b_2

Prove: $A = \frac{1}{2}h(b_1 + b_2)$

Diagram

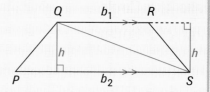

ONE WAY **Plan:** Draw diagonal $\overline{QS}$. Then find the sum of the areas of the two triangles. Because the distance between parallel lines is constant, the heights of $\triangle QRS$ and $\triangle PQS$ are both equal to h.

Statements	Reasons
❶ $PQRS$ is a trapezoid with height h and bases b_1 and b_2	Given
❷ $\overline{QR} \parallel \overline{PS}$	Def. of trapezoid
❸ Draw diagonal $\overline{QS}$	2 pts. determine a line (P05)
❹ h is the length of the altitude of $\triangle QRS$ and $\triangle QPS$	Dist. between $\parallel$ lines constant (T004)
❺ $A(\triangle QRS) = \frac{1}{2}b_1 h,\ A(\triangle PQS) = \frac{1}{2}b_2 h$	Area of a $\triangle$ formula (F24)
❻ $A(PQRS) = A(\triangle QRS) + A(\triangle PQS)$	Area + Postulate (P18)
❼ $A(PQRS) = \frac{1}{2}b_1 h + \frac{1}{2}b_2 h$	Substitution
❽ $A(PQRS) = \frac{1}{2}h(b_1 + b_2)$	Distributive prop.

ANOTHER WAY If you cut up any trapezoid, you can rearrange the pieces to make a rectangle and a triangle.

Cut off right triangles, leaving a rectangle.

The area of a rectangle is its length times its width, so the area of this rectangle is $b_1\, h$.

Push the two triangles together at their right angles. The area of this triangle is $\frac{1}{2}(b_2 - b_1)h$.

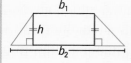

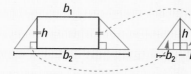

Use the distributive property and combine like terms to show that the area of the rectangle plus $\frac{1}{2}$ the area of the two triangles is equal to $\frac{1}{2}h(b_1 + b_2)$.

Consider each of the regular polygons below. Each polygon has a perimeter of 24 units. Which polygon has the greatest area?

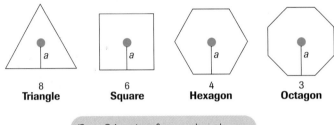

8	6	4	3
Triangle	**Square**	**Hexagon**	**Octagon**

P = 24 units for each polygon

To help you decide, recall the formula for the area of a regular polygon: $A = \frac{1}{2}aP$, where a is the length of the apothem and P is the perimeter of the polygon. Since the perimeters of these polygons are equal, their areas will increase as the lengths of their apothems increase. It seems that the polygon with the most sides has the longest apothem, and indeed this is the case.

Theorem   Of all plane figures with the same perimeter, the circle has maximum area. Isoperimetric Theorem (2-d) (T086)

If you think of a circle as a polygon with an infinite number of sides, then a circle with a 24-unit circumference should have a larger area than polygons with that perimeter.

Area of a Circle

Formula The area of a circle is π times the square of the radius; $A = \pi r^2$. (F32)

MORE HELP
See 174, 176

Diagram

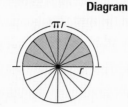

To convince yourself that the formula works, make a model. Divide a circle into 16 congruent wedges. You can do this by using a compass to draw a large circle and then folding the circle in half four times to create congruent wedges. If you unfold the circle and cut out all the congruent wedges, you can form a figure that resembles a parallelogram.

The height of this near-parallelogram approaches r, the radius of the circle. The length of the base is one half circumference $\left(\frac{1}{2} \cdot 2\pi r\right)$ of the circle, or πr. Write the equation that describes the area.

$A \approx bh$
$\quad \approx \pi r \cdot r$ By cutting your circle into more and more wedges, the
$\quad \approx \pi r^2$ near-parallelogram will look more and more like a true
parallelogram and the formula will remain the same.

EXAMPLE: You have a recipe for an 8-inch round pizza, but you want to make a pizza for your 16-inch round pan. Will doubling the recipe be enough to fill your pizza pan?

Compare the areas of the large pizza pan and the small pizza. For the small pizza, $r = 4$ in. and for the large pan, $r = 8$ in.

8 in. 16 in.

Find the area of the small pizza.

$A = \pi r^2$
$\quad = \pi(4)^2$
$\quad = 16\pi$

Find the area of the large pan.

$A = \pi r^2$
$\quad = \pi(8)^2$
$\quad = 64\pi$

MORE HELP
See 186

★ The area of the large pan is four times as great as the area of the smaller pizza. Doubling the recipe will not make enough.

In general, if the ratio of the radii of two circles is $r_1:r_2$, then the ratio of their areas is $r_1^2:r_2^2$. This is analogous to the case of similar polygons with sides in the ratio $a:b$ and area in the ratio $a^2:b^2$.

Area of a Sector

A **sector** of a circle is the region bounded by two radii of the circle and the arc they intercept.

MORE HELP
See 176–177

Just as arc length is part of the circumference of a circle, the area of a sector is part of the area of a circle. The fractional part of the area that a sector contains depends on the measure of the central angle.

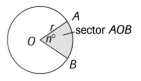

sector AOB

Formula The ratio of the area, A, of a sector to the area of its circle is equal to the ratio of the measure of the intercepted arc to 360°; $\frac{A}{\pi r^2} = \frac{m\widehat{RQ}}{360°}$. (F33)

Proof

Given: Sector AOB with $m\angle O = n°$

Prove: $\dfrac{A(\text{sector } AOB)}{\pi r^2} = \dfrac{m\widehat{AB}}{360°}$

Diagram

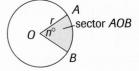

sector AOB

Plan: Since degree measure divides a circle into 360 congruent wedges, $\frac{n}{360°}$ represents the fraction of the total area of the circle that is in the sector. To find this area, multiply the fraction of the area by the total area.

Area of a fraction of a circle $= \dfrac{n°}{360°}(\pi r^2)$

Area of sector $AOB = \dfrac{m\widehat{AB}}{360°}(\pi r^2)$

$\dfrac{A(\text{sector } AOB)}{\pi r^2} = \dfrac{m\widehat{AB}}{360°}$

EXAMPLE: A Rose Parade float must be completely covered with plant material. What is the ratio of poppy seeds to sesame seeds on this portion of the float?

poppy seeds

sesame seeds

You know that the angle between hands of a clock at 4 p.m. is 120°. Use the formula to find the ratio of poppy seeds to all seeds.

$$\frac{A(\text{sector } AOB)}{\pi r^2} = \frac{m\widehat{AB}}{360°}$$

$$= \frac{120°}{360°}$$

$$= \frac{1}{3}$$

The ratio of poppy seeds to all seeds is $\frac{\text{poppy seeds}}{\text{poppy seeds } + \text{ sesame seeds}} = \frac{1}{3}$.

The ratio of poppy seeds to sesame seeds is $\frac{1}{2}$.

★ The ratio of poppy seeds to sesame seeds is $\frac{1}{2}$.

Area of a Segment of a Circle

A **segment** of a circle is a region bounded by a chord and the minor arc that it intercepts. You can find the area of the segment by subtracting the area of the triangle from the area of the sector.

MORE HELP
See 178, 182, 191, 310

Formula The area of a segment is: area of sector − area of triangle formed by the chord and two radii. (F34)

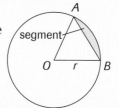

This formula follows directly from the Area Addition Postulate.

EXAMPLE: You own a wedge-shaped lot. Your city wants to buy the segment of your lot to widen the street. The price it will pay depends on the area of the segment. What is its area?

The segment is bounded by $\overline{QR}$ and $\widehat{QR}$. Now use the formula for the area of a segment. For the area of the triangle, use Hero's formula, with $s = \frac{200 \; + \; 200 \; + \; 150}{2}$ or $s = 275$.

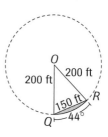

Area of segment = area of sector − area of triangle

$$= \frac{m\widehat{QR}}{360°} \cdot \pi r^2 - \sqrt{s(s-a)(s-b)(s-c)}$$

$$\approx \frac{44°}{360°}(3.14)(200)^2 - \sqrt{275(75)(75)(125)}$$

$$\approx 15{,}351.11 - 13{,}905.37$$

$$\approx 1445.74$$

★ The area of the segment is about 1446 square feet.

A region may seem too irregular to find its area accurately. However, many irregular shapes can be decomposed into familiar shapes for which you can find the area.

EXAMPLE 1: Suppose you wanted to make an envelope. How can you find out how much paper you need?

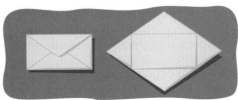

If you have an envelope to use as a model, you can unfold it and see how it was made.

★ To find the area of the envelope, first you can find the area of the rectangle in the center. Then you can find the areas of the pairs of congruent triangles that are folded over and sealed to make the envelope.

EXAMPLE 2: Every spring your high school puts a new surface on the running track. How many square meters must be resurfaced?

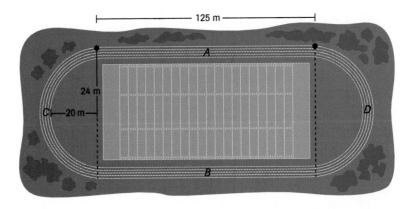

The track is composed of two congruent rectangles (A and B) and two congruent curves (C and D). You can find the area of each curved section by subtracting the area of the smaller semicircular region from the area of the larger semicircular region.

Area of the two congruent rectangles = $2bh$

$$= 2(125)(4)$$

$$= 1000$$

The difference of the two radii, 24 m − 20 m is 4 m.

Area of the two curves $= 2\left(\dfrac{1}{2}\right)\pi r_2^2 - 2\left(\dfrac{1}{2}\right)\pi r_1^2$

> Since two semicircles with the same radius form one circle, the area of a semicircular region is $\frac{1}{2}(\pi r^2)$.

$$= \pi(r_2^2 - r_1^2)$$
$$\approx 3.14(24^2 - 20^2)$$
$$\approx 3.14(576 - 400)$$
$$\approx 552.64$$

Total area $\approx 1000 + 522.64 \approx 1552.64$

★ About 1553 square meters must be resurfaced.

Suppose you are looking at a map and want to know the area of one of its regions. Here, too, you can estimate area by dividing an irregular shape into shapes for which you can easily find the area.

EXAMPLE 3: Based on this map of Indiana, estimate its area.

Look for familiar shapes that make up the area of Indiana. You can approximate the area with a rectangle and a trapezoid.

Check the map dimensions, then use the scale to write these measurements in miles. Since 1 inch = 80 miles or $\frac{1}{8}$ inch = 10 miles, you know that the dimensions are 150 miles by 220 miles for the rectangular region; b_1 is 80 miles, b_2 is 120 miles, and h is 60 miles for the trapezoidal region.

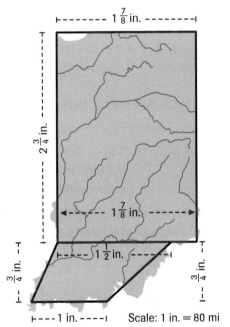

Scale: 1 in. = 80 mi

Find the area of the rectangle.

$A = bh$
$\quad = 150 \times 220$
$\quad = 33,000$

Find the area of the trapezoid.

$A = \dfrac{1}{2}h(b_1 + b_2)$
$\quad = \dfrac{1}{2}(60)(80 + 120)$
$\quad = 6000$

Total area $= 33,000 + 6000$
$\qquad\qquad = 39,000$

> The actual area of Indiana is 36,290 square miles, so the estimate is reasonable.

★ This technique gives about 39,000 square miles as the area of Indiana.

194 Square Measurement in Solids

Prisms, pyramids, cylinders, and cones have plane figures for faces. You can use their two-dimensional faces to find the areas of their entire surfaces.

195 Surface Area

You can memorize and use formulas for the areas of the surfaces of common three-dimensional figures. Or, you can use what you know about the area of circles and polygons to look at each face or group of faces separately.

MORE HELP See 326

196 Surface Area of a Prism

Formula The surface area of a right prism is $SA = 2B + Ph$; B is the area of a base, P is the perimeter of a base, and h is the height of the prism. (F35)

You can see why this formula works by using a net. Imagine that you cut this hexagonal prism along some of its edges to form its net.

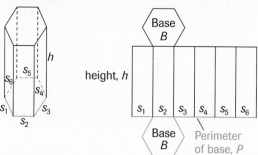

Each of the six lateral faces is a rectangle. Their total area is the product of the height of the prism and the perimeter of the base.

SA = (area of both bases) + (area of the lateral faces)

Area of bases = $2B$

Area of lateral faces $= s_1h + s_2h + \ldots + s_6h$
$= (s_1 + s_2 + \ldots + s_6)h$
$= Ph$

EXAMPLE: A door wedge is coated with a plastic seal. How many square inches of plastic do you need to cover the door wedge?

Find the surface area.

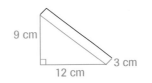

9 cm
12 cm
3 cm

MORE HELP
See 153

The right triangle is a multiple of a 3-4-5 right triangle, so the hypotenuse is 15 centimeters long and $P = 9 + 12 + 15$ or 36.

$$SA = 2B + Ph$$

Each base of the prism (with an area of B) is a right triangle, so $B = \frac{1}{2}(9)(12)$ or 54.

The height is the distance between the bases: $h = 3$.

$SA = 2B + Ph$

$= 2(54) + 36(3)$

$= 216$

★ You need 216 square centimeters of plastic.

Surface Area of a Cylinder

197

Formula
The surface area of a right circular cylinder is $SA = 2B + Ch$ or $SA = 2\pi r^2 + 2\pi rh$; B is the area of a base, C is the circumference of a base, r is the radius of a base, and h is the height of the cylinder. (F36)

MORE HELP
See 330

The net shows why the formula for the surface area of a cylinder works.

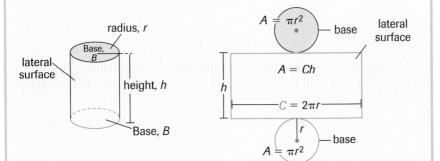

radius, r
Base, B
lateral surface
height, h
Base, B

$A = \pi r^2$ — base
lateral surface
$A = Ch$
h
$C = 2\pi r$
r — base
$A = \pi r^2$

MORE ▶

EXAMPLE: About how many square inches of sheet metal were used to make this soda can?

$SA = 2\pi r^2 + 2\pi rh$

$\approx 2(3.14)(2.5)^2 + 2(3.14)(2.5)(12)$

≈ 227.65

★ About 228 square centimeters of sheet metal were used to make the can.

198

Surface Area of a Cone

Formula   The surface area of a right cone is $SA = \pi r^2 + \pi r\ell$; r is the radius of the base, and ℓ is the slant height of the cone. (F37)

Proof

Given: Slant height ℓ and radius r of a right cone

Prove: $SA = \pi r^2 + \pi r\ell$

Plan: Use the net of a cone to show that the surface area is the sum of the areas of the circular base and a sector of a circle. Use the given information to write an expression for each piece of the net.

Diagram

slant height, ℓ

lateral surface

$A = \pi r\ell$
$C = 2\pi r$

$A = \pi r^2$

Base, B

To find the area of the sector, you don't have the angle measure given to you in degrees. Instead, you need to compare the arc length of the sector (which is equal to the circumference of the base) to the arc length of the whole circle with radius ℓ to find out how much of this larger circle is in the sector.

First, find the area of the circle.

$A = \pi r^2$

MORE HELP
See 191, 331

Next, find the area of the sector.

$$\frac{A \text{ (sector)}}{A \text{ (circle)}} = \frac{\text{Arc length of sector}}{\text{Circumference of circle}}$$

$$A(\text{sector}) = \frac{A \text{ (circle)} \cdot \text{Arc length of sector}}{\text{Circumference of circle}}$$

$\pi\ell^2$ is the area of the entire circle with radius ℓ.

$$= \frac{\pi\ell^2 \cdot 2\pi r}{2\pi\ell}$$

$2\pi r$ is the arc length, which is equal to the circumference of the smaller circle (radius r).

$$= \frac{\frac{1}{2}\pi^2\ell^2 r}{\frac{1}{2\pi_1\ell}}$$

This is the circumference of the larger circle (radius ℓ).

$$= \pi r\ell$$

Then the total surface area is $SA = \pi r^2 + \pi r\ell$, the area of the base plus the area of the sector.

Surface Area of a Pyramid

199

Formula   The surface area of a regular pyramid is $SA = B + \frac{1}{2}P\ell$; B is the area of the base, P is the perimeter of the base, and ℓ is the slant height of the pyramid. (F38)

MORE HELP
See 327

Proof

Diagram

slant height, ℓ

Given: A regular pyramid; area of base is B, perimeter of base is P, and slant height is ℓ

Prove: $SA = B + \frac{1}{2}P\ell$

The area of each lateral face is $\frac{1}{2}b\ell$ where b is the length of one side of the base. The perimeter of the base is $5b$.

$SA = (\text{Area of base}) + 5(\text{Area of lateral face})$

$$= B + 5\left(\frac{1}{2}b\ell\right)$$

$$= B + \frac{1}{2}(5b)\ell$$

$$= B + \frac{1}{2}P\ell$$

MORE HELP
See 152, 134, 327

MATH ALERT The Height and Slant Height of Pyramids and Cones are Not the Same

Don't use an *edge* or *altitude* when you need the slant height. In the formula for the surface area of a regular pyramid or a right cone, ℓ is the slant height. Remember, the slant height is the altitude of a face or lateral surface.

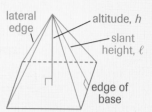

EXAMPLE 1: Find the slant height of the square pyramid.

Use the Pythagorean Theorem.

$(\text{slant height})^2 = 42^2 + 20^2$
$(\text{slant height})^2 = 2164$
$\quad\text{slant height} = \sqrt{2164}$
$\quad\quad\quad\quad\quad \approx 46.52$

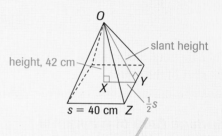

In a regular pyramid, the altitude intersects the apothem at the center of the base. If the base is a square, the length of the apothem is $\frac{1}{2}s$.

★ The slant height is about 46.5 centimeters.

EXAMPLE 2: Find the length of a lateral edge of the pyramid in Example 1.

ONE WAY Use $\triangle OYZ$.

In Example 1 you found that $OY = \sqrt{2164}$. Use this as the length of one side in the Pythagorean Theorem.

$OZ^2 = \left(\sqrt{2164}\right)^2 + 20^2$
$\quad\quad = 2164 + 400$
$\quad\quad = 2564$
$OZ \approx 50.64$

ANOTHER WAY Use $\triangle OZX$. Since the base of the pyramid is a square, the length of its diagonal is $40\sqrt{2}$. This means that $XZ = 20\sqrt{2}$. Now use the Pythagorean Theorem.

$OZ^2 = 42^2 + \left(20\sqrt{2}\right)^2$
$\quad\quad = 1764 + 800$
$\quad\quad = 2564$
$OZ \approx 50.64$

★ Either way, the length of a lateral edge is about 50.6 centimeters.

Surface Area of a Sphere

MORE HELP
See 238, 332

Formula The surface area of a sphere with radius r is $SA = 4\pi r^2$.
(F39)

This proof relies on techniques of calculus, and is beyond the scope of this book, but you can get a sense of its accuracy by comparing this formula to the formulas for the surface areas of a cone and a cylinder.

The surface area of a sphere lies between the lateral area of a double cone and the surface area of a cylinder.

  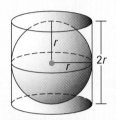

ℓ is the hypotenuse of an isosceles right triangle with legs of length r, so from the 45°-45°-90° triangle relationships, $\ell = r\sqrt{2}$.

$$
\begin{aligned}
L.A. \text{ (cones)} &= 2(\pi r\ell) \\
&= 2(\pi r \cdot r\sqrt{2}) \\
&= 2\sqrt{2}\pi r^2 \\
&\approx 2.8\pi r^2
\end{aligned}
\qquad
\begin{aligned}
SA \text{ (cylinder)} &= 2\pi r^2 + 2\pi rh \\
&= 2\pi r^2 + 2\pi r \cdot 2r \\
&= 2\pi r^2 + 4\pi r^2 \\
&= 6\pi r^2
\end{aligned}
$$

Lateral area of cones < Surface area of sphere < Surface area of cylinder

$$2.8\pi r^2 \quad < \quad 4\pi r^2 \quad < \quad 6\pi r^2$$

EXAMPLE: The radius of a baseball is about 1.45 in. About how much leather is needed to cover a baseball?

The leather covers the outer surface of a baseball. Use the formula for the surface area of a sphere with $r \approx 1.45$.

$$
\begin{aligned}
SA &= 4\pi r^2 \\
&\approx 4(3.14)(1.45)^2 \\
&\approx 26.4
\end{aligned}
$$

★ A baseball uses about 26.4 square inches of leather for its covering.

Surface Area of Similar Solids

If you take a prism or other solid and multiply each dimension by a number k, you get a new solid similar to the original. It has the same shape, but not the same size (unless $k = 1$). Two solids with equal ratios of corresponding linear measures, such as lengths, widths, heights, and radii, are called **similar solids**. The following theorem shows how any pair of corresponding areas (such as lateral, base, or surface areas) in similar solids are related.

MORE HELP
See 186

Theorem

If two solids are similar with a scale factor of $a{:}b$, then the corresponding surface areas have a ratio of $a^2{:}b^2$.

~ solids, corresp. sides $a{:}b \Rightarrow$ corresp. areas $a^2{:}b^2$ (T087)

Proof

Given: Solid A ~ solid B with corresponding sides in the ratio $a{:}b$

Prove: $\dfrac{\text{Surface area of solid A}}{\text{Surface area of solid B}} = \dfrac{a^2}{b^2}$

Form the nets of solids A and B. Since the solids are similar, so are their nets. Corresponding areas have a ratio of $a^2{:}b^2$, because they are plane figures with a ratio of corresponding linear measures of $a{:}b$.

Diagram

A

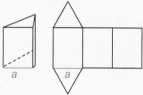

a a

B

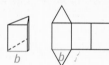

b b

Geometric Probability

Probability is the measure of the likelihood of an event occurring. It is always a number n, $0 \le n \le 1$. An event with a probability of 0 cannot occur. An event with a probability of 1 is certain to occur.

You may be familiar with the probability of an event as the ratio of the number of favorable outcomes to the number of possible outcomes when all the outcomes are equally likely.

$$P(\text{event}) = \frac{\text{number of favorable outcomes}}{\text{number of possible outcomes}}$$

Finding **geometric probability** is a similar process. When you want to find the probability of randomly selecting a particular region from within a larger region, the probability is the ratio of areas of the two regions.

Let R be a region that contains region S. If a point N in R is chosen at random, then the probability that it will also be in S is:

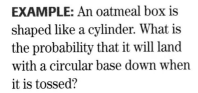

$$P(N \text{ is in S}) = \frac{\text{area of S}}{\text{area of R}}$$

EXAMPLE: An oatmeal box is shaped like a cylinder. What is the probability that it will land with a circular base down when it is tossed?

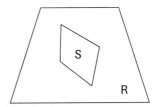

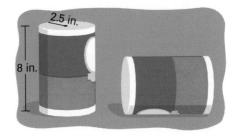

Geometric probability applies to surface areas as well as plane areas. The particular area is the area of the bases, and the total area is the total surface area of the cylinder.

$$P(\text{land on its base}) = \frac{\text{area of circular bases}}{\text{surface area of cylinder}}$$

$$= \frac{2\pi r^2}{2\pi r^2 + 2\pi rh}$$

$$= \frac{\overset{1}{\cancel{2}}\,\cancel{\pi}\,\cancel{r^2}^{r}}{\underset{1}{\cancel{2}}\,\underset{1}{\cancel{\pi}}\,\cancel{r}(r + h)}$$

$$= \frac{r}{r + h}$$

$$= \frac{2.5}{2.5 + 8}$$

$$= \frac{2.5}{10.5}$$

$$\approx 0.238$$

★ The probability that it will land on a base is about 23.8%.

The design of some containers makes them look as if they hold more than they actually do. The volume of juice, shampoo, or other material in a container depends not only on the size of the container but on the shape as well.

The **volume** of a solid is a measure of the amount of space it occupies or encloses. It is measured in cubic units, such as cubic inches (in.³), cubic feet (ft³), cubic centimeters (cm³), or cubic meters (m³).

MORE HELP
See 209, 304

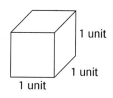

1 unit
1 unit
1 unit

1 cubic unit

To find the volume of this box, think of filling it with one-inch ice cubes. The volume is the total number of these cubes needed to fill the box. It will take 6 · 3, or 18, cubes to fill the bottom layer, and there will be five of these layers, so the box can hold 18 · 5, or 90 one-inch cubes. Its volume is 90 cubic inches.

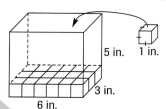

5 in. 1 in.
3 in.
6 in.

If all three dimensions of the box are doubled, then the number of cubic inches in the box is 12 · 6 · 10 or 720. In general, the volume of a box is length · width · height or ℓwh. If all three dimensions are doubled, the new volume is $2\ell \cdot 2w \cdot 2h$ or $8\,\ell wh$. Its volume becomes eight times as great.

Soap bubbles are made of soap, water, and air trapped inside the soap film. Because of surface tension, the soap takes a shape that minimizes the surface area surrounding the trapped air. The shape they form is a sphere.

MORE HELP
See 239

Theorem
Of all the solids with the same surface area, the sphere has the largest volume. Isoperimetric Theorem (3-d) (T088)

To get some idea of why this theorem is true, consider these regular polyhedrons which have a surface area of 60 square centimeters. As the number of faces increases, and the solid becomes more sphere-like, the volume increases. If you consider a sphere to be a regular polyhedron with more faces than any other, you can see why it will have the greatest volume of all.

Area of each face	15 cm²	10 cm²	3 cm²
Length of each edge	≈ 5.89 cm	≈ 3.16 cm³	≈ 2.63 cm
Volume	≈ 24.08 cm³	≈ 31.62 cm³	≈ 39.62 cm³

Volume

All of the formulas for volumes of polyhedrons are based on three postulates (the formula for volume of a cube is also a postulate). These parallel the three area postulates.

MORE HELP
See 178

Postulate
If two polyhedrons are congruent, then they have the same volume. Volume ≅ Postulate (P19)

Postulate
The volume of a solid is the sum of the volumes of all of its non-overlapping parts. Volume + Postulate (P20)

Formula
The volume of a cube is the cube of the length of its side; $V = s^3$. (F40)

To understand this formula, think about how many unit cubes would be needed to fill a cube with side length s. There will be s cubes for the length, s cubes for the width, and s cubes for the height, or $V = s^3$.

206 Cavalieri's Principle

MORE HELP
See 337

DID YOU KNOW Bonaventura Cavalieri (1598–1647) was an Italian mathematician, physicist, and follower of Galileo. He wrote the first textbook on how to find areas using calculus, called *Geometria Indivisibilibus Continuorum*, first published in 1635. The following theorem comes from his explorations in calculus.

Theorem If two solids have the same height and the same cross-sectional area at every level, then they have the same volume. Cavalieri's Principle (T089)

To understand why this theorem makes sense, consider a stack of paper in the shape of a right prism. Suppose the stack is pushed into the shape of an oblique prism. The stacks have the same volume, even if they don't look the same, because

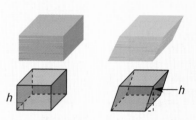

each stack is made from the same number of congruent sheets of paper. Any cross section would be one of these sheets of paper, so the figures have congruent cross sections at every height and equal heights.

Assume the areas of square A, circle B, and triangle C are all the same. Each figure has the same height, so by Cavalieri's Principle, all three figures have the same volume.

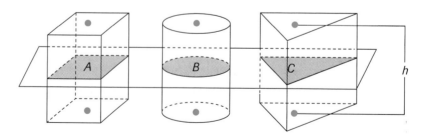

207 Volume of a Prism

MORE HELP
See 206

If the area of the base of a prism is B, then each layer that is 1 unit deep contains B cubes. The height h tells how many layers are in the cube. So the space can be filled with $B \cdot h$ cubes.

> **Formula** The volume of a prism is $V = Bh$; B is the area of a base and h is the height of the prism. (F41)
>
> Because of Cavalieri's Principle, the formula works for any prism.

> **Formula** The volume of a rectangular solid is $V = \ell wh$; ℓ is the length, w is the width, h is the height of the solid. (F42)
>
> In a rectangular prism, the area of a base is the product of the length and width, or $\ell \cdot w$. By substitution, the formula $V = Bh$ becomes $V = \ell wh$.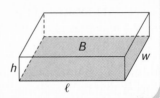

Volume of a Cylinder

> **Formula** The volume of a cylinder is $V = Bh$ and $V = \pi r^2 h$; B is the area of a base, h is the height of the cylinder, r is the radius of a base. (F43)
>
> Like a prism, a cylinder has parallel congruent bases joined by segments that join corresponding points of the two bases, so finding the volume of a cylinder is a lot like finding the volume of prism. The difference is in how you find the area of the base. Because of Cavalieri's Principle, the formula works for any cylinder.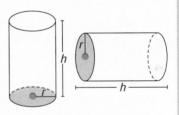

MORE HELP
See 206

EXAMPLE: How many of these bales of hay can you make from cutting 5000 cubic feet of hay?

For one bale of hay, $r = \frac{1}{2}(7) = \frac{7}{2}$ and $h = 6$.

$$V = Bh$$
$$= \pi r^2 h$$
$$\approx \frac{22}{7}\left(\frac{7}{2}\right)^2 (6)$$
$$\approx 231$$

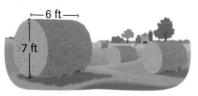

Divide to find the total number of bales: $5000 \div 231 \approx 21.6$.

★ You can make 21 bales of hay from the cutting.

Volume of Pyramids and Cones

MORE HELP
See 206

It is possible for a triangular *pyramid* to have an equilateral base and a lateral edge that is an altitude. By constructing this pyramid from the net, you can show that its volume is $\frac{1}{3}$ that of a triangular *prism* with the same base.

Formula The volume of a pyramid is $V = \frac{1}{3}Bh$; B is the area of the base, h is the height of the pyramid. (F44)

Because of Cavalieri's Principle, the formula works for any pyramid. You can see why it works by making a model from these nets. Make two copies of Pyramid 1 and one copy of Pyramid 2.

You can fit the three pieces together to form a prism. Use an equilateral triangle from each Pyramid 1 as each base of the prism. The colored isosceles triangles of Pyramid 2 match up with the colored isosceles triangle on the two copies of Pyramid 1.

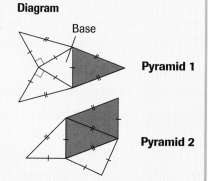

Diagram

Base

Pyramid 1

Pyramid 2

The two copies of Pyramid 1 have the same volume because they are congruent. The third pyramid also has the same volume as each Pyramid 1. This means that the volume of each pyramid is $\frac{1}{3}$ the volume of the triangular prism.

Diagram

Since, for any triangle, you can find an equilateral triangle with the same area, you can always make a pyramid whose base is an equilateral triangle that has the same volume as a given pyramid. Then the pyramid will have $\frac{1}{3}$ the volume of a prism with this base.

EXAMPLE 1: An ornament is made by joining two congruent square pyramids. The designer fills the ornament with a colored fluid. One cubic centimeter contains one milliliter of fluid. How many milliliters of fluid are needed to fill the ornament?

The inside measure of the base of each pyramid is a square with side $s = 3$, so $B = 9$.

The total volume is twice the volume of one of the pyramids.

$$V = 2\left(\frac{1}{3}Bh\right)$$

From the diagram, $h = 5$.

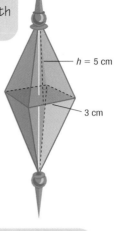

$h = 5$ cm

3 cm

$$V = 2\left(\frac{1}{3}Bh\right)$$
$$= 2\left(\frac{1}{3}\right)(9)(5)$$
$$= 30$$

The number of cubic centimeters in the volume equals the number of milliliters contained in the ornament.

★ The designer needs 30 mL of fluid to fill the ornament.

Like pyramids, cones have one vertex that is not in the plane of the base. It is not surprising that the relationship between a cone and a cylinder of the same base and height is similar to the relationship between a pyramid and a prism of the same base and height.

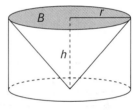

B

r

h

Formula The volume of a cone is $V = \frac{1}{3}Bh$ and $V = \frac{1}{3}\pi r^2 h$; B is the area of the base, h is the height of the cone, r is the radius of the base. (F45)

Think of a cone as a pyramid with an infinite number of sides. Then the formula follows directly from the formula for the volume of a pyramid. Because of Cavalieri's Principle, the formula works for any cone, including cones that are not right cones.

EXAMPLE 2: Windshield washer fluid is being poured into the funnel at a rate of 162 milliliters per second and flows out of the funnel at the rate of 78 milliliters per second. About how long will it take for the funnel to overflow? (1 mL $= 1$ cm^3)

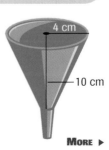

4 cm

10 cm

MORE ▶

To find how long it will take to fill the funnel, divide the volume by the rate at which fluid accumulates in the funnel.

Find the volume.

$$V = \frac{1}{3}\pi r^2 h$$

$$= \frac{1}{3}(3.14)(4)^2(10)$$

$$\approx 167.5 \qquad \boxed{167.5 \text{ cm}^3 = 167.5 \text{ mL.}}$$

Find the rate of accumulation.

RA = rate pouring in − rate flowing out

$$= 162 - 78$$

$$= 84$$

Total time ≈ 167.5 mL $\div \dfrac{84 \text{ mL}}{s}$

$$\approx 167.5 \cancel{\text{ mL}} \cdot \frac{s}{84 \cancel{\text{ mL}}}$$

$$\approx 1.99 \text{ s}$$

★ The funnel will overflow after almost 2 seconds.

210 Volume of a Sphere

Use the surface area of a sphere to help you find a formula for its volume.

MORE HELP
See 201

> **Formula** The volume of a sphere with radius r is $V = \frac{4}{3}\pi r^3$. (F46)
>
> You can think of the sphere as being made up of n pyramids, each with a height equal to the radius of the sphere and a base with area B. The volume of each pyramid is $\frac{1}{3}Br$. Because there are n such pyramids, the volume of the sphere is approximately $n(\frac{1}{3}Br)$. But the surface area of the sphere is approximately nB. Substituting the formula for the surface area of a sphere ($4\pi r^2$) yields the formula for the volume of a sphere.
>
> $$V \approx n\left(\frac{1}{3}Br\right)$$
>
> $$\approx \frac{1}{3}(nB)r$$
>
> $$= \frac{1}{3}(4\pi r^2)r$$
>
> $$= \frac{4}{3}\pi r^3$$
>
> **Diagram**
>
>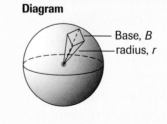
>
> Base, B
> radius, r

EXAMPLE: Members of a junior basketball clinic receive basketballs to take home at the end of the clinic. The basketballs are flat. How much air does it take to fill a basketball with an inside radius of 4.77 inches?

$$V = \frac{4}{3}\pi r^3$$

$$\approx \frac{4}{3}(3.14)(4.77)^3$$

$$\approx 454.38$$

★ It takes a little more than 454 cubic inches of air to inflate the basketball.

Volume of Similar Solids

This theorem shows how the volumes of two similar solids are related.

Theorem	If two solids are similar with a scale factor of $a:b$, then the corresponding volumes have a ratio of $a^3:b^3$.

~ solids, corresp. sides $a:b \Rightarrow$ volumes $a^3:b^3$ (T090)

Proof

Diagram

Given: Similar prisms with scale factor $a:b$

Prove: $\dfrac{\text{Volume of prism K}}{\text{Volume of prism L}} = \dfrac{a^3}{b^3}$

Plan: Consider prisms K and L, since the proof for other solids is similar.

You know the ratio of their corresponding linear elements. You can find the ratio of their corresponding areas. The ratio of their volumes is the product of these two ratios.

Statements	**Reasons**
❶ Scale factor of K to L is $a:b$	Given
❷ $\dfrac{\text{Height of K}}{\text{Height of L}} = \dfrac{a}{b}$	Def. of scale factor
❸ $\dfrac{\text{Area of base K}}{\text{Area of base L}} = \dfrac{a^2}{b^2}$	~ polygons, corresp. sides $a:b \Rightarrow$ areas $a^2:b^2$ (T085)
❹ $\dfrac{\text{Volume of K}}{\text{Volume of L}} = \dfrac{B_k\, h_k}{B_l\, h_l}$	Volume of a prism formula (F41)
❺ $\dfrac{\text{Volume of K}}{\text{Volume of L}} = \dfrac{a^2 \cdot a}{b^2 \cdot b}$	Substitution Look back at steps 2 and 3.
❻ $\dfrac{\text{Volume of K}}{\text{Volume of L}} = \dfrac{a^3}{b^3}$	Simplify

Similarity

"You can't compare me to my father. Our similarities are different."

—*Dale Berra, son of Yogi Berra*

You may say on occasion that two people are similar, because they look alike or act alike, but a friend may disagree and say that they are not similar. Both of you may be right, since *similar* is a not a precise word, except in geometry.

As with any other mathematical term, similarity has a precise meaning (otherwise you couldn't be sure of your conclusions). Geometric figures are **similar** if they have the same shape. Mathematicians use ratios to specify what *same shape* means. You think with ratios more often than you realize: *Hmmm, I'll buy the Thirst-Smasher because I get three times as much soda for only twice as much money!* Ratios really do come in handy.

When you apply ratios to angles, line segments, and figures, your thinking becomes even more powerful. Suddenly you can figure out the distance to the nearest galaxy simply by measuring an angle and making some calculations. You can plan bridges and skate parks that stand up to constant use. You can design airplanes and rockets that actually fly.

Thousands of years ago, mathematicians and engineers used ratios and similar figures to build pyramids, coliseums, and temples. Even if those civilizations didn't have computers to help with calculations and create designs, we are like them in the way we use geometry to solve problems.

A **ratio** is a comparison of two numbers or measures. If a ratio compares two different kinds of quantities, it is called a **rate**. An equation showing that two ratios are equal is called a **proportion.**

214 **Ratios**

You can compare quantities by asking *how much* more. You can also compare quantities by asking *how many times* as great.

Beth is 60 inches tall. Amy is 48 inches tall. Compare their heights.

CASE 1 Subtract to find how much taller Beth is than Amy.

Beth's height − Amy's height = 60 in. − 48 in.

Beth is 12 inches taller than Amy, or Amy is 12 inches shorter than Beth.

CASE 2 Write a ratio to compare Beth's and Amy's heights.

Beth's height $\longrightarrow$ $\dfrac{60 \text{ in.}}{48 \text{ in.}}$ or $\dfrac{5}{4}$ Amy's height $\longrightarrow$ $\dfrac{48 \text{ in.}}{60 \text{ in.}}$ or $\dfrac{4}{5}$
Amy's height $\longrightarrow$ Beth's height $\longrightarrow$

Beth is $\frac{5}{4}$, or $1\frac{1}{4}$, times as tall as Amy; Amy is $\frac{4}{5}$ as tall as Beth.

215 **Writing Ratios**

You can write ratios to compare parts of the same whole, wholes, and parts of different wholes. Here are some ratios you can use to compare Neal's and Nicki's drum sets.

Tom-tom

Snare
Drum

Bass
Drum

Compare a part to a part

Compare a part to a whole

Compare a whole to a whole

Different Ways to Write Ratios			
Ratio	Neal's bass drums to his snares	Nicki's snares to all her drums	All Neal's drums to all Nicki's drums
Use *to*	2 to 4	3 to 10	9 to 10
Use a colon	2:4	3:10	9:10
Use fraction form	$\frac{2}{4}$	$\frac{3}{10}$	$\frac{9}{10}$
Use decimal form	0.5	0.3	0.9

MATH ALERT Don't Confuse Ratios with Fractions   216

A fraction and a ratio often look alike, but they are not the same things. A fraction compares a part to a whole, so it is a ratio, but a ratio need not be a fraction. For example, the second term of a ratio can be another part rather than a whole.

Ratios can also compare two wholes. That can make a great difference when you try to compute. Consider this example.

Ratio of Boys to Girls

In Your Class

$\frac{10}{15}$

In Class Next Door

$\frac{8}{10}$

You can't find the ratio of boys to girls in the combined classes by adding the two ratios the way you would add fractions. Instead, you need to compare the *total number of boys* to the *total number of girls*.

Total number of boys →
Total number of girls → $\frac{10 + 8}{15 + 10} = \frac{18}{25}$

You *can* treat ratios like fractions when you simplify or find equivalents.

217

Rates

A **rate** is a ratio that compares two quantities that have different units, such as miles per hour, pounds per square inch, or miles per gallon. These common rates have special names—speed, pressure, and fuel economy.

EXAMPLE: Suppose you type 132 words in 5 minutes. What is your typing rate?

★ Your typing rate is $\frac{132\ words}{5\ minutes}$, or about 26 words per minute.

> 26 words per minute is a **unit rate**, because the second part of the rate is one unit.

218

Proportions

Two ratios that are equal are called a **proportion.** If you were a practical joker, you might switch the salt in the salt box with the sugar in the bag just before your sister makes fudge. Then, instead of using 32 times as much sugar as salt, she would use 32 times as much salt as sugar. The fudge would be super salty because the ingredients are **out of proportion**. That is, the ratio of sugar to salt in the salty batch is not the same as the ratio of sugar to salt in a normal-tasting batch. If you were making a double batch of cookies, to be sure they tasted okay, you would keep the recipe **in proportion** by doubling the amount of each ingredient.

219

Terms of a Proportion

To show that the ratio $\frac{a}{b}$ is equal to the ratio $\frac{c}{d}$, you can write the proportion $\frac{a}{b} = \frac{c}{d}$.

Write: $\frac{a}{b} = \frac{c}{d}$ or $a{:}b = c{:}d$ **Write:** $\frac{2}{4} = \frac{5}{10}$ or 2:4 = 5:10

Say: *a is to b as c is to d*   **Say:** *two is to four as five is to ten*

Just as the numbers in a fraction have special names—numerator and denominator—so do the numbers, or **terms**, of a proportion.

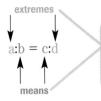

extremes

$a{:}b = c{:}d$

means

> **Extremes** is another word for **extreme** (or end) **terms**, and **means** is another word for **mean** (or middle) **terms** when a proportion is written with colons.

Properties of Proportions

When you write a proportion in equation form, it contains two fractions. Often the first thing you want to do is to clear the equation of fractions. This property is used so often to clear fractions or find missing terms that it is given a special name: the Cross Product Property.

Theorem For positive numbers a, b, c, and d, $\frac{a}{b} = \frac{c}{d}$, if and only if $ad = bc$. Cross product prop. (T091)

Proof

CASE 1 If $a{:}b = c{:}d$, then $ad = bc$.

Given: $a{:}b = c{:}d$

Prove: $ad = bc$

Plan: Use the fraction form of the proportion. The multiplication property of equality allows you to multiply both sides of the equation by bd to clear the fractions.

$$\frac{a}{b} = \frac{c}{d} \qquad \text{Write in fraction form}$$

$$\frac{a}{b}(bd) = \frac{c}{d}(bd) \qquad \times \text{ prop. of} =$$

$$\frac{abd}{b} = \frac{cbd}{d} \qquad \text{Identity prop.}$$

$$ad = bc \qquad \text{Simplify}$$

CASE 2 If $ad = bc$, then $a{:}b = c{:}d$.

Given: $ad = bc$

Prove: $a{:}b = c{:}d$

Plan: This time divide each side of the equation by the two numbers you want in the denominators.

$$\frac{ad}{bd} = \frac{bc}{bd} \qquad \div \text{ prop. of} =$$

$$\frac{a}{b} = \frac{c}{d} \qquad \text{Simplify}$$

$$a{:}b = c{:}d \qquad \text{Write in colon form}$$

You can use cross products to tell whether two ratios form a proportion (that is, whether the two ratios are equivalent). You can say that the product of the extremes equals the product of the means.

MORE ▶

If you're twice as old as your sister, you can also say that your sister is half your age. You can describe this relationship in more than one way. It's the same with proportions.

The corresponding sides of these two rectangles are in the same ratio. They are **proportional.**

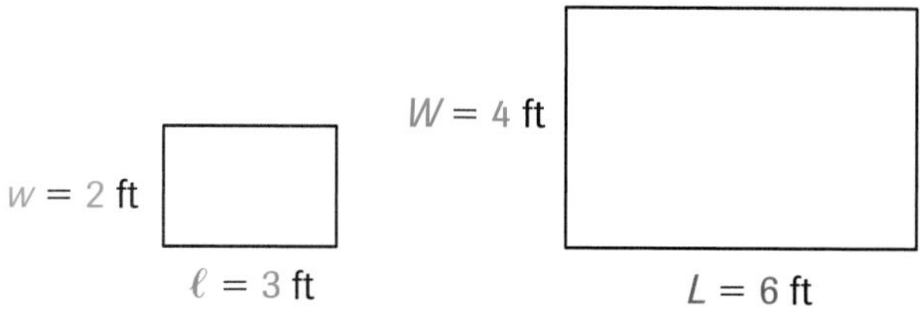

$w = 2$ ft

$\ell = 3$ ft

$W = 4$ ft

$L = 6$ ft

You can show that this is true by writing the ratios in the form of a proportion and comparing the cross products. Since the cross products are equal, the ratios form a proportion.

$3 \times 4 = 12$ — The product of the means is 12.

$$\frac{w}{\ell} = \frac{W}{L} \qquad \frac{2}{3} = \frac{4}{6}$$

$2 \times 6 = 12$ — The product of the extremes is 12.

Here are two other ways to write proportions with the same information.

$2 \times 6 = 12$

$$\frac{\ell}{w} = \frac{L}{W} \qquad \frac{3}{2} = \frac{6}{4}$$

$3 \times 4 = 12$

$3 \times 4 = 12$

$$\frac{L}{\ell} = \frac{W}{w} \qquad \frac{6}{3} = \frac{4}{2}$$

$6 \times 2 = 12$

The table summarizes some properties of proportions.

Properties of Proportions	
Cross Products	If $\dfrac{a}{b} = \dfrac{c}{d}$, then $ad = bc$.
Reciprocals	If $\dfrac{a}{b} = \dfrac{c}{d}$, then $\dfrac{b}{a} = \dfrac{d}{c}$.
Interchanging Means	If $\dfrac{a}{b} = \dfrac{c}{d}$, then $\dfrac{a}{c} = \dfrac{b}{d}$.

Solving Proportions

If one term of a proportion is unknown, you can use cross products to solve for the missing term, because the cross products of a proportion are equal.

To make an accurate model of an object or map of an area, you use a scale. **Scale** is the ratio of a length in a model or drawing to the corresponding length in the actual object or region. You can use a proportion to solve problems involving a scale.

EXAMPLE: The builders of an aviation exhibit plan to include a model of the Bell X-1, the first plane to fly faster than sound. It will be built to the scale of 1 in.:1.5 ft. The actual Bell X-1 is 31 feet long. How long will the model be?

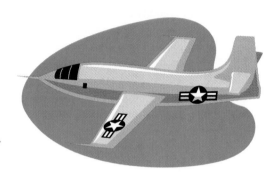

To solve this problem, write and solve a proportion. Let x represent the length of the model of the Bell X-1.

$$\text{inches} \longrightarrow \frac{1}{1.5} = \frac{x}{31} \longleftarrow \text{inches} \atop \text{feet}$$

$$1 \cdot 31 = 1.5x$$

$$\frac{31}{1.5} = x$$

> Be sure to write the correct units in your answer.

$$20.\overline{6} = x$$

★ The scale model of the Bell X-1 will be about 21 inches long.

It's a good idea to find the product of the extremes first, then the product of the means. If you don't, you may forget and multiply in the wrong order when working with inequalities.

To compare $\frac{2}{3}$ to $\frac{1}{2}$, check cross products, extremes first.

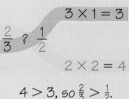

$$3 \times 1 = 3$$

$$\frac{2}{3} \ ? \ \frac{1}{2}$$

$$2 \times 2 = 4$$

$$4 > 3, \text{ so } \frac{2}{3} > \frac{1}{2}.$$

MORE HELP
See 218, 256

Polygons are **similar** if they are the same shape, but not necessarily the same size. *Same shape* means that corresponding angles are congruent and the lengths of corresponding sides are proportional. The ratio of the lengths of corresponding sides is the **similarity ratio**, or **scale factor**.

Similar Quadrilaterals

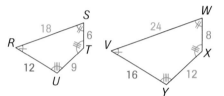

Not Similar Quadrilaterals

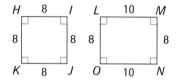

This not only names the figures that are similar, but it also sets up a correspondence between the points, just as it does for congruent figures.

Write: *RSTU ~ VWXY*

Say: *Quadrilateral R S T U is similar to quadrilateral V W X Y.*

EXAMPLE 1: What is the similarity ratio of *RSTU* to *VWXY*?

$$\frac{RS}{VW} = \frac{ST}{WX} = \frac{TU}{XY} = \frac{UR}{YV}$$

$$\frac{18}{24} = \frac{6}{8} = \frac{9}{12} = \frac{12}{16} = \frac{3}{4}$$

★ The similarity ratio of *RSTU* to *VWXY* is $\frac{3}{4}$.

Congruent polygons are always similar. For example, you know that the corresponding angles in congruent polygons are congruent. The corresponding sides in congruent polygons have a ratio of $\frac{1}{1}$, so they are proportional. That makes the polygons similar.

EXAMPLE 2: How do you know that *HIJK* and *LMNO* are not similar?

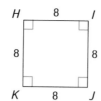

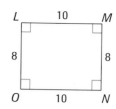

Because *HIJK* and *LMNO* are rectangles, their opposite sides are congruent.

Compare the similarity ratios of two pairs of adjacent corresponding sides.

$$\frac{HK}{LO} \overset{?}{=} \frac{HI}{LM}$$

$$\frac{8}{8} \neq \frac{8}{10}$$

> In these polygons, opposite sides do have equal ratios! Choosing adjacent sides assures that, if you're comparing a rectangle to a square, you won't come to a faulty conclusion about similarity.

★ *HIJK* is not similar to *LMNO*.

Using Similar Polygons

223

Lengths of corresponding sides of similar polygons are proportional, so you can use proportions to solve problems involving similar polygons.

Finding Side Lengths and Angle Measures

224

If two polygons are similar, all pairs of corresponding angles are congruent and the ratios of the lengths of all pairs of corresponding sides are equal.

If polygon *ABCDE* is similar to polygon *JKLMN*, then $\angle A \cong \angle J$, $\angle B \cong \angle K$ $\angle C \cong \angle L$, $\angle D \cong \angle M$ and $\angle E \cong \angle N$, and $\frac{AB}{JK} = \frac{BC}{KL} = \frac{CD}{LM} = \frac{DE}{MN} = \frac{EA}{NJ}$.

EXAMPLE 1: *PQRS* ~ *TUVW*. Find *PS* and m$\angle P$.

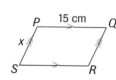

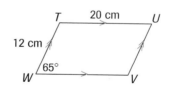

To find *PS*, write and solve a proportion.

$\dfrac{PQ}{TU} = \dfrac{PS}{TW}$	Def. of ~ polygons
$\dfrac{15}{20} = \dfrac{x}{12}$	Substitution
$15 \cdot 12 = 20x$	Cross product prop. (T091)
$\dfrac{180}{20} = x$	÷ prop. of =
$9 = x$	Simplify

MORE ▶

MORE HELP
See 160

To find m∠P, write and solve an equation using the consecutive angles of *TUVW*.

m∠W + m∠T = 180°	Parallelogram ⇒ consec. ∠s supp. (T068)
65° + m∠T = 180°	Substitution
m∠T = 115°	Subtraction prop. of =
m∠T = m∠P	Def. of ~ polygons
m∠P = 115°	Substitution

★ *PS* = 9 centimeters and m∠P = 115°.

EXAMPLE 2: You can use a photocopier to enlarge or reduce an original picture. What are the dimensions of a 5-inch by 7-inch rectangular picture that is reduced to 60%?

Reduced to 60% means the copy's dimensions are 60% of the original. *Reduced* or *reduced by 60%* would mean the dimensions of the copy are 100% − 60%, or 40%, of the original.

If an image is reduced to 60% of its original dimensions, then the similarity ratio of the copy to the original is $\frac{60}{100}$. To find the dimensions of the reduced image, write and solve two proportions.

Let x represent one dimension of the image.

$$\text{image} \rightarrow \frac{x}{5} = \frac{60}{100} \leftarrow \text{similarity ratio}$$
$$\text{original} \rightarrow$$

$$100x = 5 \cdot 60$$
$$x = \frac{5 \cdot 60}{100}$$
$$= 3$$

Let y represent the other dimension of the image.

$$\text{image} \rightarrow \frac{y}{7} = \frac{60}{100} \leftarrow \text{similarity ratio}$$
$$\text{original} \rightarrow$$

$$100y = 7 \cdot 60$$
$$y = \frac{7 \cdot 60}{100}$$
$$= 4.2$$

★ The dimensions of the reduced image are 3 inches by 4.2 inches.

MATH ALERT Use Corresponding Parts When Writing Proportions

If you are using similar figures to measure indirectly, set up the proportion carefully. Be sure the ratios use corresponding parts.

CASE 1 When triangles are separate, picture them oriented in the same direction.
$\triangle ABC \sim \triangle DEF$

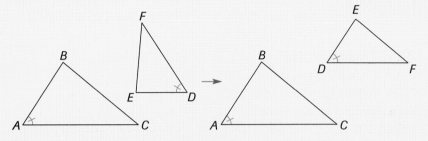

Now it is easier to see that $\frac{AB}{DE} = \frac{BC}{EF} = \frac{AC}{DF}$.

CASE 2 When triangles overlap, picture them separated.

$\overline{DE} \parallel \overline{BC}$, so $\triangle DAE \sim \triangle BAC$.

MORE HELP
See 141

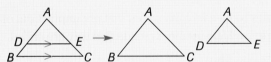

If you write a proportion using the lengths of the sides, be sure to use the lengths of corresponding sides in each ratio. For example, $\frac{AD}{AB} = \frac{AE}{AC}$, but $\frac{AD}{AB} \neq \frac{AC}{DE}$.

If you write a proportion using the lengths of two parts of a side in one ratio, be sure to use the corresponding lengths of the same parts in the other ratio. For example, $\frac{AD}{AB} = \frac{AE}{AC}$, but $\frac{AD}{BD} \neq \frac{DE}{BC}$.

Proving Triangles Similar

To find out whether two polygons are similar, you must satisfy both parts of the definition: corresponding angles must be congruent *and* the ratios of all pairs of corresponding sides must be proportional. A few postulates will give you shortcuts for proving that two triangles are similar.

AA Similarity Postulate

Postulate If two angles of one triangle are congruent to two angles of another triangle, then the two triangles are similar.
AA ~ Postulate (P21)

Because you know that
$\triangle ABC \sim \triangle DEF$, you now
know that the other pair of
corresponding angles is con-
gruent: $\angle C \cong \angle F$ (but you

MORE HELP
See 143, 260

also know that from the Third
Angles Theorem). You also
know now that the corresponding sides are proportional, so
$\frac{AB}{DE} = \frac{BC}{EF} = \frac{CA}{FD}$.

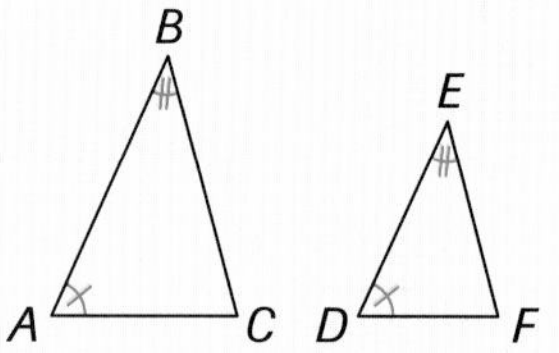

$\angle A \cong \angle D$ and $\angle B \cong \angle E$, so $\triangle ABC \sim \triangle DEF$

You can use similar triangles to measure distances that are impractical or impossible to measure directly. Measurements made this way are called **indirect measurements**.

MORE HELP
See 076

DID YOU KNOW To calculate the height of the Great Pyramid in Egypt, the Greek mathematician Thales (640–546 B.C.) used the AA Similarity Postulate? He placed a rod at the tip of the pyramid's shadow. He then measured the distance from the center of the pyramid to the tip of the pyramid's shadow and the distance from the rod to the tip of the rod's shadow.

EXAMPLE: Use Thales' method to find the height of the pyramid in the diagram.

$\angle GHI \cong \angle KIJ$ because both are right angles. $\angle GIH \cong \angle KJI$ because the sun's rays, represented by $\overline{GI}$ and $\overline{KJ}$, are parallel and $\overline{HJ}$ is a transversal.

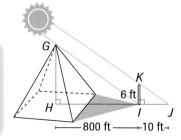

According to the AA Similarity Postulate, $\triangle GHI \sim \triangle KIJ$, so write and solve a proportion. Let x represent GH, the height of the pyramid.

$\dfrac{GH}{KI} = \dfrac{HI}{IJ}$	Def. of $\sim \triangle$s
$\dfrac{x}{6} = \dfrac{800}{10}$	Substitution
$10x = 6 \cdot 800$	Cross product prop.
$x = \dfrac{4800}{10}$	$\div$ prop. of $=$
$= 480$	Simplify

★ The height of the pyramid is 480 feet.

SAS Similarity Theorem

Theorem   If an angle of one triangle is congruent to an angle of a second triangle and the lengths of the sides including these angles are proportional, then the two triangles are similar. SAS Similarity Theorem (T092)

Proof

Given: $\angle 1 \cong \angle 2, \dfrac{LM}{OP} = \dfrac{NL}{QO}$

Prove: $\triangle LMN \sim \triangle OPQ$

Plan: Use parallel lines and congruent triangles to prove that the two triangles are similar. Begin by constructing $\overline{RS}$ in $\triangle OPQ$ so that $\overline{RS} \parallel \overline{OQ}$ and $RP = LM$. Then show $\triangle OPQ \sim \triangle RPS$ and $\triangle LMN \cong \triangle RPS$ in order to make your point.

MORE HELP
See 373, 432, 434

Diagram

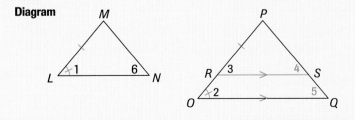

Statements	Reasons
❶ Locate R on $\overline{OP}$ so $RP = LM$	Ruler Postulate (P08)
❷ Construct $\overline{RS} \parallel \overline{OQ}$	Construction
❸ $\angle 3 \cong \angle 2$; $\angle 4 \cong \angle 5$	Corresp. $\angle$s Postulate (P15)
❹ $\triangle RPS \sim \triangle OPQ$	AA $\sim$ Postulate (P21)
❺ $\dfrac{RP}{OP} = \dfrac{SP}{QP} = \dfrac{SR}{QO}$	Def. of $\sim$ $\triangle$s
❻ $\dfrac{LM}{OP} = \dfrac{NL}{QO}$	Given
❼ $\dfrac{LM}{OP} = \dfrac{RP}{OP} = \dfrac{NL}{QO} = \dfrac{SR}{QO}$	Substitution *See steps 1, 5, and 6.*
❽ $NL = SR$	$\times$ prop. of $=$
❾ $\angle 1 \cong \angle 2$; $\angle 1 \cong \angle 3$	Given; Substitution *See step 2.*
❿ $\triangle LMN \cong \triangle RPS$	SAS $\cong$ Postulate (P23) *See steps 5, 8, and 9.*
⓫ $\angle 6 \cong \angle 4$; $\angle 6 \cong \angle 5$	CPCTC; Substitution
⓬ $\triangle LMN \sim \triangle OPQ$	AA $\sim$ Postulate (P21)

Look back at steps 9 and 11.

229

MATH ALERT In SAS, the Angle Must Be Included

MORE HELP
See 228

When using the SAS Similarity Theorem, you need to specify two sides and an angle in each triangle. Be sure the angle is *between* the two sides (it is included). Otherwise the triangles may not be similar, as these two triangles show.

In these two triangles, two pairs of sides are proportional: $\dfrac{RT}{UV} = \dfrac{ST}{WV}$. $\angle R \cong \angle V$, but $\angle R$ is not the angle between the proportional sides, $\overline{RT}$ and $\overline{ST}$. By looking at the other angle measures, you can see that the triangles are not similar.

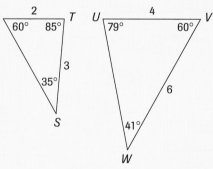

SSS Similarity Theorem

Theorem	If corresponding sides of two triangles are proportional, then the two triangles are similar. SSS Similarity Theorem (T093)

MORE HELP
See 153, 376, 432, 434

Proof

Given: $\dfrac{a}{d} = \dfrac{b}{e} = \dfrac{c}{f}$

Prove: $\triangle ABC \sim \triangle DEF$

Diagram

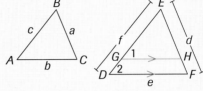

Plan: Construct $\overline{GH}$ in $\triangle DEF$ so that $\overline{GH} \parallel \overline{DF}$ and $GE = AB$. Then $\triangle GEH \sim \triangle DEF$. Now you can prove that $\triangle ABC \cong \triangle GEH$ to get $\triangle ABC \sim \triangle DEF$.

Statements	**Reasons**
❶ $\dfrac{a}{d} = \dfrac{c}{f} = \dfrac{b}{e}$	Given
❷ $af = cd,\ ce = bf$	Cross product prop. (T091)
❸ $a = \dfrac{cd}{f},\ \dfrac{ce}{f} = b$	÷ prop. of =
❹ Locate G on $\overline{ED}$ so that $EG = c$	Ruler Postulate (P08)
❺ Construct $\overline{GH} \parallel \overline{DF}$	Construction
❻ $\angle E \cong \angle E$	Reflexive prop. of $\cong$ (T105)
❼ $\angle 1 \cong \angle 2$	Corresp. $\angle$s Postulate (P15)
❽ $\triangle GEH \sim \triangle DEF$	AA $\sim$ Postulate (P21)
❾ $\dfrac{EH}{d} = \dfrac{EG}{f},\ \dfrac{GH}{e} = \dfrac{EG}{f}$	Def. of $\sim$ $\triangle$s
❿ $\dfrac{EH}{d} = \dfrac{c}{f},\ \dfrac{GH}{e} = \dfrac{c}{f}$	Substitution See steps 4 and 9.
⓫ $EH \cdot f = cd,\ GH \cdot f = ce$	Cross product prop. (T091)
⓬ $EH = \dfrac{cd}{f},\ GH = \dfrac{ce}{f}$	÷ prop. of =
⓭ $EH = a,\ GH = b$	Substitution See steps 3 and 12.
⓮ $\triangle ABC \cong \triangle GEH$	SSS $\cong$ Postulate (P22) See steps 4 and 13.
⓯ $\triangle ABC \sim \triangle DEF$	Substitution See steps 8 and 14.

MORE ▶

You can use the SSS Similarity Theorem to generate whole numbers that satisfy the Pythagorean Theorem ($a^2 + b^2 = c^2$). All you have to do is to start with a Pythagorean Triple that you already know, such as 3-4-5 or 5-12-13. Then enlarge or reduce the triangle using a whole number scale factor.

EXAMPLE: The side lengths of right $\triangle IJK$ are 3, 4, and 5. $\triangle IJK \sim \triangle LMN$. Name two possible sets of side lengths for $\triangle LMN$.

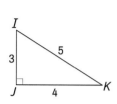
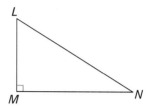

MORE HELP
See 152, 222

Suppose the similarity ratio of $\triangle IJK$ to $\triangle LMN$ is 1:2 or 1:3. Then you can write these proportionality statements.

$$\frac{IJ}{LM} = \frac{JK}{MN} = \frac{KI}{NL} = \frac{1}{2}$$

$$\frac{3}{LM} = \frac{4}{MN} = \frac{5}{NL} = \frac{1}{2}$$

$$\frac{3}{6} = \frac{4}{8} = \frac{5}{10} = \frac{1}{2}$$

$$\frac{IJ}{LM} = \frac{JK}{MN} = \frac{KI}{NL} = \frac{1}{3}$$

$$\frac{3}{LM} = \frac{4}{MN} = \frac{5}{NL} = \frac{1}{3}$$

$$\frac{3}{9} = \frac{4}{12} = \frac{5}{15} = \frac{1}{3}$$

★ Two possible sets of side lengths for $\triangle LMN$ are 6, 8, 10 and 9, 12, 15.

> The number of sets of possible side lengths for $\triangle LMN$ is infinite!

231

Using Similar Triangles in Proof

You can use what you know about similar triangles to prove theorems about parallel lines and angle bisectors.

232

Parallel Lines Proofs

MORE HELP
See 058

Theorem If a line parallel to one side of a triangle intersects the other two sides, then it divides the two sides proportionally. △ Proportionality Theorem (T094)

Proof

Given: $\overline{ST} \parallel \overline{PR}$

Prove: $\dfrac{SP}{QS} = \dfrac{TR}{QT}$

MORE HELP
See 027, 076, 220, 432, 434

Plan: If you can prove that $\triangle SQT \sim \triangle PQR$, then you can show that their sides are proportional. Use what you know about parallel lines and transversals to complete the proof.

Diagram

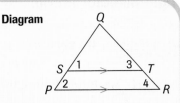

Statements	Reasons
❶ $\overline{ST} \parallel \overline{PR}$	Given
❷ $\angle 1 \cong \angle 2; \angle 3 \cong \angle 4$	Corresp. $\angle$s Postulate (P15)
❸ $\triangle SQT \sim \triangle PQR$	AA $\sim$ Postulate (P21)
❹ $\dfrac{QP}{QS} = \dfrac{QR}{QT}$	Def. of $\sim \triangle$s
❺ $QP = QS + SP, QR = QT + TR$	Seg. + Postulate (P09)
❻ $\dfrac{QS + SP}{QS} = \dfrac{QT + TR}{QT}$	Substitution *Look back at steps 4 and 5.*
❼ $\dfrac{QS}{QS} + \dfrac{SP}{QS} = \dfrac{QT}{QT} + \dfrac{TR}{QT}$	Distributive prop.
❽ $1 + \dfrac{SP}{QS} = 1 + \dfrac{TR}{QT}$	Simplify
❾ $\dfrac{SP}{QS} = \dfrac{TR}{QT}$	Subtraction prop. of =

Theorem

If a line divides two sides of a triangle proportionally, then it is parallel to the third side. Converse of $\triangle$ Proportionality Theorem (T095)

MORE HELP
See 228, 432, 434

Proof

Diagram

Given: $\dfrac{VX}{XU} = \dfrac{VY}{YW}$

Prove: $\overline{XY} \parallel \overline{UW}$

You're given that $\frac{VX}{XU} = \frac{VY}{YW}$. By the Segment Addition Postulate, $VX + XU = VU$, or $XU = VU - VX$, and $VY + YW = VW$, or $YW = VW - VY$. By substitution, $\frac{VX}{VU - VX} = \frac{VY}{VW - VY}$. You can simplify this to $\frac{VX}{VU} = \frac{VY}{VW}$. You know that $\angle 1 \cong \angle 1$. The SAS Similarity Theorem tells you that $\triangle XVY \sim \triangle UVW$ since the corresponding sides of the triangles are proportional. The definition of similar triangles tells you $\angle 2 \cong \angle 3$ and $\angle 4 \cong \angle 5$. The Corresponding Angles Postulate then allows you to conclude that $\overline{XY} \parallel \overline{UW}$.

Angle Bisector Proofs

Theorem   If a ray bisects an angle of a triangle, then it divides the opposite side into segments whose lengths are proportional to the lengths of the other two sides. △; ∠ bisector ⇒ opp. side segs. proportional to other 2 sides. (T096)

Proof

Given: $\overrightarrow{LP}$ bisects $\angle MLN$

Prove: $\dfrac{MP}{PN} = \dfrac{LM}{LN}$

Diagram

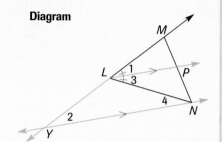

MORE HELP
See 056, 376, 432, 434

Plan: Construct $\overleftrightarrow{YN} \parallel \overrightarrow{LP}$. Extend $\overline{ML}$ to intersect $\overleftrightarrow{YN}$. Then you can use the Triangle Proportionality Theorem on $\triangle MYN$ and substitute LN for LY to complete the proof.

Statements	Reasons
❶ Extend $\overline{ML}$	Def. of line segment
❷ $\overleftrightarrow{YN} \parallel \overrightarrow{LP}$	Construction
❸ $\dfrac{MP}{PN} = \dfrac{LM}{LY}$	△ Proportionality Theorem (T094)
❹ $\angle 2 \cong \angle 1$	Corresp. ∠s Postulate (P15)
❺ $\overrightarrow{LP}$ bisects $\angle MLN$	Given
❻ $\angle 1 \cong \angle 3$	Def. of ∠ bisector
❼ $\angle 3 \cong \angle 4$	Alt. Int. ∠s Theorem (T027)
❽ $\angle 2 \cong \angle 4$	Substitution Look at steps 4, 6, and 7.
❾ $\overline{LY} \cong \overline{LN}$	Converse of Base ∠s Theorem (T051)
❿ $LY = LN$	Def. of ≅
⓫ $\dfrac{MP}{PN} = \dfrac{LM}{LN}$	Substitution Look back at steps 3 and 10.

Recall that in right triangles the side opposite the right angle is the hypotenuse, and the other two sides are the legs.

The Pythagorean Theorem relates the lengths of the sides of a right triangle: $a^2 + b^2 = c^2$ (a and b are the lengths of the legs and c is the length of the hypotenuse). Other right triangle theorems involve the similar triangles formed by the altitude to the hypotenuse.

MORE HELP
See 066, 150, 152

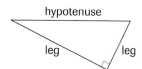

Proportions in Right Triangles

235

| **Theorem** | If the altitude is drawn to the hypotenuse of a right triangle, then the two triangles formed are similar to the original triangle and to each other. Altitude to hypotenuse $\Rightarrow$ 2 new $\triangle$s ~ to original and to each other (T097) |

MORE HELP
See 068, 137, 275, 281, 432, 434

Proof

Given: $\overline{BD}$ is an altitude of right $\triangle ABC$

Prove: $\triangle ADB \sim \triangle ABC \sim \triangle BDC$

Diagram

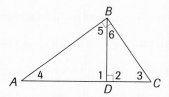

Plan: To prove this theorem, you can prove each smaller right triangle similar to the original right triangle and then show that the smaller right triangles are similar to each other.

$\angle 1 \cong \angle ABC$ because both are right angles. $\angle 4 \cong \angle 4$ by the Reflexive Property of Congruence. This means that $\triangle ADB \sim \triangle ABC$ by the AA Similarity Postulate.

You can use similar reasoning to prove $\triangle BDC \sim \triangle ABC$. Since corresponding angles of similar triangles $\triangle ADB$ and $\triangle ABC$ are congruent, you know that $\angle 6 \cong \angle 4$. You also know that $\angle 1 \cong \angle 2$, because both are right angles. Thus, $\triangle ADB \sim \triangle BDC$ by the AA Similarity Postulate.

MORE ▶

To help you better understand this theorem, look at the three similar triangles, $\triangle ADB$, $\triangle BDC$, and $\triangle ABC$. They have been separated and rotated or reflected to show them in the same orientation.

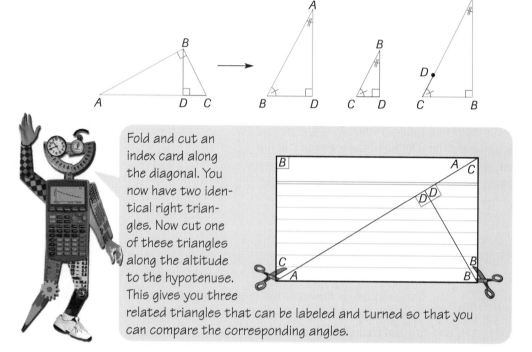

Fold and cut an index card along the diagonal. You now have two identical right triangles. Now cut one of these triangles along the altitude to the hypotenuse. This gives you three related triangles that can be labeled and turned so that you can compare the corresponding angles.

EXAMPLE: Find the length of the altitude, XZ, of triangle WXY.

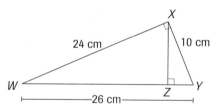

Because $\overline{XZ}$ is the altitude to the hypotenuse, $\triangle WZX \sim \triangle WXY$. To find XZ, you can set up and solve a proportion involving corresponding sides of the similar triangles. Let $x = XZ$.

$$\frac{XZ}{XY} = \frac{WX}{WY}$$
$$\frac{x}{10} = \frac{24}{26}$$
$$26x = 240$$
$$x \approx 9.2$$

★ The length of $\overline{XZ}$ is about 9.2 centimeters.

Geometric Mean Theorems

MORE HELP
See 219–220

When the middle terms, or means, of a proportion are equal, that value is the **geometric mean** of the extremes. If $\frac{a}{x} = \frac{x}{b}$, then x is the geometric mean of a and b and is equal to the positive square root of ab.

EXAMPLE 1: What is the geometric mean of 10 and 20?

Let $a = 10$, $b = 20$, and let x represent the geometric mean of a and b.

$$\frac{10}{x} = \frac{x}{20}$$

$$10 \cdot 20 = x^2$$

$$200 = x^2$$

$$\sqrt{200} = x$$

$$14.14 \approx x$$

★ The geometric mean of 10 and 20 is approximately 14.14.

MORE HELP
See 226

You can use the fact that the corresponding sides of similar triangles are proportional to prove the next two theorems. You can then use these theorems to make indirect measurements.

Theorem

In a right triangle, the altitude divides the hypotenuse into two segments. The length of the altitude is the geometric mean of the lengths of the two segments. Altitude to hypotenuse $\Rightarrow \frac{\text{seg}_1}{h} = \frac{h}{\text{seg}_2}$ (T098)

Proof

Given: $\overline{BD}$ is an altitude of right $\triangle ABC$

Prove: $\dfrac{AD}{BD} = \dfrac{BD}{CD}$

Diagram

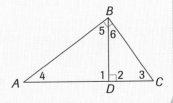

$\triangle ADB \sim \triangle BDC$, because the triangles formed by the altitude to the hypotenuse are similar to each other. Because the corresponding sides of similar triangles are proportional, $\frac{AD}{BD} = \frac{BD}{CD}$.

MORE ▶

EXAMPLE 2: To estimate the height of a sculpture, you hold a corner of a square sheet of paper in front of one eye and move back until the top edge of the paper lines up with the top of the sculpture and the bottom edge lines up with the ground. The distance between you and the sculpture is 20 feet and the distance between your eyes and the ground is 5.5 feet. About how tall is the sculpture?

The distance between you and the sculpture is the altitude of a right triangle that divides the hypotenuse into two segments. You can set up and solve a proportion to find the height of the sculpture.

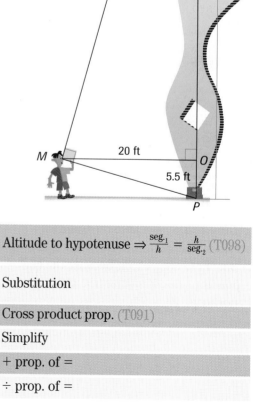

$\dfrac{NO}{MO} = \dfrac{MO}{OP}$	Altitude to hypotenuse $\Rightarrow \dfrac{\text{seg.}_1}{h} = \dfrac{h}{\text{seg.}_2}$ (T098)
$\dfrac{NP - 5.5}{20} = \dfrac{20}{5.5}$	Substitution
$5.5(NP - 5.5) = 20^2$	Cross product prop. (T091)
$5.5\,NP - 30.25 = 400$	Simplify
$5.5\,NP = 430.25$	+ prop. of =
$NP \approx 78.2$	÷ prop. of =

★ The height of the sculpture is about 78 feet.

Theorem In a right triangle, the altitude divides the hypotenuse into two segments. Each leg is the geometric mean of the hypotenuse and the segment of the hypotenuse that is adjacent to that leg. Altitude to hypotenuse ⇒ leg = geo. mean of hypotenuse and seg. adj. to leg (T099)

Proof

Diagram

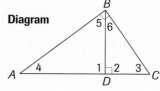

Given: $\overline{BD}$ is an altitude of right △ABC

Prove: $\dfrac{AC}{AB} = \dfrac{AB}{AD}$ and $\dfrac{AC}{CB} = \dfrac{CB}{DC}$

The proof of this theorem follows reasoning similar to that of the previous theorem except that △ADB ~ △ABC and △BDC ~ △ABC.

One proof of the Pythagorean Theorem is based on the areas of a square and a triangle. Here is a different proof of the same theorem.

MORE HELP
See 027, 152, 220, 375, 432, 434

Theorem In a right triangle, the square of the length of the hypotenuse is equal to the sum of the squares of the lengths of the legs. Pythagorean Theorem (T059)

Proof

Diagram

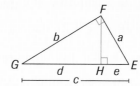

Given: right △EFG

Prove: $c^2 = a^2 + b^2$

Plan: If you construct the altitude to the hypotenuse, you can use the geometric mean.

Statements	Reasons
❶ △EFG is a right triangle	Given
❷ $\overline{FH}$ is the altitude to hypotenuse	Construction
❸ $\dfrac{c}{a} = \dfrac{a}{e}$ and $\dfrac{c}{b} = \dfrac{b}{d}$	Altitude to hypotenuse ⇒ leg = geo. mean of hypotenuse and seg. adj. to leg (T099)
❹ $ce = a^2$ and $cd = b^2$	Cross product prop. (T091)
❺ $ce + cd = a^2 + b^2$	+ prop. of =
❻ $c(e + d) = a^2 + b^2$	Distributive prop.
❼ $e + d = c$	Seg. + Postulate (P09) Look at the diagram.
❽ $c^2 = a^2 + b^2$	Substitution Look at steps 6 and 7.

Special Right Triangles

MORE HELP
See 152, 236

In special right triangles—triangles with specific angle measures—you find special relationships among the hypotenuse and the legs. The special right triangles have angle measures of 45°-45°-90° and 30°-60°-90°.

Isosceles Right Triangles

An isosceles right triangle has two congruent sides and two congruent base angles. Therefore, it has two 45° angles and one 90° angle.

MORE HELP
See 134, 143, 246, 434

Theorem   In a 45°-45°-90° triangle, the hypotenuse is $\sqrt{2}$ times as long as each leg. 45-45-90 $\triangle \Rightarrow c = a\sqrt{2} = b\sqrt{2}$ (T100)

Proof

Given: JKL is a 45°-45°-90° triangle

Prove: $k = \ell\sqrt{2} = j\sqrt{2}$

By the Converse of the Base Angles Theorem, $j = \ell$. The Pythagorean Theorem tells you that $k^2 = \ell^2 + j^2$. Substitute ℓ for j and you get $k^2 = \ell^2 + \ell^2$, or $k^2 = 2\ell^2$. Solving for k you get $k = \ell\sqrt{2}$. Now go back and substitute j for ℓ and you get $k^2 = j^2 + j^2$ or $k = j\sqrt{2}$.

Diagram

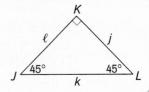

EXAMPLE: A ramp at a skateboard park has a 45° angle of elevation. The ramp is 50 feet long. To the nearest foot, how far above the ground is the top of the ramp?

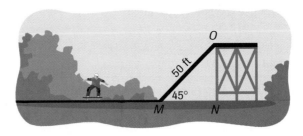

$\triangle MNO$ is a 45°-45°-90° triangle. This means that the length of the hypotenuse, MO, is $\sqrt{2}$ times as long as the length of each leg.

> Remember, distance in a case like this means the perpendicular distance.

$MO = \sqrt{2}\ ON$	45-45-90 $\triangle \Rightarrow c = a\sqrt{2} = b\sqrt{2}$ (T100)
$50 = \sqrt{2}\ ON$	Substitution
$\dfrac{50}{\sqrt{2}} = ON$	÷ prop. of =

★ The top of the ramp is $\frac{50}{\sqrt{2}}$ feet above the ground. This is about 35.4 feet.

> $\frac{50}{\sqrt{2}}$ may be written without the radical in the denominator by multiplying both numerator and denominator by $\sqrt{2}$. Then the answer is $\frac{50\sqrt{2}}{2}$, or $25\sqrt{2}$. This is called **rationalizing the denominator** and was a very common form for presenting a solution before calculators were commonplace. It lets you avoid dividing by a divisor with several decimal places. Of course, your calculator doesn't care about dividing with complicated decimals!

30°-60°-90° Triangles

239

Theorem	In a $30°$-$60°$-$90°$ triangle, the hypotenuse is twice as long as the shorter leg and the longer leg is $\sqrt{3}$ times as long as the shorter leg. 30-60-90 $\triangle \Rightarrow c = 2a;\ b = \sqrt{3}a$ (T101)

Proof

Diagram

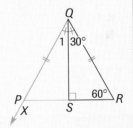

ONE WAY

Given: QSR is a $30°$-$60°$-$90°$ triangle.

Prove: $QR = 2RS$, $QS = RS\sqrt{3}$

Plan: A $30°$-$60°$-$90°$ triangle is half of an equilateral triangle. By constructing the other half of the equilateral triangle, you find that the shortest side of the $30°$-$60°$-$90°$ triangle is half the length of the shorter side of the equilateral triangle, which is also the length of the hypotenuse of the $30°$-$60°$-$90°$ triangle. Use the Pythagorean Theorem to find the length of the longer leg.

MORE HELP
See 152, 432, 434

MORE ▶

Statements	Reasons
❶ QSR is a 30°-60°-90° triangle	Given
❷ Draw $\overrightarrow{QX}$ so that m∠1 = 30°	Protractor Postulate (P12)
❸ Mark P on $\overrightarrow{QX}$ so that $QP = QR$	Ruler Postulate (P08)
❹ $\overline{QS} \cong \overline{QS}$	Reflexive prop. of $\cong$ (T105)
❺ $\triangle QSP \cong \triangle QSR$	SAS $\cong$ Postulate (P23)
❻ $\overline{PS} \cong \overline{RS}$; $PS = RS$	CPCTC; def. of $\cong$
❼ $PR = RS + SP$	Seg. + Postulate (P09)
❽ $PR = RS + RS$	Substitution
❾ $PR = 2RS$	Distributive prop.
❿ m∠R = m∠P = 60°	CPCTC
⓫ m∠RQP = 60°	∠ + Postulate (P13)
⓬ $\triangle PQR$ is equiangular	Def. of equiangular $\triangle$
⓭ $\triangle PQR$ is equilateral	Equilateral $\triangle \Leftrightarrow$ equiangular $\triangle$ (T052)
⓮ $PR = QR$	Def. of equilateral
⓯ $QR = 2RS$	Substitution *See steps 9 and 14.*
⓰ $QR^2 = QS^2 + RS^2$	Pythagorean Theorem (T059)
⓱ $(2RS)^2 = QS^2 + RS^2$	Substitution *Look at step 15.*
⓲ $4RS^2 = QS^2 + RS^2$	Simplify
⓳ $4RS^2 - RS^2 = QS^2 + RS^2 - RS^2$	Subtraction prop. of =
⓴ $3RS^2 = QS^2$	Simplify
㉑ $RS\sqrt{3} = QS$	Simplify

ANOTHER WAY You could start with an equilateral triangle. Drop an altitude to create a 30°-60°-90° triangle, QSR, then use the Pythagorean Theorem as in steps 16–21 above to complete the proof.

EXAMPLE 1: The pitch of a symmetrical roof on a house that is 12 meters wide is 30°. What is the length of the rafter, TV, to the nearest tenth of a meter?

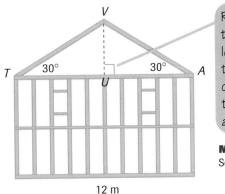

Remember, the longer leg of a triangle is opposite the larger angle.

MORE HELP
See 140

$\triangle TAV$ is isosceles. Its vertex angle has a measure of 120° ($180 - 30 - 30 = 120$). The altitude from the vertex of an isosceles triangle bisects the vertex angle, so $\triangle TUV$ is a 30°-60°-90° triangle. Its longer leg is 6 meters, half the width of the house.

The length of the longer leg, b, is $\sqrt{3}$ times the length of the shorter leg, a. The length of the hypotenuse, c, is twice the length of the shorter leg, a.

$6 = a\sqrt{3}$

$\dfrac{6}{\sqrt{3}} = a$

$3.46 \approx a$

$c = 2a$

$\approx 2(3.46)$

≈ 6.92

★ The rafter is about 6.9 meters long.

You can also use the relationships in a 30°-60°-90° triangle to find the height of an equilateral triangle and the length of the apothem of a regular hexagon. The **apothem** is the perpendicular distance from the center of a regular polygon to a side.

MORE HELP
See 129, 131

EXAMPLE 2: Find the length of the apothem, OP, of regular hexagon $EFGHIJ$ to the nearest tenth of a centimeter.

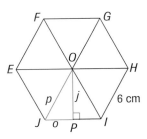

The measures of the interior angles of a regular hexagon are 120°, so the diagonals connecting opposite vertices intersect at the center to form equilateral triangles. Half of a diagonal, $\overline{OJ}$; the apothem, $\overline{OP}$; and half of a side, $\overline{PJ}$ form the 30°-60°-90° triangle JOP. Each side of $EFGHIJ$ is 6 centimeters long, so PJ is 3 centimeters long.

$j = o\sqrt{3}$

$j = 3\sqrt{3}$

≈ 5.2

★ The apothem of hexagon $EFGHIJ$ is about 5.2 centimeters long.

MORE HELP
See 234, 422

Trigonometry comes from the Greek language and means *triangle measurement*. Thousands of years ago, astronomers and mathematicians understood that, if the ratio of two sides of a right triangle were known, they could determine the measures of the acute angles. That's because all right triangles with acute angles of 27° and 63° are similar, as are all right triangles with acute angles of 33° and 57°, and so on.

Mathematicians in other ancient civilizations made tables to show the ratio of side lengths for each angle measured in fractions of degrees. During the Middle Ages, mathematicians converted the fractions in these tables to decimals. These trigonometric tables are still used today, although you might prefer to use your calculator to find these values. Calculators with keys SIN, COS, and TAN have these ratios built into their memory.

DID YOU KNOW The first known table of trigonometric values was compiled by Ptolemy in his book *Syntaxis mathematica* in about 150 A.D. It gave the ratios for the sides of right triangles for all acute angles between 0° and 90° in 15′ increments. It was the standard reference for trig ratios until Copernicus published a table correct to five decimal places 1400 years later.

Write: *15′*
Say: *15 minutes*

Just as with time, a minute is $\frac{1}{60}$ of a degree, so $15' = \frac{1}{4}°$.

Trigonometric Ratios

A right triangle has three sides, so only three pairs of sides can be compared: leg 1 and leg 2, leg 1 and the hypotenuse, and leg 2 and the hypotenuse. **Trigonometric ratios** (also called trig functions) are ratios that compare the lengths of two sides of a right triangle.

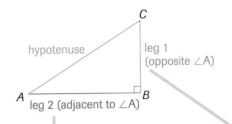

hypotenuse

leg 1 (opposite ∠A)

A

leg 2 (adjacent to ∠A)

B

The leg adjacent to ∠A has A as an endpoint.

The leg opposite ∠A does not contain point A.

Name of Ratio (Always refers to one of the acute angles.)	Ratio
Sine of ∠A (sin A)	$\dfrac{\text{length of leg opposite } \angle A}{\text{length of hypotenuse}}$, or $\dfrac{BC}{AC}$
Cosine of ∠A (cos A)	$\dfrac{\text{length of leg adjacent to } \angle A}{\text{length of hypotenuse}}$, or $\dfrac{AB}{AC}$
Tangent of ∠A (tan A)	$\dfrac{\text{length of leg opposite } \angle A}{\text{length of leg adjacent to } \angle A}$, or $\dfrac{BC}{AB}$

To remember these ratios, you can think SOH-CAH-TOA:

sine = opposite over hypotenuse

cosine = adjacent over hypotenuse

tangent = opposite over adjacent

Three other trigonometric ratios are the reciprocals of the three shown. They were usually used to avoid dividing by a long decimal number. These are rarely used today, because calculators, not human beings, are doing the dividing.

Cotangent A (or cot A) $= \dfrac{1}{\tan A}$

Secant A (or sec A) $= \dfrac{1}{\cos A}$

Cosecant A (or csc A) $= \dfrac{1}{\sin A}$

MORE ▶

You can find the sine, cosine, and tangent of an angle in several ways, depending on the information you have.

CASE 1 If you are given the side lengths of a right triangle, you can write ratios as decimals rounded to four decimal places.

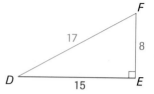

EXAMPLE 1: Find sine, cosine, and tangent of $\angle D$.

$$\sin D = \frac{\text{length of leg opposite } \angle D}{\text{length of hypotenuse}} = \frac{8}{17} \text{ or about } 0.4706$$

$$\cos D = \frac{\text{length of leg adjacent to } \angle D}{\text{length of hypotenuse}} = \frac{15}{17} \text{ or about } 0.8824$$

$$\tan D = \frac{\text{length of leg opposite } \angle D}{\text{length of leg adjacent to } \angle D} = \frac{8}{15} \text{ or about } 0.5333$$

★ The sine of $\angle D$ is approximately 0.4706, the cosine of $\angle D$ is approximately 0.8824, and the tangent of $\angle D$ is approximately 0.5333.

CASE 2 If you are given the measure of an acute angle of a right triangle, you can use a calculator or a table.

MORE HELP
See 390

EXAMPLE 2: Find sine, cosine, and tangent of $\angle G$.

ONE WAY To use your calculator, be sure to set it in degree mode. Your calculator may use different keystrokes. Round to four decimal places.

SIN 5 0 ENTER	.7660444431	Round to 0.7660
COS 5 0 ENTER	.6427876097	Round to 0.6428
TAN 5 0 ENTER	1.191753593	Round to 1.1918

MORE HELP
See 422

ANOTHER WAY To use the Table of Trigonometric Functions in the Almanac of this book, find the measure of $\angle G$ in the first column. Then read across.

Angle	Sine	Cosine	Tangent
50°	.7660	.6428	1.1918

★ Either way, the sine of $\angle G$ is approximately 0.7660, the cosine of $\angle G$ is approximately 0.6428, and the tangent of $\angle G$ is approximately 1.1918.

MATH ALERT There are Two Ways to Measure Angles

242

Angles can be measured in either degrees or radians. In radian measure, the size of the angle is a ratio that compares the length of the arc with endpoints on the angle to the radius of the arc. For example, the measure of a 360° angle is 2π radians and the measure of a 90° angle is $\frac{\pi}{2}$ radians.

MORE HELP
See 392, 416

If your calculator is not in degree mode, it will interpret 30° as 30 radians, an angle whose measure is very different from 30°.

Inverse Trigonometric Ratios

243

If you know the sine, cosine, or tangent of an acute angle of a right triangle, you can use an inverse trigonometric function to find the measure of that acute angle. The inverse trig function will give you the measure of the angle when you know the ratio of two sides.

MORE HELP
See 422

EXAMPLE 1: Find m∠D to the nearest degree.

Use the sine function. Find the ratio of the side opposite ∠D to the hypotenuse and write it as a decimal.

$\sin D = \dfrac{4}{5} = 0.8$

ONE WAY If you are using a table, find in the Sine column the number closest to 0.8. Read the angle measure in the first column. This will be the closest approximation to the size of your angle.

Angle	Sine
52°	.7880
53°	.7986
54°	.8090

.7986 is closest to 0.8, so m∠D ≈ 53°.

> You could have found m∠D from the table using either the cosine or the tangent function as well.

MORE ▶

ANOTHER WAY You can't work backward from a table when you're using a calculator, but you can use inverse trig functions. ($\sin^{-1}$, $\cos^{-1}$, $\tan^{-1}$). $\mathrm{Sin}\,D \approx 0.8$, so $\sin^{-1} 0.8 \approx m\angle D$.

MORE HELP
See 390

Write: $\sin^{-1} x$

Say: *the inverse sine of x* or *the angle whose sine is x*

Use the following sequence of keystrokes or a sequence appropriate to your calculator. Be sure the calculator is in degree mode.

| 2nd | SIN | (| . | 8 | ENTER | 53.13010235 |

★ Either way, the measure of $\angle D$ to the nearest degree is 53°.

244 Solving Right Triangles

How do scientists measure the distance to the sun or other stars? They certainly don't lay out a giant tape measure! Mathematicians, astronomers, other scientists, and engineers have long used trigonometric ratios to indirectly measure distances that cannot be measured directly. They use the ratios to find the length of one or more sides or the measure of one or both acute angles in a right triangle.

245 Sketching and Labeling Information

You know that drawing a diagram can help you solve some problems. This is especially true when making indirect measurements.

EXAMPLE: You have a furniture moving company and need to get ramps for your new fleet of trucks. The ramps need to rise $2\frac{1}{2}$ feet at a 15° angle to be most efficient for your workers. How long should the ramps be, to the nearest inch?

Begin by sketching what you know.

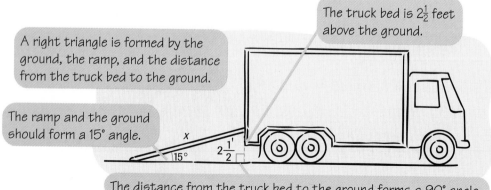

The truck bed is $2\frac{1}{2}$ feet above the ground.

A right triangle is formed by the ground, the ramp, and the distance from the truck bed to the ground.

The ramp and the ground should form a 15° angle.

x

$2\frac{1}{2}$

15°

The distance from the truck bed to the ground forms a 90° angle.

What you know:

MORE HELP
See 241

■ an angle measure, and

■ the length of the side opposite the known angle.

What you need to find out:

■ the length of the hypotenuse.

The sine ratio relates all three of these items. Use it to find the unknown length, x.

$$\text{sine of ramp angle} = \frac{\text{length of opposite side}}{\text{length of hypotenuse}}$$

$$\sin 15° = \frac{2.5}{x}$$

$$x \cdot \sin 15° = 2.5$$

$$x = \frac{2.5}{\sin 15°}$$

$$\approx 9.66$$

Don't be fooled! 0.66 is *not* 0.66 inches, but 0.66 feet. 0.66 feet · 12 inches in one foot ≈ 8 inches.

★ The ramps should be about 9.66 feet long. This is 9 feet 8 inches to the nearest inch.

Angles of Elevation and Depression

246

Suppose you are standing on the ground looking up at the top of an observation tower. The angle that your line of sight makes with a horizontal line is the **angle of elevation**. If you are standing at the top looking down, the angle that your line of sight makes with a horizontal line is the **angle of depression**.

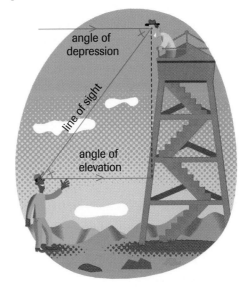

EXAMPLE: As a plane begins its final approach to an airport, it is 8.8 miles from the airport. It will descend at a 15° angle. To the nearest foot, what is the plane's current altitude?

MORE ▶

MORE HELP
See 241

The vertical distance from the plane to the ground itself, the ground, and the plane's flight path form a right triangle. The angle at which the plane is descending is an angle of depression. It is congruent to the angle of elevation in the diagram. They are alternate interior angles formed by parallel lines and a transversal.

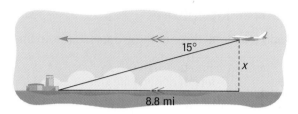

What you know:

- an acute angle of a right triangle, and
- the length of the adjacent side.

What you need to find:

- the length of the side opposite the acute angle.

Use the tangent ratio because it compares the length of the side opposite an angle to the length of the adjacent side.

$$\sin 15° = \frac{\text{length of opposite side}}{\text{length of adjacent side}}$$

$$\sin 15° = \frac{x}{46,464} \qquad 8.8 \text{ mi} \cdot \frac{5280\text{ ft}}{1\text{ mi}} = 46,464 \text{ ft}$$

$$46,464 \cdot \tan 15° = x$$

$$12,450 \approx x$$

★ The plane's altitude is about 12,450 feet.

247 Solving Non-Right Triangles

Although trigonometric ratios are derived from right triangles, they can be used to find unknown lengths and angle measures in acute and obtuse triangles as well. The next few pages show how to find missing lengths in acute triangles.

248 Law of Sines

If you know the measures of two angles of a triangle and the length of one side, you can use the Law of Sines to find the lengths of the other two sides.

Theorem In any triangle ABC, $\frac{\sin A}{a} = \frac{\sin B}{b} = \frac{\sin C}{c}$. Law of Sines
(T102)

Proof

Given: Any acute triangle ABC

Prove: $\dfrac{\sin A}{a} = \dfrac{\sin B}{b} = \dfrac{\sin C}{c}$

Plan: Begin with any acute triangle, and draw two altitudes, forming some right triangles. Next, use these triangles to find the sine of each angle in the original triangle. Algebra will help you show the relationship you're trying to prove.

> This formula also applies to obtuse triangles, but the algebra is more complex, because some of the right triangles fall outside the given triangle.

Diagram

Statements	Reasons
❶ Acute triangle ABC	Given
❷ Construct altitudes from A and C to their opposite sides. Call their lengths h and i	Construction
❸ $\sin A = \dfrac{h}{b}$, $\sin B = \dfrac{h}{a}$ $\sin B = \dfrac{i}{c}$, $\sin C = \dfrac{i}{b}$	Def. of sine ratio
❹ $b \sin A = h$, $a \sin B = h$ $c \sin B = i$, $b \sin C = i$	$\times$ prop. of $=$
❺ $b \sin A = a \sin B$ $c \sin B = b \sin C$	Substitution
❻ $\dfrac{\sin A}{a} = \dfrac{\sin B}{b}$ $\dfrac{\sin B}{b} = \dfrac{\sin C}{c}$	$\div$ prop. of $=$
❼ $\dfrac{\sin A}{a} = \dfrac{\sin B}{b} = \dfrac{\sin C}{c}$	Transitive prop. of $=$

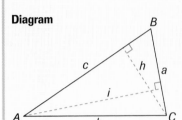
$$\frac{\cancel{b} \sin A}{a\cancel{b}} = \frac{\cancel{a} \sin B}{\cancel{a}b}$$
$$\frac{\cancel{c} \sin B}{b\cancel{c}} = \frac{\cancel{b} \sin C}{\cancel{b}c}$$

MORE HELP
See 137, 241, 375

Law of Cosines

If you know the lengths of three sides of a triangle, you can use the Law of Cosines to find the measures of the angles. If you know the lengths of two sides of a triangle and the measure of the included angle, you can also use this law to find the length of the third side.

MORE HELP
See 137, 241, 375, 432, 434

Theorem In any triangle ABC, $a^2 = b^2 + c^2 - 2bc \cos A$.
Law of Cosines (T103)

Proof

Diagram

Given: Any triangle ABC

Prove: $a^2 = b^2 + c^2 - 2bc \cos A$

Plan: Start with any triangle and draw an altitude from the largest angle. Then apply the Pythagorean Theorem to both right triangles formed by the altitude and the sides of the original triangle.

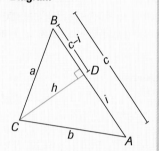

Look at $\triangle BDC$.

$a^2 = h^2 + (c - i)^2$

$\quad = h^2 + c^2 - 2ci + i^2$

$\quad = h^2 + i^2 + c^2 - 2ci$ — In $\triangle ACD$, $\cos A = \frac{i}{b}$, so $b \cos A = i$

In $\triangle ACD$, $b^2 = h^2 + i^2$

Substitute b^2 for $h^2 + i^2$ and $b \cos A$ for i.

$a^2 = h^2 + i^2 + c^2 - 2ci$

$\quad = b^2 + c^2 - 2bc \cos A$

Another form of the Law of Cosines is $c^2 = a^2 + b^2 - 2ab \cos C$.

The Golden Rectangle was considered by the Greeks to be the most aesthetically pleasing of all rectangular shapes. It is called a Golden Rectangle because the ratio of the lengths of the longer side to the shorter side is the golden ratio. Both the Golden Rectangle and fractals are examples of geometric figures seen in everyday life.

Golden Ratio _____

251

A segment is divided into two lengths that form a **golden ratio** if the longer of the two segments is the geometric mean of the shorter segment and the whole segment, $\frac{a+b}{b} = \frac{b}{a}$.

MORE HELP
See 214–215, 236

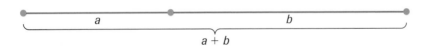

$$a \qquad b$$
$$a + b$$

> **DID YOU KNOW**   Pythagoras and his followers were particularly intrigued by the golden ratio. They adopted the pentagram as a symbol of their alliance because it contained so many ratios that were golden ratios.
>
>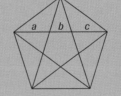
>
> Golden ratios in the pentagram:
>
> $$\frac{a+b+c}{b+c} = \frac{b+c}{c} = \frac{c}{b}$$

Fibonacci Sequence

252

If you are looking for whole numbers that will form a golden ratio, one place to start is with the Fibonacci sequence:

MORE HELP
See 214–215

1, 1, 2, 3, 5, 8, 13, 21, 34, 55, 89 . . .

> Each term (after the second) is found by adding the previous two terms. For example $55 = 34 + 21$.

If you form ratios of two successive terms, such as $\frac{3}{2}$, $\frac{5}{3}$, and $\frac{8}{5}$, you will come closer and closer to a true golden ratio. With some good algebra skills, you can prove that this ratio is $\frac{1 + \sqrt{5}}{2}$ or about 1.618.

Golden Rectangle

A **golden rectangle** is a rectangle whose length and width are proportional to the golden ratio. Throughout history, golden rectangles have appeared in architecture and art because their dimensions were considered pleasing to the eye.

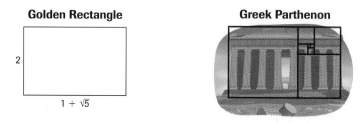

Golden Rectangle

2

$1 + \sqrt{5}$

Greek Parthenon

EXAMPLE: A property of a golden rectangle is that it can be cut into a square and a rectangle, such that the smaller rectangle is also a golden rectangle. Show that this is true.

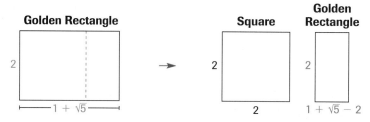

Golden Rectangle

2

$1 + \sqrt{5}$

Square

2

2

Golden Rectangle

2

$1 + \sqrt{5} - 2$

MORE HELP
See 222

You can use what you know about corresponding parts of similar polygons to prove that this property exists. If the larger and smaller rectangles are both golden rectangles, they are similar and this proportion is true. Here's why.

$$1 + \sqrt{5} : 2 \stackrel{?}{=} 2 : 1 + \sqrt{5} - 2$$

$$\frac{1 + \sqrt{5}}{2} \stackrel{?}{=} \frac{2}{1 + \sqrt{5} - 2}$$

$$\frac{1 + \sqrt{5}}{2} \stackrel{?}{=} \frac{2}{^-1 + \sqrt{5}}$$

$$(1 + \sqrt{5})(^-1 + \sqrt{5}) \stackrel{?}{=} 2^2$$

$$^-1 + 5 \stackrel{?}{=} 4$$

$$4 = 4$$

★ Since the cross products are equal; the proportion is true.

Fractals

Fractals are objects that have self-similarity, like the fronds of a fern or a snowflake. **Self-similarity** means that one part of the object can be enlarged to look like the whole object. If you were to magnify one part of a fractal, you would think you were looking at the whole fractal.

DID YOU KNOW The term *fractal* was first used by Benoit Mandelbrot (1924–), an early researcher of objects with self-similarity. Using a high-speed computer, he created one of the most well-known fractals, the Mandelbrot set.

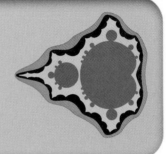

Many fractals are formed by **iteration**, the repetition of a sequence of steps. Look at these steps for drawing another well-known fractal, the Koch curve.

1. Draw a segment of length 1.

2. Replace the middle third of the segment with two segments of length $\frac{1}{3}$.

3. Replace the middle third of each segment with two segments of length $\frac{1}{9}$.

4. To continue, replace the middle third of each segment with two segments of length $\frac{1}{27}, \frac{1}{81}, \frac{1}{243}$, and so on.

If you were to join three Koch curves, you would create the shape known as the Koch snowflake.

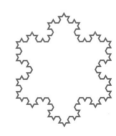

Congruence

"How can it be that mathematics, being after all a product of human thought independent of experience is so admirably adapted to the objects of reality?"

—*Albert Einstein*

Tell me again about that position thing.

The cartoon makes it clear that where you are or which direction you're facing can have a big effect on the shape you're in. In fact, your shape can change drastically in a few seconds. When life is more normal, however, size and shape don't change when location or orientation change.

In geometry, it often pays to know whether two figures have the same size and shape, regardless of position and orientation. If they are the same size and shape, then all the relationships in one figure are also true for the other.

For instance, suppose you have these rectangular frames. A diagonal wire on one frame forms an angle of about 30° with the 52-inch side. Since the second frame has the identical size and shape as the first, its diagonal and long side will form an angle of exactly the same measure as on the first.

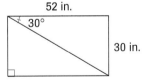

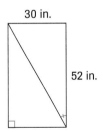

That's why paying attention to size and shape is so important. If you know something about one figure, then you know the same thing about all the figures that have the same size and shape. The frames are congruent even though their orientations and positions make them look different, but you don't have to worry about position and orientation when you're checking for congruence. Of course an oncoming train could change the story altogether.

Congruent figures have exactly the same size and the same shape. Notice that congruent figures can have different orientations and still be congruent. **Congruent segments** are segments that have the same length. **Congruent angles** are angles that have the same measure.

Congruent Figures   **Not Congruent Figures**

 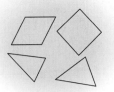

If two polygons are congruent, they share many properties. For example, the corresponding angles are congruent and the corresponding sides are congruent. Possibly the most frequently used abbreviation in geometry is CPCTC: corresponding parts of congruent triangles are congruent. CPCPC, for polygons, is also a useful abbreviation.

The notation $ABCD \cong QRST$ uses the symbol $\cong$ to show that these two quadrilaterals are congruent. The order of the letters used to name each figure is important, because this order shows how the vertices in $ABCD$ correspond to the vertices in $QRST$.

Write: $ABCD \cong QRST$

Say: *Figure A B C D is congruent to figure Q R S T.*

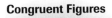

Corresponding Vertices	Corresponding Sides	Corresponding Angles
$A \longleftrightarrow Q$	$\overline{AB} \cong \overline{QR}$	$\angle A \cong \angle Q$
$B \longleftrightarrow R$	$\overline{BC} \cong \overline{RS}$	$\angle B \cong \angle R$
$C \longleftrightarrow S$	$\overline{CD} \cong \overline{ST}$	$\angle C \cong \angle S$
$D \longleftrightarrow T$	$\overline{DA} \cong \overline{TQ}$	$\angle D \cong \angle T$

Other corresponding parts, such as diagonals, are also congruent.

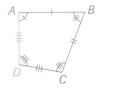

You can name the first figure in many ways, as long as adjacent letters name adjacent vertices. Once the first figure is named, however, there is only one way to name the second. For example, if you name the first figure *CBAD*, then you need to write *CBAD* ≅ *SRQT*, so that the correspondence between the vertices is still true.

A figure that is symmetric has a line of reflection, called the **line of symmetry**. Because the parts of the figure on either side of the line of symmetry are the same size and the same shape, the symmetric halves of the figure are congruent. Since the halves are congruent, they have corresponding parts. This observation leads to the following theorem.

MORE HELP
See 275, 279

Theorem   If a figure is symmetric, then any pair of corresponding parts under the symmetry is congruent. Symmetric fig. ⇒ corresp. parts ≅ (T104)

Proof

Diagram

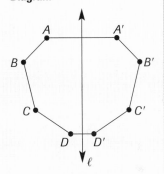

Given: Symmetric figure *ABCDD'C'B'A'*, ℓ is a line of symmetry

Prove: Corresponding segments are congruent, corresponding angles are congruent

If a figure is symmetric, then there is a line ℓ that divides the figure into two congruent halves. One half is the reflected image of the other half about this line. If *ABCD* represents any part of one half, then its image about the line of reflection is *A'B'C'D'*. Because reflections preserve distances and angle measures, all the corresponding segments and angles are congruent, so the two parts must also be congruent.

Equivalence Relations

These three properties all involve equivalence:

■ Reflexive property: Every object is equivalent to itself.

MORE HELP
See 033, 116

■ Symmetric property: If *a* is equivalent to *b*, then *b* is equivalent to *a*.

■ Transitive property: If *a* is equivalent to *b* and *b* is equivalent to *c*, then *a* is equivalent to *c*.

If all three properties are true for a relation, then the relation is called an **equivalence relation**. Equivalence relations can apply both to equality and to congruence.

MORE ▶

MORE HELP
See 058, 061

EXAMPLE: Which of these relations are equivalence relations?

a. *equality* for real numbers

b. *is parallel to* for lines

c. *is perpendicular to* for lines

Refer to the diagram. For each relation listed, the chart shows statements to represent the reflexive, symmetric, and transitive properties. The chart also shows whether the statement is true or false. Remember, if all three statements are true, the relation is an equivalence relation.

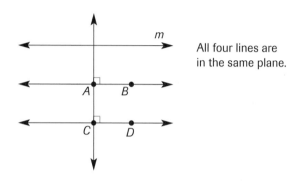

All four lines are in the same plane.

Property	equality	is parallel to	is perpendicular to
Reflexive	$AB = AB$: true	$\overleftrightarrow{AB} \parallel \overleftrightarrow{AB}$: false	$\overleftrightarrow{AB} \perp \overleftrightarrow{AB}$: false
Symmetric	If $AB = CD$, then $CD = AB$: true	If $\overleftrightarrow{AB} \parallel \overleftrightarrow{CD}$, then $\overleftrightarrow{CD} \parallel \overleftrightarrow{AB}$: true	If $\overleftrightarrow{AB} \perp \overleftrightarrow{AC}$, then $\overleftrightarrow{AC} \perp \overleftrightarrow{AB}$: true
Transitive	If $AB = CD$ and $CD = AC$, then $AB = AC$: true	If $\overleftrightarrow{AB} \parallel \overleftrightarrow{CD}$, and $\overleftrightarrow{CD} \parallel m$, then $\overleftrightarrow{AB} \parallel m$: true	If $\overleftrightarrow{AB} \perp \overleftrightarrow{AC}$ and $\overleftrightarrow{AC} \perp \overleftrightarrow{CD}$ then $\overleftrightarrow{AB} \perp \overleftrightarrow{CD}$: false

★ Since all three properties are true for *equality* of real numbers, this is an equivalence relation. Since only one or two of the properties are true for *is parallel to* and *is perpendicular to*, these are not equivalence relations.

In most geometry textbooks, the equivalence statements about congruent segments and congruent angles are definitions. However, in some books, only one definition of congruence is given, and it must apply to all figures. The definition of congruence these books use is similar to the following.

In an **isometry**, every distance in the image equals the corresponding distance in the preimage. Two figures are **congruent** if and only if there is a sequence of isometries that assigns exactly one point of the second figure to each point of the first figure.

To show that two segments or two angles are congruent you must find a sequence of isometries that will match the points of the first figure to the points of the second. The proofs of both statements use the same sequence of isometries. First translate the figure so that an endpoint or the vertex of the angle coincide. Then use a rotation about this point to match the remaining points, as shown in the diagram.

Given: $AB = PQ$
Prove: $\overline{AB} \cong \overline{PQ}$

Given: $m\angle BAC = m\angle QPR$
Prove: $\angle BAC \cong \angle QPR$

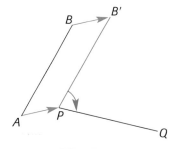

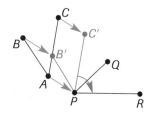

Translate $\overline{AB}$ to $\overline{PB'}$.
Rotate $\overline{PB'}$ to $\overline{PQ}$.

Translate $\angle BAC$ to $\angle B'PC'$.
Rotate $\angle B'PC'$ to QPR.

Reflexive, Symmetric, and Transitive Properties of Congruence

Congruence of segments and of angles are equivalence relations, because each relation is defined in terms of equal measures, which are real numbers. It follows then that congruence of polygons is an equivalence relation, as the following theorems show. Each proof is based on the equivalence properties of congruence for segments and for angles.

MORE HELP
See 033–036

A **figure** can be a segment, an angle, an arc, a circle, or a polygon.

Theorem — Every figure is congruent to itself. Reflexive prop. of $\cong$ (T105)

Proof

Given: $\angle A$ is an angle
Prove: $\angle A \cong \angle A$

Diagram

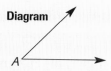

Since angle measures are real numbers, by the Reflexive Property of Equality, $m\angle A = m\angle A$. By definition of congruence, $\angle A \cong \angle A$.

Use a similar argument to show that any other figure is congruent to itself.

MORE ▶

Theorem   If figure A is congruent to figure D, then figure D is congruent to figure A. Symmetric prop. of $\cong$ (T106)

Proof

Diagram

A ————— B

C ————— D

Given: $\overline{AB} \cong \overline{CD}$

Prove: $\overline{CD} \cong \overline{AB}$

Plan: Use what you know about the definition of congruence.

Statements	Reasons
❶ $\overline{AB} \cong \overline{CD}$	Given
❷ $AB = CD$	Def. of $\cong$
❸ $CD = AB$; $\overline{CD} \cong \overline{AB}$	Symmetric prop. of $=$; def. of $\cong$

Use a similar argument to prove this theorem true for any other figure.

Theorem   If figure A is congruent to figure D and figure D is congruent to figure G, then figure A is congruent to figure G. Transitive prop. of $\cong$ (T107)

Proof

Diagram

P ————— B

C ————— Q

E ————— F

Given: $\overline{PB} \cong \overline{CQ}$ and $\overline{CQ} \cong \overline{EF}$

Prove: $\overline{PB} \cong \overline{EF}$

Plan: Use what you know about the definition of congruence.

Statements	Reasons
❶ $\overline{PB} \cong \overline{CQ}, \overline{CQ} \cong \overline{EF}$	Given
❷ $PB = CQ$, $CQ = EF$	Def. of $\cong$
❸ $PB = EF$; $\overline{PB} \cong \overline{EF}$	Transitive prop. of $=$; def. of $\cong$

Use a similar argument to prove this theorem true for any other figure.

You can apply the Properties of Congruence to a sheet of stamps. By the Reflexive Property of Congruence, each stamp is congruent to itself. By the Symmetric Property of Congruence, any pair of stamps is congruent. By the Transitive Property of Congruence, all the stamps on the sheet are congruent to each other.

When you make a duplicate key for a lock, it will only work if it has the same size and shape as the original key. The original key and the duplicate must be congruent. Otherwise, the duplicate will not open the lock.

To show that two polygons are congruent, you can use these methods.

1. Use the definition of congruence to show that all pairs of corresponding sides are congruent and all pairs of corresponding angles are congruent.

2. Use the equivalence properties of congruence.

Congruence of Triangles

260

If △ABC is congruent to △RST, then there is a correspondence between their angles and sides such that the corresponding angles are congruent and the corresponding sides are congruent.

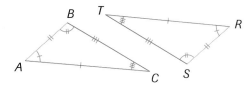

Side-Side-Side Congruence Postulate

261

Postulate If three sides of one triangle are congruent to three sides of a second triangle, then the two triangles are congruent. SSS ≅ Postulate (P22)

If Side $\overline{AB} \cong \overline{LM}$
  Side $\overline{BC} \cong \overline{MN}$
  Side $\overline{AC} \cong \overline{LN}$

Then △ABC ≅ △LMN

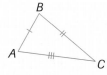

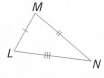

MORE ▶

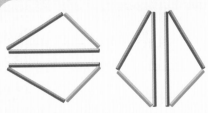

To see why this postulate works, consider six drinking straws that form two triangles. If the straws are all the same length, it is easy to see that all the triangles formed will be congruent.

Similarly, even if the three corresponding pairs of straws are different lengths, constructing a few triangles will convince you that whatever triangles you form will be congruent.

You can try this yourself using strips of posterboard and brads. Any triangle you can make will be rigid. You cannot change the measures of the angles unless you bend or shorten the strips. As long as the sides of the triangles stay congruent, the measures of the angles will also be congruent.

EXAMPLE: If $\overline{DE} \cong \overline{GF}$, and $\overline{DF} \cong \overline{GE}$, prove that $\triangle DEF \cong \triangle GFE$.

Proof

Diagram

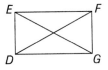

Given: $\overline{DE} \cong \overline{GF}, \overline{DF} \cong \overline{GE}$

Prove: $\triangle DEF \cong \triangle GFE$

Plan: Find a third pair of congruent sides and use the SSS Congruence Postulate to show that the two triangles are congruent.

Statements	Reasons
❶ $\overline{DE} \cong \overline{GF}$; $\overline{DF} \cong \overline{GE}$	Given
❷ $\overline{EF} \cong \overline{EF}$	Reflexive prop. of $\cong$ (T105)
❸ $\triangle DEF \cong \triangle GFE$	SSS $\cong$ Postulate (P22)

Because of the SSS Congruence Postulate, if the sides of a triangle are fixed, the size and shape of the triangle cannot change. The rigidity of the triangles means that triangular supports are stable and will retain their shape as long as they stay connected. A rectangular support, however, can change shape even when the sides stay attached. A basketball hoop with a triangular support will remain stable, even during a game!

Side-Angle-Side Congruence Postulate

The Side-Angle-Side Congruence Postulate provides another shortcut for proving two triangles are congruent. This works because once you establish the measure of an angle and the lengths of the two sides forming the angle, you've made sure that only one triangle can be made.

Postulate	If two sides and the included angle of one triangle are congruent to two sides and the included angle of a second triangle, then the two triangles are congruent.

SAS ≅ Postulate (P23)

If Side $\overline{DE} \cong \overline{QR}$
  Angle $\angle E \cong \angle R$
  Side $\overline{EF} \cong \overline{RS}$
Then $\triangle DEF \cong \triangle QRS$

If Side $\overline{AB} \cong \overline{LM}$
  Angle $\angle B \cong \angle M$
  Side $\overline{BC} \cong \overline{MN}$
Then $\triangle ABC \cong \triangle LMN$

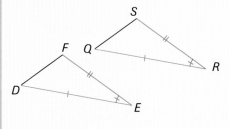

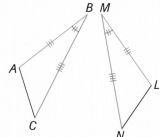

To understand why this postulate is reasonable, consider a hinge. If you set the two sides of the hinge so that the angle that is included between the two sides is fixed, a triangle is established. If you set another hinge that is the same size with the same included angle, the triangle that it forms is congruent to the triangle formed by the original hinge.

EXAMPLE 1: A contractor is building a roof truss following the design shown in the diagram. Can she conclude that $\triangle JKM$ is congruent to $\triangle LKM$?

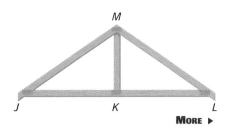

MORE ▶

Proof

Diagram

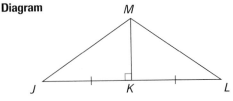

Given: $\overline{JK} \cong \overline{KL}$, $\overline{KM} \perp \overline{JL}$

Prove: $\triangle JKM \cong \triangle LKM$

Plan: One pair of congruent sides is given. Find a pair of congruent angles and another pair of congruent sides. Use the SAS Congruence Postulate to prove the triangles are congruent.

Statements	Reasons
❶ $\overline{JK} \cong \overline{KL}$, $\overline{KM} \perp \overline{JL}$	Given
❷ $\angle MKJ$ and $\angle MKL$ are rt. $\angle$s	$\perp$ lines $\Rightarrow$ 4 rt. $\angle$s (T011)
❸ $\angle MKJ \cong \angle MKL$	All rt. $\angle$s $\cong$ (T020)
❹ $\overline{KM} \cong \overline{KM}$	Reflexive prop. of $\cong$ (T105)
❺ $\triangle JKM \cong \triangle LKM$	SAS $\cong$ Postulate (P23)

★ The contractor can conclude that the two triangles are congruent.

You can use the same reasoning to prove that any point on a perpendicular bisector of a line segment is equidistant from the endpoints of that segment (part of the Perpendicular Bisector Theorem in 056).

EXAMPLE 2: Given the diagram as marked, prove $\triangle ABC \cong \triangle CDA$.

Proof

Diagram

Given: $\overline{AB} \parallel \overline{DC}$, $\overline{AB} \cong \overline{DC}$

Prove: $\triangle ABC \cong \triangle CDA$

Plan: One pair of congruent sides is given. Since $\overline{AB} \parallel \overline{DC}$, a pair of congruent alternate interior angles are formed by $\overline{AC}$. Using the Reflexive Property of Congruence, you can find another pair of congruent sides. The SAS Congruence Postulate will apply.

Statements	Reasons
❶ $\overline{AB} \cong \overline{DC}$; $\overline{AB} \parallel \overline{DC}$	Given
❷ $\angle 1 \cong \angle 2$	Alt. Int. $\angle$s Theorem (T027)
❸ $\overline{AC} \cong \overline{AC}$	Reflexive prop. of $\cong$ (T105)
❹ $\triangle ABC \cong \triangle CDA$	SAS $\cong$ Postulate (P23)

Angle-Side-Angle Congruence Theorem

Theorem	If two angles and the included side of one triangle are congruent to two angles and the included side of a second triangle, then the two triangles are congruent. ASA ≅ Theorem (T108)

Proof

Diagram

Given: Angle $\angle E \cong \angle K$; Side $\overline{DE} \cong \overline{JK}$
Angle $\angle D \cong \angle J$

Prove: $\triangle DEF \cong \triangle JKL$

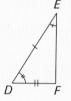

Plan: Do an indirect proof. Mark point F' on $\overrightarrow{JL}$ so that $JF' = DF$. Then $\triangle DEF \cong \triangle JKF'$. Show that F' cannot be between J and L nor can L be between J and F'. Then the only alternative left is for L to *be* F'. Therefore $\triangle DEF \cong \triangle JKL$.

Mark point F' on $\overrightarrow{JL}$ so that $JF' = DF$, which is possible by the Ruler Postulate. $\overline{DE} \cong \overline{JK}$ and $\angle D \cong \angle J$ from the given information, so $\triangle DEF \cong \triangle JKF'$ by the SAS Congruence Postulate.

If F' is between J and L, then it is in the interior of $\angle K$. But then $m\angle JKL = m\angle JKF' + m\angle F'KL$, by the Angle Addition Postulate. This means that $m\angle JKF' < m\angle JKL$ which, from the given, is congruent to $\angle E$. However, $\angle JKF' \cong \angle E$ from CPCTC. Since $m\angle JKF'$ cannot be both less than and equal to $m\angle E$ at the same time, F' is not between J and L.

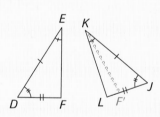

If L is between J and F', then L is in the interior of $\angle JKF'$ and by the Angle Addition Postulate $m\angle JKF' = m\angle JKL + m\angle LKF'$. This means that $m\angle JKF' > m\angle JKL$ which, from the given, is congruent to $\angle E$. However, $m\angle JKF' = m\angle E$. Since $m\angle JKF'$ cannot be both greater than and equal to $m\angle E$ at the same time, L cannot be between J and F'. The only place that F' can fall on $\overrightarrow{JL}$ is at the same point as L. Since $\triangle DEF \cong \triangle JKF'$, it follows that $\triangle DEF \cong \triangle JKL$.

MORE ▶

EXAMPLE: Given the diagram as marked, prove $\triangle PQR \cong \triangle STR$.

Proof   **Diagram**

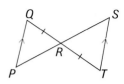

Given: $\overline{PQ} \parallel \overline{TS}$, $\overline{QR} \cong \overline{RT}$

Prove: $\triangle PQR \cong \triangle STR$

Plan: The vertical angles in the diagram are congruent. Because $\overline{PQ}$ is parallel to $\overline{TS}$, the alternate interior angles are congruent. The included sides, $\overline{PQ}$ and $\overline{TS}$, between those pairs of angles are congruent, so ASA will prove your point.

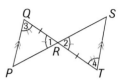

Statements	Reasons
❶ $\overline{QR} \cong \overline{RT}$; $\overline{PQ} \parallel \overline{TS}$	Given
❷ $\angle 3 \cong \angle 4$	Alt. Int. $\angle$s Theorem (T027)
❸ $\angle 1 \cong \angle 2$	Vert. $\angle$s $\cong$ (T023)
❹ $\triangle PQR \cong \triangle STR$	ASA $\cong$ Theorem (T108)

264

MATH ALERT Be Careful about Correspondence and Inclusion

Two sides of a triangle form an angle. This angle is called the **included angle.**

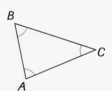

$\angle A$ is the included angle between $\overline{AB}$ and $\overline{AC}$.
$\angle B$ is the included angle between $\overline{AB}$ and $\overline{BC}$.
$\angle C$ is the included angle between $\overline{AC}$ and $\overline{CB}$.

If the congruent angles are not the included angles, you cannot use the SAS Congruence Postulate. It may lead you to false conclusions.

$\triangle ABC$ is not congruent to $\triangle JKL$, because $\angle A$ and $\angle J$ are not formed by corresponding congruent sides, so they are not the included angles. The SAS Congruence Postulate does not apply.

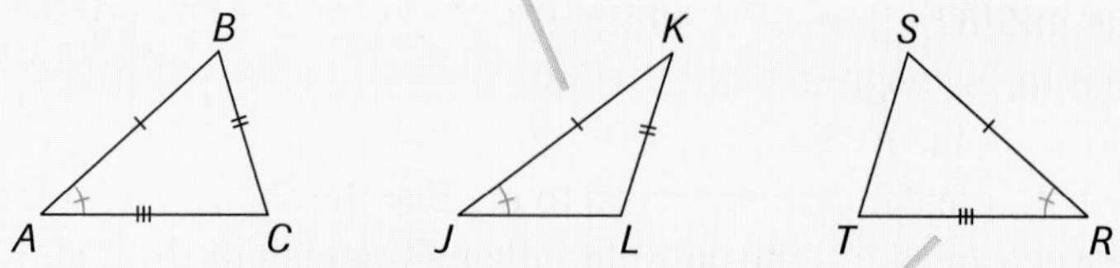

$\triangle ABC \cong \triangle RST$ by the SAS Congruence Postulate.

Two angles of a triangle share a common side.
This side is called the **included side.**

$\overline{AB}$ is the included side between $\angle A$ and $\angle B$.
$\overline{BC}$ is the included side between $\angle B$ and $\angle C$.
$\overline{AC}$ is the included side between $\angle A$ and $\angle C$.

If the congruent sides are not the included side, you cannot use the ASA Congruence Theorem.

EXAMPLE: Can you prove that
$\triangle ABC \cong \triangle DEF$? Explain.

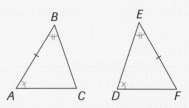

★ The triangles are not congruent. In
$\triangle ABC$, $\overline{AB}$ is the included side between $\angle A$ and $\angle B$. In $\triangle DEF$, $\overline{EF}$ is the
included side between $\angle E$ and $\angle F$. In order for the triangles to be congruent by the ASA Congruence Theorem, the included side in $\triangle DEF$ would
have to be $\overline{DE}$.

Angle-Angle-Side Congruence Theorem

The Angle-Angle-Side Congruence Theorem follows directly from the
Angle-Side-Angle Congruence Theorem and the Third Angles Theorem.

MORE HELP
See 143, 263

Theorem   If two angles and a nonincluded side of one triangle are
congruent to two angles and the corresponding non-
included side of a second triangle, then the triangles
are congruent. AAS $\cong$ Theorem (T109)

Proof   **Diagram**

Given: $\angle A \cong \angle D$, $\angle B \cong \angle E$, $\overline{AC} \cong \overline{DF}$

Prove: $\triangle ABC \cong \triangle DEF$

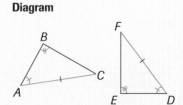

Plan: If two pairs of angles in two
triangles are congruent, then the third
pair of angles must also be congruent by
the Third Angles Theorem. This means you
can use the ASA Congruence Theorem.

Because two angles of $\triangle ABC$ are congruent to two angles of $\triangle DEF$
($\angle A \cong \angle D$ and $\angle B \cong \angle E$), $\angle C \cong \angle F$ by the Third Angles Theorem. Now
$\overline{AC}$ is the included side between $\angle A$ and $\angle C$ and $\overline{DF}$ is the included side
between $\angle D$ and $\angle F$. By the ASA $\cong$ Theorem, $\triangle ABC \cong \triangle DEF$.

266

MATH ALERT Watch Out For Methods That Do *Not* Establish Congruence

MORE HELP
See 222

Although Side-Side-Side (SSS) shows congruence between two triangles, the same is not true for Angle-Angle-Angle (AAA). Consider these triangles. While the corresponding angles of both triangles are congruent, the triangles *are not* congruent, but they *are* similar.

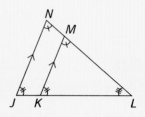

If you look at these two triangles in isolation, you can see why you might get confused.

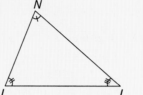

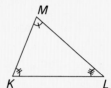

Although Angle-Angle-Side (AAS) shows congruence between two triangles, the same is not true for Side-Side-Angle (SSA). Look at △ANP. Think of side $\overline{AN}$ as a pendulum that you can swing toward point P. Eventually, the pendulum forms a vertex at point Q.

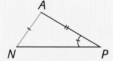

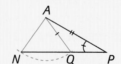

You've created a new triangle, △AQP. In △ANP and △AQP, $\overline{AN} \cong \overline{AQ}$ (both segments are the pendulum); $\overline{AP} \cong \overline{AP}$; and ∠APN ≅ ∠APQ. The two triangles have two pairs of corresponding sides and a pair of non-included angles (SSA) congruent. However, $\overline{NP}$ is not congruent to $\overline{QP}$ and ∠ANP is not congruent to ∠AQP. The two triangles are not congruent.

Side-Side-Angle (SSA) does not prove congruence. Two triangles with SSA correspondence and congruence CAN be congruent, but you don't know for sure unless you examine other angles and sides to see whether the pairs of corresponding parts are congruent.

Congruence of Right Triangles

Right triangles have special properties associated with them. It should not be surprising that they also have special congruence theorems.

MORE HELP
See 150, 266

Hypotenuse-Leg Congruence Theorem

The Hypotenuse-Leg (H-L) Congruence Theorem is a special case of Side-Side-Angle that does work. Remember SSA does not generally guarantee congruence.

MORE HELP
See 306–307

If a leg of a right triangle is pivoted about its non-right vertex, the only place it intersects the other leg is at the right angle. This is related to the fact that a radius is perpendicular to a tangent to the circle at their point of intersection.

| **Theorem** | If the hypotenuse and a leg of a right triangle are congruent to the hypotenuse and leg of a second right triangle, then the triangles are congruent. H-L ≅ Theorem (T110) |

Proof

Diagram

Given: $c = f$ and $b = e$ in right triangles ABC and DEF

Prove: $\triangle ABC \cong \triangle DEF$

ONE WAY **Plan:** Use the Pythagorean Theorem to show that $a = d$. Then use the SSS Congruence Postulate to complete the proof.

Statements	Reasons
❶ $\triangle ABC$ and $\triangle DEF$ are right triangles; $c = f, b = e$	Given
❷ $c^2 = f^2, b^2 = e^2$	× prop of =
❸ $a^2 + b^2 = c^2; d^2 + e^2 = f^2$	Pythagorean Theorem (T059)
❹ $a^2 + b^2 = d^2 + e^2$	Transitive prop. of =
❺ $a^2 + e^2 = d^2 + e^2$	Substitution Look back at step 3.
❻ $a^2 = d^2$	Subtraction prop. of =
❼ $a = d$	Simplify
❽ $\overline{AC} \cong \overline{DF}; \overline{AB} \cong \overline{DE}; \overline{BC} \cong \overline{FE}$	Def. of ≅
❾ $\triangle ABC \cong \triangle DEF$	SSS ≅ Postulate (P22)

MORE ▶

ANOTHER WAY Translate the second triangle so that the corresponding legs are coincident. The new triangle is an isosceles triangle, so the base angles are congruent. This makes the two original triangles congruent by AAS.

Diagram

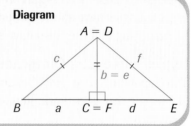

EXAMPLE: The guy wires on a tower are the same length. The tower is perpendicular to the ground. Prove that the wires must all be attached to the ground at the same distance from the base of the tower.

Given: $\overline{DB} \perp \overline{AC}$, $\overline{DA} \cong \overline{DC}$

Prove: $\overline{AB} \cong \overline{BC}$

Diagram

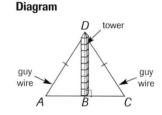

Plan: Use the Hypotenuse-Leg Congruence Theorem.

You are given that $\overline{DB}$ and $\overline{AC}$ are perpendicular. Because perpendicular lines form right angles, $\angle DBA$ and $\angle DBC$ are right angles. You are given that the hypotenuses of these two triangles are congruent. By the Reflexive Property of Congruence, you know that $\overline{DB} \cong \overline{DB}$. Then you know that $\triangle DBA \cong \triangle DBC$ by the Hypotenuse-Leg Congruence Theorem. This means that $\overline{AB} \cong \overline{BC}$ because they are corresponding parts of congruent triangles.

Hypotenuse–Acute Angle Congruence Theorem

This is a special case of the Angle-Angle-Side Congruence Theorem.

269

MORE HELP
See 265

Theorem If the hypotenuse and an acute angle of a right triangle are congruent to the hypotenuse and an acute angle of a second right triangle, then the triangles are congruent.
H-A $\cong$ Theorem (T111)

Proof

Given: In right triangles ABC and DEF, $\overline{AB} \cong \overline{DE}$, and $\angle B \cong \angle E$

Prove: $\triangle ABC \cong \triangle DEF$

You are given that $\triangle ABC$ and $\triangle DEF$ are right triangles, $\overline{AB} \cong \overline{DE}$, and $\angle B \cong \angle E$. Because all right angles are congruent, you also know that $\angle C \cong \angle F$. Then you know that $\triangle ABC \cong \triangle DEF$ by the AAS Congruence Postulate.

Diagram

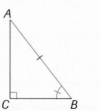
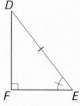

Leg-Leg Congruence Theorem

This is a special case of the Side-Angle-Side Congruence Theorem.

MORE HELP
See 262

Theorem If both legs of a right triangle are congruent to the corresponding legs of a second right triangle, then the triangles are congruent. L-L ≅ Theorem (T112)

Proof

Diagram

Given: In right triangles JKL and QRS, $\overline{JK} \cong \overline{QR}$, $\overline{JL} \cong \overline{QS}$

Prove: $\triangle JKL \cong \triangle QRS$

Since the right angles are included between the corresponding congruent sides, and all right angles are congruent, the two triangles are congruent by the SAS Congruence Postulate.

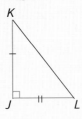
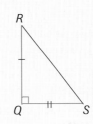

EXAMPLE: Given rectangle $ABCD$, prove $\triangle BAD \cong \triangle DCB$.

Given: Rectangle $ABCD$

Prove: $\triangle BAD \cong \triangle DCB$

Diagram

Plan: Since a rectangle has four right angles and its opposite sides are congruent, use the Leg-Leg Congruence Theorem.

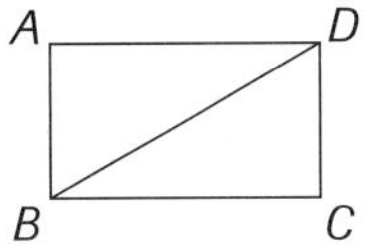

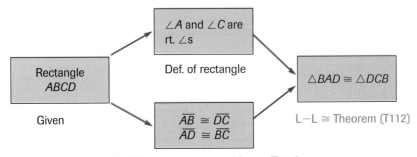

Congruence of Quadrilaterals

Two quadrilaterals are congruent if their corresponding angles and corresponding sides are congruent. However, the next two theorems give you shortcuts for showing that two quadrilaterals are congruent. It is sufficient to show that five corresponding parts, instead of all eight, are congruent.

MORE ▶

Theorem If three sides and the included angles of one quadrilateral are congruent to the corresponding three sides and included angles of another quadrilateral, then the quadrilaterals are congruent. SASAS ≅ Theorem (T113)

Proof

Given: $\overline{AB} \cong \overline{JK}$, $\angle B \cong \angle K$, $\overline{BC} \cong \overline{KL}$, $\angle C \cong \angle L$, $\overline{CD} \cong \overline{LM}$

Prove: $ABCD \cong JKLM$

Plan: Draw the diagonals $\overline{AC}$ and $\overline{JL}$. Then show that the two pairs of triangles are congruent. Now you can use CPCTC to show that the other corresponding parts are congruent. This lets you use the definition of congruent quadrilaterals to prove congruence.

Diagram

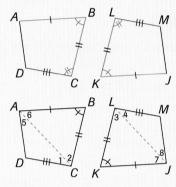

Statements	Reasons
❶ $\overline{AB} \cong \overline{JK}$, $\angle B \cong \angle K$, $\overline{BC} \cong \overline{KL}$, $\angle C \cong \angle L$, $\overline{CD} \cong \overline{LM}$	Given
❷ $AB = JK$, $BC = KL$, $CD = LM$; $m\angle B = m\angle K$, $m\angle C = m\angle L$	Def. of ≅
❸ $\triangle ABC \cong \triangle JKL$	SAS ≅ Postulate (P23)
❹ $\angle 2 \cong \angle 3$, $\angle 6 \cong \angle 7$; $\overline{AC} \cong \overline{JL}$; $m\angle 2 = m\angle 3$; $m\angle 6 = m\angle 7$; $AC = JL$	CPCTC; def. of ≅
❺ $m\angle 1 + m\angle 2 = m\angle C$ $m\angle 3 + m\angle 4 = m\angle L$	∠ + Postulate (P13)
❻ $m\angle 1 + m\angle 2 = m\angle 3 + m\angle 4$	Substitution *Look back at step 2.*
❼ $m\angle 1 = m\angle 4$; $\angle 1 \cong \angle 4$	Subtraction prop. of =; def. of ≅
❽ $\triangle ACD \cong \triangle JLM$	SAS ≅ Postulate (P23)
❾ $\angle D \cong \angle M$; $\overline{AD} \cong \overline{JM}$; $\angle 5 \cong \angle 8$; $m\angle 5 = m\angle 8$	CPCTC; def. of ≅
❿ $m\angle 5 + m\angle 6 = m\angle 7 + m\angle 8$	+ prop. of = *See steps 4 and 9.*
⓫ $m\angle 5 + m\angle 6 = m\angle A$; $m\angle 7 + m\angle 8 = m\angle J$	∠ + Postulate (P13)
⓬ $m\angle A = m\angle J$; $\angle A \cong \angle J$	Substitution; def. of ≅
⓭ $ABCD \cong JKLM$	Def. of ≅ *See steps 1, 9, and 12.*

(note beside step 8) $\overline{CD} \cong \overline{LM}$; $\angle 1 \cong \angle 4$; $\overline{AC} \cong \overline{JL}$

Theorem If three angles and the included sides of one quadrilateral are congruent to the corresponding three angles and included sides of another quadrilateral, then the quadrilaterals are congruent. ASASA ≅ Theorem (T114)

Given: $\angle A \cong \angle J$, $\overline{AB} \cong \overline{JK}$, $\angle B \cong \angle K$, $\overline{BC} \cong \overline{KL}$, $\angle C \cong \angle L$

Prove: $ABCD \cong JKLM$

Diagram

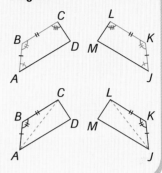

Plan: The proof is similar to the previous one. Begin by drawing diagonals $\overline{AC}$ and $\overline{JL}$. You can show that $\triangle ABC \cong \triangle JKL$ by the SAS Congruence Postulate, and then that $\triangle ADC \cong \triangle JML$ by the ASA Congruence Postulate. Then use CPCTC to show congruence by the SASAS Congruence Theorem.

MATH ALERT SSSS and AAAA Do Not Prove Congruence

Even if all sides of two quadrilaterals are congruent, the two quadrilaterals may not be congruent. Consider the rectangle and the parallelogram below. All the pairs of corresponding sides are congruent. However, you can tell by looking at the quadrilaterals that they are not congruent because the corresponding angles are not congruent.

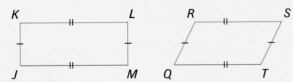

Similarly, even if all angles of two quadrilaterals are congruent, the two quadrilaterals may not be congruent. Consider quadrilaterals *ABEF* and *ACDF* in this diagram. All the pairs of angles are congruent. However, it is obvious that the two quadrilaterals can't be congruent, because corresponding sides are not congruent.

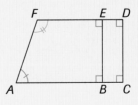

Transformations

"Plus ça change, plus c'est la méme chose."

"The more things change, the more they stay the same."

—Alphonse Karr in <u>Les Guepes</u>

A man wakes up to find himself transformed into a six-foot cockroach. That's the premise of a famous story by Franz Kafka, but fortunately it's not the type of transformation we talk about in geometry. Instead, we'll be looking at changes in which at least some of the characteristics of the original are preserved.

For example, take something more pleasant than a giant insect. Imagine a gymnast practicing. She runs backward across the studio, does a somersault with a half twist, lands on her feet with her right hand raised, and checks her posture in the mirror on the wall in front of her. These actions involve transformations, because some things have changed. By running, she has moved to a different spot. By twisting during her backflip she is facing the opposite direction. And her image in the mirror is raising the left hand instead of the right.

Yet, through all these changes, the gymnast still looks the same (maybe just a bit more tired). Some transformations, like translations, reflections, and rotations (also called slides, flips, and turns), don't change the figure itself, only its position or orientation or both. Others, like dilations, change the size of a figure, but not the shape.

MORE HELP
See 292

When you stand in front of a mirror, the image you see looks just like you. Another way of saying this is that an isometry preserves size and shape.

Transformations like this that create **images** that are congruent to the original figures, or **preimages,** are known as **rigid transformations**, or **isometries.** *Isometry* comes from the Greek phrase meaning *equal measure* and each measure on your image, like the width of your smile, is the same as on you—the original. Three basic isometries are reflections, rotations, and translations.

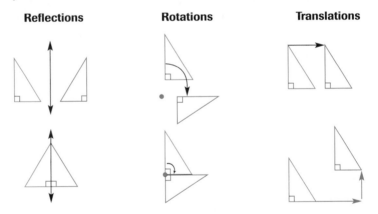

| Reflections | Rotations | Translations |

You may know these better as flips, turns, and slides because when you flip, turn, or slide a figure, it maps the figure onto its image. **Maps onto** means that the new image is always congruent to the original image, even though the location or orientation has changed.

Trapezoid $A'B'C'D'$ is the reflection image of trapezoid $ABCD$. A' is the image of A. You can write $ABCD \longrightarrow A'B'C'D'$ to show that $ABCD$ maps onto $A'B'C'D'$.

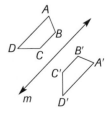

Write: A'
Say: *A prime*

Theorem	Every isometry preserves angle measure, betweenness, collinearity, and distance (length of segments). Prop. of isometries (T115)

Proof

Given: $\triangle A'B'C'$ is a reflection, rotation, or translation of $\triangle ABC$; M is the midpoint of $\overline{AB}$

Prove: Angle measure, betweenness, collinearity, and distance are preserved

Diagram

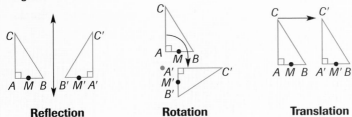

Reflection	**Rotation**	**Translation**

You can see that when a figure is reflected, rotated, or translated, the lengths of its segments and the measures of its angles are preserved (that is, they stay the same). The preimage maps onto the image, and by definition of a transformation, a figure and its image are congruent. Point M is the midpoint of $\overline{AB}$. Notice that the image point of M, M', is the midpoint of the image of $\overline{AB}$, $\overline{A'B'}$. A midpoint is halfway between two other points on the same segment, so you can say that betweenness and collinearity are also preserved.

MORE HELP
See 048, 256

Some people call this theorem the ABCD Theorem.

Angle measure—If one angle is the image of another angle, both angles are congruent.

Betweenness—If one point is between two other points, the image of that point is between the images of the two other points.

Collinearity—If three points are on a line, the images of those points are on a line.

Distance—If one line segment is the image of another line segment, the segments are the same length and the distance between two points on the preimage and the corresponding points on the image stays the same.

Reflections

A **reflection** is the image of a figure that has been flipped over a **line of reflection**. A reflection image may be called a **mirror image** or **flip**.

A **reflection** has all the properties of an isometry—angle measure, betweenness, collinearity, and distance, but the defining property of a reflection is that the line of reflection is the perpendicular bisector of the line segments connecting corresponding points of a figure and its reflection.

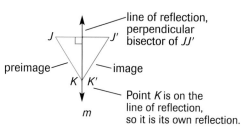

line of reflection, perpendicular bisector of *JJ'*

preimage

image

Point *K* is on the line of reflection, so it is its own reflection.

Theorem

If A and B are points and A is the reflection of B over a line, then B is the reflection of A over the same line.
Point flip-flop (T116)

Proof

Diagram

Given: A is the reflection of B over m.

Prove: B is the reflection of A over m.

MORE HELP
See 056

By the definition of a reflection, m is the perpendicular bisector of $\overline{AB}$. $\overline{AB}$ and $\overline{BA}$ are the same segment, so m is also the perpendicular bisector of $\overline{BA}$ and B is the reflection of A over m.

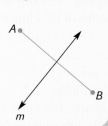

Theorem

If A and B are figures and A is the reflection of B over a line, then B is the reflection of A over the same line.
Figure flip-flop (T117)

Given: Figure A is the reflection of figure B over m.

Diagram

Prove: Figure B is the reflection of figure A over m.

A is the reflection of B, so the Point flip-flop theorem says that points in A are all reflections of corresponding points in B. This means that m is the perpendicular bisector of every segment connecting a point in A to its image in B. The reasoning in the proof of the Point flip-flop theorem now proves this theorem.

Isometry in Reflections

To prove that a reflection is an isometry, prove that distance is preserved.

Theorem   A reflection is an isometry. (T118)

Proof

Given: R' and S' are the reflection images of R and S over m.

Prove: $RS = R'S'$

Plan: Show that the distance between the two points, and between their reflections is preserved. Draw $\overline{RR'}$, $\overline{SS'}$, $\overline{RU}$, and $\overline{R'U}$ and use what you know about congruent triangles.

Diagram

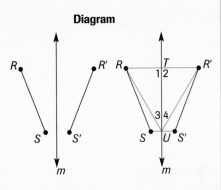

MORE HELP
See 432, 434

Statements	Reasons
❶ R' and S' are the reflection images of R and S over m	Given
❷ Draw $\overline{RR'}$, $\overline{SS'}$, $\overline{RU}$, and $\overline{R'U}$	2 pts. determine a line (P05)
❸ m is $\perp$ bisector of $\overline{RR'}$ and $\overline{SS'}$	Def. of reflection
❹ T is midpt. of $\overline{RR'}$; U is midpt. of $\overline{SS'}$; $\angle 1$, $\angle 2$, $\angle TUS$, and $\angle TUS'$ are rt. $\angle$s	Def. of $\perp$ bisector
❺ $\angle 1 \cong \angle 2$	Def. of rt. $\angle$
❻ $\overline{RT} \cong \overline{R'T}$	Def. of midpt.
❼ $\overline{TU} \cong \overline{TU}$	Reflexive prop. of $\cong$ (T105)
❽ $\triangle RTU \cong \triangle R'TU$	SAS $\cong$ Postulate (P23)
❾ $\overline{RU} \cong \overline{R'U}$; $\angle 3 \cong \angle 4$	CPCTC
❿ $\overline{SU} \cong \overline{S'U}$	Def. of midpt.
⓫ $\angle TUS \cong \angle TUS'$	Def. of rt. $\angle$
⓬ $m\angle TUS = m\angle 3 + m\angle RUS$; $m\angle TUS' = m\angle 4 + m\angle R'US'$	$\angle +$ Postulate (P13)
⓭ $m\angle 3 + m\angle RUS = m\angle 4 + m\angle R'US'$	Substitution *See steps 9–12.*
⓮ $\angle RUS \cong \angle R'US'$	Subtraction prop. of $=$
⓯ $\triangle RUS \cong \triangle R'US'$	SAS $\cong$ Postulate (P23)
⓰ $\overline{RS} \cong \overline{R'S'}$; $RS = R'S'$	CPCTC; def. of $\cong$

MORE ▶

EXAMPLE: Two office buildings are being constructed alongside each other, but they are not the same distance from the road. They will share the same entrance from the road. Where should that entrance be placed so the driveways are as short as possible?

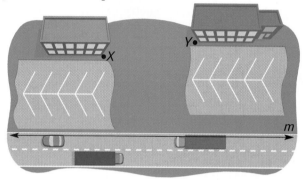

To solve the problem, you need to locate Z on m so that $XZ + ZY$ is as short as possible. This distance would be shortest if X, Z, and Y could be collinear. Since that is not possible, locate X', the reflection of X over m. Because a reflection is an isometry, $XZ = X'Z$. So $XZ + ZY = X'Z + ZY$. Locate Z where $X'Y$ intersects m.

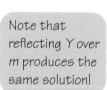

Note that reflecting Y over m produces the same solution!

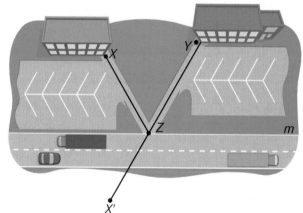

★ To minimize the driveways XZ and ZY, locate Z where $X'Y$ intersects m.

Drawing a Reflection

ONE WAY To draw a reflection over a line, you can use graph paper to locate images of points of a figure.

For Point H, the image H' is on the other side of the line of reflection and is the same number of units from it. Repeat for other key points of your figure.

Same number of units.

ANOTHER WAY You can use a plastic image reflector to draw a reflection over a line.

Place the reflector along the line. Look through the reflector from the same side as the preimage. Use your pencil to trace the reflection on the other side of the reflector.

m

ANOTHER WAY Use patty paper.

Reflections on a Coordinate Plane

Reflections that are drawn on the coordinate plane are usually reflections over one of the coordinate axes or over a line through the origin at a 45° angle to the axes ($y = x$).

If $P(x, y)$ is reflected over the x-axis, its image is $P'(x, \,^-y)$.

If $P(x, y)$ is reflected over the y-axis, its image is $P'(\,^-x, y)$.

If $P(x, y)$ is reflected over the line $y = x$, its image is $P'(y, x)$.

You might want to trace this diagram and fold along the lines of reflection to see that the rules work.

For P(4, 2), the reflection over the y-axis is ($^-$4, 2).

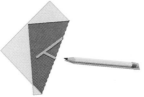

For P(4, 2), the reflection over the line $y = x$ is (2, 4).

For P(4, 2), the reflection over the x-axis is (4, $^-$2).

You may be able to program your graphing calculator to use matrices to produce reflections. Look up translations or reflections in the index of your calculator manual for more information.

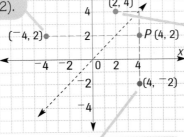

Line Symmetry

A figure that can be folded along a line so that it has two parts that are reflections of each other has **line symmetry**. The fold line is called the **line of symmetry**. A figure can have no lines of symmetry, one line of symmetry, or more than one line of symmetry.

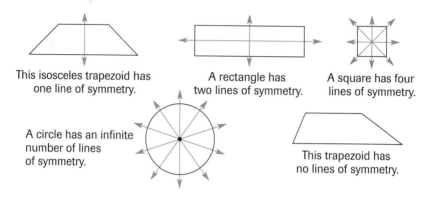

This isosceles trapezoid has one line of symmetry.

A rectangle has two lines of symmetry.

A square has four lines of symmetry.

A circle has an infinite number of lines of symmetry.

This trapezoid has no lines of symmetry.

MATH ALERT The Diagonal of a Parallelogram Is Not Usually a Line of Symmetry

A diagonal of a square or a rhombus is a line of symmetry. To check, trace each figure and fold on the diagonals. The halves of each figure will fold on top of each other to match exactly.

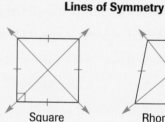

Lines of Symmetry

Square

Rhombus

Although they look like they may be lines of symmetry, the diagonals of other parallelograms, including rectangles, are not lines of symmetry. Again, you can check by tracing and folding each figure. The halves of each figure may come close to matching, but they will not match exactly.

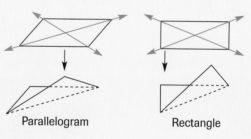

Not Lines of Symmetry

Parallelogram

Rectangle

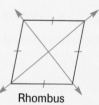

Rotations

The two line segments marked by the windshield wiper blade on the back window of a vehicle are rotation images of each other. $\overline{EF} \longrightarrow \overline{E'F'}$ by a 120° counterclockwise rotation about point D.

A rotation is a transformation that is informally called **a turn**. A rotation turns a figure about a point called the **center of rotation.** That point may or may not be on the figure. When describing a rotation, be sure to include:

- the amount of turn, or the **angle of rotation**;

- the direction of the turn, clockwise or counterclockwise;

- and the center of rotation.

A **rotation** has all the properties of an isometry. In addition, the distance from the center of rotation to a point is the same as the distance from the center of rotation to the point's image. Also, each point of a figure rotates the same number of degrees, unless the point is the center of rotation.

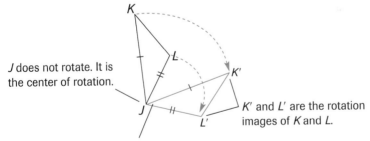

J does not rotate. It is the center of rotation.

K′ and L′ are the rotation images of K and L.

$\overline{JK} \cong \overline{JK'}$, $\overline{JL} \cong \overline{JL'}$, and $\angle KJK' \cong \angle LJL'$.

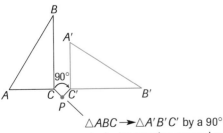

$\triangle ABC \longrightarrow \triangle A'B'C'$ by a 90° clockwise rotation around point P.

MATH ALERT In a Rotation, All Points Do Not Move the Same Distance

In a rotation, each point of a figure rotates the same number of degrees, but not the same distance. Have you ever seen a line of ice skaters in formation turning in a circle?

The skater closest to the center travels very little distance while the skater on the outside travels much farther. They may rotate the same number of degrees, but the skater on the outside is traveling on a circle with a much longer radius.

Isometry in Rotations

MORE HELP
See 276

You can use the defining property of a rotation to prove that a rotation is an isometry by proving that distance (length of segments) is preserved in a rotation.

> **Theorem** A rotation is an isometry. (T119)
>
> **Proof**
>
> **Diagram**
>
> **Given:** T' and U' are the rotation images of T and U after a rotation about S
>
> **Prove:** $\overline{TU} \cong \overline{T'U'}$
>
> **Plan:** Choose any two points T and U and show that after a rotation about point S, $\overline{TU}$ is congruent to $\overline{T'U'}$. Show that $\triangle TSU$ and $\triangle T'SU'$ are congruent and then use the fact that corresponding parts of congruent triangles are congruent to show that segment lengths are preserved.

Statements	Reasons
❶ T' and U' are the rotation images of T and U after a rotation about S	Given
❷ $\overline{ST} \cong \overline{ST'}$, $\overline{SU} \cong \overline{SU'}$, $\angle TST' \cong \angle USU'$	Def. of rotation
❸ $m\angle TST' = m\angle USU'$	Def. of $\cong$
❹ $m\angle 1 + m\angle 2 = m\angle TST'$, $m\angle 3 + m\angle 2 = m\angle USU'$	$\angle$ + Postulate (P13)
❺ $m\angle 1 + m\angle 2 = m\angle 3 + m\angle 2$	Substitution *See steps 3 and 4.*
❻ $m\angle 1 = m\angle 3$	Subtraction prop. of =
❼ $\triangle TSU \cong \triangle T'SU'$	SAS $\cong$ Postulate (P23)
❽ $\overline{TU} \cong \overline{T'U'}$	CPCTC

MORE HELP
See 432, 434

Rotation as Two Reflections

284

The next theorem describes a relationship between rotations and reflections.

MORE HELP
See 054, 275

Theorem If two lines, ℓ and m, intersect at a point O, then a reflection in ℓ followed by a reflection in m is a rotation about point O. The angle of rotation is $2x°$; $x°$ is the measure of the acute or right angle between ℓ and m. ℓ and $m \cap$ at O, reflection in ℓ + reflection in m is rotation about O; angle of rotation = $2x°$ (T120)

This symbol means intersect or intersection.

When talking about reflections, in m means the same as over m;

When talking about rotations, about O means the same as around O.

Diagram

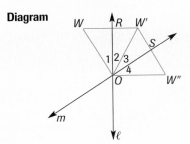

MORE ▶

Proof

Two primes is read as *double prime*.

Given: ℓ and m intersect at O, W' is the reflection image of W over ℓ, W'' is the reflection image of W' over m.

Prove: $\overline{OW''}$ is the rotation image of $\overline{OW}$; $m\angle WOW'' = 2\,m\angle ROS$.

Diagram

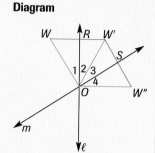

MORE HELP
See 056, 432, 434

Since W' and W'' are reflection images of W and W' respectively, $\overline{OW} \cong \overline{OW'}$ and $\overline{OW'} \cong \overline{OW''}$. By the Transitive Property of Congruence, $\overline{OW} \cong \overline{OW''}$, so by the definition of a rotation, $\overline{OW''}$ is the rotation image of $\overline{OW}$.

Because $\overline{OW}$ is reflected over ℓ, ℓ is the perpendicular bisector of $\overline{WW'}$. By the same reasoning, m is the perpendicular bisector of $\overline{W'W''}$. This gives you $\overline{WR} \cong \overline{RW'}$ and $\overline{W'S} \cong \overline{SW''}$. $\overline{OR} \cong \overline{OR}$ and $\overline{OS} \cong \overline{OS}$ by the Reflexive Property of Congruence and you've already said that $\overline{OW} \cong \overline{OW'} \cong \overline{OW''}$, so the SSS Congruence Postulate tells you that $\triangle WOR \cong \triangle W'OR$ and $\triangle W'OS \cong \triangle W''OS$. By CPCTC, $\angle 1 \cong \angle 2$ and $\angle 3 \cong \angle 4$. By the Angle Addition Postulate, $m\angle 1 + m\angle 2 + m\angle 3 + m\angle 4 = m\angle WOW''$ and $m\angle 2 + m\angle 3 = m\angle ROS$. By substitution, $m\angle 1 + m\angle 4 = m\angle ROS$ and $m\angle WOW'' = \angle mROS + m\angle ROS$, or $2m\angle ROS$.

285

Rotational Symmetry

A figure that can be mapped onto itself by a rotation of 180° or less is said to have **rotational symmetry**.

Any equilateral triangle has rotational symmetry because it can be mapped onto itself by a 120° rotation. The center of symmetry is the center of the triangle.

Mapping a figure onto itself means that the transformation moves each point so that it overlaps another point on the figure.

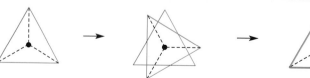

A 90° rotation does not map the triangle onto itself.

A 120° rotation maps the triangle into itself.

Rotational Symmetry

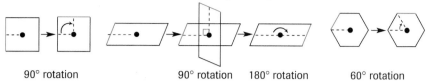

90° rotation   90° rotation   180° rotation   60° rotation

No Rotational Symmetry

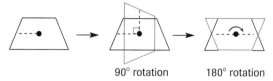

90° rotation   180° rotation

This trapezoid does not map onto itself until it is rotated 360°.

To check whether a figure has rotational symmetry, trace it. Fold to establish the center, then hold your tracing over the original figure with your pencil at its center. See whether the tracing maps over the original figure in a half-turn (180°) or less.

Some figures have both line symmetry and rotational symmetry.

MORE HELP
See 279

| **Theorem** | If a figure has two lines of symmetry, intersecting at a point, then it is rotation symmetric with a center of rotation at that point. Figs., ∩ lines of symmetry ⇒ center of rotation at ∩ (T121) |

The proof is beyond the scope of this book. The figures shown are rotation-symmetric.

A figure is **rotation-symmetric** if the figure is its own image after a rotation, and only the center point remains fixed.

Diagram

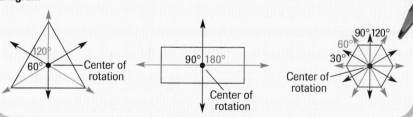

Translations

When you open a sliding
patio door, you are translating the door panel about
3 feet to the left or to the
right. A translation is a transformation that is informally
called a **glide** or a **slide**.
A **translation** has all the
properties of an isometry.
In addition, the line segments
connecting the corresponding points of a
figure and its translation image are congruent and parallel. (By contrast, in a reflection,
the line segments are congruent, but not
necessarily parallel.)

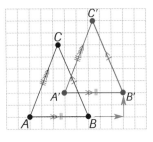

$\triangle A'B'C'$ is the translation image of $\triangle ABC$.
The **slide arrows** show that $\triangle ABC$ was
shifted 3 units right and 2 units up.

Isometry in Translations

You can use the defining property of a translation to prove that distance is
preserved and a translation is an isometry.

MORE HELP
See 058, 157,
255, 274, 376,
434

Theorem A translation is an isometry. (T122)

Proof

Diagram

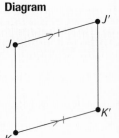

Given: $\overline{JJ'} \cong \overline{KK'}$, $\overline{JJ'} \parallel \overline{KK'}$

Prove: $JK = J'K'$

Plan: Since the line segments connecting the
corresponding points of a figure and its translation
image are congruent and parallel, construct a
parallelogram with $\overline{JJ'}$ and $\overline{KK'}$ as one pair of
sides. Use the figure to show that distance
(segment length) is preserved for the other pair of sides.

If one pair of opposite sides of a quadrilateral is parallel and congruent,
then the quadrilateral is a parallelogram. $\overline{JJ'}$ and $\overline{KK'}$ are parallel and
congruent, so $JJ'K'K$ is a parallelogram. Since the opposite sides of a
parallelogram are congruent, $\overline{JK} \cong \overline{J'K'}$ and $JK = J'K'$.

Translation as Two Reflections

The next theorem describes a relationship between reflections and translations.

MORE HELP
See 058, 275

Theorem   If lines ℓ and m are parallel, then a reflection in line ℓ followed by a reflection in line m is a translation. If P'' is the image of P after the two reflections, then $\overline{PP''}$ is perpendicular to ℓ; d is the distance between ℓ and m and $PP'' = 2d$. $\ell \parallel m \Rightarrow$ reflection in ℓ + reflection in m is translation; $\overline{PP''} \perp \ell$ and $PP'' = 2d$ (T123)

Proof

Given: $\ell \parallel m$; d is the distance between ℓ and m; P'' is the image of P after reflections over ℓ and m

Prove: $\overline{P''Q''}$ is the translation image of $\overline{PQ}$, $\overline{PP''} \perp \ell$, $PP'' = 2d$

Plan: It's easy to show $\overline{PP''} \perp \ell$: ℓ is the perpendicular bisector of $\overline{PP'}$ because P' is the reflection of P over ℓ. You can't tell just by watching what happens to P whether two reflections over parallel lines is really a translation. Expand your diagram so that you're watching what happens to a line segment. Show that $PP''Q''Q$ is a parallelogram and use the fact that the opposite sides of a parallelogram are congruent to prove that $\overline{P''Q''}$ is the translation image of $\overline{PQ}$.

Diagram

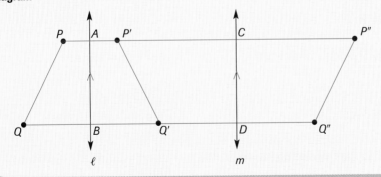

More Help
See 056, 379,
432, 434

Statements	Reasons
❶ $\ell \parallel m$; d is the distance between ℓ and m; P'' is the image of P after reflections over ℓ and m	Given
❷ $\overline{P'Q'}$ is the reflection of $\overline{PQ}$ over ℓ, $\overline{P''Q''}$ is the reflection of $\overline{P'Q'}$ over m	Construction
❸ ℓ is the perpendicular bisector of $\overline{PP'}$ and $\overline{QQ'}$ and m is the perpendicular bisector of $\overline{P'P''}$ and $\overline{Q'Q''}$	Def. of reflection
❹ $AP' + P'C = AC$, or d, and $PA + AP' + P'C + CP'' = PP''$; $BQ' + Q'D = BD$, or d, and $QB + BQ' + Q'D + DQ'' = QQ''$	Seg. + Postulate (P09)
❺ $\overline{PP''} \perp \ell$ and m; $PA = AP'$; $P'C = CP''$; $\overline{QQ'} \perp \ell$ and m; $QB = BQ'$ and $Q'D = DQ''$	Def. of $\perp$ bisector
❻ $PP'' = PA + AP' + P'C + CP''$ $\quad = 2(AP' + P'C) = 2d$; $QQ'' = QB + BQ' + Q'D + DQ''$ $\quad = 2(BQ' + Q'D) = 2d$	Substitution *Look back at steps 4 and 5.*
❼ $PP'' = QQ''$	Substitution
❽ $PP'' \parallel QQ''$	2 lines in plane $\perp$ 3rd line $\Rightarrow \parallel$ (T010) *Look back at step 5.*
❾ $PP''Q''Q$ is a parallelogram	Quadrilateral; opp. sides $\parallel$ and $\cong \Rightarrow$ parallelogram (T065)
❿ $PQ = P''Q''$	Parallelogram $\Rightarrow$ opp. sides $\cong$ (T063)
⓫ $\overline{P''Q''}$ is the translation image of $\overline{PQ}$.	A translation is an isometry (T122)

289

Translations on a Coordinate Plane

A **vector** is a quantity with both direction and magnitude. **Magnitude** is another word for *size*. Sometimes a vector is called a **directed line segment**. An arrow is used to represent a vector, and a vector can identify a translation.

The **initial**, or starting, point of vector RS is R and its **terminal**, or ending, point is S. $\overrightarrow{RS}$ has two components: a horizontal component of $^-6$, and a vertical component of 4. The component form of $\overrightarrow{RS}$ is written $<^-6, 4>$.

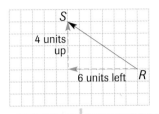

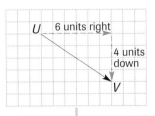

You always consider the horizontal component first, then the vertical, just as with coordinate pairs.

$\overrightarrow{RS} = <^-6, 4>$ Left six, up four $\overrightarrow{UV} = <6, ^-4>$ Right six, down four

Write: $\overrightarrow{RS}$

Say: *vector RS*

Write: $<^-6, 4>$

Say: *the vector with horizontal displacement $^-6$ and vertical displacement 4* or *the vector with components $^-6$ and 4*

A vector looks a lot like a ray, but it is not a ray. A ray has an initial point and then continues with no end. Remember that a vector has initial *and* terminal points.

You can use vectors to show translations on a coordinate plane.

EXAMPLE: A triangle has vertices $L(^-5, 2)$, $M(^-4, 4)$, and $N(^-2, 1)$. What are the coordinates of the image's vertices after a translation of $(x, y) \longrightarrow (x + 2, y - 4)$?

The translation $(x, y) \longrightarrow (x + 2, y - 4)$ moves each point of the triangle 2 units right and 4 units down.

ONE WAY Make a table.

To find the coordinates of L', M', and N', you can make a table. Add 2 to the x-coordinates of L, M, and N. Subtract 4 from the y-coordinates of L, M, and N.

Vertices of Triangle *LMN*	Vertices of Triangle *L′M′N′*
$L(^-5, 2)$	$L'(^-3, ^-2)$
$M(^-4, 4)$	$M'(^-2, 0)$
$N(^-2, 1)$	$N'(0, ^-3)$

MORE ▶

ANOTHER WAY Use matrices.

MORE HELP
See 275, 286

Vertices of Preimage	Translation Matrix	Vertices of Image

$$\begin{matrix} L & M & N \\ \begin{bmatrix} {}^-5 & {}^-4 & {}^-2 \\ 2 & 4 & 1 \end{bmatrix} \end{matrix} + \begin{bmatrix} 2 & 2 & 2 \\ {}^-4 & {}^-4 & {}^-4 \end{bmatrix} = \begin{matrix} L' & M' & N' \\ \begin{bmatrix} {}^-3 & {}^-2 & 0 \\ {}^-2 & 0 & {}^-3 \end{bmatrix} \end{matrix}$$

The top row of each matrix contains the x-coordinates. The bottom row contains the y-coordinates. Since the x-coordinate translates 2 units, you add 2 to each x-coordinate of the preimage vertices to get each x-coordinate in the image. Since the y-coordinate translates $^-4$ units, you add $^-4$ to each y-coordinate of the preimage vertices to get each y-coordinate in the image.

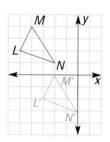

★ Either way the image has vertices L' ($^-3$, $^-2$), M' ($^-2$, 0), and N' (0, $^-3$).

290

Glide Reflections

A **glide reflection** is a transformation that is a combination or **composition** of a translation, or glide, and a reflection.

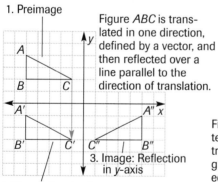

1. Preimage

Figure *ABC* is translated in one direction, defined by a vector, and then reflected over a line parallel to the direction of translation.

3. Image: Reflection in *y*-axis

2. Translation, $(x, y) \rightarrow (x, y - 5)$

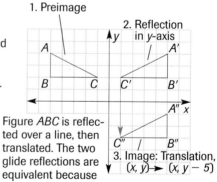

1. Preimage

2. Reflection in *y*-axis

Figure *ABC* is reflected over a line, then translated. The two glide reflections are equivalent because the image and preimage are in corresponding positions.

3. Image: Translation, $(x, y) \rightarrow (x, y - 5)$

Theorem The composition of two or more isometries is an isometry. 2+ isometries = isometry (T124)

You can use the defining properties of a reflection, rotation, and translation to prove this theorem. Since each is an isometry, two or more reflections, rotations, or translations must also be an isometry.

Dilations   **292**

When you make a reprint of a photograph in the same size as the original photograph, it is considered a rigid transformation since the size has not changed. However, when a photograph is enlarged or reduced, the original photograph and the new photograph are no longer the same size. This is an example of a **non-rigid** transformation.

Dilations _____

When you enlarge a photograph, it still looks like the same photo, but it's a different size. Dilations change the size but not the shape of a figure.

A **dilation** is considered a non-rigid transformation because a dilation causes the points of a figure to move further apart or closer together. That's why the preimage and image of a figure are similar, not congruent.

292

MORE HELP
See 222

Reduction

Original

Enlargement

For every dilation, there is a **center** point C and a scale factor, or size change, k. An image point P' lies on $\overleftrightarrow{CP}$ such that $k = \frac{CP'}{CP}$, but $k \neq 1$. A dilation is a reduction if $0 < k < 1$. It is an enlargement if $k > 1$.

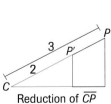
Reduction of $\overline{CP}$
$$k = \frac{CP'}{CP} = \frac{2}{3}$$

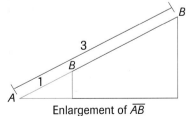
Enlargement of $\overline{AB}$
$$k = \frac{AB'}{AB} = \frac{3}{1} = 3$$

Dilations on a Coordinate Plane

To draw a dilation on a coordinate plane with the origin as the center, multiply the x- and y-coordinates of the vertices of a figure by a number, k. The preimage points are (x, y), so the image points are (kx, ky).

EXAMPLE: Draw the image of $\triangle ABC$ under a dilation centered at the origin with scale factor 2.

Since the scale factor is greater than one, the image will be larger than the preimage.

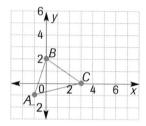

You can use matrices to find the coordinates of the vertices of $\triangle A'B'C'$. Multiply each coordinate of each point by the scale factor, 2. The preimage matrix has a row for x-values and a row for y-values. The image matrix has a row for $2x$ values and a row for $2y$ values.

$$2 \cdot \begin{matrix} A & B & C \\ \begin{bmatrix} -1 & 0 & 3 \\ -1 & 2 & 0 \end{bmatrix} \end{matrix} = \begin{matrix} A' & B' & C' \\ \begin{bmatrix} -2 & 0 & 6 \\ -2 & 4 & 0 \end{bmatrix} \end{matrix}$$

★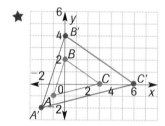

The scale factor refers to the change in length of segments, it does not refer to the change in the area of the transformed figure.

Properties of Dilations	
Attribute	**Key Element of Proof**
In a dilation, a line and its image are parallel.	Parallel lines have the same slope.
In a dilation, every point (x, y) of the preimage maps onto (kx, ky), so the scale factor is k.	The distance formula shows that the distance between points is $k \cdot$ the distance between points on the preimage.
Every dilation preserves angle measure, betweenness, and collinearity, but not distance.	A dilation produces a similar figure, not a congruent figure.

Transformation Patterns 294

Some things in nature, art, and architecture may have caught your eye because of the repeated patterns of shapes. You probably did not say to yourself, *Look at the transformations!* or *Look at the isometries!* but that's exactly what you were looking at.

Frieze Patterns

295

This beading pattern is an example of a **frieze** (or **strip**) **pattern**. It can be extended infinitely to the left or right by horizontal translations.

MORE HELP
See 274, 290

Frieze patterns are classified according to the types of transformations that will map the pattern onto itself. This table shows some frieze patterns that can be made by using the letter *b* as the initial shape.

Transformations	Example
translations only	b b b b b b
translations and 180° rotations	b q b q b q
translations and reflections about a vertical line	b d b d b d
translations and reflections about a horizontal line	b b b b b b p p p p p p

A 180° rotation is also referred to as a half-turn. A 90° rotation is referred to as a quarter-turn.

For more information on frieze patterns, you can go to
http://nrich.maths.org/mathsf/journalf/mar99/art1/ or
http://www.ucs.mun.ca/~mathed/Geometry/Transformations/frieze.html

Tessellations

MORE HELP
See 274

A **tessellation**, or **tiling**, is the complete covering of a plane with a re-peating pattern of figures so that no gaps or overlaps occur. Tessellations may be composed of one or more shapes, and the shapes may be trans-formed by rotations, reflections, translations, or glide reflections. They differ from frieze patterns in that their elements repeat in all directions whereas a frieze pattern repeats in one direction.

DID YOU KNOW The Dutch artist Maurits S. Escher (1898-1972) was inspired by tile patterns he saw at the Alhambra while traveling in Spain during the 1930s. The Alhambra, built during the 1200s, contains many fine examples of the precise geometric art of Islamic artists.

MORE HELP
See 128

Some tessellations, like the honeycomb, are **regular tessellations** because they are composed of congruent images of one regular polygon. For polygons to fill the space around a vertex without leaving a gap or overlapping, the sum of the measures of the angles that meet at any vertex must equal 360°. This may surprise you, but there are only three regular tessellations.

Equilateral Triangle Tessellation	Square Tessellation	Regular Hexagon Tessellation
360° ÷ 60° = 6	360° ÷ 90° = 4	360° ÷ 120° = 3

Look at what happens if you try to tessellate a regular pentagon. The figures overlap.

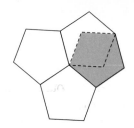

$360° \div 108° \approx 3.33$ This means that $3\frac{1}{3}$ pentagons surround a point— you can't force the pentagon to tessellate.

Semiregular tessellations are composed of congruent images of more than one regular polygon which meet in the same order at each vertex. Again, the sum of the measures of the angles that meet at the vertex must equal 360°.

There are eight different semiregular tessellations. One example of a semiregular tessellation is the regular octagon-square combination, in which two regular octagons and a square meet at each vertex point.

$135° + 135° + 90° = 360°$

Some other tessellations are composed of images of one or more nonregular polygons.

Rectangle Tessellation

Parallelogram and Triangle Tessellation

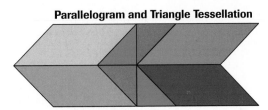

Still other tessellations, like Escher-type drawings, are composed of figures that are not polygons at all. One way to create such tessellations is to start with a regular polygon such as a square, that you know tessellates.

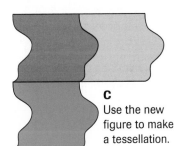

A
Draw a curve from one vertex to an adjacent vertex.

B
Cut along the curve. Tape the cutout to the opposite side of the square.

C
Use the new figure to make a tessellation.

Circles

"She saw every personal relationship as a pair of intersecting circles. . . . Probably perfection is reached when the area of the two outer crescents, added together, is exactly equal to that of the leaf-shaped piece in the middle. On paper there must be some neat mathematical formula for arriving at this; in life, none."

–Jan Struther in *Mrs. Miniver*

It was time to get out a pump — Elaine's bicycle tire had ceased to be circular.

Toss a pebble in a pond and watch the ripples. Why do they form circles? Twirl a sparkler with your arm straight. Why does the glittering light trace out a circle? Coast on a bicycle or skates on an even surface. Why do circular wheels give such a smooth ride?

The answers to all these questions are based on what makes a circle so special — every point on a circle is the same distance from the center.

Consider the pebble in the pond. Waves move out in all directions at the same speed. At any instant, every part of a ripple has moved the same distance from where the pebble hit the water.

When you twirl the sparkler with a straight arm, it stays the same distance from the center of your spin.

A circular wheel rolls smoothly because its center stays the same distance above the ground. No matter which point of the wheel is touching the ground, the center is always the same distance away.

You can use this section to learn how circles are related to polygons, lines, line segments, and angles. As you do, think about ripples, sparklers, and wheels. They'll help you remember what makes circles so special.

Circle Relationships

Although it may be easy to recognize a circle, defining it may be more difficult. However, there is a precise mathematical definition of this familiar figure.

A **circle** is the set of all points in a plane which are the same distance from a point called the **center** of the circle. A circle with center C is often called *circle C* or $\odot C$. The points inside the circle form the **interior** of the circle. The interior of the circle, including the center, is *not* part of the circle. The points outside the circle form its **exterior**.

MORE HELP
See 113

If you fold a circle in half along a diameter, you form two congruent half circles, called **semicircles.** A diameter intersects a circle at the endpoints of two semicircles.

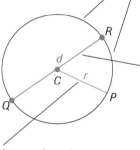

The **diameter** of a circle is a segment connecting two points on the circle and containing the center of the circle. The length of that segment is also called the diameter, which is twice the radius, or $d = 2r$. All the diameters of a circle are congruent.

The **radius** of a circle is the distance from the center to a point on the circle. The segment connecting the center with a point on the circle is also called the radius. The radius of a circle is half its diameter, or $r = \frac{1}{2}d$. By definition, all radii of a circle are congruent.

Semicircles are reflections of each other across the diameter, which is a line of symmetry of a circle. These ideas lead to the next theorem.

MORE HELP
See 275, 310

Theorem A diameter is a line of reflection for a circle.
Diameter ⇒ line of reflection (T125)

Proof

Diagram

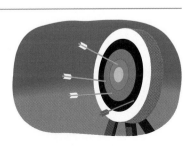

Given: ⊙C with line ℓ, containing diameter $\overline{AB}$

Prove: $\overparen{APB}$ is a reflection of $\overparen{AP'B}$

Plan: Show that the reflection image of any point on the circle also lies on the circle and that every point on the circle is an image of another point on the circle. That would prove that a circle reflects on itself because all points on the circle and *only* points on the circle are reflections of points on the circle.

Let P be any point on ⊙C and let P′ be the reflection of the point over line ℓ, which contains a diameter. Then $\overline{CP}$ is a radius of the circle. Since C is on ℓ, the reflection of C is C by the definition of reflection. Because reflections preserve distance $CP = CP'$. So, P′ is on the circle by the definition of circle. Likewise, the reflection image of each point on ⊙C is also on ⊙C. Thus every point on the circle is the image of some point on the circle. This means that the diameter is a line of reflection for ⊙C.

Congruent Circles

299

Two circles are **congruent** if and only if they have equal radii.

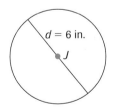

$d = 6$ in.

J

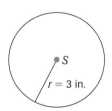

S

$r = 3$ in.

Radii is the plural of radius.

Since $d = 2r$; both circles have a radius of three inches. They are congruent.

Concentric Circles

300

Concentric circles are two or more co-planar circles that share the same center but not the same radius. Concentric circles have *no* points of intersection. An archery target is composed of several circles that share a common center. The circles on the target are concentric.

301

Tangent Circles

A line in a plane can intersect a circle in no points, in two points (a secant line) or in exactly one point. Place two coins next to each other so that they are touching. They touch at one point. The coins are tangent to each other.

MORE HELP
See 115, 241

Coplanar circles that intersect in exactly one point are called **tangent circles**. Circles can be **internally tangent** or **externally tangent**. A coplanar line is tangent to a circle if it intersects the circle at exactly one point. A line or segment that is tangent to two coplanar circles is called a **common tangent**.

Internally Tangent Circles

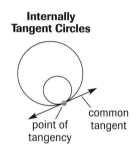

point of tangency   common tangent

Externally Tangent Circles

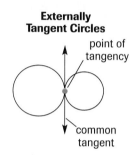

point of tangency

common tangent

A tangent segment is related to the tangent ratio. The **unit circle**, a circle with a one-unit radius centered at the origin, intersects the positive x-axis at B. Choose any point A so that $\overleftrightarrow{AB}$ is a tangent to the circle at B. In right triangle OBA, $\tan \angle AOB = \frac{AB}{OB} = \frac{AB}{1} = AB$; $\tan \angle AOB$ is equivalent to AB.

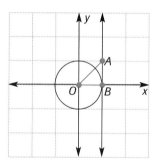

302

Inscribed Circles

A circle is **inscribed** in a polygon if each side of the polygon is tangent to the circle, so an inscribed circle touches each side of the polygon at exactly one point.

Inscribed Circles

MORE HELP
See 139

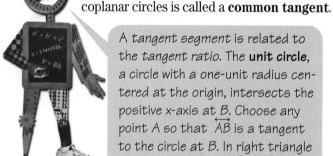

Circles inscribed in triangles

Circle inscribed in a square

Circle inscribed in a pentagon

Circumscribed Circles

A circle is **circumscribed** about a polygon if each vertex of the polygon lies on the circle. A circumscribed circle passes through each vertex of the polygon.

MORE HELP
See 138

> When a circle is inscribed in a polygon, then the polygon is circumscribed about the circle. When a circle is circumscribed about a polygon, then the polygon is inscribed in the circle.

Circumscribed Circles

| Circle circumscribed about a triangle | Circle circumscribed about a square | Circle circumscribed about a quadrilateral | Circle circumscribed about a hexagon |

MORE HELP
See 115, 176

DID YOU KNOW In the third century B.C., the Greek mathematician Archimedes used regular polygons inscribed and circumscribed about a circle to approximate the value of π. He compared the perimeter of a regular polygon inscribed in a circle with a diameter of one unit to the perimeter of the polygon circumscribed about the same circle. Remember that the circumference of a circle is πd. But d = 1 unit, so the perimeter of the circle Archimedes used was π. The perimeter, or circumference of the circle is less than the perimeter of the circumscribed polygon. Likewise, the circumference of the circle is greater than the perimeter of the inscribed polygon.

1 unit

Archimedes then used the following inequality to approximate π.

Perimeter of inscribed hexagon < π < Perimeter of circumscribed hexagon

As the number of sides of the regular polygon increases, the perimeter gets closer to π.

Archimedes sandwiched the value of π between two perimeters that he could compute exactly. His approximation was $3\frac{10}{71} < \pi < 3\frac{1}{7}$.

The circle is a geometric figure that you see everywhere you look. There are many mathematically interesting relationships among the angles, lines, and line segments within and around circles.

305 Special Segments in Circles

There are special segments and lines that are used to investigate circles.

A **diameter** is a chord that passes through the center of the circle. $\overline{DE}$ is a diameter.

A **chord** is any line segment whose endpoints are points on the circle. $\overline{AB}$ and $\overline{DE}$ are chords.

A **secant** is a line that intersects the circle in two points. It contains a chord. $\overleftrightarrow{AB}$ is a secant.

A **radius** is any line segment from the center of the circle to a point on the circle. $\overline{CF}$, $\overline{CE}$, and $\overline{CD}$ are radii of $\odot C$.

A **tangent** is a line that intersects a circle at one point, the **point of tangency**. $\overleftrightarrow{FG}$ is a tangent. It is tangent to $\odot C$ at point F.

306 Properties of Tangents

Consider a penny rolling on its edge. The penny touches the table at only one point of its edge at a time. It is tangent to the table.

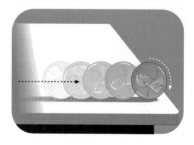

A **tangent** is a line in the plane of a circle that intersects the circle in exactly one point.

Theorem	If a line is tangent to a circle, then it is perpendicular to the radius drawn to the point of tangency. Tan to ⊙ ⊥ radius (T126)

Proof

Diagram

Given: ℓ is tangent to ⊙C at P

Prove: $\ell \perp$ radius $\overline{CP}$

Plan: Use an indirect proof. Assume ℓ and $\overline{CP}$ are *not* perpendicular. Show that this leads to a contradiction.

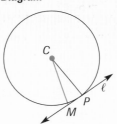

Assume ℓ and $\overline{CP}$ are not perpendicular. Then the ⊥ segment from C to ℓ must intersect ℓ at some other point M. Because ℓ is a tangent and can only intersect the circle at one point, M cannot be on or in the interior of ⊙C. So, $CM > CP$. If $\overline{CM}$ is the ⊥ segment from C to ℓ, then $\overline{CM}$ must be the shortest segment from C to ℓ, so $CM < CP$. But CM cannot be both greater than and less than CP. This means that the assumption that point M exists must be false and $\ell \perp \overline{CP}$.

The converse of this theorem is also true.

Theorem	In a plane, if a line is perpendicular to a radius of a circle at its endpoint on the circle, then the line is tangent to the circle. $\ell \perp$ radius $\Rightarrow \ell$ tan to ⊙ (T127)

Proof

Given: ℓ is in the plane of ⊙C;
$\ell \perp$ radius $\overline{CP}$ at P

Prove: ℓ is tangent to ⊙C

Plan: Use an indirect proof. Assume ℓ is not tangent to ⊙C. Show that this leads to a contradiction.

Diagram

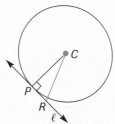

Assume ℓ is not tangent to ⊙C at P. Then there must be another point R on ℓ that is also on ⊙C. That would mean $CR = CP$ because both would be radii. But the ⊥ segment from C to ℓ is the shortest such segment, so $CR > CP$. CR cannot be both equal to and greater than CP. This means that the assumption that point R exists must be false and ℓ is tangent to ⊙C at P.

MORE ▶

The following example shows how you can use the properties of tangents.

MORE HELP
See 337

EXAMPLE: How far is it to the horizon from point P that is 400 feet above the ground?

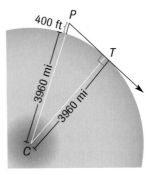

Assume Earth is a sphere with center C and radius exactly 3960 miles. The diagram shows a circular cross section. A tangent line from P to Earth intersects Earth at the horizon. Use this and the Pythagorean theorem to find PT. Get out your calculator.

First write 400 feet in miles:

$$400 \text{ ft} \left(\frac{1 \text{ mi}}{5280 \text{ ft}}\right) = \frac{400 \text{ mi}}{5280} \approx 0.076 \text{ mi}$$

Then $CP \approx 3960.076 \text{ mi}$

Use the Pythagorean Theorem.
$$(PT)^2 + 3960^2 \approx 3960.076^2$$
$$(PT)^2 \approx 3960.076^2 - 3960^2$$
$$(PT)^2 \approx 602$$
$$PT \approx \sqrt{602}$$
$$\approx 24.5$$

★ If there is nothing in the way, it is about 24.5 miles from a point 400 feet above the ground to the horizon.

From an exterior point of a circle, you can draw exactly two different tangents to a circle. The following theorem relates the two segments.

> You should develop this mathematical habit: call points *exterior* or *interior*; call segments *external* or *internal*.

Theorem If two segments from the same exterior point are tangent to a circle, then the segments are congruent. 2 segs. from 1 ext. pt. tan to $\odot$ ⇒ segs. $\cong$ (T128)

Proof

MORE HELP
See 268

Given: $\overleftrightarrow{AD}$ is tangent to $\odot C$ at A; $\overleftrightarrow{BD}$ is tangent to $\odot C$ at B
Prove: $\overline{AD} \cong \overline{BD}$

Plan: Draw radii $\overline{CA}$ and $\overline{CB}$ from the center to the tangents and connect the exterior point to point C. Since a radius is perpendicular to a tangent, right triangles are formed. Prove that $\triangle CAD \cong \triangle CBD$ and use corresponding parts of the congruent triangles to make your point.

Diagram

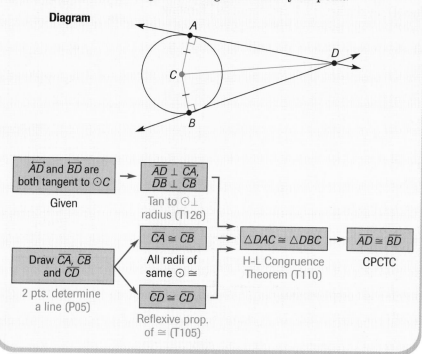

$\overrightarrow{AD}$ and $\overrightarrow{BD}$ are both tangent to $\odot C$	$\rightarrow$	$\overline{AD} \perp \overline{CA}$, $\overline{DB} \perp \overline{CB}$		
Given		Tan to $\odot \perp$ radius (T126)		

| | | $\overline{CA} \cong \overline{CB}$ | $\rightarrow$ | $\triangle DAC \cong \triangle DBC$ | $\rightarrow$ | $\overline{AD} \cong \overline{BD}$ |

Draw $\overline{CA}$, $\overline{CB}$ and $\overline{CD}$

2 pts. determine a line (P05)

$\overline{CA} \cong \overline{CB}$

All radii of same $\odot \cong$

$\triangle DAC \cong \triangle DBC$

H-L Congruence Theorem (T110)

$\overline{AD} \cong \overline{BD}$

CPCTC

$\overline{CD} \cong \overline{CD}$

Reflexive prop. of $\cong$ (T105)

Intersecting Tangents, Secants, and Chords _____

Theorem If a tangent and a chord intersect at a point on a circle, then the measure of each angle formed is half the measure of its intercepted arc. Tan and chord $\cap$ at pt. on $\odot$ $\Rightarrow$ each $\angle = \frac{1}{2}$ of its intercepted arc (T129)

MORE HELP See 068, 318

Proof

Given: $\overleftrightarrow{QR}$ is tangent to the circle at R, $\overline{RS}$ is a chord

Prove: $m\angle QRS = \frac{1}{2}m\widehat{RS}$

Diagram

Plan: Draw diameter $\overline{RT}$ and chord $\overline{ST}$, forming $\triangle RST$. Use the fact that $\angle RTS$ is an inscribed angle. Show that $\angle RTS \cong \angle QRS$, since both are complements of $\angle SRT$.

Statements	Reasons
❶ $\overleftrightarrow{QR}$ is a tangent; $\overline{RS}$ is a chord	Given
❷ Draw diameter $\overline{RT}$ and chord $\overline{ST}$	2 pts. determine a line (P05)
❸ $\angle RST$ is a rt. $\angle$	$\angle$ inscribed in $\odot$ is rt. $\angle$ $\Leftrightarrow$ corresp. arc is semicircle (T140)
❹ $\triangle RST$ is a rt. $\triangle$	Def. of rt. $\triangle$
❺ $\angle RTS$ is complementary to $\angle SRT$	Acute $\angle$s of rt. $\triangle$ comp. (T058)
❻ $\overline{RT} \perp \overleftrightarrow{RQ}$	Tan to $\odot \perp$ radius (T126)
❼ $\angle QRT$ is a right angle	$\perp$ lines $\Rightarrow$ 4 rt. $\angle$s (T011)
❽ $\angle QRS$ is complementary to $\angle SRT$	Def. of comp. $\angle$s
❾ $\angle RTS \cong \angle QRS$; $m\angle RTS = m\angle QRS$	Comps. of $\cong \angle$s $\cong$ (T021); def. of $\cong$
❿ $m\angle RTS = \frac{1}{2}m\widehat{RS}$	$\angle$ inscribed in $\odot \Rightarrow$ measure is $\frac{1}{2}$ intercepted arc (T138)
⓫ $m\angle QRS = \frac{1}{2}m\widehat{RS}$	Substitution

You can also show $m\angle SRM = \frac{1}{2}m\widehat{RTS}$

Theorem

If two chords intersect in the interior of a circle, then the measure of each angle formed is half the sum of the measures of their intercepted arcs. 2 chords $\cap$ $\Rightarrow$ each $\angle = \frac{1}{2}$ sum of intercepted arcs (T130)

Proof

Diagram

Given: Chords $\overline{AD}$ and $\overline{BC}$ intersect

Prove: $m\angle 1 = \frac{1}{2}(m\widehat{CD} + m\widehat{AB})$

Plan: Use the Exterior Angle Theorem to show $m\angle 2 + m\angle 3 = m\angle 1$. Then relate the measures of angles 1 and 4 to their intercepted arcs.

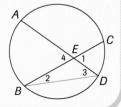

Statements	Reasons
❶ Draw $\overline{BD}$	2 pts. determine a line (P05)
❷ ∠1 and ∠4 are vertical ∠s intercepting $\widehat{CD}$ and $\widehat{AB}$	Def. of vertical ∠; def. of intercepted arc
❸ m∠1 = m∠2 + m∠3	Exterior ∠ Theorem (T048)
❹ m∠2 = $\frac{1}{2}$m$\widehat{CD}$, m∠3 = $\frac{1}{2}$m$\widehat{AB}$	∠ inscribed in ⊙ ⇒ measure is $\frac{1}{2}$ intercepted arc (T138)
❺ m∠1 = $\frac{1}{2}$m$\widehat{CD}$ + $\frac{1}{2}$m$\widehat{AB}$	Substitution
❻ m∠1 = $\frac{1}{2}$(m$\widehat{CD}$ + m$\widehat{AB}$)	Distributive prop.

> Look back at steps 3 and 4.

MORE HELP
See 144

EXAMPLE: Find the measure of ∠1.

$$m\angle 1 = \frac{1}{2}(m\widehat{CD} + m\widehat{AB})$$

$$= \frac{1}{2}(40 + 80)$$

$$= \frac{1}{2}(120)$$

$$= 60$$

★ The measure of ∠1 is 60°.

MORE HELP
See 310

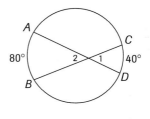

Segment Product Properties

Secant segments and tangent segments share some special properties.

A **tangent segment** is a line segment that is tangent to the circle at an endpoint. $\overline{AB}$ is a tangent segment.

A **secant segment** is a line segment that contains a chord of the circle. $\overline{DB}$ is a secant segment that contains chord $\overline{DC}$ and **external secant segment** CB.

308

> **Theorem** If two secant segments are drawn to a circle from an exterior point, then the product of the lengths of one secant segment and its external secant segment is equal to the product of the lengths of the other secant segment and its external secant segment. 2 secant segs. to ⊙ from ext. pt. ⇒ seg$_1$ · external part$_1$ = seg$_2$ · external part$_2$ (T131)

MORE HELP
See 220, 227, 311, 318

MORE ▶

Proof

Diagram

Given: $\overline{ED}$ and $\overline{EB}$ are secant segments.

Prove: $EB \cdot EA = ED \cdot EC$

Plan: Draw $\overline{AD}$ and $\overline{BC}$. Show that $\triangle BCE$ and $\triangle DAE$ are similar. Then use the fact that corresponding sides of similar triangles are proportional to prove your point.

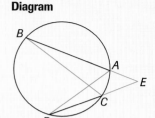

$\angle B$ and $\angle D$ intercept the same arc, $\overset{\frown}{AC}$, so $\angle B \cong \angle D$. $\angle E \cong \angle E$ by the Reflexive Property of Congruence. Then $\triangle BCE \sim \triangle DAE$ by the Angle-Angle Similarity Postulate. Since lengths of corresponding sides of similar triangles are proportional, $\frac{EA}{EC} = \frac{ED}{EB}$. Cross products in a proportion are equal, so $EA \cdot EB = EC \cdot ED$.

Theorem If a tangent segment and a secant segment are drawn to a circle from an exterior point, then the square of the length of the tangent segment is equal to the product of the lengths of the secant segment and its external segment. Tan seg. (t) and secant seg. to $\odot$ from ext. pt. $\Rightarrow t^2 =$ seg. $\cdot$ external seg. (T132)

Proof

Diagram

Given: $\overline{EA}$ is a tangent segment and $\overline{ED}$ is a secant segment

Prove: $(EA)^2 = ED \cdot EC$

Plan: Draw $\overline{AD}$ and $\overline{AC}$. Show that $\triangle EAC \sim \triangle EDA$, then use the fact that corresponding sides of similar triangles are proportional. Flip the triangles into the same orientation to show the corresponding parts.

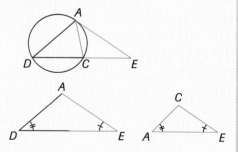

MORE HELP
See 318

Draw $\overline{AD}$ and $\overline{AC}$. $\angle E \cong \angle E$ by the Reflexive Property of Congruence. $m\angle D = \frac{1}{2}m\overset{\frown}{AC}$ since the measure of an inscribed angle is one half the measure of its intercepted arc. $m\angle EAC = \frac{1}{2}m\overset{\frown}{AC}$ since tangent $\overline{AE}$ and chord $\overline{AC}$ intersect on a circle, so the measure of each angle formed is one half the measure of its intercepted arc. By the Transitive Property of Equality, $m\angle D = m\angle EAC$, so $\angle D \cong \angle EAC$. Then $\triangle EAC \sim \triangle EDA$ by the Angle-Angle Similarity Postulate. Corresponding sides of similar triangles are proportional, $\frac{EA}{ED} = \frac{EC}{EA}$, so $(EA)^2 = ED \cdot EC$.

> **Theorem** If a tangent and a secant, two tangents, or two secants in-
> tersect in the exterior of a circle, then the measure of the
> angle formed is half the difference of the measures of the
> intercepted arcs. Tan and secant, 2 tans, 2 secants ∩ in
> ext. of ⊙ ⇒ ∠ = ½ difference of intercepted arcs. (T133)
>
> There are three cases to consider: a tangent and a secant, two tangents,
> and two secants.
>
>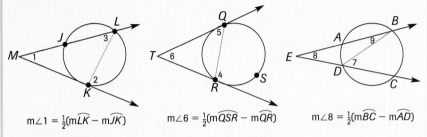
>
> $m\angle 1 = \frac{1}{2}(m\widehat{LK} - m\widehat{JK})$ $m\angle 6 = \frac{1}{2}(m\widehat{QSR} - m\widehat{QR})$ $m\angle 8 = \frac{1}{2}(m\widehat{BC} - m\widehat{AD})$
>
> The proof of this theorem is very similar to the proof of the first theorem
> in this item.

A satellite in a geostationary orbit moves in a circle concentric to Earth's
equator. Because the satellite completes an orbit of Earth in 24 hours, it
appears to hover directly over a point on the equator.

> A geostationary orbit allows a satellite to stay
> in the same position relative to a point on Earth.

EXAMPLE: A camera on a
weather monitoring satellite is
in a geostationary orbit. The
length of the equator that the
camera can view is 6000 km,
which is an arc of 54°. Find the
angle of view of the camera.

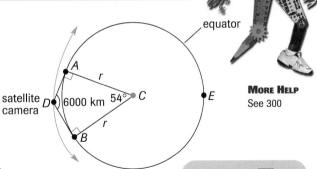

MORE HELP
See 300

The angle of view of the camera
is an angle formed by two tangents.

$m\angle ADB = \frac{1}{2}(m\widehat{AEB} - m\widehat{AB})$

$\quad = \frac{1}{2}(306 - 54)$

$\quad = \frac{1}{2}(252)$ $m\widehat{AEB} = 360° - 54°, \text{ or } 306°$

$\quad = 126$

> Notice that $\overline{DA}$ and
> $\overline{DB}$ are tangent to
> ⊙ C.

★ The angle of view of the camera is 126°.

There are a number of mathematically interesting relationships between arcs and angles, between arcs and chords, and between angles in a circle.

310

Naming Arcs and Angles

Any two spokes of a wheel form an angle called a *central angle* because its vertex is the *center* of the circle.

An angle whose vertex is the center of a circle and is in the same plane is a **central angle** of the circle. The sides of a central angle are radii of the circle. Remember, a complete revolution is 360°, so the sum of all the central angles in a circle is 360°.

Each central angle of a circle splits the circumference of the circle into two parts. An arc greater than a semicircle (or greater than 180°) is a **major arc**. An arc less than a semicircle (or less than 180°) is a **minor arc**.

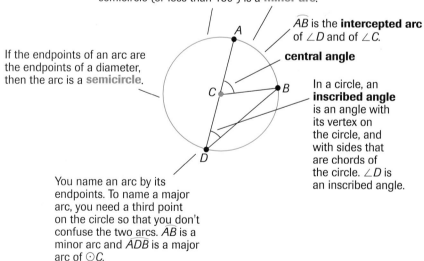

$\overarc{AB}$ is the **intercepted arc** of $\angle D$ and of $\angle C$.

central angle

If the endpoints of an arc are the endpoints of a diameter, then the arc is a **semicircle**.

In a circle, an **inscribed angle** is an angle with its vertex on the circle, and with sides that are chords of the circle. $\angle D$ is an inscribed angle.

You name an arc by its endpoints. To name a major arc, you need a third point on the circle so that you don't confuse the two arcs. $\overarc{AB}$ is a minor arc and $\overarc{ADB}$ is a major arc of $\odot C$.

Arc Measure

Arcs are measured by their corresponding central angles. The measure of a semicircle is 180°.

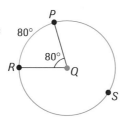

The **measure of a minor arc** is the measure of its central angle. So, $m\overset{\frown}{PR} = m\angle PQR$. You can write the measure of an arc next to the arc.

The **measure of a major arc** is the difference between 360° and the measure of its associated minor arc; $m\overset{\frown}{RSP} = 360° - 80° = 280°$.

Arc Addition Postulate

Two arcs of the same circle are **adjacent** if they intersect at exactly one point.

| **Postulate** | The measure of an arc formed by two adjacent arcs is the sum of the measures of the two arcs.
Arc + Postulate (P24) | 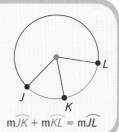 |

$$m\overset{\frown}{JK} + m\overset{\frown}{KL} = m\overset{\frown}{JL}$$

Congruent Arcs

Two arcs are **congruent** if they have the same measure.

| **Postulate** | In the same circle, or in congruent circles, two arcs are congruent if and only if their central angles are congruent. 2 arcs $\cong$ ⇔ central $\angle$s $\cong$ (P25) |

Some geometry texts present this as a theorem. The proof involves definitions of $\cong$ angles, arc length, and $\cong$ arcs.

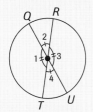

$\angle 2 \cong \angle 4$ and $\angle 1 \cong \angle 3$, so $\overset{\frown}{QR} \cong \overset{\frown}{TU}$ and $\overset{\frown}{QT} \cong \overset{\frown}{RU}$.

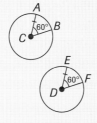

$\odot C \cong \odot D$ because the radii are congruent, so $\overset{\frown}{AB} \cong \overset{\frown}{EF}$.

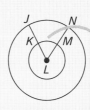

$m\overset{\frown}{JN} = m\overset{\frown}{KM}$ but $\overset{\frown}{JN} \ncong \overset{\frown}{KM}$.

In circles that are not congruent, arcs that have the same measure are not congruent.

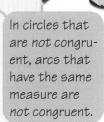

Arc and Chord Relationships

As you might expect, chords and arcs of circles have some special properties.

Theorem — In the same circle, or in congruent circles, two minor arcs are congruent if and only if their corresponding chords are congruent. 2 minor arcs ≅ ⟺ corresp. chords ≅ (T134)

When a minor arc and a chord share the same endpoints, we call the arc the **arc of the chord.**

To prove the theorem, you need to cover four cases.

CASE 1 In the same circle if two chords are congruent, then their corresponding minor arcs are congruent.

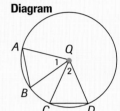

Diagram

Proof

Given: $\overline{AB} \cong \overline{DC}$

Prove: $\overset{\frown}{AB} \cong \overset{\frown}{DC}$

$\overline{QA}$, $\overline{QB}$, $\overline{QD}$, and $\overline{QC}$ are all radii of $\odot Q$, so $\overline{QA} \cong \overline{QB} \cong \overline{QD} \cong \overline{QC}$. It is given that $\overline{AB} \cong \overline{DC}$. By the SSS Congruence Postulate, $\triangle AQB \cong \triangle CQD$. Since corresponding parts of congruent triangles are congruent, $\angle 1 \cong \angle 2$. $\angle 1$ and $\angle 2$ are central angles of $\odot Q$, so $m\overset{\frown}{AB} = m\overset{\frown}{DC}$. Then $\overset{\frown}{AB} \cong \overset{\frown}{DC}$, by the definition of congruent arcs.

CASE 2 In the same circle, if two minor arcs are congruent, then their corresponding chords are congruent.

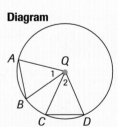

Diagram

Proof

Given: $\overset{\frown}{AB} \cong \overset{\frown}{DC}$

Prove: $\overline{AB} \cong \overline{DC}$

Since $\overset{\frown}{AB} \cong \overset{\frown}{DC}$, $\angle 1 \cong \angle 2$ by the definition of congruent arcs. $\overline{QA}$, $\overline{QB}$, $\overline{QD}$, and $\overline{QC}$ are all radii of $\odot Q$, so $\overline{QA} \cong \overline{QB} \cong \overline{QD} \cong \overline{QC}$. Then $\triangle AQB \cong \triangle CQD$ by the SAS Congruence Theorem. Since corresponding parts of congruent triangles are congruent, $\overline{AB} \cong \overline{DC}$.

You can use similar arguments for cases involving congruent circles.

Diameter Perpendicular to a Chord

A point B is called the **midpoint** of $\overset{\frown}{ABC}$ if $\overset{\frown}{AB} \cong \overset{\frown}{BC}$.
Any line, segment, or ray that contains B **bisects** $\overset{\frown}{ABC}$.

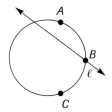

Theorem	If a diameter of a circle is perpendicular to a chord, then the diameter bisects the chord and its arc. Diameter $\perp$ chord $\Rightarrow$ diameter bisects chord and arc (T135)

Proof

Diagram

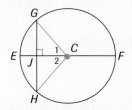

Given: $\overline{EF}$ is a diameter of $\odot C$, $\overline{EF} \perp \overline{GH}$

Prove: $\overline{JG} \cong \overline{JH}$, $\overset{\frown}{GE} \cong \overset{\frown}{EH}$

Plan: Draw radii $\overline{CG}$ and $\overline{CH}$. Use congruent triangles to show $\overline{JG} \cong \overline{JH}$ and $\angle 1 \cong \angle 2$. Then show that $\overset{\frown}{GE} \cong \overset{\frown}{EH}$.

Draw radii $\overline{CG}$ and $\overline{CH}$; $\overline{CG} \cong \overline{CH}$. $\overline{CJ} \cong \overline{CJ}$ by the Reflexive Property of Congruence. $\overline{EF} \perp \overline{GH}$, so $\angle CJG$ and $\angle CJH$ are both right angles. Then $\triangle CJG$ and $\triangle CJH$ are right triangles and $\triangle CJG \cong \triangle CJH$ by the Hypotenuse-Leg Congruence Theorem. Since corresponding parts of congruent triangles are congruent, $\overline{JG} \cong \overline{JH}$ and $\angle 1 \cong \angle 2$. By the definition of congruent arcs, $\overset{\frown}{GE} \cong \overset{\frown}{EH}$.

Theorem	If a chord is a perpendicular bisector of another chord, then it is a diameter. Chord$_1$ $\perp$ bisector of chord$_2$ $\Rightarrow$ chord$_1$ is diameter (T136)

Proof

Diagram

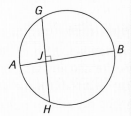

Given: $\overline{AB}$ is the $\perp$ bisector of $\overline{GH}$

Prove: $\overline{AB}$ is a diameter of $\odot C$.

Plan: Use an indirect proof. Assume the center is not on $\overline{AB}$ and draw radii $\overline{CH}$ and $\overline{CG}$. Prove that $\triangle GCJ \cong \triangle HCJ$, so $\overline{JC} \perp \overline{GH}$. Show that this leads to a contradiction, since there can't be two lines through point J that are both perpendicular to $\overline{GH}$.

MORE ▶

MORE HELP
See 061

Assume the center of the circle, C, is not on $\overline{AB}$. Draw $\overline{JC}$. You know that $\overline{AB}$ is the perpendicular bisector of $\overline{GH}$, so $\overline{JG} \cong \overline{JH}$. You're assuming $\overline{CH}$ and $\overline{CG}$ are radii, so they must be congruent. $\overline{JC} \cong \overline{JC}$ by the Reflexive Property of Congruence. By the SSS Congruence Theorem, $\triangle GCJ$ would be congruent to $\triangle HCJ$ and since corresponding parts of congruent triangles are congruent, $\angle GJC$ would be congruent to $\angle HJC$.

Diagram

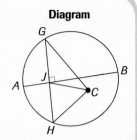

Since they would be congruent adjacent angles that form a straight line, $\angle GJC$ and $\angle HJC$ must be right angles and $\overline{JC} \perp \overline{GH}$. But it is given that $\overline{AB} \perp \overline{GH}$ and by the Perpendicular Postulate there is only one line perpendicular to a given line through a point on that line. Therefore the assumption must be false and C must really be on $\overline{AB}$, which makes $\overline{AB}$ a diameter of the circle.

316

Congruent Chords

Theorem In the same circle, or in congruent circles, two chords are congruent if and only if they are equidistant from the center. 2 chords $\cong$ $\Leftrightarrow$ equidistant from center (T137)

To prove, you need to cover four cases.

MORE HELP
See 268

CASE 1 In congruent circles, if two chords are equidistant from the center, then they are congruent.

Diagram

Proof

Given: $\odot C \cong \odot D$, $\overline{CR} \perp \overline{QS}$, $\overline{DU} \perp \overline{TV}$, $\overline{CR} \cong \overline{DU}$

Prove: $\overline{QS} \cong \overline{TV}$

Draw radii $\overline{CQ}$, $\overline{CS}$, $\overline{DT}$ and $\overline{DV}$. Since $\overline{CR} \perp \overline{QS}$ and $\overline{DU} \perp \overline{TV}$, the triangles formed are right triangles. The radii are congruent and it is given that $\overline{CR} \cong \overline{DU}$. By the Hypotenuse-Leg Congruence Theorem, $\triangle CRQ \cong \triangle CRS \cong \triangle DUT \cong \triangle DUV$. Because corresponding parts of congruent triangles are congruent, $\overline{RQ} \cong \overline{RS} \cong \overline{UT} \cong \overline{UV}$. By the Segment Addition Postulate, $\overline{QS} \cong \overline{TV}$.

CASE 2 In congruent circles, if two chords are congruent, then they are equidistant from the center.

Given: $\odot C \cong \odot D$, $\overline{QS} \cong \overline{TV}$

Prove: $\overline{CR} \cong \overline{DU}$

Diagram

Proof

Draw radii $\overline{CS}$ and $\overline{DV}$. It is given that $\overline{QS} \cong \overline{TV}$. Construct $\overline{CR} \perp \overline{QS}$ and $\overline{DU} \perp \overline{TV}$, forming right triangles CRS and DUV. $\overline{CR}$ bisects $\overline{QS}$ and $\overline{DU}$ bisects $\overline{TV}$ since $\overline{CR}$ is part of a diameter and a diameter perpendicular to a chord bisects the chord. Since $\overline{QS} \cong \overline{TV}$, half of $\overline{QS}$ is congruent to half of $\overline{TV}$, or $\overline{RS} \cong \overline{UV}$. By the Hypotenuse-Leg Congruence Theorem, $\triangle CRS \cong \triangle DUV$. By CPCTC, $\overline{CR} \cong \overline{DU}$.

You can use similar arguments for cases involving the same circle.

Special Angle Relationships in Circles _____

Recall that the vertex of a central angle is at the center of a circle. The vertex of an inscribed angle is *on* the circle.

Inscribed Angles and Intercepted Arcs

A carpenter's square is like two rulers that form a right angle.

A carpenter can use a carpenter's square to find the center of a circle. Suppose you place a carpenter's square inside a circle, with the vertex on the circle. Notice that the carpenter's

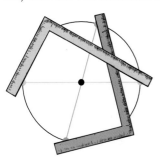

square corresponds to an inscribed angle in the circle. The legs, or sides, of the carpenter's square are secant segments of the circle. Draw a segment connecting the two points where the legs intersect the circle. Move the vertex of the carpenter's square to another point on the circle and draw another segment connecting the points where the legs intersect the circle. The two segments will intersect in the center of the circle.

You can try to find the center of a circle yourself using this method. Just use the corner of an index card instead of a carpenter's square. This method is called the **right-angle method** and it works because an inscribed right angle intercepts an arc of 180°, so the chords you draw are diameters.

MORE HELP
See 132, 302

Theorem If an angle is inscribed in a circle, then its measure is half the measure of its intercepted arc. ∠ inscribed in ⊙ ⇒ measure is $\frac{1}{2}$ intercepted arc (T138)

To prove, you need to cover three cases.

CASE 1 The center of the circle lies on a side of the inscribed angle.

Diagram

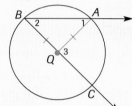

Proof

Given: ∠2 is inscribed in ⊙Q; Q lies on $\overrightarrow{BC}$

Prove: m∠2 = $\frac{1}{2}$m$\widehat{AC}$

Draw radius $\overline{QA}$. Since △AQB is isosceles, m∠1 = m∠2. Call this measure x. By the Exterior Angle Theorem, m∠3 = 2x. The measure of an arc equals the measure of its central angle, so m$\widehat{AC}$ = 2x. 2x = 2 · m∠2, so m∠2 = $\frac{1}{2}$m$\widehat{AC}$.

CASE 2 The center of the circle is in the interior of the inscribed angle.

Diagram

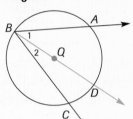

Proof

Given: ∠ABC is inscribed in ⊙Q; Q is in the interior of ∠ABC

Prove: m∠ABC = $\frac{1}{2}$m$\widehat{AC}$

Plan: Use the Angle Addition Postulate and Case 1 to prove Case 2.

Statements	Reasons
❶ Draw $\overrightarrow{BD}$ through the center of circle Q	2 pts. determine a line (P05)
❷ m∠ABC = m∠ABD + m∠DBC	∠ + Postulate (P13)
❸ m∠ABD = $\frac{1}{2}$m$\widehat{AD}$; m∠DBC = $\frac{1}{2}$m$\widehat{DC}$	Case 1
❹ m∠ABC = $\frac{1}{2}$m$\widehat{AD}$ + $\frac{1}{2}$m$\widehat{DC}$	Substitution
❺ m∠ABC = $\frac{1}{2}$(m$\widehat{AD}$ + m$\widehat{DC}$)	Distributive prop.
❻ m∠ABC = $\frac{1}{2}$m$\widehat{AC}$	Arc + Postulate (P24)

Point Q is on a side of ∠ABD and on a side of ∠DBC.

CASE 3 The center of the circle is in the exterior of the inscribed angle.

Draw $\overrightarrow{BD}$ through the center of ⊙Q. Now the proof is like the proof of Case 2. Here m∠1 = m∠ABD − m∠2.

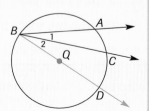

| **Theorem** | If two inscribed angles of a circle intercept the same arc, then the angles are congruent. 2 inscribed ∠s intercept same arc ⇒ ≅ ∠s (T139) |

Proof

Given: ∠1 intercepts $\widehat{AB}$, ∠2 intercepts $\widehat{AB}$

Prove: ∠1 ≅ ∠2

Plan: Show that both inscribed angles have the same measures. Since the measures are equal, the angles must be congruent.

Diagram

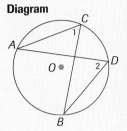

Statements	Reasons
❶ ∠1 intercepts $\widehat{AB}$, ∠2 intercepts $\widehat{AB}$	Given
❷ $m\angle 1 = \frac{1}{2}m\widehat{AB}$, $m\angle 2 = \frac{1}{2}m\widehat{AB}$	∠ inscribed in ⊙ ⇒ measure is $\frac{1}{2}$ intercepted arc (T138)
❸ $m\angle 1 = m\angle 2$	Transitive prop. of =
❹ ∠1 ≅ ∠2	Def. of ≅

| **Theorem** | An angle that is inscribed in a circle is a right angle if and only if its corresponding arc is a semicircle. ∠ inscribed in ⊙ is rt. ∠ ⇔ corresp. arc is semicircle (T140) |

You need to prove two cases of this theorem.

CASE 1 If an angle that is inscribed in a circle is a right angle, then its corresponding arc is a semicircle.

Diagram

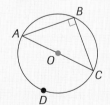

Proof

Given: ∠ABC is a right angle

Prove: $\widehat{ADC}$ is a semicircle

By definition, m∠ABC is 90°. Because ∠ABC is an inscribed angle, its measure is $\frac{1}{2}$ of its intercepted arc; $90° = \frac{1}{2}m\widehat{ADC}$ so $180° = m\widehat{ADC}$. By definition, $\widehat{ADC}$ is a semicircle.

CASE 2 If an arc is a semicircle, then its corresponding inscribed angle is a right angle.

Proof

Diagram

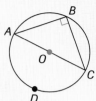

Given: $\overset{\frown}{ADC}$ is a semicircle

Prove: $\angle ABC$ is a right angle

By definition, $m\overset{\frown}{ADC} = 180°$. Because $\angle ABC$ is inscribed in a circle, its measure is $\frac{1}{2}$ of its intercepted arc, so $\frac{1}{2} \times 180° = m\angle ABC$ and $m\angle ABC = 90°$. By definition, $\angle ABC$ is a right angle.

Inscribed Quadrilaterals

A quadrilateral is **inscribed** in a circle if all of its vertices lie on the circle.

Theorem A quadrilateral can be inscribed in a circle if and only if its opposite angles are supplementary. Quadrilateral inscribed in $\odot \Leftrightarrow$ opp. $\angle$s supp. (T141)

You need to prove two cases of this theorem.

CASE 1 If a quadrilateral is inscribed in a circle, then its opposite angles are supplementary.

Diagram

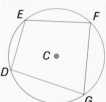

Proof

Given: $DEFG$ is inscribed in $\odot C$

Prove: $\angle D$ and $\angle F$ are supplementary, $\angle E$ and $\angle G$ are supplementary

The Arc Addition Postulate says that $m\overset{\frown}{EFG} + m\overset{\frown}{GDE} = 360°$. Since $\angle D$ is an inscribed angle that intercepts $\overset{\frown}{EFG}$ and $\angle F$ is an inscribed angle that intercepts $\overset{\frown}{GDE}$, $m\angle D = \frac{1}{2}\overset{\frown}{EFG}$ and $m\angle F = \frac{1}{2}m\overset{\frown}{GDE}$. Then by the Addition property of equality $m\angle D + m\angle F = \frac{1}{2}m\overset{\frown}{EFG} + \frac{1}{2}m\overset{\frown}{GDE}$. By the Distributive property, $m\angle D + m\angle F = \frac{1}{2}(m\overset{\frown}{EFG} + m\overset{\frown}{GDE})$. By substitution, $m\angle D + m\angle F = \frac{1}{2}(360°)$, or $180°$. So, $\angle D$ and $\angle F$ are supplementary by definition. Since the sum of the angles of a quadrilateral is $360°$, if one pair of opposite angles is supplementary, the other pair, $\angle E$ and $\angle G$, must also be supplementary.

CASE 2 If the opposite angles of a quadrilateral are supplementary, then the quadrilateral can be inscribed in a circle.

Proof

Given: ∠1 and ∠2 are supplementary

Prove: *DEFG* is inscribed in ⊙*C*

Plan: Use an indirect proof to show that the circle also passes through *G*. You must show that *G* can't be either outside or inside the circle.

❶ G is inside the circle.	❷ G is outside the circle.
Draw the circle that passes through *D*, *E*, and *F*. Assume that *G* lies in the *interior* of the circle. Let *DG⃗* intersect the circle at *H*. From Case 1, ∠1 would be supplementary to ∠3. You are given that ∠1 is supplementary to ∠2, so ∠2 ≅ ∠3 because supplements of the same angle are congruent. Since ∠2 and ∠3 form congruent corresponding angles, *GF* would be parallel to *HF*. But these segments intersect at *F*, so this is impossible. Therefore, the assumption that *G* lies in the *interior* of the circle is false.	If you assume that *G* lies in the *exterior* of the circle, a similar argument leads to the conclusion that this too is impossible.
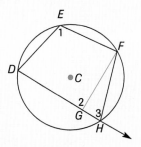	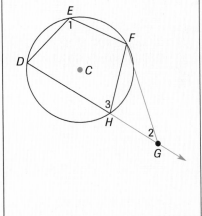

Both cases lead to a contradiction. *G* does not lie in the interior nor in the exterior of the circle. Therefore, *G* must lie on the circle and *DEFG* is inscribed in the circle.

Solids

". . . treat Nature by the sphere, the cylinder, and the cone . . ."

—Paul Cézanne

Columbus, the cartoon character, had a REALLY hard time trying to convince others that the world was round.

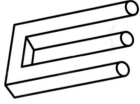

Look closely at the drawing. If you cover the right part with your hand, the figure appears to have two prongs. But if you cover the left part, you see three prongs. What's going on?

Illusions like this often arise when you try to display the three-dimensional world on a two dimensional surface such as the page of a book, but since there's no easy way to actually draw in three dimensions, people rely more than they might think on flat representations with a three dimensional look.

Even though you live in a world where objects have length, width, and depth, you often use pictures with length, width, and only the appearance of depth. As you learn about points, lines, surfaces, and regions of space, you'll need to visualize in three dimensions, but be careful! As the pronged figure indicates, there's a fine line between visualization and illusion.

321 Classification of Solids

Solid figures, or simply **solids**, are three-dimensional figures. They enclose a region of space. They are classified by the types of surfaces they have. These surfaces may be flat, curved, or both.

322 Polyhedrons

MORE HELP See 081, 128

A **polyhedron** is a solid bounded by polygons. Both *polyhedrons* and *polyhedra* refer to more than one polyhedron.

A vertex is a point of intersection of three or more edges.
Each planar region is a face.
An edge is a line segment formed by the intersection of two faces. (Remember, the intersection of two planes is a line.)

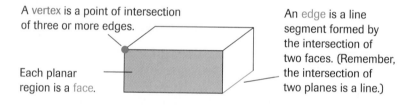

Polyhedrons

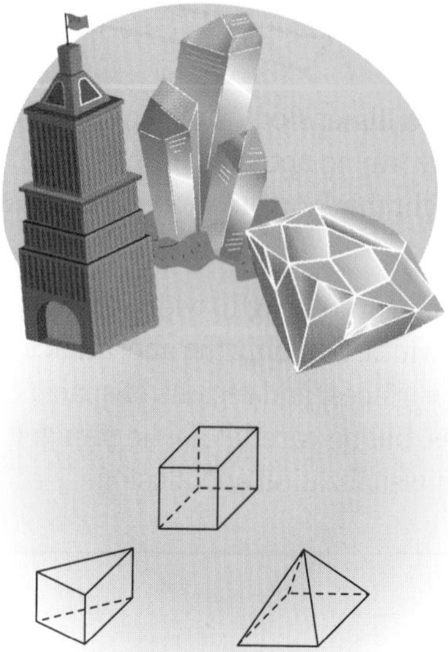

Not Polyhedrons

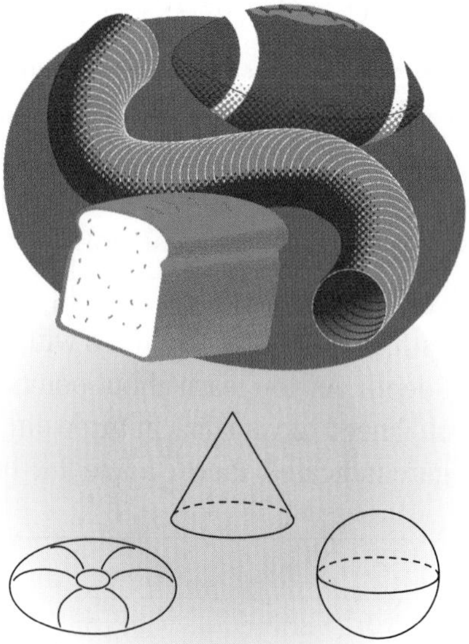

Polyhedrons, just like polygons, may be convex or nonconvex. If a segment that connects any two points on the surface of a polyhedron is completely inside or on the polyhedron, the polyhedron is **convex**. Otherwise, it is non-convex (or concave).

MORE HELP
See 128

Convex Polyhedron

$\overline{FG}$ is in the polyhedron.

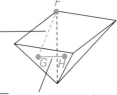

$\overline{GH}$ is on the polyhedron.

Non-convex Polyhedron

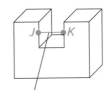

$\overline{JK}$ is outside the polyhedron.

Euler's Theorem

323

The Swiss mathematician Leonhard Euler (**Oil** er) lived from 1707 to 1783. He proved a theorem relating the number of faces, vertices, and edges of a polyhedron. This formula is known as Euler's Theorem for Polyhedrons.

Theorem   The number of faces, F, vertices, V, and edges, E of a polyhedron are related by $F + V = E + 2$. (T142)

The proof of this theorem is beyond the scope of this book.

$F + V = E + 2$					
Type of Polyhedron	**Drawing of Polyhedron**	**Number of Faces**	**Number of Vertices**	**Number of Edges**	**Test Euler's Theorem**
Square Pyramid		5	5	8	$5 + 5 = 8 + 2$
Tetrahedron		4	4	6	$4 + 4 = 6 + 2$
Cube		6	8	12	$6 + 8 = 12 + 2$
Pentagonal Prism		7	10	15	$7 + 10 = 15 + 2$

MORE ▶

EXAMPLE: Use these polyhedrons to test Euler's formula.

Hexagonal Pyramid

Triangular Prism

$F = 7$, $V = 7$, and $E = 12$

$F + V = E + 2$

$7 + 7 \overset{?}{=} 12 + 2$

$14 = 14$

$F = 5$, $V = 6$, and $E = 9$

$F + V = E + 2$

$5 + 6 \overset{?}{=} 9 + 2$

$11 = 11$

★ The formula checks for these polyhedrons.

324

Platonic Solids

In a **regular polyhedron**, or **Platonic solid**, the faces are all regular congruent polygons. The same number of edges meet at each vertex. Although an infinite number of *polygons* are regular, only five *polyhedrons* are regular.

> **DID YOU KNOW** The ancient Greeks believed there were only five elements and that they could be matched with the five Platonic solids.
>
> Plato was a Greek mathematician and philosopher who lived from 429 to 347 B.C. He assigned one of the regular polyhedrons to each of the five known elements: regular tetrahedron for fire, regular hexahedron for earth, regular octahedron for air, regular dodecahedron for the cosmos, and regular icosahedron for water.

The Five Platonic Solids

Regular Tetrahedron

Regular Hexahedron

Regular Octahedron

Regular Dodecahedron

Regular Icosahedron

Archimedean Solids

In a **semiregular polyhedron,** or **Archimedean solid,** the faces consist of more than one type of regular polygon, and the same number of each type meets at each vertex in the same order. These thirteen solids are named after the Greek mathematician Archimedes (287–212 B.C.).

MORE HLEP
See 370–371

An icosidodecahedron is made up of 20 equilateral triangles and 12 regular pentagons.

Archimedean Solids

Cuboctahedron

Snub Cube

Icosidodecahedron

Snub Dodecahedron

Truncated Tetrahedron

Truncated Cube

Truncated Octahedron

Truncated Dodecahedron

Truncated Icosahedron

Small Rhombicuboctahedron

Great Rhombicuboctahedron

Small Rhombicosidodecahedron

Great Rhombicosidodecahedron

Do the names of the Platonic and Archimedean solids sound like some kind of foreign language? If so, that's because most of the names are derived from Greek words. Refer to the lists of prefixes and suffixes in the Almanac for help translating.

Dodecahedron

Truncated Dodecahedron

Two English words in these names that may be new to you are **truncated,** which means cut off, and **snub,** which means rounded.

If you look at a truncated dodecahedron, you can see that it started as a polyhedron with twelve faces. A cut was then made at each vertex to create a new solid.

A truncated dodecahedron no longer has 12 faces. It has 12 regular decagons and 15 equilateral triangles.

Prisms

MORE HELP
See 060–061,
196

A box shape is a very common type of polyhedron. It is a type of prism. A **prism** is a polyhedron that has two congruent and parallel faces joined by faces that are parallelograms. In the box shape, or **rectangular prism**, the congruent parallel faces (bases) are rectangles. The bases in other types of prisms are other congruent polygons. In a **right prism**, the lateral edges are perpendicular to the bases (so, they are also altitudes). In an **oblique prism**, the lateral edges are not perpendicular to the bases. Its **slant height** is the length of a lateral edge.

Right Rectangular Prism

Oblique Rectangular Prism

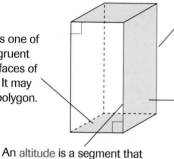

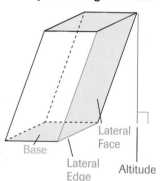

A base is one of the congruent parallel faces of a prism. It may be any polygon.

A lateral edge is an edge of a lateral face that joins corresponding vertices of the bases.

An altitude is a segment that is perpendicular to the planes of the bases. Its length is the **height** of the prism.

A lateral face of a prism is not a base, It is a parallelogram and is congruent to the other lateral faces only if the bases are regular.

Lateral Face

Base

Lateral Edge

Altitude

Prisms are classified by the shapes of their bases. The base of a prism need not be a regular polygon. If all of the faces of a polyhedron are parallelograms, it is a **parallelepiped.**

Pentagonal Prism **Hexagonal Prism** **Octagonal Prism** **Square Prism (Parallelepiped)**

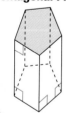

A **regular prism** is one whose base is a regular polygon.

The bases of a prism are not always the top and bottom of a prism. The only requirements for the bases of a prism are that they are congruent and parallel.

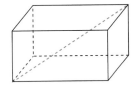

MORE HELP
See 152

The **diagonal** of a solid is a segment that joins two vertices and contains points in the interior of the solid. In a rectangular prism, its endpoints are a vertex of one base and the opposite vertex of the other base.

The formula for the length of a diagonal in a rectangular prism is based on the Pythagorean Theorem.

Formula   In a rectangular solid with dimensions ℓ, w, and h the length, d, of the diagonal is $d = \sqrt{\ell^2 + w^2 + h^2}$. (F47)

Proof

Given: Rectangular prism with dimensions ℓ, w, and h and diagonal of length d

Prove: $d = \sqrt{\ell^2 + w^2 + h^2}$

Plan: Think of the diagonal of the rectangular prism as the hypotenuse of a right triangle whose legs are the diagonal of the base of the prism and the height of the prism. You'll need to use the Pythagorean Theorem twice.

$d^2 = (\text{diagonal of base})^2 + h^2$

$d^2 = (\ell^2 + w^2) + h^2$

$d = \sqrt{\ell^2 + w^2 + h^2}$

Diagram

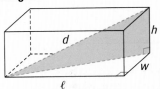

EXAMPLE: A packing box is 6 inches by 6 inches by 30 inches. Can a 32-inch pole be shipped in this box?

The longest straight distance in the box is its diagonal, so use the formula for the diagonal of a rectangular prism to see whether the pole would fit in the box if it were placed at an angle.

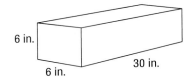

$d = \sqrt{\ell^2 + w^2 + h^2}$

$d = \sqrt{30^2 + 6^2 + 6^2}$

$d = \sqrt{972}$ or about 31.2

★ The 32-inch pole is longer than the diagonal of the packing box, so the pole cannot be shipped in this box.

Pyramids

MORE HELP
See 199, 209

From the monuments of ancient Egypt to the Trans America Building in San Francisco, pyramids have inspired builders by their beauty and simplicity. A **pyramid** is a polyhedron with at least three triangular faces that meet at a point and one other face (the base) that can be any type of polygon. A **regular** pyramid is a right pyramid with a regular polygon for its base. The altitude of a **right** pyramid intersects the base at its center.

A vertex (or **apex**) is the point at which the triangular faces meet.

A lateral edge joins the vertex of the pyramid to a vertex of the base.

The slant height of a regular pyramid is the height of any of the lateral faces. Pyramids that are not regular do not have slant heights.

An altitude is a segment from the vertex perpendicular to the plane of the base. Its length is the **height** of the pyramid.

A lateral face is a triangle.

The base is the face of a pyramid that need not be a triangle.

Vertex

Lateral Edge

Lateral Face

Altitude

A base edge is a side of the polygonal base.

Base

Base Edge

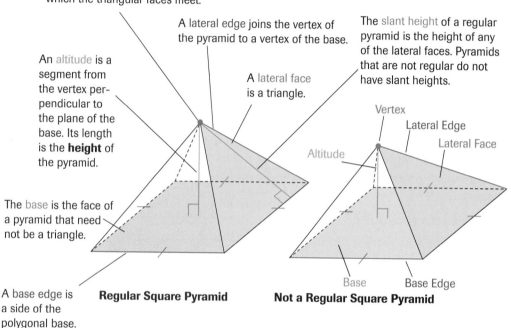

Regular Square Pyramid

Not a Regular Square Pyramid

As with prisms, pyramids are classified by the shapes of their bases.

MORE HELP
See 322, 324

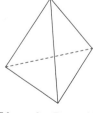

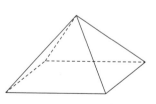

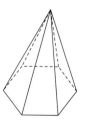

Triangular Pyramid   **Rectangular Pyramid**   **Hexagonal Pyramid**

MATH ALERT A Regular Pyramid May Not Be a Regular Polyhedron

MORE HELP
See 327

328

When you see the word *regular* in both terms—regular pyramid and regular polyhedron—it's easy to think that, because a pyramid is a polyhedron, a regular pyramid must be a regular polyhedron. However, that's not usually the case.

The faces (including any bases) of a regular polyhedron must all be regular congruent polygons. This means that the only pyramid which could be a regular polyhedron must be triangular, and a triangular pyramid is regular only if its base is an equilateral triangle. In order for a regular triangular pyramid to be a regular polyhedron, the lateral faces must also be equilateral triangles.

Regular Polyhedron

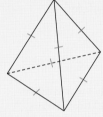

Not a Regular Polyhedron

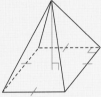

Regular Triangular Pyramid (Tetrahedron)
The base and faces are congruent equilateral triangles.

Regular Triangular Pyramid
The base and faces are all triangles, but they are not all congruent.

Regular Square Pyramid
The base is a regular polygon, but it is not congruent to the faces.

Prismoids

329

MORE HELP
See 326–327

Sometimes you may see a solid that looks something like a pyramid, except that it doesn't have a vertex, and something like a prism, except that its bases aren't congruent. You can classify it as a **prismoid**, a polyhedron that has two parallel bases that are not necessarily congruent. This prismoid is a truncated square pyramid.

All prisms are prismoids but not all prismoids are prisms.

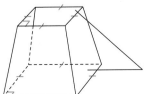

These bases are parallel but not congruent.

330 Cylinders

MORE HELP
See 176, 190, 197, 208, 297

You are probably familiar with cylinders because of their many uses from cans to automobile parts. A **cylinder** is a solid formed from two congruent and parallel circular regions and a curved surface joining the two. In a **right cylinder**, a segment joining the centers of the bases is perpendicular to each base. This segment is an altitude. In an **oblique cylinder**, the segment joining the centers of the bases is not perpendicular to the bases; the altitude does not join the centers.

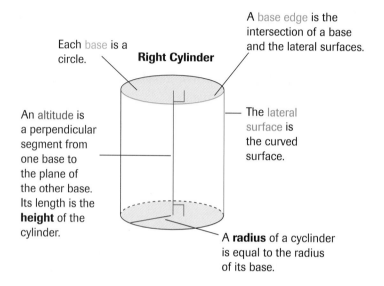

A base edge is the intersection of a base and the lateral surfaces.

Each base is a circle.

Right Cylinder

An altitude is a perpendicular segment from one base to the plane of the other base. Its length is the **height** of the cylinder.

The lateral surface is the curved surface.

A **radius** of a cyclinder is equal to the radius of its base.

Oblique Cylinder

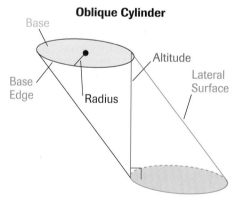

Base

Altitude

Base Edge

Lateral Surface

Radius

331 Cones

MORE HELP
See 176, 190, 198, 209, 297

The shape of ice cream cones and funnels is called a cone. A **cone** is a solid with a circular base and one curved surface. In a **right cone**, the altitude intersects the base at its center. In an **oblique cone**, the altitude does not intersect the base at its center.

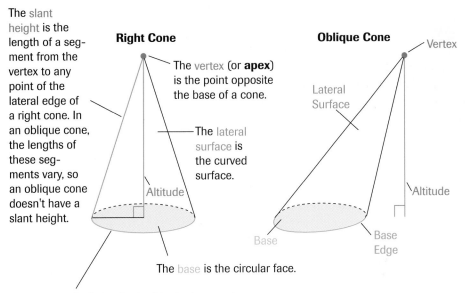

The slant height is the length of a segment from the vertex to any point of the lateral edge of a right cone. In an oblique cone, the lengths of these segments vary, so an oblique cone doesn't have a slant height.

Right Cone

The vertex (or **apex**) is the point opposite the base of a cone.

The lateral surface is the curved surface.

Altitude

The base is the circular face.

Oblique Cone

Vertex

Lateral Surface

Altitude

Base

Base Edge

The base edge (or **lateral edge**) is the intersection of the base and the lateral surface.

Spheres

332

A circle is all points *in a plane* equidistant from a given point. A **sphere** is all points *in space* equidistant from a given point, called its **center**.

MORE HELP
See 201, 210, 297, 332, 337

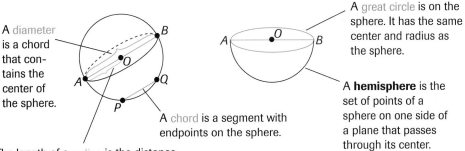

A diameter is a chord that contains the center of the sphere.

A chord is a segment with endpoints on the sphere.

The length of a radius is the distance from the center to a point on a sphere.

A great circle is on the sphere. It has the same center and radius as the sphere.

A **hemisphere** is the set of points of a sphere on one side of a plane that passes through its center.

333 Visualization of Solids

When you draw a picture of an object on paper, you are representing a three-dimensional object on a two-dimensional surface. There are different ways to draw three-dimensional objects, not just different in amount of detail, but also different in general approach.

334 Sketching

A sketch is not meant to be perfectly to scale, but it should show all relevant details. Since a picture is worth a thousand words, it pays to know how to sketch some common solids.

MORE HELP
See 326, 330

Here are some steps for sketching a prism or a cylinder.

- Start by drawing a base. Distances that are parallel to your line of sight should be shorter than a similar distance that is perpendicular to your line of sight.

Base of a Prism   **Base of a Cylinder**

- Next draw a congruent, parallel base. Offset it a bit if you'll need to draw in segments behind it. Since you are looking directly at it, make the segments solid.

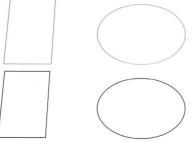

Bases of a Prism   **Bases of a Cylinder**

To make a right prism or cylinder, draw the second base almost directly over the first. To make it oblique, shift it to the right or left.

- Finally, draw segments connecting corresponding points of the bases. Dash any segments that would be hidden from view.

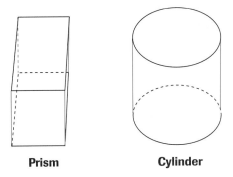

Prism   **Cylinder**

You can sketch a pyramid and a cone the same way you sketch a prism and a cylinder, except that you draw a point above the base instead of a parallel base.

- Draw the base. A circular base will appear elliptical, and a rectangular base will appear to be a parallelogram. Dash hidden parts of the base.

- Draw the vertex. Shift it to the right or left if you need to draw any segments behind the front face.

- Connect the vertex to points of the base. Dash hidden segments.

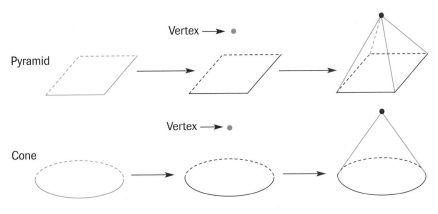

Perspective Views

Isometric drawings and orthographic drawings are two kinds of drawings commonly used by architects and engineers. An **isometric drawing** provides a corner view of an object. One view shows three sides of an object.

Isometric Drawing of a House

MORE ▶

An **orthographic drawing** or **orthographic projection** provides three separate views to show three sides of an object: a top view, a front view, and a side view of an object.

Orthographic Drawing of a House

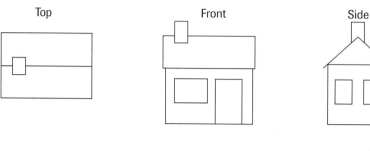

To make an isometric drawing and an ortho-graphic drawing of a simple solid, such as a stack of cubes, its helpful to use dot paper and graph paper.

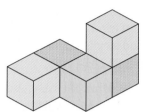

Use isometric dot paper for the isometric drawing. First sketch three axes on the paper. Then, in order to maintain the correct perspective, make all the lines in your isometric drawing paral-lel to these axes.

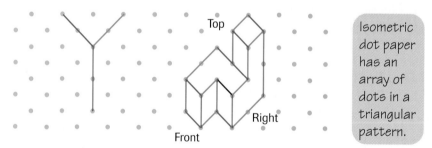

Isometric dot paper has an array of dots in a triangular pattern.

Use graph paper for the orthographic drawing. Use solid lines to show all edges.

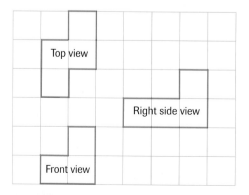

Nets

Have you ever watched an employee of a doughnut shop assemble your doughnut box? If so, you have probably seen a net. A **net** is a two-dimensional pattern that can be folded to form a solid. A net shows all the faces of a solid and their positions in relation to each other. It can be folded, like your doughnut box, into a solid.

MORE HELP
See 326–327,
330–331

Net for a Rectangular Prism

Net for a Triangular Prism

Net for a Cylinder

Net for a Cone

The net for a doughnut box also contains flaps that tuck in to hold the box together. A true net for a solid doesn't have any extra parts, such as flaps. It only includes the faces or surfaces of the solid.

Some solids, such as a sphere, can't be built from a net. Other solids may have more than one net. For example, a cube has twelve nets, not including any rotations or reflections of these twelve. Here are four of them.

MORE HELP
See 321

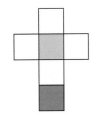
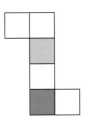
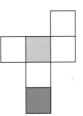
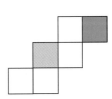

If the red square forms one base of the cube, the blue square will form the opposite base.

Cross Sections

MORE HELP
See 048, 052

A **cross section** is the intersection of a plane and a solid. Have you ever seen a cross section of a tree trunk? It is made by a saw slicing through the nearly cylindrical tree trunk. You can think of a geometric cross section as what you would see if you sliced though a solid figure like a tree trunk.

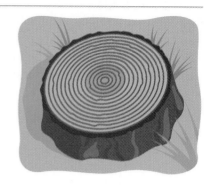

Depending on how a plane slices a solid, a cross section may be a point, a line segment, or a region of a plane.

MORE HELP
See 332

A plane can intersect a sphere at a single point, or it can intersect a sphere to form a circle. If that circle includes the center of the sphere (that is, the plane slices the sphere at the diameter), it is a **great circle**.

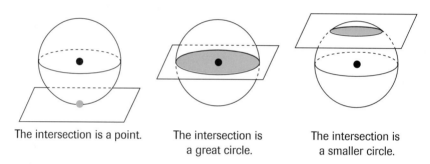

| The intersection is a point. | The intersection is a great circle. | The intersection is a smaller circle. |

MORE HELP
See 128, 326

A plane can intersect a cube at a point or a segment. It can also intersect a cube to form a triangle, a trapezoid, a square, a rectangle, pentagon, or a hexagon.

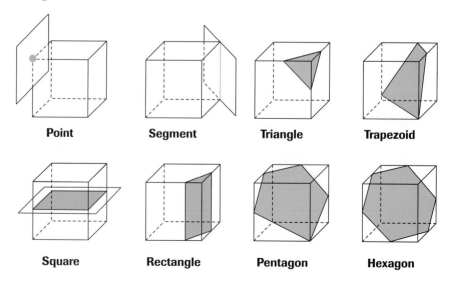

| **Point** | **Segment** | **Triangle** | **Trapezoid** |

| **Square** | **Rectangle** | **Pentagon** | **Hexagon** |

Conic Sections

Conic sections are formed by the cross sections of a solid known as a **double napped right cone**. Unlike a true cone, the double napped cone has no bases. The surfaces extend without end. The **axis** of this cone is the vertical line through the vertex of each nap or half. Any line on the cone that contains the vertex is an **element** of this cone.

MORE HELP
See 298, 331

Conic Sections

Slicing perpendicular to the axis forms a circle. The axis intersects the circle at its center.

Slicing parallel to an element forms a parabola. The axis intersects the parabola at a point called the **focus**.

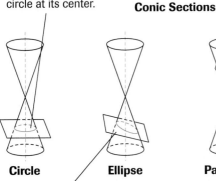

Slicing through both cones parallel to the axis forms a hyperbola.

Circle   **Ellipse**   **Parabola**   **Hyperbola**

Slicing oblique to the axis, but intersecting every element of the cone forms an ellipse. The axis intersects the ellipse at a point called a **focus**. There is another focus that is a point symmetric to the first.

A plane can also intersect a double napped cone at a point, a line, or a pair of intersecting lines. These cross sections are known as **degenerate conic sections**.

You may recall from your study of algebra that parabolas and hyperbolas are the graphs of quadratic and reciprocal functions. These equations give you a way to draw these curves.

MORE HELP
See 110–116

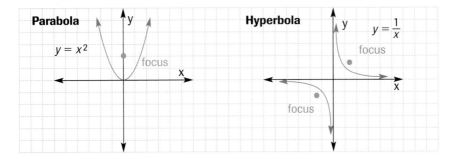

Parabola $y = x^2$ focus

Hyperbola $y = \frac{1}{x}$ focus   focus

Problem Solving

"For every problem, there is one solution which is simple, neat, and wrong."

—*H.L. Mencken*

Being a good problem solver, Rachel easily figured out what was wrong with the family car.

Figuring things out comes naturally for you. As an infant, you figured out how to spin the dials on your activity toys. When you were two, you figured out how to get to those cookies your mom left in the kitchen. Later you figured out more complicated things like how to open the refrigerator.

Now you solve even more complex problems, like finding your way around school, fixing your car or bicycle, or wrapping an odd-shaped present.

A lot of the problems you're so good at solving are geometric. They involve visualizing things and thinking logically. Of course, as with any problem, to solve a geometry problem it helps to know what's going on and what you're supposed to find out. It helps to know methods that have worked for you before. It helps to care about finding a solution. You may be surprised to see how much of what you already do can help you solve geometry problems.

Don't be too surprised that you know so much about solving math problems. After all, you're a natural-born problem solver.

Keep trying.

Just imagine if Tiger Woods had quit golf because he missed a putt, or if Michelle Kwan stopped skating after one fall. No one's perfect. That's especially true in problem solving. The best problem solvers make lots of mistakes; but part of what makes them so good is that they don't give up. When you work on a problem, your first try may not work out. That's OK. Just look at what you've done and give it another try. To a good problem solver, a wrong turn is just another step to success.

Take chances.

Have you ever wanted to meet someone but were too nervous to talk? That happens to everyone. It's understandable, but there's no reason to be shy when you're solving a math problem. After all, a problem can't remember the tries that didn't work. The next time you think you can't solve a problem, just go ahead and give it a shot. You've got nothing to lose.

Use what you know.

You take your new digital camera to the prom, but when you try to click your first picture you realize you forgot to charge the battery. If you're lucky, that hasn't happened to you, but if it has, you'll probably always remember to make sure there's a fully charged battery in your camera or in any battery-operated device you take somewhere. Experience is a very good teacher. When you solve geometry problems, use your experience. Look for things that are familiar. Maybe the problem you're working on reminds you of one you've solved before and maybe the method you used then will work now.

Practice.

Do you believe the saying *practice makes perfect*? Well, maybe not perfect, but if you dance, swim, play the guitar, or do any other activity, you know that practice makes you better. It's the same with problem solving. Each time you work on a problem, you learn something new. You become a better problem solver.

Watch what you do.

As you work on a problem, keep an eye on your progress. Take a look at the method you're using. Are you getting closer to a solution or to the final step of your proof, or are you just grinding out calculations and writing steps that won't help? If you think you're on the right track, stay on it. If you think you're not getting anywhere, stop and look around. You may want to try a different path.

Take a break.

You're tired. You're getting nowhere. All your ideas have bombed and you've run out of new ones. Those are signs that it may be time to get away from the problem for awhile. Take a short break and let your brain refresh itself.

A Four-Step Problem-Solving Plan

Getting stuck on a problem is like being lost. In both cases, a map sure would help. Here is a problem-solving plan that acts like a map. It won't solve the problem or write the proof, but it can help you find your way.

 If you found yourself in a game and you had no clue about the object or the rules, you wouldn't have much chance of winning, unless you found out what you were supposed to do. It's like that in problem solving. If you don't understand what's going on, ask yourself, *What am I given? What do I need to prove or find out?* If you don't understand the problem, use these hints.

- Read the problem again slowly. Take notes or draw pictures to help.

- If there are charts or diagrams, study them.

- Look up any words or symbols you don't know.

- Try to explain the problem to someone else.

 Take a little time to think about how to solve a problem. Redrawing or taking apart the diagram may give you ideas; so can reviewing related theorems. For example, you know a lot about triangles. Even if the current problem isn't about triangles, can you make it so?

 Try the method you picked. Work carefully. Keep thinking while you work. Remember, if your first try doesn't work, try something else.

 After you find an answer or finish a proof, go over what you've done.

- Check for reasonableness. Does your answer make sense?

- Does it really answer what the problem is asking or prove what you're supposed to prove?

- Did you use correct mathematics?

- Does your reasoning flow smoothly from one step to the next?

- If you try another way, do you get the same result?

Problem-Solving Strategies

Walking, riding in a car, biking, taking a bus, train, or plane—there are many ways to get from one place to another. Solving a problem is like going somewhere. There are lots of different methods, or strategies, you can use to help get an answer.

Keep in mind a few things about strategies.

- Strategies are not recipes; they are more like guides. They will help you find your way, but they won't give you step-by-step directions.

- You can use more than one strategy on a single problem.

- You can use a strategy that's not on the list (even one that you make up yourself).

- You can use whatever strategy works for you. Strategies are not right or wrong. Your friend might work backward to solve a problem. You might write an equation to solve the same problem. It's not necessary for everyone to solve a problem the same way.

Make a Visual Representation

When you draw a diagram to explain a play in soccer or football, you keep it simple. You use X's and O's to stand for people. To make a diagram to solve a problem, you don't have to be an artist. Just be sure to include the important information.

MORE HELP
See 203

EXAMPLE 1: Suppose you toss a nickel at random onto a chessboard made of five-centimeter squares. What is the probability that a nickel landing on the board will be entirely within a square?

- A nickel will be tossed at random toward the chessboard.

- Each square is five centimeters long.

- Find the probability that a nickel that lands on the board will not overlap any side of any square.

First look up or measure the diameter of a nickel (it's two centimeters). Then, make a diagram to show the region in which the nickel can land without crossing a side of a square. Then compare the area of the favorable region to the total area of the board.

Make a diagram of one square. Since the radius of the nickel is one centimeter, the center of the nickel must land at least one centimeter from any side of the square.

Draw a square three centimeters on each side to show the region in which the center of the nickel must land. Don't worry about drawing exactly to scale. You can use labels to show distances and other measures.

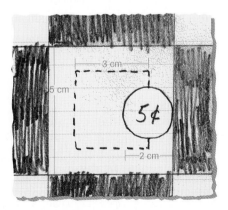

Probability of landing in favorable region = $\dfrac{\text{Total target area}}{\text{Total area of chessboard}}$ = $\dfrac{n(9 \text{ cm}^2)}{n(25 \text{ cm}^2)}$

> The number of squares on the chessboard is represented by n.

MORE ▶

4 Is it reasonable that we used the area of the chessboard as the total area? If the center of the nickel can go beyond the edge, that would increase the total area. But if its center is past an edge, the nickel would fall off and would not count. Using the area of the chessboard as the total area makes sense.

★ The probability of the nickel not overlapping a line is $\frac{9}{25}$, or 0.36.

Sometimes it is useful to make an accurate scale drawing and then measure what you need to find.

EXAMPLE 2: What is the outside diameter of the largest cylindrical pipe that will fit through the triangular opening shown in the diagram?

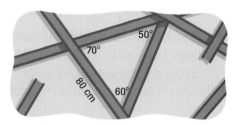

1
- The interior angles and one side length of the triangle are given.
- The diagram may not be to scale.
- Find the outside diameter of the largest pipe that can fit through.

2 Make an accurate scale drawing because you'll want to take measurements from it. Then inscribe a circle in the triangle and measure its diameter.

You could also use the fact that you know the angle measures to construct two angle-bisectors that locate the center. Then construct a perpendicular from the center to the base to give you the radius of the cylinder, whose length you can compute using the tangent ratio.

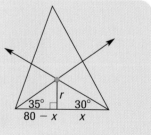

$$\tan 35° = \frac{r}{80-x} \qquad \tan 30° = \frac{r}{x}$$

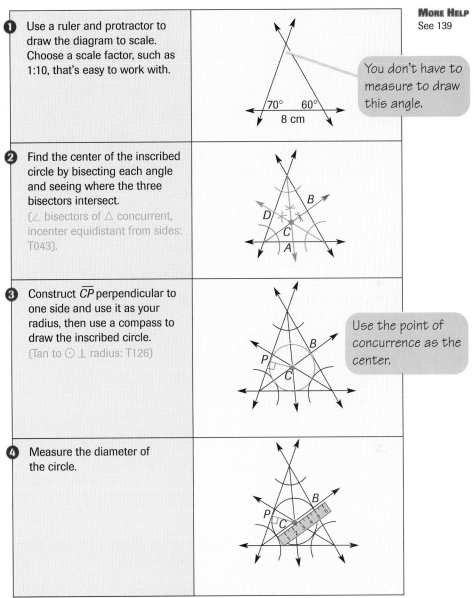

MORE HELP
See 139

TRY
3

1 Use a ruler and protractor to draw the diagram to scale. Choose a scale factor, such as 1:10, that's easy to work with.

You don't have to measure to draw this angle.

70°   60°
8 cm

2 Find the center of the inscribed circle by bisecting each angle and seeing where the three bisectors intersect.
(∠ bisectors of △ concurrent, incenter equidistant from sides: T043).

3 Construct $\overline{CP}$ perpendicular to one side and use it as your radius, then use a compass to draw the inscribed circle.
(Tan to ⊙ ⊥ radius: T126)

Use the point of concurrence as the center.

4 Measure the diameter of the circle.

LOOK BACK
4

■ Check the lengths and angle measures on your diagram (especially if your angle bisectors do not look concurrent).

■ Is your answer reasonable? Since the diameter in the drawing is five centimeters, the actual diameter would be 50 centimeters. Does it make sense that a 50-centimeter pipe will fit through the opening described?

★ The outside diameter of the largest cylindrical pipe that can fit through the opening is 50 cm.

MORE ▶

Sometimes you are given a diagram, but adding to it or changing it in some way can help you solve the problem.

EXAMPLE 3: *E* is the center of square *ABCD*. Find the area of quadrilateral *EFCD*.

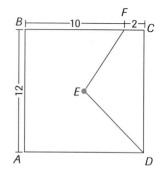

 UNDERSTAND 1

- *E* is at the center of a square 12 units on a side.

MORE HELP
See 129, 181, 188

- *C* and *D* are vertices of the square and *F* is two units from *C*.

- What is the area of quadrilateral *EFCD*?

PLAN 2

Draw a segment to break *EFCD* into parts that have known area formulas.

TRY 3

Construct $\overline{EG} \perp \overline{CD}$ to break *EFCD* into a triangle and a trapezoid.

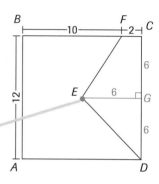

> You know that $\overline{EG}$, $\overline{GD}$, and $\overline{CG}$ are 6 units long because *E* and *G* would be the midpoints of 12-unit segments.

Area of $EGD = \frac{1}{2}bh$

$= \frac{1}{2}(6)(6)$

$= 18$

Area of $EFCG = \frac{1}{2}(b_1 + b_2)h$

$= \frac{1}{2}(2 + 6)6$

$= 24$

Area of $EFCD = 18 + 24$

$= 42$

LOOK BACK 4

- Make sure your geometric reasoning is sound. $EG = CG = GD = 6$ because *E* is the center of the square and $\overline{EG} \perp \overline{CD}$. $\overline{EG}$ is an altitude of $\triangle EGD$ because $\overline{EG} \perp \overline{CD}$. $\overline{EG} \parallel \overline{FC}$ because both are perpendicular to the same line.

- Check your calculations. Are your results reasonable?

> You could have also solved the problem by drawing a vertical segment through *E* to divide the square in half and then subtracting the area of the two triangles formed from the area of half the square.

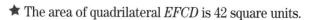

★ The area of quadrilateral *EFCD* is 42 square units.

Sometimes you can visualize or draw intersecting sets to solve a problem.

MORE HELP
See 299, 305

EXAMPLE 4: By measuring shock waves, seismologists can tell the distance but not direction to the **epicenter** of an earthquake, the place on the ground directly above the origin of the quake. From each measuring station, they can plot a circle to show all the places the epicenter could be. From how many stations do they need to take measurements in order to determine the location of the epicenter?

- Measurements from one station can tell you how far the epicenter is from that location.

- From how many different stations do you need to take measurements so you can tell exactly where the epicenter is?

Draw a diagram with circles, because a circle shows all the points in a plane that are the same distance from a given point.

❶ The measurements from one station tell you the epicenter is somewhere on a particular circle.	A• The epicenter could be any point on circle A.
❷ The measurements from a second station tell you the epicenter must be somewhere on a different circle, so, it could be either of the the two points where the circles intersect.	A• •B Either point of intersection could be the epicenter; another reading is required.
❸ The measurements from a third station will tell you which of those two possible points is the actual epicenter location.	C• P A• •B All three readings intersect at P. This is the epicenter.

In special cases you might not need a third circle. Just two circles could tell you where the epicenter is, if the circles are tangent. That's not likely, but if it did happen, then measurements from only those two stations would be enough to locate the epicenter. However, scientists cannot count on such a special case occurring.

★ Scientists need to take measurements from three different stations.

Find and Use a Pattern

You're playing a video game and the computer keeps blocking your path with colored pyramids and prisms. Then you notice that each blue prism is making the same move every time. You're seeing a behavior pattern. You can use that pattern to anticipate the move and get past the prism. Patterns can help you play video games. They can also help you solve math problems.

EXAMPLE: You can place a hexagonal ring of pennies around a central penny. Then you can place a second hexagonal ring of pennies around the first. How many pennies, not counting the central penny, will it take to make ten hexagonal rings of pennies?

 UNDERSTAND 1

- You're arranging pennies in a hexagonal pattern around a central penny over and over.

- Each penny is tangent to all adjacent pennies.

- If you make ten such hexagonal rings, how many pennies will you use?

- Don't count the central penny.

> You could try using real pennies to show all ten rings and then counting them. But looking for a pattern would be simpler and more practical.

 PLAN 2

Keep track of how many pennies are in the first few rings, and then look for a pattern to figure out how many pennies are in the larger rings.

 TRY 3

Ring	Diagram	Number of Pennies
First		6

Ring	Diagram	Number of Pennies
Second		12
Third		18

It looks like each ring you add has six more pennies than the previous ring.

$$6 + 12 + 18 + 24 + 30 + 36 + 42 + 48 + 54 + 60 = 330$$

4 Is it reasonable to assume that the pattern you used will really continue? In this case, it will continue because each new hexagon will always have one more penny per side than the previous hexagon.

★ It will take 330 pennies to form ten hexagonal rings around a central penny.

Find and Use a Pattern is often used with other strategies.

Check out:
  Account for All Possibilities [347]
  Start with a Simpler Problem [348]
  Organize the Data [349]
  Model with an Equation [353]

MATH ALERT Patterns Don't Necessarily Continue

Whenever you use a pattern to solve a problem, ask yourself, *Can I be sure the pattern will continue?* Suppose you noticed that a bean sprout grew a centimeter one day, two centimeters the next day, and three centimeters the third day. Is it reasonable to assume that, if you continue to measure daily, the plant will follow this growth pattern? It may be reasonable for as much as a week, but what about for a year? Sometimes a pattern like this will continue, but in this case, it is not reasonable to assume the pattern is permanent.

Guess, Check, and Revise

You forget the combination to your locker, so you keep trying different combinations. That strategy can take more time than you have because one guess is as good as another. In many math problems, however, you can learn a lot from a wrong guess, so your guesses can keep getting better. Pretty soon you've locked onto the answer.

EXAMPLE 1: You count the sides on a group of 15 polygons, all triangles and pentagons. You count 63 sides. How many of each polygon are in the group?

 UNDERSTAND

- There are 15 polygons. Some are triangles. The rest are pentagons.

- The polygons have a total of 63 sides.

- How many triangles and how many pentagons are there?

 PLAN

Make a guess and check it. If it's right, great. If it's not right, decide whether it's too high or too low and use that information to improve your next guess.

TRY
3

❶ Guess (sum must be 15)	❷ Check (number of sides must be 63)	❸ Think and revise
8 triangles 7 pentagons (8 + 7 = 15)	8(3) + 7(5) = 24 + 35 = 59	Too low! Make a guess that raises the total. Try more pentagons and fewer triangles.
5 triangles 10 pentagons (5 + 10 = 15)	5(3) + 10(5) = 15 + 50 = 65	Too high, but close. Make a guess that lowers the total a little. Try fewer pentagons and more triangles.
6 triangles 9 pentagons (6 + 9 = 15)	6(3) + 9(5) = 18 + 45 = 63	Just right!

LOOK BACK
4

- Is the total number of sides 63? Yes, $6(3) + 9(5) = 63$.

- Is the total number of polygons 15? Yes, $6 + 9 = 15$.

MORE HELP
See 353

★ There are 6 triangles and 9 pentagons.

> You could have also solved this problem by writing and solving a system of equations where t is the number of triangles and p is the number of pentagons.
> $$3t + 5p = 63 \rightarrow \quad 3t + 5p = 63$$
> $$t + p = 15 \rightarrow \quad \underline{-3t - 3p = -45}$$
> $$2p = 18$$
> $$p = 9$$
> $$\text{so } t = 6$$

EXAMPLE 2: You're building a pen for your dog at the back of the garage. You plan to use the wall as one side of a rectangle, and 24 feet of fencing for the other three sides. What whole-number dimensions could you use to enclose the greatest area possible?

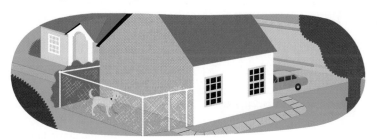

- You have 24 feet of fence for three sides of the rectangle.

- The wall will be the fourth side.

- You want to enclose as much area as you can.

- How long and how wide should the rectangle be?

Make some guesses and check them. When you find one where you can't make the area any larger, you've got it. Close in on the answer by evaluating and refining your guesses.

❶ Guess (total fencing must be 24 ft)	❷ Check	❸ Think and revise
8' ⌐8'⌐ 8' — 8'	8(8) = 64	Will different dimensions increase the area? Try making the rectangle stick out more from the wall.
10' 10' — 4'	10(4) = 40	Changing the shape that way makes the area smaller. Try changing the shape the other way.
7' 7' — 10'	7(10) = 70	That makes it greater. Keep changing the dimensions in this direction to see what happens.
6' 6' — 12'	6(12) = 72	That's even greater. Try again.
5' 5' — 14'	5(14) = 70	That area is smaller again. Looks like 6' × 12' gives you the maximum area.

4 ■ Is the total amount of fencing 24 feet? Yes, $2(6) + 12 = 24$.

■ Is this the greatest area possible? Yes, if you change the dimensions by one foot either way, the area decreases.

★ The rectangle should be six feet from the wall and 12 feet long.

MORE HELP
See 353, 392

You also could have solved this problem with a graphing calculator. Write and graph an equation for the area and then use the zoom feature on your calculator to find the length when the area is greatest.

Account for All Possibilities

347

You're planning a camping trip. You try to account for all the things that could go wrong, so you can plan for them. Accounting for all possibilities can also help you solve some math problems.

When you list possibilities, a pattern can help you make sure you don't leave out or repeat items. Even with a pattern, though, you have to count carefully. Two items may look different but may actually be the same.

EXAMPLE 1: You're building regular hexagons with colored straws that are all the same length. Each side can be a whole red or blue straw. How many hexagons with different color schemes can you make?

1 ■ The side of a regular hexagon can be red or blue.

■ How many different hexagons can be formed?

2 Try making an organized set of diagrams. Use letters for colors.

3 Start with hexagons that have three red sides and three blue sides.

Three adjacent reds   At most two adjacent reds   No adjacent reds

Since regular hexagons are symmetric, these are the only three possibilities with three red sides and three blue sides. Any other such hexagon can be rotated or flipped to form one of the three arrangements shown.

MORE ▶

Find the rest of the hexagons in an organized way, using a pattern. First, look at four red sides and two blue sides.

Blues adjacent

Blues one side apart

Blues two sides apart

There are only three possibilities with two blue sides, because if the blues are three sides apart, that's the same as 1 side apart. Now look at five red sides and one blue side. The reds must be adjacent, so there is only one possibility.

What about six red sides and no blue sides?

4 **Results so far:**

| 3 red, 3 blue | 3 | 5 red, 1 blue | 1 |
| 4 red, 2 blue | 3 | 6 red, 0 blue | 1 |

We left out possibilities with no red, one red, and two reds. Fortunately, there's an easy way to include these. Since there are three possibilities for two blue sides, then there must also be three possibilities for two red sides, (just change *r* to *b* and *b* to *r* in the diagrams.) Similarly, there must be as many hexagons with one red side as with one blue side and as many with two reds as with two blues.

★ You can build 13 different regular hexagons.

Straws Needed	Possible Hexagons
0 red, 6 blue	1
1 red, 5 blue	1
2 red, 4 blue	3
3 red, 3 blue	3 same same same
4 red, 2 blue	3
5 red, 1 blue	1
6 red, 0 blue	1

Start with a Simpler Problem _____

Artists often draw something complicated, like an animal or person, by starting with a simpler version.

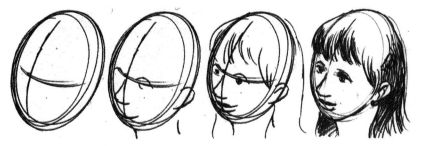

Solving the simplest form of a math problem and then changing it little by little may lead you to a solution of the original problem. Sometimes, a simpler problem may have the same answer as the original problem.

EXAMPLE: In how many different ways can you place a dot in the center of each of four sides of a cube?

1 ■ How many different ways can you place a dot on each of four faces?

■ Each dot must be placed the same way—at the center of a face.

2 Figuring out all the four-face combinations can be tedious. Instead, you can solve a simpler but equivalent version of the problem. For every way you dot four faces, there are two faces you don't dot. Finding all the ways of dotting two faces will solve the problem.

3 On a cube, two faces are either adjacent or opposite.

The two dots can be on adjacent faces.

The two dots can be on opposite faces.

Any other way you might place the dots can be duplicated by simply rotating one of these two cubes. There are only two ways to dot two faces of a cube. That means there must also be only two ways to dot four faces of a cube. The two blank faces must be either adjacent or opposite.

4 Make sure your reasoning makes sense.

★ There are exactly two different ways you can place a dot in the center of each of four faces of a cube.

Organize the Data

Libraries are organized so that it's easy for you to find the book you need and for the library to keep track of its books. Likewise in math problems, organizing information—using tables, diagrams, and graphs—can make it easy to find and keep track of things.

EXAMPLE 1: In a cartoon, a teenager studying for a geometry test imagines the three sides of a triangle separating. Each side grows into a square. Next, each square separates into four sides, which in turn become pentagons. Then each pentagon becomes five hexagons. If this pattern continues, how many decagons will form in this side-splitting animation?

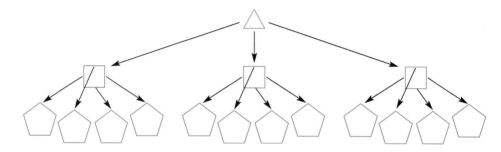

- At every stage, each side of a polygon becomes a new polygon with one more side than the parent polygon.

- How many 10-sided polygons will be formed?

Organize the information to keep track of the polygons at each stage.

MORE HELP
See 322, 418

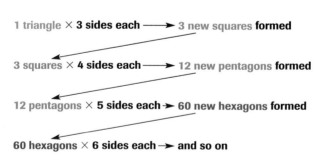

1 triangle × **3 sides each** ⟶ **3 new squares formed**

3 squares × **4 sides each** ⟶ **12 new pentagons formed**

12 pentagons × **5 sides each** ➤ **60 new hexagons formed**

60 hexagons × **6 sides each** ➤ **and so on**

Notice the pattern. With each stage, the number of sides in each polygon increases by one. If you multiply that number by the number of sides formed in the previous stage, you will get the number of new polygons formed.

Continue the pattern.

$$60 \times 6 = 360 \text{ 7-sided polygons}$$
$$360 \times 7 = 2520 \text{ 8-sided polygons}$$
$$2520 \times 8 = 20{,}160 \text{ 9-sided polygons}$$
$$20{,}160 \times 9 = 181{,}440 \text{ 10-sided polygons}$$

 LOOK BACK 4 Make a table to show your results, then check for reasonableness.

Initial Figure	△	□	⬠	⬡
New Figure	□	⬠	⬡	⬭
Number of New Figures	1 x 3	4 x 3	5 x 12	6 x 60

★ 181,440 decagons will be formed.

EXAMPLE 2: Based on this inventory of geometric blocks, how many blocks are there altogether?

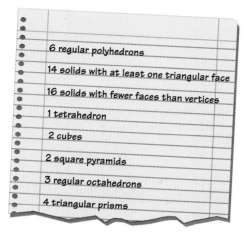

6 regular polyhedrons
14 solids with at least one triangular face
16 solids with fewer faces than vertices
1 tetrahedron
2 cubes
2 square pyramids
3 regular octahedrons
4 triangular prisms

 UNDERSTAND 1
- The inventory lists how many blocks have certain characteristics and how many of each of the listed shapes there are.

- How many blocks are there?

MORE ▶

PLAN

2

You can't find the total just by adding all the numbers listed, because some blocks belong to more than one category and so were counted twice. Organize the information with a Venn diagram.

TRY

3

MORE HELP
See 323–325

1 Use circles to show the three choices. Regions where circles overlap show multi-category blocks. Fill in the data that you know:
- The **tetrahedron** fits all three categories.
- The two **cubes** fit both the *regular* category and the *fewer faces than vertices* category.
- The three **octahedrons** fit the *regular* category and the *triangular face* category.
- Four **triangular prisms** fit both the *fewer faces than vertices* category and the *triangular face* category.
- Two **square pyramids** fit only the *triangular faces* category.

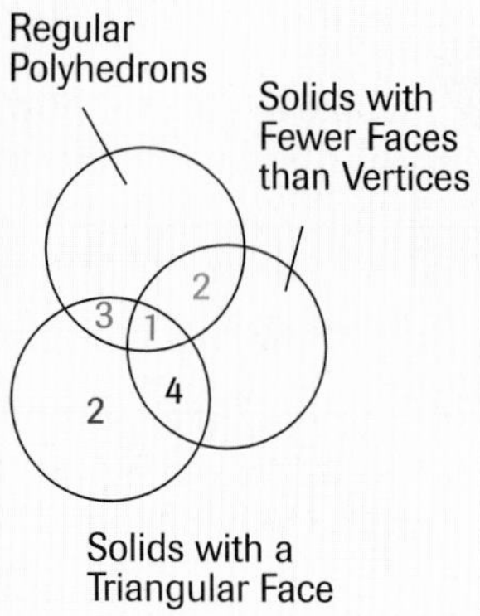

Regular Polyhedrons / Solids with Fewer Faces than Vertices

3 / 1 / 2 / 4 / 2

Solids with a Triangular Face

2 So far, the diagram shows seven solids with fewer faces than vertices, but you know there are 16 such solids in all. Since 16 − 7 = 9, there must be **nine** other solids with fewer faces than vertices that don't fit any of the other categories.

Regular Polyhedrons / Solids with Fewer Faces than Vertices

3 / 1 / 2 / 4 / 2 / 9

Solids with a Triangular Face

3 Similarly, there must be **four more** solids with a triangular face that don't fit the other categories, and there must be **no other regular solids** because all six are already shown.

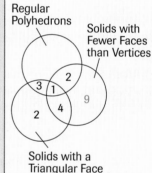

Regular Polyhedrons / Solids with Fewer Faces than Vertices

0 / 3 / 1 / 2 / 4 / 9 / 6

Solids with a Triangular Face

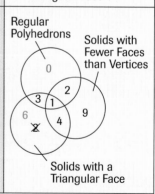

LOOK BACK

4 Make sure you entered the numbers correctly in the diagram. Find the sum of the entries in the diagram and check to be sure that your answer is reasonable.

★ There are 25 blocks in all.

Change Your Point of View

Hold this page a few inches from your face. Can you tell what's in the picture? Now try looking at it from further away. Sometimes changing your point of view puts things in focus. That's especially true with math problems. You may stare and stare in vain until you look at the problem in a different way.

EXAMPLE: A communications satellite consists of eight antennae extending symmetrically from the center of a small sphere. Each antenna is ten meters long. What is the shortest distance from the tip of one antenna to the tip of another?

You should assume, from this word, that the angles between antennae are equal.

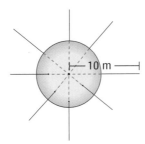

 Working with an unusual three-dimensional figure can be difficult, but if you change your point of view, you might be able to think of this figure in relation to a common solid.

 Imagine a cube with its four diagonals each 20 meters long. You can think of each antenna as half a diagonal of the cube. Then the distance from one tip to the next is the length of a side of the cube. So simply find the length of the side of a cube whose diagonals are 20 meters long.

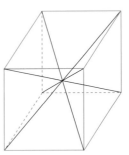

MORE ▶

MORE HELP
See 326, 421

3 Picture the right triangle formed by a diagonal of a cube, a side of the cube, and a diagonal of the face of a cube.

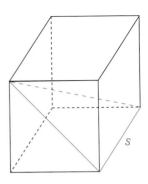

Use the formula for the length of a diagonal of a rectangular prism.

$$d = \sqrt{\ell^2 + w^2 + h^2}$$

Substitute what you know into the equation:

$$20 = \sqrt{3s^2}$$
$$= s\sqrt{3}$$
$$s = \frac{20}{\sqrt{3}}$$
$$\approx 11.5$$

> In a cube, ℓ, w, and h, are all the same.

4 Find or make a cube to make sure your change of view did not change the problem. Make sure all calculations are correct.

★ The shortest distance from the tip of one antenna to the tip of another is about 11.5 meters.

> When you solve problems, don't put unnecessary restrictions on yourself. Think out of the box.

351

Use Logical Reasoning

Do you ever figure things out, like where you left your backpack or who ate the leftover pizza? You often use logic, like a detective, to solve life's daily mysteries. You can use this same skill to solve math problems, too.

EXAMPLE 1: Follow the clues to detect how many sides the polygon has.

Clue 1: There is a regular polygon that has fewer than 12 sides.
Clue 2: Each of its interior angles measures more than 90°.
Clue 3: The diagonals connecting opposite vertices are concurrent.
Clue 4: Each interior angle measures less than 125°.

- Regular polygon with 3-11 sides.

- Use clues to figure out how many sides it has.

PLAN

2 Use logical reasoning to eliminate possible polygons. Make a chart to keep track.

TRY

3 From Clue 1, you can tell that the mystery polygon has 3 to 11 sides.

MORE HELP
See 131

Number of Sides	3	4	5	6	7	8	9	10	11
Possible?									

From Clue 2, you can tell that the mystery polygon cannot be a triangle or a square because a regular triangle has 60° angles and a square has 90° angles. Mark in your chart to show that.

Number of Sides	3	4	5	6	7	8	9	10	11
Possible?	X	X							

From Clue 3, you can tell that the polygon cannot have an odd number of sides because only polygons with an even number of sides have an opposite vertex. Mark in your chart to show that.

Number of Sides	3	4	5	6	7	8	9	10	11
Possible?	X	X	X		X		X		X

From Clue 4, you can tell that each of the interior angles must measure less than 125°. The mystery polygon cannot have seven sides or more. Mark in your chart to show that.

A regular polygon with 6 sides has interior angles of $180° \frac{(6-2)}{6}$, or 120°.

A regular polygon with 10 sides has interior angles of $180° \frac{(10-2)}{10}$, or 144°.

Number of Sides	3	4	5	6	7	8	9	10	11
Possible?	X	X	X		X	X	X	X	X

A regular polygon with 8 sides has interior angles of $180° \frac{(8-2)}{8}$, or 135°.

LOOK BACK

4 Make sure the reason for each X is logical.

★ The polygon has six sides.

MORE ▶

Sometimes, logical reasoning can make a hard problem very easy.

EXAMPLE 2: You are setting up a chess tournament. The person who wins a match goes on to the next round. The loser is out. There are 64 people in the tournament. How many matches will be played until there is a champion?

Group A, MHHS Chess Tournament			Monday-Wednesday	
Round 1	**Round 2**	**Round 3**	**Round 4**	**Group A Winner**
Susan D.				
Sarah R.				
Carol H.				
Joe D.				
Ed R.				
Ed D.				
Dana K.				
Bill S.				
Pearl L.				
Richard S.				
Justine D.				
Marlys M.				
Randy G.				
Pat B.				
Amy G.				
Ed M.				

Group A winner plays Group B winner Thursday. Group A-B winner plays Group C-D winner Friday.

Think about the tournament. After each match, one more player is out. To have a champion, 63 players must be out, so you need 63 matches.

★ 63 matches will be played.

Work Backward

If you've ever taken something apart you know that you have to reverse your steps to put it back together. If the cover was the first thing you removed, it will be the last thing you put back. Notice that you not only do the steps in reverse, but each step is the opposite. You can work backward to solve some math problems. If you know the end and the steps in between, you can find the beginning by going step by step in reverse.

EXAMPLE 1: You have directions from your house to a friend's house. What directions can you write to go from your friend's house back to your house?

Walk out your front door to the sidewalk on King Road.

Turn left and go 5 blocks to Gem Street

Turn left.

Go $\frac{3}{4}$ mile to Bell Avenue.

Turn right.

Go $3\frac{1}{2}$ blocks to the green house on the left.

■ If you follow the directions from your house, you end up at your friend's house.

■ Write directions from your friend's house back to your house.

 Trace the directions in reverse order on a grid.

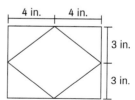

 Trace the route and follow the directions both ways.

★ ■ Stand on the sidewalk on Bell Ave.
■ Turn right.
■ Go $3\frac{1}{2}$ blocks to Gem Street.
■ Turn left.
■ Go $\frac{3}{4}$ mile to King Road.
■ Turn right.
■ Go 5 blocks to your house on the right.

EXAMPLE 2: Start with a rectangle.

■ Shorten the length so it's $\frac{2}{3}$ of the original length.

■ Add three inches to the width.

■ Connect the midpoints of the 4 sides.

■ What rectangle do you start with so that you end up with the figure shown?

 ■ Start with a rectangle and follow the directions.

■ The result is the figure shown.

■ Find the dimensions of the starting rectangle.

Since you know the end figure and all the steps, you can work backward to find the starting figure.

MORE ▶

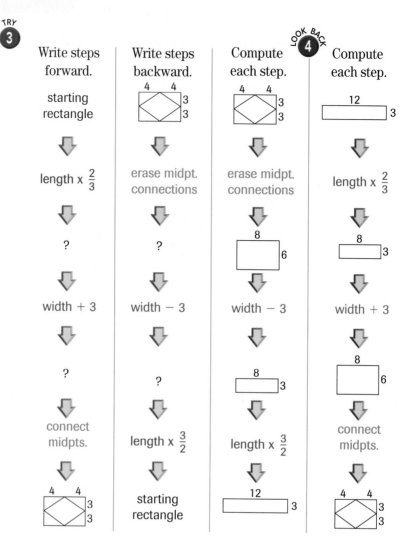

TRY
3

Write steps forward.	Write steps backward.	Compute each step.	**LOOK BACK 4** Compute each step.
starting rectangle			
length x $\frac{2}{3}$	erase midpt. connections	erase midpt. connections	length x $\frac{2}{3}$
?	?		
width + 3	width − 3	width − 3	width + 3
?	?		
connect midpts.	length x $\frac{3}{2}$	length x $\frac{3}{2}$	connect midpts.
	starting rectangle		

★ The starting rectangle is 12 inches long and 3 inches wide.

Model with an Equation

Not all models are made of materials like wood, metal, or plastic. Mathematical models are often made of equations. The equations can predict how cables, beams, and coaster cars will perform in real life. You can solve many math problems by writing equations to model the situation.

EXAMPLE: If this pattern made of unit squares continues, what will be the perimeter of Figure 75?

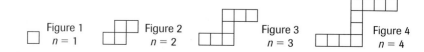

Figure 1
$n = 1$

Figure 2
$n = 2$

Figure 3
$n = 3$

Figure 4
$n = 4$

■ Squares are added to each figure according to a rule.

■ What will be the perimeter when $n = 75$?

 You can write an equation to relate the perimeter to the figure number.

Let n be the figure number and p the perimeter. For the first figure $n = 1$ and $p = 4$, for the second, $n = 2$ and $p = 10$, and so on. Organize the data in a table. Look for a pattern.

n	p
1	4
2	10
3	16
4	22

It looks like the perimeter increases by six with each figure. That makes sense since with each successive figure three squares are added but each new square adds only two more units

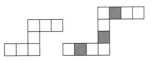

■ If $n = 1$, then $6n = 6$, so $6n$ by itself will not work.

■ If you subtract two, you get the correct perimeter: $6n - 2 = 4$ when $n = 1$.

That also works for $n = 2$, $n = 3$, and so on, so you can write $p = 6n - 2$.

For Figure 75, $n = 75$.
$$p = 6n - 2$$
$$= 6(75) - 2$$
$$= 448$$

 ■ Make sure your equation models the situation correctly.

■ Check your calculations for reasonableness.

★ Figure 75 will have a perimeter of 448 units.

> Model with an Equation is often used with other strategies.
> Check out:
> Make a Visual Representation [343]
> Change Your Point of View [350]
> Work Backward [352]
> Identify Subgoals [354]

Identify Subgoals

You want to play that new song on your keyboard but it's too long to learn all at once, so you learn the intro, then you learn the rest, part by part. Breaking up the task makes it more manageable. With math problems too, a complicated task can be made simpler by breaking it into smaller tasks.

MORE ▶

EXAMPLE: If a billiard ball is struck as shown in the diagram, where will it first hit the east cushion of the table? The ball has no lateral spin so it reflects like a beam of light; the angle at which it approaches the wall is congruent to the angle at which it leaves the wall.

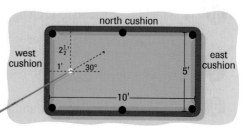

■ You know the dimensions of the pool table.

■ You know where the ball begins and the direction it travels.

■ You know how the ball caroms off a cushion.

■ Where will it first hit the east cushion?

Find where the ball first hits the north cushion. Then find where the ball will hit the east cushion after bouncing off the north cushion.

MORE HELP
See 239, 241, 422

① Find where the ball hits the north cushion. Let d be the distance from the west cushion to where the ball strikes the north cushion. The path is the hypotenuse of a 30°-60°-90° triangle with leg lengths a and 2.5 feet. Since $d = a + 1$, if you find a you'll know d. Use the tangent function to find a:

$$\tan 30° = \frac{2.5}{a}$$

$$a = \frac{2.5}{\tan 30°}$$

$$= \frac{2.5}{0.577}$$

$$\approx 4.33$$

Then $d \approx 1 + 4.33$, or about 5.3. The ball strikes the north cushion at about 5.3 feet from the west cushion.

② Find where the ball hits the east cushion. You know that the ball hits the north cushion about 5.3 feet from the west cushion, which is about 4.7 feet from the east cushion. The ball bounces off the north cushion at an angle of 30° because it hit the cushion at that angle. The path of the ball is the hypotenuse of a 30°-60°-90° triangle with leg lengths h and 4.7 feet. To find h, use the tangent function.

$$\tan 30° = \frac{h}{4.7}$$

$$h = 4.7 \tan 30°$$

$$= 4.7(0.577)$$

$$\approx 2.71$$

The ball hits the east cushion about 2.7 feet from the north cushion.

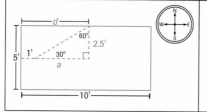

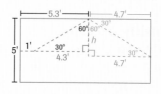

4

■ Make a freehand sketch reasonably to scale to see whether the answer makes sense.

■ Check calculations and tangent values.

★ The ball will first strike the east cushion about 2.7 feet down from the north cushion.

Consider Special Cases

When you solve a problem or prove a general statement, you often draw a diagram, but the way you arrange things in your diagram may affect whether a statement is true or false. For example, if you're trying to prove something about the altitude of a triangle, you might think it true if you draw the altitude inside the triangle. It may not be true, however, if the altitude is outside the triangle or on the triangle. That's why it makes sense to choose cases so that you cover all possibilities.

EXAMPLE 1: Which of the three choices below describes the following statement?

The distance (d_c) between the centers of two circles is $R + r + \ell$, where R and r are the radii of the two circles and ℓ is the shortest distance between the circles.

a) always true　**b)** sometimes true　**c)** never true

1

■ Is the statement true for every configuration of two circles?

■ Is the statement true for at least one configuration and false for at least one other?

■ Is the statement false for every possible configuration?

2

What if the circles don't intersect, the circles are tangent, the circles intersect at two points, or the circles are concentric?

Configuration	ℓ	Result
	$\ell > 0$	$d_c = r + \ell + R$ In this case, the statement is true.
	$\ell = 0$	$d_c = r + R$ but since $\ell = 0$, $d_c = r + \ell + R$ In this case, the statement is true.
	The radii overlap each other and ℓ	$d_c \neq r + \ell + R$ In this case, the statement is false.

You don't need to test any more cases, because the statement is true in at least one case and false in another and you can now answer the question. Although they weren't needed in this solution, you might have tested other special cases, such as concentric circles and intersecting circles where one circle passes through the center of the other.

LOOK BACK
4
- Check the reasoning you used for each case.

- Since you found at least one case where the statement is true and one case where it is not true, then the statement is sometimes true.

★ The answer is choice b.

Sometimes you can choose a special case or special cases to simplify your calculations.

EXAMPLE 2: An architect needs to design concrete paths that will connect the four corners of a square park. He wants the total length of the paths to be as small as possible. Will two diagonal paths provide the minimum total length?

UNDERSTAND
1
- The four corners of a square must be connected by paths.

- Show whether a different design of paths will have a shorter total length than two diagonals.

PLAN

2 Curved paths will be longer. Try straight paths that are not diagonals. Then calculate the total path length to see if it is shorter than two diagonals.

MORE HELP
See 163, 239

TRY

3 Because the diagonals of a rhombus bisect its vertices, and a square is a rhombus, m $\angle 1$ = 45°. Try something less than 45° for the measure of $\angle 2$. For simplicity, choose an angle measure easy to work with, like 30°. Make the angle measure 30° for each of the four paths starting at a corner.

You'll need to calculate the altitude of the triangles, so choose a side-length of 2 units for the square so that the base of each 30°-60°-90° triangle is one unit.

In a 30°-60°-90° triangle, the length of the long leg is $\sqrt{3}$ times the length of the short leg. Since the length of the long leg is 1, the short leg is $\frac{1}{\sqrt{3}}$, or $\frac{\sqrt{3}}{3}$. Also, the hypotenuse is twice the length of the short leg, so the length of the hypotenuse is $\frac{2\sqrt{3}}{3}$.

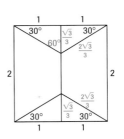

MORE HELP
See 421

For this configuration of paths:

Total length = length of 4 hypotenuses + length of short vertical path

$$= 4 \cdot \frac{2\sqrt{3}}{3} \qquad\qquad + \quad 2 - \frac{\sqrt{3}}{3} - \frac{\sqrt{3}}{3}$$

$$\approx 4.62 \qquad\qquad\qquad + \quad 0.85$$

$$\approx 5.47$$

The diagonal of a square is $\sqrt{2}$ times as long as the side.

Total length of diagonal paths = $2\sqrt{2} + 2\sqrt{2}$

$$\approx 2.83 + 2.83$$

$$\approx 5.66$$

LOOK BACK

4

- Make sure your geometric reasoning is correct.

- Make sure all calculations are correct.

★ Two diagonal paths do not provide the minimum path length for connecting the four corners of a square.

List Properties

For some problems, it helps to write down everything you know about a figure. Then you can look at your list to find a property that can help you solve the problem.

MORE HELP
See 157, 163, 261

EXAMPLE 1: In rhombus *ABCD*, point *E* is on diagonal $\overline{AC}$. Prove that $\angle ADE \cong \angle ABE$.

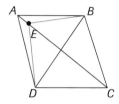

 1

- Quadrilateral *ABCD* is a rhombus.
- *E* is on diagonal $\overline{AC}$.
- Prove $\angle ADE \cong \angle ABE$.

 2

List the properties of a rhombus to see if there's some relationship you can use to help show that $\triangle ADE \cong \triangle ABE$. If so, you can easily use the fact that corresponding parts of congruent triangles are congruent to show that $\angle ADE \cong \angle ABE$.

TRY
3

List what you know about any rhombus.
1. All sides are congruent.
2. Opposite angles are congruent.
3. Adjacent angles are supplementary.
4. The diagonals bisect each other.
5. The diagonals are perpendicular to each other.
6. Opposite sides are parallel to each other.
7. The diagonals bisect the opposite angles.

Since you want to prove $\triangle ADE \cong \triangle ABE$, it would help to know about corresponding parts of the two triangles.

- The first property on our list tells us that $\overline{AD} \cong \overline{AB}$.

- The fourth and fifth properties tell us that diagonal $\overline{AC}$ is the perpendicular bisector of diagonal $\overline{DB}$, which means that *E* is equidistant from *B* and *D*; making $\overline{BE} \cong \overline{DE}$.

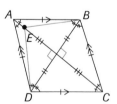

Since you already know that $\overline{AE} \cong \overline{AE}$, you now know enough to use the Side-Side-Side Congruence Theorem to prove $\triangle ADE \cong \triangle ABE$. You also have enough information to use SAS.

 4

Make sure your reasoning is valid and complete before writing up the proof.

★ One possible proof: $\overline{AC}$ is the perpendicular bisector of $\overline{DB}$ because they are the diagonals of a rhombus. It's given that Point E is on $\overline{AC}$, so $\overline{ED} \cong \overline{EB}$ because any point on a perpendicular bisector of a line segment is equidistant from the two endpoints of that segment. $\overline{AD} \cong \overline{AB}$ because they are both sides of the same rhombus. $\overline{AE} \cong \overline{AE}$ by the reflexive property of congruence. The Side-Side-Side Congruence Theorem makes $\triangle ADE \cong \triangle ABE$; $\angle ADE \cong \angle ABE$ by CPCTC.

Create a Simulation

You're on a simulation ride, one moment racing through a jungle and the next moment plunging mid-air into a deep canyon. You know it's just a ride, but it sure feels real. Simulations imitate reality because reality is not always practical. You can use simulations to solve math problems by acting out the problem in a practical way.

EXAMPLE 1: Nine circles are arranged in an equilateral triangle. Form a parallelogram arrangement with all nine circles by moving only two of them.

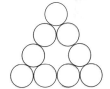

- Nine circles are arranged as shown.

- Move only two to form a parallelogram shape.

PLAN

2 Use objects like coins to model the circles. Then try moving coins until you find a solution.

TRY

3 Place nine pennies in triangular pattern. Try moving two pennies to see whether you can form a parallelogram arrangement.

	Not a solution—one circle is not in the parallelogram pattern.
	Not a solution—needs another penny to complete the parallelogram.
	Not a solution—one circle is outside the parallelogram.
	This works.

All the conditions are satisfied. Only two coins were moved. A parallelogram arrangement with equally spaced circles was formed. The problem didn't state that the parallelogram couldn't have circles on the inside, so the answer is reasonable.

MORE HELP
See 152, 241, 422

When you create a simulation, you don't always have to carry it out to the end. Sometimes you can also use a simple model, such as folded patty paper, to simulate a situation just to get a clearer sense of what's going to help you find a simple way to solve the problem.

EXAMPLE 2: Two rectangles are each 6 inches by 4 inches. They share a common six-inch side and they form a dihedral angle of 30°. What is the greatest distance between a vertex of one rectangle and any vertex of the other?

- Two 6" × 4" rectangles are connected along their 6" sides.

- They are not in the same plane. They form a dihedral angle of 30°.

- Find two vertices that are furthest apart and find that distance.

Make a model with patty paper to help picture the situation.

TRY
3 **①** Create an approximate version of the rectangles described in the problem by folding a sheet of patty paper.

② Look at your model. You have two rectangles: *ABCD* and *ABEF*. If the paper forms an angle of about 30°, vertices *A* and *C* may be further apart than *D* and *E*, even if it doesn't look that way when you draw it.

③ Look at Rectangle *ABCD*. You can see that you can find *AC* by using the Pythagorean Theorem because △*ABC* is a right triangle.
$$AC = \sqrt{(BC)^2 + (AB)^2}$$
$$= \sqrt{4^2 + 6^2} = \sqrt{52}$$
$$\approx 7.2$$

④ You can also use the Pythagorean Theorem to find *DE* once you know *DF*, and you can find *DF* by using a trigonometric function.
$$\sin 15° = \frac{DG}{4}$$
$$DG = 4 \sin 15°$$
$$\approx 1.04$$
$$DF = 2\,DG$$
$$\approx 2.1$$

⑤ $DE = \sqrt{(DF)^2 + (EF)^2}$
$$\approx \sqrt{2.1^2 + 6^2}$$
$$\approx 6.4$$

LOOK BACK
4
- *AC > DE*, so the greatest distance between two vertices is any diagonal of either rectangle.

- Since *A* is a vertex of both rectangles, *AC* is a distance from the vertex of one rectangle to a vertex of the other.

- Check your model again to see that the distances you found are reasonable.

★ The greatest distance between two vertices is almost $7\frac{1}{4}$ inches.

Problem-Solving Skills

It takes more than one skill to do most things. For example, to drive a car you need to know how to judge distance and speed, how to steer and brake, how to use the gas pedal and other controls, and how to use mirrors to know what's going on behind you. In problem solving, too, you need many skills, and the more you have, the better all-around problem solver you'll be.

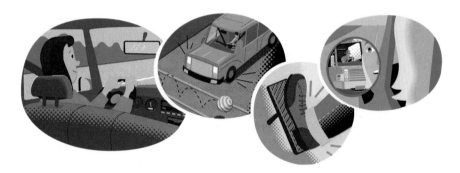

359

Be Ready for Multiple Answers

MORE HELP
See 346, 357

You miss the bus to school. Maybe you ask your parents for a ride. Maybe you call a friend. Maybe you bike, skate, or walk. There's more than one solution to the problem. Some math problems are like that. They may have more than one correct answer.

EXAMPLE 1: How can you cut all of the six pieces listed from a single panel eight feet long and four feet wide?

You might make a diagram and use *Guess, Check, and Revise*. You might *Create a Simulation* by cutting out and using a scale model of the pieces. Either way, you would discover that one or more solutions exist.

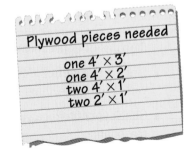

Plywood pieces needed

one 4′ × 3′
one 4′ × 2′
two 4′ × 1′
two 2′ × 1′

Here are three of the many possible solutions.

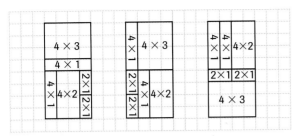

EXAMPLE 2: An explorer travels due south for one mile, then due east for one mile, and then due north for one mile. She is then back where she started. Where did she start?

One answer is the North Pole.

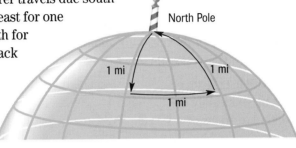

North Pole

1 mi   1 mi

1 mi

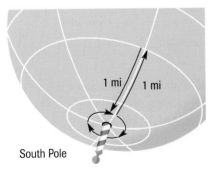

South Pole

1 mi   1 mi

Another answer is, near the South Pole: The explorer could also have started a little more than a mile north of the South Pole. After traveling one mile south she is so close to the South Pole that when she walks east one mile, she walks in a complete circle.

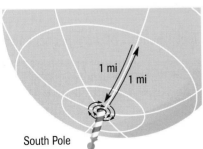

South Pole

1 mi   1 mi

She also might have started a little further south. So, after walking one mile south, she gets close enough to the South Pole that walking one mile east makes two complete circles.

★ Mathematically, there are an infinite number of answers to this problem. Depending on her starting point, she could make any number of complete circles when she walks one mile east.

Choose an Estimate or Exact Amount

Suppose you worked for the city of Chicago and needed to report how many people had watched a parade. Could you find out the exact number? Probably not.

one million thirty-seven, one million thirty-... Hey, stay where you are! Can't you see I'm trying to count!

Sometimes you have to estimate because you cannot get an exact amount. Sometimes an estimate is all you need. And sometimes an estimate just won't do. When you solve math problems, think about the situation before deciding whether you can estimate or whether you need an exact amount.

MORE HELP
See 176, 420

EXAMPLE 1: Metal cables move steadily beneath the streets of San Francisco, and they propel anything that grabs onto them, particularly cable cars. At the city's Cable Car Museum you can see the turning wheels that keep the cables in motion, as shown in this very simplified diagram.

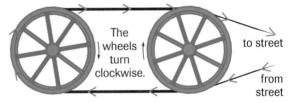

The wheels turn clockwise.

to street

from street

You are told that the cable cars can travel at about $9\frac{1}{2}$ mph. Since the cable cars move by grabbing the cable, the cable must also move at about $9\frac{1}{2}$ mph. You decide to check whether that speed makes sense. First, you estimate the diameter of the wheels to be about 15 feet. Then you count revolutions for a minute and determine that the wheels turn at a rate of about 18 rpm, which is 0.3 revolutions per second.

speed in $\frac{\text{ft}}{\text{s}}$ = circumference of wheel in feet · number of turns per second

$= \pi d \cdot 0.3$

$\approx 3(15)(0.3)$

≈ 13.5

> Use 3 for π. The turning rate and wheel diameter are very rough estimates, so this will not harm your estimate.
>
> $\frac{13.5\text{ ft}}{1\text{ s}} \cdot \frac{1\text{ mi}}{5280\text{ ft}} \cdot \frac{3600\text{ s}}{1\text{ h}} \approx \frac{9.2\text{ mi}}{1\text{ h}}$

★ Your estimates tell you that a speed of $9\frac{1}{2}$ mph is reasonable.

EXAMPLE 2: You are placing hash marks along the sides of a basketball court according to the diagram. What is the distance between the insides of the long hash marks?

In this situation, you need an exact amount. Look at a diagram that exaggerates the thickness of the hash marks:

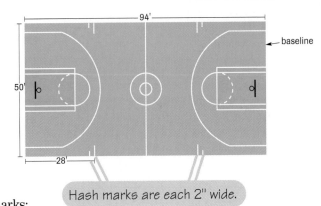

Hash marks are each 2" wide.

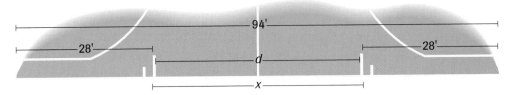

Find the distance between the outsides of the marks.

$$x = 94' - 2(28')$$
$$= 38'$$

Find the distance between the insides (d is 4" shorter than x).

$$d = 38' - 4"$$

★ The inside distance between the long hash marks is 37 feet 8 inches.

Check by Using Another Method

When you add, you could check your answer by adding again. You are more likely to catch an error if you change your method when you add again, perhaps by putting the addends in a different order. In more complicated math problems, you can check your result by solving the problem a different way. If you get the same result, you can be more sure it's right.

MORE HELP
See 207

EXAMPLE: How many cubic inches of foam will be in the block shown in the diagram?

You might find the volume by thinking of the block in parts. (You have to be careful not to overlap parts.)

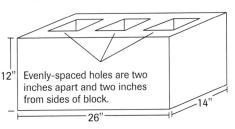

12" Evenly-spaced holes are two inches apart and two inches from sides of block.

26"

14"

MORE ▶

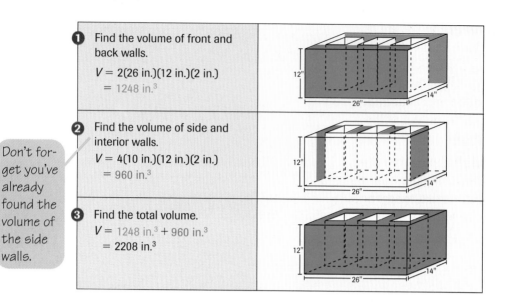

① Find the volume of front and back walls.

$V = 2(26 \text{ in.})(12 \text{ in.})(2 \text{ in.})$
$\quad = 1248 \text{ in.}^3$

② Find the volume of side and interior walls.

$V = 4(10 \text{ in.})(12 \text{ in.})(2 \text{ in.})$
$\quad = 960 \text{ in.}^3$

③ Find the total volume.

$V = 1248 \text{ in.}^3 + 960 \text{ in.}^3$
$\quad = 2208 \text{ in.}^3$

> Don't forget you've already found the volume of the side walls.

To check your answer, you could use a different method.

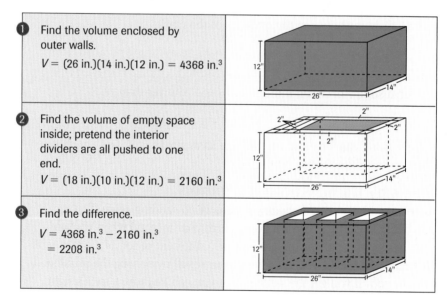

① Find the volume enclosed by outer walls.

$V = (26 \text{ in.})(14 \text{ in.})(12 \text{ in.}) = 4368 \text{ in.}^3$

② Find the volume of empty space inside; pretend the interior dividers are all pushed to one end.

$V = (18 \text{ in.})(10 \text{ in.})(12 \text{ in.}) = 2160 \text{ in.}^3$

③ Find the difference.

$V = 4368 \text{ in.}^3 - 2160 \text{ in.}^3$
$\quad = 2208 \text{ in.}^3$

★ Both methods give the same result, 2208 cubic inches.

Find Information You Need

You're going to a movie. You know where it's playing but you don't know when it starts. You've been in situations like these where you need more information. To find out when the movie starts, you could look in the paper or call the theater. Knowing what information you need and how to find it can come in handy when you solve math problems, too.

Ask yourself:

- What information could help me solve the problem?
- Can I look up the information?
- Can I ask someone?
- Can I take a measurement?
- Can I use an estimate?

EXAMPLE: Which of the choices would provide the information you need to determine the total length of the diagonals of rhombus *ABCD* with three-inch sides?

a) $\angle A$ and $\angle D$ are supplementary.

b) The diagonals bisect each other.

c) Point *E* is located so that $ED = 2$ and $EC = 2$.

d) $\angle A$ and $\angle C$ are supplementary.

e) none of the above

MORE HELP
See 157, 163, 164

The first choice looks like it provides a new relationship, but this relationship is true for every parallelogram and, therefore, every rhombus, so choice **a)** provides no information that couldn't be deduced from what you already know.

Choice **b)** looks like it provides another relationship, but it, too, is something that you already know.

Choice **c)** introduces a new element, point *E*, but since you know nothing else about point *E*, you are not getting any useful information about the rhombus.

Choice **d)** gives you information that is not true for all rhombuses. In fact, since the opposite angles of any parallelogram are congruent, this gives you enough information to figure out m$\angle A$ and m$\angle C$.

- m$\angle A$ + m$\angle C$ = 180°
- Since m$\angle A$ = m$\angle C$, both angles must be right angles.
- Since adjacent angles of a rhombus are supplementary, the other angles must also be right angles. So rhombus *ABCD* is a square. Each diagonal of a square is $\sqrt{2}$ times as long as a side.

$$AC + BD = 3\sqrt{2} + 3\sqrt{2}$$
$$= 6\sqrt{2}$$
$$\approx 8.49$$

★ Choice **d)** is the useful one.

Non-Euclidean Geometry

"When asked about what it was like to set about proving something, the mathematician likened proving a theorem to seeing the peak of a mountain and trying to climb to the top. One establishes a base camp and begins scaling the mountain's sheer face, encountering obstacles at every turn, often retracing one's steps and struggling every foot of the journey. Finally when the top is reached, one stands examining the peak, taking in the view . . . and then noting the automobile road up the other side!"

      —*Robert J. Kleinhenz*

One rule changes and geometry class will never again be the same.

Change a single word in the rules for a game and you might change the game completely. Take chess, for example. One rule is: *If your king cannot escape, you lose.* Now change the word *lose* to the word *win*. Suddenly the strategy for winning turns itself upside down. You're not playing the same game anymore. What you're playing is definitely a game, but it's not chess—even though you are using the same board, the same pieces, and the same rules, except of course for one change in one rule.

That's the case with non-Euclidean geometry. It's not Euclidean geometry (the geometry you're used to), but it still is geometry, just as the new chess-like game is still a game even though it's not chess. Non-Euclidean geometry uses the same logic as Euclidean geometry. It uses the same terms, like *point, line, plane,* and *triangle.* It also uses some of the same postulates.

You may recall that in Euclidean geometry, the parallel postulate says: *If you have a line and a point off the line, there is exactly one line through the point that is parallel to the given line.* Now make a small change: Replace the words *exactly one* with *two* or with *none* or with *an infinite number of.* With each change you have created a new geometry, one that turns Euclidean geometry on its head, just as one simple rule change turned the game of chess upside down. And just as the new chess-like game seems unnatural, these non-Euclidean geometries present some astounding results that run counter to your normal view of the world.

MORE HELP
See 058

Euclidean geometry is based on a set of postulates first formulated
by Euclid over 2000 years ago. Euclid's fifth postulate—the parallel
postulate—is unique among them.

> **Postulate**　If there is a line and a point not on the line, then there is
> exactly one line through the point and parallel to the
> given line. ‖ Postulate (P10)
>
>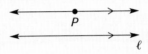

For a long time, mathematicians puzzled over the parallel postulate
because it seemed as if they should be able to prove it. In the nineteenth
century, several mathematicians investigated what would happen if they
changed the parallel postulate. They played this *what if* game with two
new forms of the postulate. Georg Friedrich Bernhard Riemann and Ludwig
Schläfi in the late 1800s investigated one form of the parallel postulate. This
led to a non-Euclidean geometry called **spherical geometry** and a slight
modification by Felix Klein in the early 1900s called **elliptic geometry**.

MORE HELP
See 332

> **Postulate**　Through a given point not on a given line there are *no*
> *lines* parallel to the given line. Spherical Parallel
> Postulate (P26)
>
> You can use the surface　**Euclidean Geometry**　**Spherical Geometry**
> of a sphere to model
> spherical geometry. In
> Euclidean geometry, a
> plane is a flat surface
> that extends forever.　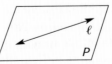　
> In spherical geometry,
> a plane is the sphere
> itself and a line is a great circle of the sphere.

Plane *P* contains line ℓ.　Sphere *S* contains
great circle *C. C* is a
line on sphere *S*.

Every great circle of a sphere has the same center, so their planes intersect, and two of these points of intersection are on the sphere. This means that in spherical geometry, any two lines must intersect.

Elliptic geometry calls the *two points* of intersection of two lines in spherical geometry *one point*. The theorems in spherical (and elliptic) geometries are consistent with each other, but often at odds with Euclidean theorems, and to your own intuition, yet they still form an important part of mathematics.

Euclid's geometry describes flat surfaces and finite portions of space. Non-Euclidean geometries provide a better description of space for astronomers and physicists. While the results of Euclidean and non-Euclidean geometries are essentially the same for relatively short distances, they are very different over long distances. Non-Euclidean geometries are better suited to the vast distances of outer space and to the physics of wave propagation and relativity. In fact, Albert Einstein developed his Theory of Relativity using one non-Euclidean geometry as a model.

DID YOU KNOW One of the non-Euclidean geometries also applies to more earthly matters. Riemannian geometry was developed by Bernhard Riemann in 1854. This geometry is the domain of sailors who voyage over curved oceans of the globe and of pilots who use great circles to chart the shortest distance between cities on the globe. It may seem surprising at first, but the shortest distance between two cities on the globe is not a straight line distance on a map. Rather it is the arc of the great circle that connects the two cities.

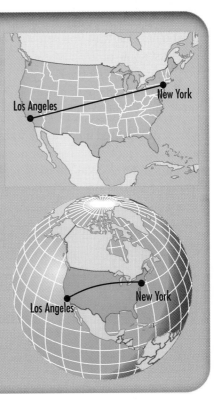

Points, Lines, and Angles in Euclidean and Spherical Geometries

You may recall that points, lines, and planes are undefined terms in geometry. The postulates define the relationships among these elements. You are used to visualizing these relationships, because they match the way you see the world around you. When you change the postulates in geometry, you must also change the way you visualize these relationships. The new geometry still remains a logical, well-defined system, but with different *pictures*.

MORE HELP
See 332

In spherical geometry, a plane is the surface of a sphere. The lines in this geometry are all great circles of this sphere and points on a sphere behave differently, depending on where they are located.

In this figure, points A and A' are the two endpoints of a diameter of a great circle and are called **polar points**. Infinitely many great circles pass through a pair of polar points. However, if you place another pair of polar points, B and B', on the sphere, then only one great circle can pass through all four points: A, A', B, and B'.

In spherical geometry, a pair of polar points is considered to be a single point. That way, you can use at least some of the postulates from Euclidean geometry. Every point lies on an infinite number

An infinite number of lines passes through A. Naming a non-polar point B leaves only one possible line that contains both points.

of lines, but two non-polar points will determine exactly one line.

Angles are measured much as they are in plane Euclidean geometry. For example, on a globe, the equator meets any meridian (a great circle that passes through the poles) at right angles. These lines are perpendicular. You should also be able to see that vertical angles exist and that they are congruent.

Perpendicular great circles intersect at two points, form eight right angles, and divide the sphere into four congruent, finite regions that can be called quarter-spheres.

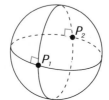

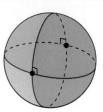

The table contrasts and compares some facts about lines in Euclidean geometry and great circles in spherical geometry.

Euclidean Geometry	Spherical Geometry	Example	
1 Lines have no endpoints.	Great circles have no endpoints.		*A and A′ are a pair of polar points, but A and B are a pair of non-polar points.*
2 A straight line is infinitely long.	A great circle has finite length and returns to its original starting point.		
3 There is a unique straight line passing through any two points.	There is a unique great circle passing through any pair of non-polar points.		$\overline{CD}$ *is the shortest path from C to D.*
4 A line segment is the shortest path between two points.	An arc of a great circle is the shortest path between two points.		
5 If three points are collinear, exactly one is between the other two.	If three points are collinear, any one of the three points is between the other two.		*B is between A and C.*

In spherical geometry, Euclid's first four postulates are true:

- you can draw a line between any two points,
- you can extend any segment indefinitely,
- you can draw a circle with given center and radius, and
- all right angles are equal.

The Segment Addition Postulate also holds true. For example, in the diagram for fact 5 in the table above, $m\widehat{ABC} = m\widehat{AB} + m\widehat{BC}$. All theorems in Euclidean geometry that were proved using only these postulates are also still true in spherical geometry.

When you reach Euclid's fifth postulate—the parallel postulate— things begin to change. In Euclidean geometry, lines in the same plane could be parallel. In spherical geometry, there is *no* line parallel to a given line. Because all great circles containing P intersect ℓ (and lines in spherical geometry are always great circles), there exists no line through point P that is parallel to ℓ.

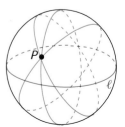

Lunes and Triangles

In spherical geometry, a closed figure can be formed from two semicircles (of a great circle) that have the same endpoints. The closed figure has only two sides! This figure is called a **lune**.

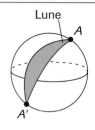

Lune

MORE HELP
See 058, 143

Spherical geometry has triangles, but they may look a bit different from the ones you're used to.

The proof of the Triangle Sum Theorem in Euclidean geometry depends upon the Parallel Postulate. You might expect different results for the sum of the measures of a triangle in spherical geometry. This is, in fact, the case.

Figure A

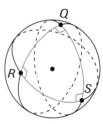

Each pair of sides in Figure A meets at right angles. So, the sum of angle measures is $90° + 90° + 90° = 270°$. The sum of the measures of the triangle is greater than 180°! In fact, the sum of the measures of every triangle in spherical geometry is greater than 180°, but less than 540° (because each angle has a measure less than 180°).

Spherical Coordinates

MORE HELP
See 117, 121

In spherical geometry, it helps to use a three-dimensional version of polar coordinates called **spherical coordinates**. In this system, a point P (not the origin) is represented by an ordered triple (ρ, ϕ, θ).

Write: (ρ, ϕ, θ)

Say: *coordinates roe, fie, thay-ta*

The first coordinate is ρ, the length of $\overline{OP}$. Because ρ is a length, it is

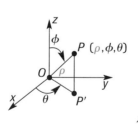

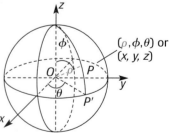

always positive. The second coordinate, ϕ, is the angle between the positive z-axis and $\overrightarrow{OP}$. It must be at least 0° and not more than 180°. The third coordinate, θ, is a polar angle associated with the point P', which is the projection of P onto the xy-plane.

Carl Friedrich Gauss, Nikolai Lobachevsky, and Janos Bolyai indepen-
dently developed a non-Euclidean geometry that stemmed from changing
the Euclidean parallel postulate. Their postulate allowed infinitely many
lines parallel to a given line through a point not on the line. The resulting
geometry was called **hyperbolic geometry**.

Postulate   Through a given point not on a given line there is more
than one line parallel to the given line. Hyperbolic
Parallel Postulate (P27)

It is hard to describe hyperbolic geometry. In fact, it can be hard to accept
the postulate that is its foundation. But if you accept it on purely mathematical terms and let go your intuition, it is easier to understand.

You can visualize hyperbolic geometry in many ways. Think of the plane as
circular. A common model was developed by Henri Poincaré and is called a
Poincaré disk. The Poincaré disk consists of all the points in the interior of
an infinitely large circle. The *lines* of this hyperbolic
plane are arcs within the circle. The arcs have their endpoints on the circle and are perpendicular to the boundary circle at both endpoints. Diameters of the boundary
circle are also allowed. Since the Poincaré disk contains
all the points in the interior of the circle, the endpoints
of these lines are not actually part of the line.

In the hyperbolic plane, you cannot measure distance with a traditional ruler. The lines are defined to have infinite length. This means that segments that look congruent may have lengths that are very different.

You can measure angles in this model, much as you do in Euclidean geometry. To measure the angle formed by a pair of lines, measure the angles formed by the tangents to the arcs at their point of intersection.

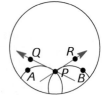

$$m\angle APB = m\angle QPR$$

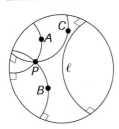

In this diagram, lines *AP*, *BP*, and *CP* intersect at point *P*. None of these lines intersect ℓ, so they are all parallel to line ℓ. In this geometry, there is *more than one line* parallel to a given line through a given point.

You can think of hyperbolic geometry in terms of very small differences. In fact, it appears today that the universe itself is hyperbolic and the Euclidean universe is an impression caused by our small size. What you see in your daily life is just an infinitesimal piece of the universe.

Here are a few of the theorems of hyperbolic geometry, which give you an idea of how strange a new parallel postulate can make geometry.

- Two perpendicular lines can be parallel to the same line.

- The sum of the measures of the angles of a triangle is less than 180°.

- The Pythagorean theorem is *not* true.

- Similar triangles are impossible. As the size of a triangle changes, so do the measures of its angles.

- As the area of a triangle increases, the sum of its angles decreases. If two triangles have the same angle sum, they have the same area.

- There is an upper limit on the area of a triangle.

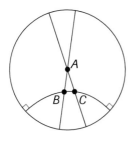

$$m\angle A + m\angle B + m\angle C \approx 176°$$

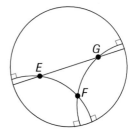

$$m\angle E + m\angle F + m\angle G \approx 100°$$

Almanac

"Knowledge is of two kinds. We know a subject ourselves, or we know where we can find information upon it."

—*Samuel Johnson*

Prefixes are added at the beginning of words or suffixes to provide consistent meaning.

Prefix	Definition	Example
alti-	high	altitude: the height of a figure
bi-	two	bisected: something divided into two equal parts
circum-	around	circumference: distance around a circle
co-	joint, jointly, together	coplanar: lying in the same plane A and B are coplanar.
col-, com-, con-, cor-	with, together	collinear: on the same line M and N are collinear.
dec, deca-, deka-	ten	decagon: polygon with ten sides
di-	two, twice, double	dihedral: having two plane surfaces
dia-	through, across	diameter: a segment through the center of a circle with endpoints on the circle
dodeca-	twelve	dodecagon: polygon with twelve sides
equi-	equal, equally	equiangular: having all angles equal
ex-	outside	exterior of a figure: the points outside the figure
hemi-	half	hemisphere: half of a sphere
hepta-	seven	heptagon: polygon with seven sides
hex-, hexa-	six	hexagon: polygon with six sides

Prefix	Definition	Example
icosi-, icosa-	twenty	icosahedron: polyhedron with twenty faces
in-	not, without	inequality: not equal $A \quad B \quad C$ $AB > BC$
in-	inside	interior of a figure: the points inside the figure
inter-	between, mutual	intersecting lines: lines that cross or meet at a common point
iso-, is-	equal	isometric: having equal measure
mid-	middle	midpoint: point on a line segment midpoint that divides it into two congruent segments
nona-	ninth, nine	nonagon: polygon with nine sides
octa-, octo-, oct-	eight	octagon: polygon with eight sides
para-, par-	beside, along-side	parallel lines: lines that run beside each other, an equal distance apart at every point
penta-, pent-	five	pentagon: polygon with five sides
poly-	many	polygon: a closed figure composed of many line segments that meet only at their endpoints
pre-	before	preimage: the original figure before its transformation
quad-	four	quadrilateral: a polygon with four sides
rhomb-, rhombo	object that can be turned	rhombus: polygon with four congruent sides. It can be turned to map onto itself.
semi-	half	semicircle: half-circle
tetra-	four	tetrahedron: polyhedron with four faces
trans-	across, over	transversal: a line that intersects (cuts across) two other lines at two distinct points transversal
tri-	three	triangle: polygon with three angles

Suffixes are added at the end of prefixes or words to provide consistent meaning.

Suffix	Definition	Example
-gon	having a specified number of interior angles	polygon: many-angled figure hexagon: six-angled figure
-hedral	surfaces or faces of a given number	dihedral: formed by two planes
-hedron	having a given number of faces or surfaces	dodecahedron: a solid whose twelve faces are polygons
-oid	form, shape	trapezoid: shape with four sides, two of which are parallel
-lateral	of, at, or relating to sides	equilateral: having all sides equal
-metry	science or process of measuring	geometry: mathematics of properties, measurement, and relationships of points, lines, angles, surfaces, and solids
-sect	cut, divide	trisect: cut or divide into three equal parts

Constructions

Are you ready for a game? Greek mathematicians played a game in which they tried to construct different geometric figures with limited tools.

You wouldn't have much trouble drawing an accurate square, for example, if you had a ruler and protractor (and a pencil, of course). Now imagine your ruler had no markings, so you could use it to draw straight lines but not to measure. In fact, such a device is called a **straightedge.** Next, imagine you had a compass instead of a protractor, so you could draw arcs and circles, but you couldn't measure angles. To draw a square with only these tools is more of a challenge, but it *is* possible.

As you'll see in this section, it's possible to construct many other figures as well if you use what you know about geometric relationships and take advantage of what the compass can do. Although you can't use it to measure in standard units, you can use a compass to:

- mark off one length equal to another, and

- draw a set of points on a plane that are all the same distance from a point you choose.

Constructing Congruent Figures

Patty papers are those small squares of waxed paper people put between uncooked hamburger patties. You can find patty paper in the kitchens of restaurants, at grocery store butcher counters, and in geometry classrooms.

MORE HELP
See 054, 062, 256, 309

Patty-paper constructions of congruent line segments and angles are very easy to do. Simply place a patty paper over the given line segment or angle and trace. If you'd like, use a straightedge to help keep your lines straight.

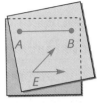

Now look at constructions using a compass and straightedge.

If you set your compass to the length of a segment, you can use it to construct other line segments that have the same length as the given segment. Each of these line segments will be congruent to the given segment.

EXAMPLE 1: Construct line segment *CD* congruent to line segment *AB*.

A   B

1. Use your straightedge to draw a segment longer than $\overline{AB}$. Label one endpoint *C*.

C

2. Set your compass to the length of $\overline{AB}$.

3. Place the point of your compass on *C*. Draw an arc that intersects the line segment. Label the point of intersection *D*.

C   D

$\overline{CD}$ is congruent to $\overline{AB}$.

MORE HELP
See 261

Since only one triangle with three given side lengths is possible, you can copy the sides of a triangle and, when you fit them together, the new triangle will be congruent to the original. The SSS Congruence Postulate proves this.

EXAMPLE 2: Construct △*MNO* congruent to △*JKL*.

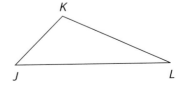

1. Construct $\overline{MO}$ congruent to $\overline{JL}$.

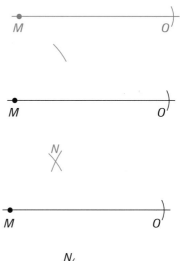

2. Set your compass to the length of JK. Keeping the compass opening the same, place the compass point on M and draw an arc.

3. Reset your compass to KL. Keeping the compass opening the same, place the compass point on O. Draw an arc that intercepts the arc you drew in Step 2. Label the point of intersection N.

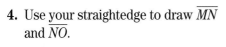

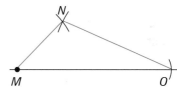

4. Use your straightedge to draw $\overline{MN}$ and $\overline{NO}$.

$\triangle MNO$ is congruent to $\triangle JKL$.

EXAMPLE 3: Construct $\angle H$ congruent to $\angle E$.

1. With your compass open to any radius, put the point at E and swing an arc. Label the intersections with the sides of the angle A and B.

2. Make the same arc from point H.

3. Set your compass to AB. Place the point of the compass at A′ and make an arc. Label the intersection with your previous arc B′.

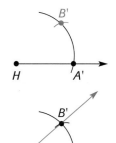

4. Draw $\overrightarrow{HB'}$. $\angle E \cong \angle H$ because $\triangle EAB \cong \triangle HA'B'$ by the SSS Congruence Postulate and E and H are corresponding parts of the congruent triangles.

Constructing Bisectors

MORE HELP
See 056, 073

Recall that a bisector divides a figure into two congruent parts. To construct the bisector of a line segment or angle using patty paper, fold the paper so that one part of the line segment exactly matches the other part or one side of an angle matches the other side. The fold lines are the bisector of $\overline{PQ}$ and the bisector of $\angle R$. The intersection of the fold line and $\overline{PQ}$ is the midpoint of $\overline{PQ}$.

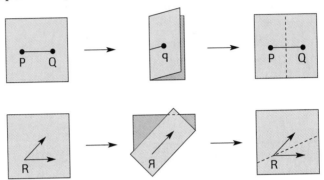

Following are compass and straightedge constructions of bisectors.

MORE HELP
See 056, 275

EXAMPLE 1: Construct a perpendicular bisector of line segment PQ. Locate the midpoint M of $\overline{PQ}$.

Use the fact that the points on the perpendicular bisector must be equidistant from P and Q. Use your compass to mark two such equidistant points, then connect them to draw the perpendicular bisector.

1. Place the point of your compass on P. Set its opening more than half the length of $\overline{PQ}$. Draw an arc.

2. Keeping your compass opening the same, place the compass point on Q. Draw an arc that intersects the first arc in two places.

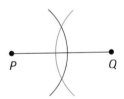

3. Use your straightedge to draw a line segment through the two points of intersection. This line segment is a bisector of $\overline{PQ}$. The point where it intersects $\overline{PQ}$, M, is the midpoint of $\overline{PQ}$.

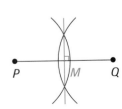

EXAMPLE 2: Construct a bisector of ∠R.

MORE HELP
See 363

Use the fact that the diagonals of a rhombus are angle bisectors.

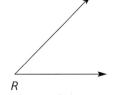

1. Place the point of your compass on R. Draw an arc that intersects the sides of ∠R. Label the points of intersection S and U.

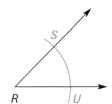

2. Keeping your compass opening the same, place the point of your compass on S and then on U and draw intersecting arcs in the interior of ∠R. Label the point of intersection T.

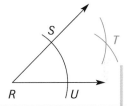

> If you used your straightedge to draw $\overline{ST}$ and $\overline{TU}$, RSTU is a rhombus because all four sides are the same length (from the same compass setting).

3. Use your straightedge to draw $\overline{RT}$. Because $\overline{RT}$ is a diagonal of a rhombus, $\overline{RT}$ bisects ∠R.

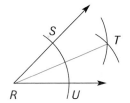

Constructing Perpendicular Lines

375

There is one patty-paper construction method for constructing perpendicular lines, and there is one method for using a straightedge and compass.

To construct a line perpendicular to line ℓ using patty paper, draw ℓ and point P on the paper. Fold so that P is on the fold line and ℓ folds onto itself.

MORE HELP
See 056

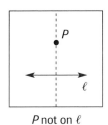

P not on ℓ

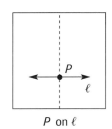

P on ℓ

MORE ▶

MORE HELP
See 374

The compass and straightedge construction calls for constructing the perpendicular bisector of a segment. Use the compass to find points equidistant from two endpoints.

EXAMPLE 1: Construct a line that is perpendicular to line ℓ and passes through point P. P is not on ℓ.

1. Place the point of your compass on P. Draw two arcs with the same radius that intersect ℓ. Label the points of intersection U and V.

2. Keeping your compass opening the same, place the point of your compass on U and then on V and draw intersecting arcs on the side of the line opposite P. Label the point of intersection Q.

3. Use your straightedge to draw a line through P and Q. $\overleftrightarrow{PQ}$ is perpendicular to ℓ and passes through P.

EXAMPLE 2: Construct a line that is perpendicular to line ℓ and passes through point P. P is on ℓ.

Follow steps similar to those for the case where P is not ℓ.

1. Draw arcs from P. 2. Draw slightly larger arcs from U and V. 3. Draw $\overleftrightarrow{QP}$.

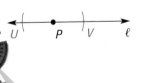
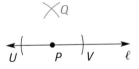
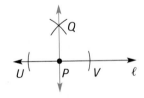

A line tangent to a circle is perpendicular to a radius of the circle. So you can use what you know about constructing perpendicular lines to construct tangents.

Constructing Parallel Lines

There is a theorem that says *if two coplanar lines are perpendicular to the same line, then they are parallel to each other* (T010). This theorem makes it possible for you to construct a line parallel to another line.

MORE HELP
See 058, 432

EXAMPLE 1: Construct a line that is parallel to line ℓ and passes through point P.

1. Draw line ℓ on the patty paper. Draw a point, P, not on line ℓ.

2. Fold the paper through P so one part of ℓ lies on the other part of ℓ. Unfold the paper. ℓ is perpendicular to the fold line.

3. Construct a second line perpendicular to the fold line. Fold the patty paper through P so one part of the first fold lies on its other part. Unfold. The second fold line is perpendicular to the first fold line, so the second fold line is parallel to ℓ.

You can also use the Corresponding Angles Postulate to construct parallel lines.

EXAMPLE 2: Construct a line that is parallel to line ℓ and passes through point P.

MORE HELP
See 373

1. Mark points A and B on ℓ. Use your straightedge to draw $\overleftrightarrow{AP}$.

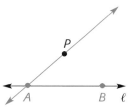

2. Copy $\angle A$ at point P. $\angle QPR$ is congruent to $\angle PAB$, so the line containing $\overline{PR}$ is parallel to line ℓ.

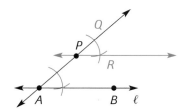

Dividing a Line Segment Into Equal Parts

MORE HELP
See 058

There is a theorem that says *if three parallel lines intersect two transversals, then they divide the transversals proportionally* (T009). You can use this theorem and the steps for constructing parallel lines to divide a line segment into equal parts.

EXAMPLE: Divide $\overline{GH}$ into three equal parts.

Draw a ray on which you can mark off three points at equal intervals. Then, construct parallel lines through those points to divide $\overline{GH}$ proportionally.

1. Mark point I so that it is not on $\overleftrightarrow{GH}$. Use your straightedge to draw $\overrightarrow{GI}$.

2. Use your compass to mark off three congruent segments on $\overrightarrow{GI}$.

3. Use your straightedge to draw $\overleftrightarrow{LH}$.

MORE HELP
See 373

4. Copy $\angle 1$ at J and K. Because the corresponding angles are congruent, $\overleftrightarrow{JM}$, $\overleftrightarrow{KN}$, and $\overleftrightarrow{LH}$ are parallel lines cut by transversals $\overrightarrow{GI}$ and $\overrightarrow{GH}$.
$GJ = JK = KL$, so $GM = MN = NH$. $\overline{GH}$ is divided into three equal parts.

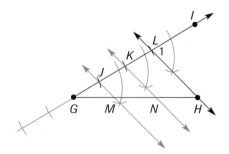

Constructing Special Segments in Triangles ____

You can use patty-paper constructions or compass and straightedge to construct special segments in triangles and locate concurrent points.

To construct medians and locate the centroid:

MORE HELP
See 136, 374

1. Construct a bisector and locate the midpoint of each side of the triangle.

2. To construct the medians, draw segments connecting each vertex to the midpoint of its opposite side.

3. The intersection of the medians is the centroid.

To construct altitudes and locate the orthocenter:

MORE HELP
See 137, 375

1. Construct a line that passes through each vertex and is perpendicular to the opposite side (or the line containing the opposite side) of the triangle.

2. The intersection of the altitudes is the orthocenter.

To locate the circumcenter:

MORE HELP
See 138, 374

1. Construct the perpendicular bisector of each side of the triangle.

2. The intersection of the perpendicular bisectors is the circumcenter.

To locate the incenter:

MORE HELP
See 139

1. Construct the bisector of each angle of the triangle.

2. The intersection of the angle bisectors is the incenter.

To construct midsegments:

MORE HELP
See 141, 374

1. Construct a bisector and locate the midpoint of each side of the triangle.

2. To construct the midsegments, draw segments connecting pairs of midpoints.

You can also use geometry software to demonstrate the special characteristics of the centroid, orthocenter, circumcenter, in-center, and midsegment.

Constructing Transformations _____

Patty papers make construction of reflections, rotations, and translations quite easy.

MORE HELP
See 275

Construct a reflection.

1. Draw a preimage and a line of reflection.

2. Fold the patty paper on the line of reflection. Trace the preimage.

3. Unfold. The reflection image will be visible from the reverse side of the paper.

 →  →

MORE HELP
See 281

Construct a rotation.

1. Draw a preimage, a point in the preimage, and a point for the center of rotation. Draw an angle of rotation by drawing two rays from the center of rotation. One ray should pass through the point on the preimage.

2. Place a second patty paper on top of the first and trace the preimage, its point, the center of rotation, and the ray that passes through the point in the preimage.

3. Place the point of your pencil on the center of rotation. Rotate the second patty paper until the ray on it lines up with the other ray on the first paper.

 → →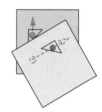

MORE HELP
See 286, 289

Construct a translation.

1. Draw a preimage. On the same paper, show the translation vector.

2. Place a second patty paper on top of the first and trace the preimage and the line segment.

3. Slide the second patty paper along the line segment until the endpoint inside the preimage is on the other end-point of the segment on the first patty paper.

 → →

You can use the properties of reflections, rotations, and translations to help construct these transformations with a compass and straightedge.

MORE HELP
See 275, 375

EXAMPLE 1: Construct the reflection of △*PQR* over line ℓ.

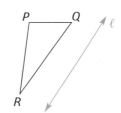

Remember that the defining property of a reflection is that the line of reflection is the perpendicular bisector of the line segments connecting corresponding points of a figure and its reflection.

1. Construct lines perpendicular to ℓ that pass through each vertex of △*PQR*. Label the points of intersection with ℓ *S, T,* and *U*. The reflections of *P, Q,* and *R* must lie on $\overleftrightarrow{PT}$, $\overleftrightarrow{QS}$, and $\overleftrightarrow{RU}$.

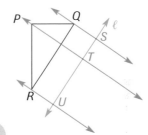

We've erased the construction marks because they overlap on such a small diagram. Your teacher will probably want you to leave them in place.

2. Mark off each reflection point with your compass so that ℓ is the perpendicular bisector of segments *PP′, QQ′,* and *RR′*. Set your compass to *SQ*. Place the compass point on *S*. Draw an arc that intersects $\overleftrightarrow{QS}$. Label the point of intersection *Q′*. Repeat to locate points *P′* and *R′*.

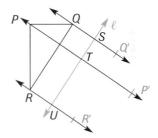

3. Use your straightedge to draw line segments connecting *P′, Q′,* and *R′*. △*P′Q′R′* is the reflection image of △*PQR* over ℓ.

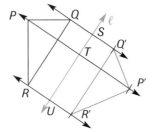

MORE ▶

MORE HELP
See 281, 373
The defining properties of a rotation are (1) that the distance from the center of rotation to a point is the same as the distance from the center of rotation to the point's image and (2) that each point of a figure rotates the same number of degrees.

EXAMPLE 2: Construct the image of △*ABC* after a counterclockwise rotation about *P*. The measure of the angle of rotation is the measure of ∠*APD*.

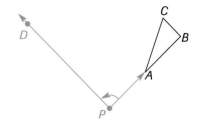

1. Set your compass to *PA*. Place the compass point on *P*. Draw an arc that intersects $\overrightarrow{PD}$. Label the point of intersection *A′*. Set the compass to *AB*, then with the compass point at *A*, draw an arc to locate *B′*.

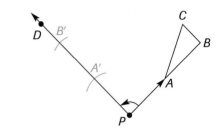

2. Use your straightedge to draw $\overrightarrow{PC}$. Construct ∠*CPE* congruent to ∠*APD*.

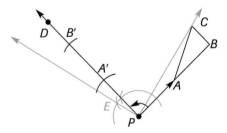

3. Copy $\overline{PC}$ on $\overrightarrow{PE}$. Use your straightedge to draw line segments connecting *A′*, *B′*, and *C′*. △*A′B′C′* is the rotation image of △*ABC*.

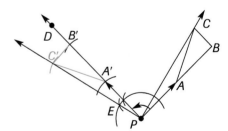

MORE HELP
See 286, 376

The defining property of a translation is that the line segments connecting the corresponding points of a figure and its image are congruent and parallel.

EXAMPLE 3: Construct the image of △*FGH* after the translation shown by the translation vector (slide arrow).

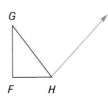

1. Extend $\overline{GH}$ and $\overline{FH}$ to use as transversals as you construct lines parallel to the slide arrow that pass through the other vertices of △*FGH*. Make ∠1 ≅ ∠2 and ∠*JHK* ≅ ∠*J'GK*.

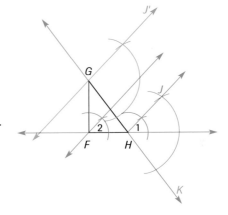

2. Set your compass to the length of the slide arrow. Place the compass point on *F*. Draw an arc that intersects the line passing through *F*. Label the point of intersection *F'*. Repeat to locate *G'*.

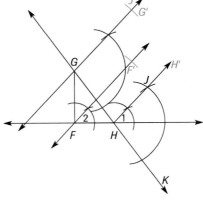

3. Use your straightedge to draw line segments connecting *F"*, *G'*, and *H'*. △*F'G'H'* is the translation image of △*FGH*.

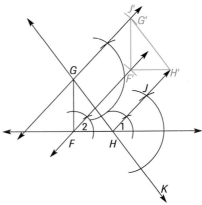

Constructing Regular Inscribed Polygons _____

An inscribed polygon is a polygon whose vertices all lie on a circle. You can use a compass and straightedge to construct an inscribed regular hexagon and an inscribed equilateral triangle.

MORE HELP
See 130,
136–138, 281

To inscribe a regular hexagon, use the fact that six equilateral triangles tessellate about a point ($60° \times 6 = 360°$). The sides of these triangles are the radii of the circle in which you inscribe the hexagon. Since the sides and base of an equilateral triangle are congruent, the radius is what you use to mark off equal arcs on the circle.

1. Use your compass to construct a circle.

2. Keeping your compass opening the same as the radius of the circle, place the compass point on the circle. Draw an arc that intercepts the circle.

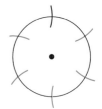

3. Still keeping your compass opening the same, place the compass point on the point of intersection you located in Step 2. Draw an arc that intercepts the circle. Repeat until you have drawn all six arcs.

4. To construct a regular hexagon, connect the six points of intersection. To construct an equilateral triangle, skip every other point when connecting the points of intersection.

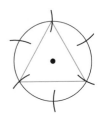

For thousands of years, the tools of geometry have been a straightedge, compass, and a writing implement. Today you can use a computer to make the same geometric constructions in a fraction of the time it took previously. Computers also allow you to research applications of geometry in the world around you.

DID YOU KNOW Archimedes of Syracuse (287–212 B.C.E.) used geometric constructions to calculate the value of π correct to three decimal places. He began by inscribing and circumscribing a hexagon about a circle. Then he bisected the angles formed by the diagonals four times to construct a regular 96-gon. Using similar triangles, he found the lengths of the sides of these polygons. From the perimeters of these polygons he concluded that

$$3\frac{10}{71} < \pi < 3\frac{1}{7}.$$

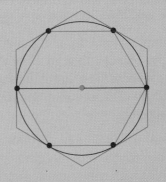

This was a major accomplishment and the precision of the value of π was not improved for over 200 years. Now you can duplicate this result on a computer in a few hours or less.

Geometric Construction Software

382

Geometric construction software lets you be a geometer, like Euclid, Archimedes, and Hilbert, quickly and easily. It allows you to conjure up your own geometric relationships and try them out on dozens of cases in a very short time. You can watch a geometric model change, and see what other elements change at the same time. It won't prove theorems for you, but it will help you decide which relationships are worth trying to prove!

MORE ▶

Each diagram you make is created on a nearly blank screen called a sketch or worksheet. Beside or above each worksheet is a set of buttons, called **tools**. These contain the basic commands that let you create a diagram on your worksheet.

Using Software for Basic Constructions

A geometric construction program has a set of figures that can be drawn by a simple point-and-click method. These figures may include points, lines, rays, segments, circles, and polygons. These figures are called **objects**.

To draw a segment, for example, point and click on the segment option in the list of tools. Then go to the worksheet with the cursor, and click and drag to draw the segment. Releasing the cursor button marks the second endpoint of the segment. See your manual or the *Help* feature for how to label points.

Using this option, you can draw a sequence of connected segments by starting each new segment where you left off on the last one. You can also create a sequence of disconnected segments by moving the cursor without depressing the cursor button between segments.

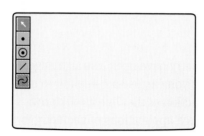

Once you know how to draw points, lines, and circles, you can now make all the constructions possible with straightedge and compass. For example, you can construct a line perpendicular to $\overleftrightarrow{AB}$ through a point D.

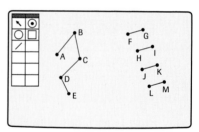

1. Draw circles with centers at A and B passing through D.

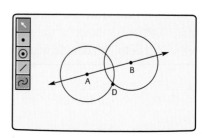

2. Draw $\overleftrightarrow{DG}$, where G is the other point of intersection of the two circles. $\overleftrightarrow{DG}$ is perpendicular to the original line and contains D.

MORE HELP
See 375

This construction may not look exactly like the straightedge and compass construction you have done in geometry class. It contains two complete circles, rather than simply arcs, but the procedures used in both types of constructions are alike.

Using Software for Other Constructions

384

Because some constructions are used so often, shortcut methods for drawing them are built into the software. Parallel and perpendicular lines fall into this category. Here's how these short-cut constructions work. The steps here might not be the same as those required in your construction program, but your manual or *Help* button will give you guidance if you need it.

All short-cut constructions require that you highlight the objects needed to determine the construction. For example, to draw a segment, you begin by highlighting two points of your diagram, because two points determine a line. Then in the list of possible constructions, choose *Segment*. A segment will appear joining the two highlighted points.

The way to highlight an object depends on the program you are using. Some programs let you point and click on the object. Others let you name the object using labels on the diagram. When using a point-and-click method, you may need to hold down the shift key while you highlight a second or third object.

To draw a line parallel to a given line, begin by highlighting a line and a point not on the line. Then, when you select Parallel Line from the list of constructions, a line parallel to the highlighted line through the highlighted point will appear.

You may be able to use the same method of highlighting to measure objects in your diagram, such as distances, angle measures, circumferences, and arc lengths. After you highlight the object, go to the list of

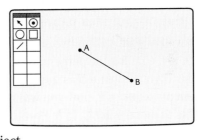

Measurement options and choose the appropriate type of measurement.

Dynamic Geometry

Dynamic geometry means that within a diagram, some selected objects can move while others stay in the same place. This is the basis of geometric experimentation. Usually, you can move the selected object by clicking on it and dragging it around on your screen.

In dynamic geometry, you can draw a triangle and, by highlighting a vertex, move that vertex while the other two vertices stay fixed. By highlighting a side, you can move this side while the opposite vertex stays fixed. (The other two sides will have one moveable endpoint and one fixed endpoint.) If you show the lengths of the sides and their sum on your sketch, then you will see the changing lengths and perimeters as you move the side.

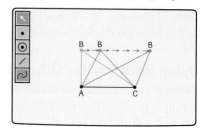

To move a point, it must be the intersection of only two lines or arcs. If it is the intersection of three or more arcs or lines, the point will stay fixed. To allow it to move, you may redefine it (using a *Construction* option) as the intersection of two of these objects. This will allow the point to move, and the other objects that intersect at this point will also move.

For example, suppose you draw $\overline{AB}$ and a line perpendicular to it through C. Then draw $\triangle ABC$. Point C will not move because it is on two segments, $\overline{CA}$ and $\overline{CB}$, and the perpendicular line. If you redefine C as the intersection of $\overline{CA}$ and $\overline{CB}$, now you will be able to move point C. In the process,

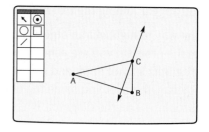

the perpendicular line will also move, staying perpendicular to $\overline{AB}$ through C.

Using Software for Transformations

Geometric construction programs allow you to make transformations of an object. These transformations may include rotations, reflections, translations, and dilations. The important thing to remember when doing these operations is that the software can perform the operation only when it is uniquely identified. For example, if you want to translate a triangle, the software can only do this after you define the distance and direction of the translation.

When you choose a transformation option, a screen will appear that asks you for the information needed to define the transformation. The information you need to provide includes the following.

- *Translation:* distance and direction

- *Rotation:* angle and a center (the angle will be in a counterclockwise direction, unless you specify it as a negative angle)

- *Reflection:* a reflection line

- *Dilation:* a ratio of enlargement or reduction and a center

What kinds of relationships will these help you to understand? Consider the following geometric statement.

A sequence of two transformations about two perpendicular lines of reflection is equivalent to a single half-turn transformation about the point of intersection of the two lines of reflection.

MORE HELP
See 284

To see that this is true, begin by drawing a triangle and two perpendicular lines. Reflect the triangle about one line, then reflect the image triangle about the second line. Then hide the middle image triangle.

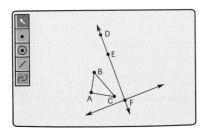

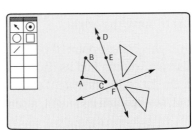

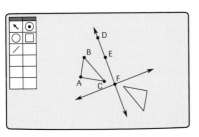

Now take the original triangle and rotate it 180° about the point of intersection of the two perpendicular lines. You will find that it is the same triangle as the second image triangle you formed from the reflections.

MORE ▶

MORE HELP
See 129, 131, 346

You can construct regular polygons with construction software using a series of rotations of a single segment, based on the measure of an interior angle of the polygon you wish to construct. For example, to construct a regular hexagon, begin with a single line segment, $\overline{AB}$. Rotate it 120° about B to get $\overline{BC}$. Rotate this segment 120° about C to get $\overline{CD}$, and so on.

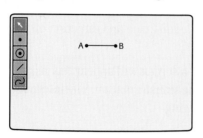

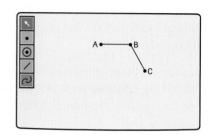

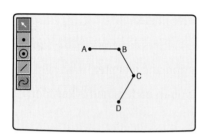

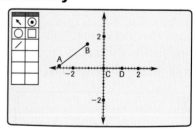

387

Using Software for Coordinate Geometry

Your geometry software may allow you to place your diagram on a coordinate grid. The software will place the grid in standard position, although there may be an option that allows you to move the origin.

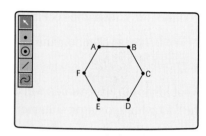

By highlighting a point of your diagram you can find its coordinates in the list of *Measurement* options. By highlighting a segment, you can find its slope and its length, again using the *Measurement* options.

Internet

The **Internet** is a network of computers that allows them to communicate with each other. Once you connect your home computer to the network, you can gather information from computers around the world.

To connect your home computer to the Internet, you need a telephone line (wired or wireless) or a cable line and a way to connect to that line. Cable companies will supply you with a cable connection. With telephone lines you will need a **modem**, although most new models of home computers have a built-in modem. You will also need an **Internet Service Provider (ISP)** who will give you access to the Internet, usually for a monthly fee.

The **World Wide Web (WWW)** is a system of resources available on the Internet. Anyone who purchases a web address can design a screen (called a **web page**) that contains information they want other Internet users to see. Some web pages are published by businesses that want to sell their products, but many organizations and government agencies publish data they have collected. The World Wide Web has become a major source of information in only a few short years.

When gathering information from the Web, you should remember that any person can write any information, true, false, or pure guesswork, on the web. You should check all information you gather from the web against other sources to be sure the information is accurate and truthful.

Using the Graphing Calculator

This section shows you how to use some of the features available on a graphing calculator.

The Graphing Calculator

A graphing calculator is an amazing tool. It allows you to perform a large variety of mathematical operations. You can see the graph of a function or the outline of a circle by just pressing the right keys. Your graphing calculator will probably look similar to this one.

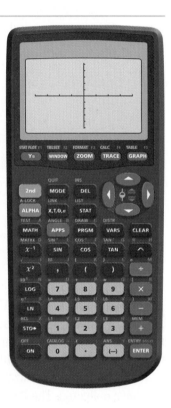

The best way to learn how to use your graphing calculator is simply to use it. This section can guide you, but it can't substitute for hands-on practice. Try different commands and work through some of the specific examples that are shown in the manual. Read through the table of contents and examine the index. Just being familiar with these sections will help you locate specific instructions when you want to try something new. The commands in your manual may be different than those shown in this handbook, but your calculator will most likely perform the functions.

A word of advice about consulting your calculator manual. Don't let it intimidate you! It's just a tool. If the instructions confuse you, try the examples shown in the manual. They will help you understand how to use the commands.

A graphing calculator is set up much like a regular calculator. The display or screen is at the top of the calculator. All of the operations (+, −, ×, ÷) are located near each other along the right side of the calculator. The number keys are also placed together in their standard calculator order. The ENTER key replaces = found on other calculators. Notice the (−) key next to ENTER. You press this key to enter the negative sign for a negative number instead of the − key or the +/− key.

The ^ key is used to raise a number to a power. To evaluate 2^3 on this calculator, use the keystrokes 2 ^ 3 ENTER. The answer, 8, will be displayed on the right side of the screen.

A graphing calculator has many more keys and symbols than an ordinary calculator. It is also color coded to show more than one function for each key. The 2nd key in the upper lefthand corner is a different color than the other keys. So is the ALPHA key below it. These keys allow you to access commands built into the calculator by pushing buttons whose primary use is for something else. The different commands or functions are color coded on the face of the calculator above the key that they correspond to. So, if your 2nd key is yellow, the yellow characters above the keys become active for the next keystroke after you press 2nd.

Suppose you want to find the square root of a number. On this calculator, the square root is color coded yellow above the x^2 key. To find $\sqrt{16}$, press the 2nd key and then x^2 1 6 ENTER. A typical screen might look like this:

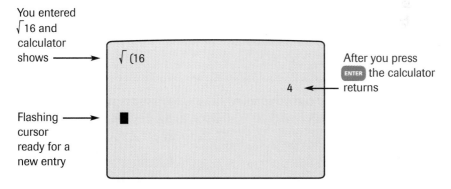

You entered $\sqrt{16}$ and calculator shows ⟶ $\sqrt{(16}$

After you press ENTER the calculator returns ⟵ 4

Flashing ⟶ cursor ready for a new entry

The graphing keys are the keys directly beneath the screen. On this calculator they are the Y=, WINDOW, ZOOM, TRACE, and GRAPH keys. These keys allow you to access the graphing features of the calculator.

The arrow keys on the upper right of the calculator are the editing keys that allow you to move the cursor up, down, left, or right on the screen.

391 ⊙

MATH ALERT Check Your Manual

Your calculator may look different or have different keys that do the same thing. Check the directions in the manual for your calculator.

392

Math Functions, Operations, and Modes

A graphing calculator follows a particular sequence to evaluate expressions:

1. functions that are entered before a number, such as $\sqrt{}$

2. functions that are entered after a number, such as x^2

3. powers and roots

4. permutations and combinations

5. multiplication and division

6. addition and subtraction

To override this sequence, you can use parentheses ⬛ and ⬛.

EXAMPLE: Evaluate $^-2^2$ and $(^-2^2)$.

If you enter ⬛ ⬛ ⬛ ⬛, a graphing calculator will perform the squaring function. Then it will multiply the result by $^-1$, giving $^-4$.

If you enter ⬛ ⬛ ⬛ ⬛ ⬛ ⬛, the calculator will evaluate the expression within the parentheses first. It will then square the result, giving 4.

★ $^-2^2 = {}^-4$ and $(^-2)^2 = 4$.

A graphing calculator can do so many things that it is not practical to have a separate key for each function. In addition to the keyboard mathematical functions, such as ⬛, ⬛, and ⬛, there are other functions built into the calculator.

If you press 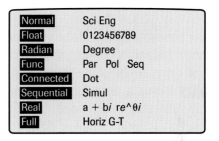, the screen might display a menu similar to this one, the math menu. Using the arrow keys to move up and down the list, you can change an answer to a fraction, find the cube of a number, or find the cube root of a number. Using the arrow keys to move across the top line will change the active menu. For example, NUM accesses the MATH NUM menu. You can use this menu to find the absolute value of a number or to round a number.

MATH	NUM	CPX	PRB
1 : abs(			
2 : round(			
3 : iPart(			
4 : fPart(			
5 : int(			
6 : min(			
7↓ max(			

When using your graphing calculator, do not round until you reach your final answer. This will give you a more precise answer.

If you press MODE, you can see how your graphing calculator will display and interpret numbers and graphs. The highlighted settings are the current settings. You can change any setting by using the arrow keys to move to a new setting and pressing ENTER. For example, to use the trigonometric functions of your calculator, put it in the Degree mode (third line).

If you are trying to find a specific function, remember to look it up directly in the index of your calculator manual or the catalog on the calculator itself. If you want a more general discussion, the table of contents may have a chapter about *MATH Operations* that will explain how to access each function. There may also be an appendix with tables and reference information.

Normal	Sci Eng
Float	0123456789
Radian	Degree
Func	Par Pol Seq
Connected	Dot
Sequential	Simul
Real	a + bi re^θi
Full	Horiz G-T

As you use your calculator, remember to clear the home screen before starting a new calculation. The table of contents may address this in the very first section of the manual. Probably there will also be an entire chapter on *Memory*. Check the index under *memory*, with a subentry for *reset* or *resetting*.

MATH ALERT **Error Messages**

Don't panic if you get an error message. It doesn't always mean you made a mistake.

For example, you'll get an error message if you press (2) (7) (^) (1) (0) (0) (ENTER) because the answer has too many digits to fit on the calculator display.

If you can't figure out what the error message means, check your manual. Error conditions will probably be covered in the first chapter of the manual. An appendix may explain each type of error in detail. Looking in the index under *error* should direct you to help.

> ERR: OVERFLOW
> **1:** Goto
> 2: Quit

Variables on a Graphing Calculator

Suppose you want to use a value or a numerical expression more than once. Instead of entering the number or expression over and over again, you can store the value or expression to a variable letter. A key such as (STO▸) is usually used to store the value. The variable letters used to name the value may be activated with (ALPHA). There is also a special key for commonly-used variables, (X,T,θ,n). You can even store an answer to a variable. Check your manual for details on how to *store*, *display*, and *recall* the variables. The initial chapter on operating instructions should have details, or check the index under *store*.

Programming a Graphing Calculator

Many graphing calculators are programmable. This means that you can store a set of instructions in the calculator to make specific calculations as the values of the variables change. This is especially useful for formulas that you might use over and over. To produce the desired output, it is important that you understand how input flows through the program you enter.

EXAMPLE: Write a formula to find the slope of a line. Use the formula to find the slope of a line that goes through the points (2, 5) and (8, 9).

MORE HELP
See 098

First create the program, using steps similar to these.

1. Press `PRGM` `▷` `▷` to display the PRGM NEW menu.

2. Press `ENTER` to select Create New. You are asked to name the program, and the *A* flashing on the screen shows that the alpha-lock is on. Press `LN` `)` `7` `8` `SIN` `ENTER` to name it SLOPE.

3. To enter the first line of SLOPE, press `PRGM` `▷` `2`. Let *A*, *B*, *C*, and *D* represent the *x*- and *y*-coordinates of the two points a line passes through. Press `ALPHA` `MATH` `,` `ALPHA` `MATRIX` `,` `ALPHA` `PRGM` `,` `ALPHA` `x⁻¹` `ENTER`.

4. On the next line, enter the slope formula and store it as the variable *M*. Press `(` `ALPHA` `x⁻¹` `−` `ALPHA` `MATRIX` `)` `÷` `(` `ALPHA` `PRGM` `−` `ALPHA` `MATH` `)` `STO▸` `ALPHA` `÷`.

5. Use `2nd` `MODE` to return to the home screen.

Now you are ready to **execute**, or use, your program using steps similar to these.

1. Press `PRGM` to display the PRGM EXEC menu. If necessary, move the cursor to SLOPE. Then press `ENTER`.

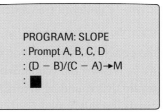

```
PROGRAM: SLOPE
: Prompt A, B, C, D
: (D − B)/(C − A)→M
: ■
```

2. Press `ENTER` to begin executing the program. Enter 2 for *A*, 5 for *B*, 8 for *C*, and 9 for *D*, pressing `ENTER` after each entry.

3. The slope is displayed in decimal form. If you wish to display the slope as a fraction, press `MATH` `ENTER` `ENTER`.

★ The slope of the line that goes through the points (2, 5) and (8, 9) is $\frac{2}{3}$.

```
prgm SLOPE
A = ? 2
B = ? 5
C = ? 8
D = ? 9
            .6666666667
Ans > Frac    2/3
```

Consult your manual for specific programming details. Check the table of contents for a chapter on *Programming* or look up *programming* in the index.

Function Graphing on a Graphing Calculator _____

Here are some of the most common keys used to graph a function.

More Help
See 095, 109

(Y=) Use this screen to enter the function(s) you want graphed.

(WINDOW) Use this screen to set the part of the coordinate plane you want to have appear in the viewing window. Xmin, Xmax, Ymin, and Ymax define the minimum, or least, and maximum, or greatest, values that will appear on the x- and y-axes in the window. Xscl and Yscl define the scale, or distance between the tick marks on the x- and y-axes. Xres defines the resolution, or the frequency along the x-axis at which functions are evaluated and graphed.

(ZOOM) Use the ZOOM menu to adjust the viewing window of the graph. With the ZOOM feature, you can look closer at a particular section of the graph or at a larger portion of the graph. *ZBox* draws a box to define the viewing window. You can move the zoom cursor to define a box around the part of the graph in which you want to use the Zoom feature. *Zoom In* magnifies the part of the graph around the cursor, while *Zoom Out* views more of a graph around the cursor. *Zoom factors* define the magnification used to *Zoom In* or *Zoom Out* around a point.

(TRACE) You can use the cursor to trace along the graph of a function or the data points of a plot. It will display variable values for its location as you move it along the graph. When using Trace to find points on a graph, be aware that rounding errors may affect the coordinate values being displayed on the screen.

(GRAPH) Use this key to display the graph screen. It graphs the selected functions entered in (Y=) .

Make sure you check your manual to find out exactly which keys you need to use to enter a function, to graph the function, and to access options available with the graph. In particular, your graphing calculator probably has a menu that will allow you to calculate a y-value for a given x-value of a function, find a zero (x-intercept) of a function, and find a maximum and/or minimum value of a function.

Did you know that how you study can be more important than how long you study? If you don't like to study, or you don't have very much time, you can use the tips in this section to make the most of your study time.

Taking Notes and Keeping a Journal

You can think of notes as your own customized review book. Notes can help you remember what you learned in class. They can guide you when you try exercises on your own. A math notebook is a good place to record examples and proofs that you think are especially helpful. Write about new vocabulary and theorems, use symbols with examples, and draw diagrams or illustrations. Include descriptions of how geometry is used in the world around you. There is often more than one way to solve a problem, so include alternate methods when you can.

Some students like to use a two-column format for their notes. Others like to keep their definitions, postulates, and theorems in special sections.

Wherever you take notes, have a good set of tools with you: a pencil or two with good erasers, a highlighter, colored pens or pencils, straightedge, compass, protractor, plenty of lined paper, and graph paper or patty paper, too, for when you need it.

How to Take Notes

Your math notebook can take different forms. You can write math notes on cards and keep them in an envelope. To keep this card-journal handy, punch holes in the envelope and place it in your loose-leaf binder. You can also write your notes in a separate notebook. Date your notes to keep track of the order in which topics were introduced, studied, or reviewed in class.

Your notes can take different forms. You can use an outline form or write full sentences. You should draw lots of diagrams. You don't have to use the same form all the time. Just try to make your notes as useful as possible.

Try to make connections in class. Try to reflect the connections in your notes so you can make the same connections outside of class.

MORE ▶

MORE HELP
See 260

Oct. 4   Congruent Triangles

All corresponding angles congruent.

All corresponding sides congruent.

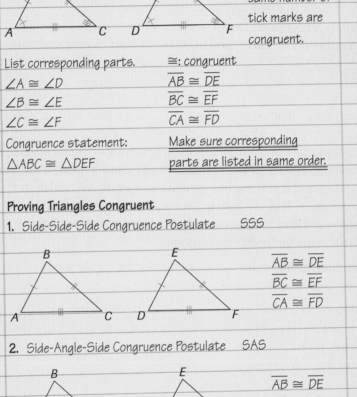

Angles or segments with the same number of tick marks are congruent.

List corresponding parts.   ≅: congruent

∠A ≅ ∠D $\overline{AB} \cong \overline{DE}$

∠B ≅ ∠E $\overline{BC} \cong \overline{EF}$

∠C ≅ ∠F $\overline{CA} \cong \overline{FD}$

Congruence statement: Make sure corresponding

△ABC ≅ △DEF   parts are listed in same order.

Listen as actively as possible to explanations and include in your notes any comments that might be helpful to you later.

Proving Triangles Congruent

1. Side-Side-Side Congruence Postulate   SSS

$\overline{AB} \cong \overline{DE}$
$\overline{BC} \cong \overline{EF}$
$\overline{CA} \cong \overline{FD}$

2. Side-Angle-Side Congruence Postulate   SAS

$\overline{AB} \cong \overline{DE}$
∠A ≅ ∠D
$\overline{AC} \cong \overline{DF}$

★ Remember: ★

The included angle must be between the two sides.

It's hard to remember everything covered in class, so copy all notes written on the board. If an example is worked out in detail, try to include in your notes the comments your teacher makes.

Listen carefully. That means, think about what the teacher is saying and how the problem is being solved or the theorem is being proved. Reword what the teacher is saying in terms that you understand and can apply—thinking is more important than writing every word you hear. If you are uncertain about a particular step or part of a solution and have a question, ask. Don't be afraid to ask, since others probably have the same question in mind and will thank you for your question. Remember to include the answer in your notes. Try to work through similar problems on your own as soon as you can.

> If your teacher will allow it, tape-recording the lesson may help you check later to be sure your notes are accurate and complete.

Evaluating Your Notes

The easier to read and more complete your notes are, the more they can help you study for tests. If one way of taking notes isn't as helpful as you'd like it to be, try something new.

- If writing in paragraphs doesn't work, write in outline form instead.

- If you can't find what you need in your notes because they are too brief, try to fill in some of the details. When you copy a problem from the board, define new symbols and explain the steps in the solution. Try to record comments that help you understand the procedure.

- If you have too many details, concentrate on only the most important points, but be careful here. Use your class time to understand new concepts being taught and record what you think is important. When you read through your notes, you can always use a highlighter to mark the most important details.

- Try to look over your notes every day while the material is still fresh in your mind. Try to use them to help you with a few practice problems. If you don't understand what you've written, you'll need to improve your notes by checking another source and filling in the gaps.

- Look over your notes before you do your homework. If something is unclear, check your textbook and this handbook, too. If you still have a question, write it in the margin of your notebook so you'll remember to ask your teacher.

- Don't wait until just before a test to look through all of your notes. Regularly look back at what you did earlier in the week, last week, or last month.

Guidelines for Improving Note-Taking Skills

Taking effective notes is tricky. A short word or phrase that seems clear when you write it may be a mystery when you read it sometime later.

- **Be attentive.** Listen carefully as your teacher explains how to solve a problem, prove a theorem, or use a procedure. Carefully read explanations in your textbook or this handbook. Write down parts of the explanation that seem to help you understand the problem and its solution.

- **Keep it simple.** Write only things that help you understand how to solve problems or prove theorems.

- **Be organized.** Number all items presented in a list. Highlight items that you do not understand so that you can look them up or ask about them later.

- **Summarize.** Write a brief summary after class before you forget what went on. Just a few sentences might be what you need to jog your memory later on and give you insight into how much you really understood.

- **Communicate.** Mathematics is about reasoning. Use your notes to communicate with yourself. Your thoughts, ideas, and insights are valuable. Don't take them for granted.

- **Look for another way.** If different methods are used to solve a problem, write them down. It makes you more mathematically flexible, and it may give you another point of view and a more thorough understanding.

Keeping a Journal

Keep a journal in a separate part of your notebook or in a completely separate book. In it, record your reflections on your work. You may want to start by recording what your goals are for studying geometry, what you are looking forward to in your study, and what makes you nervous. Name some specific steps you can take to reach your goals. From time to time, review what you first wrote and record the progress you are making in reaching your goals. You may also record in your journal important concepts or procedures you learn. Be sure to tell why they are important.

Reading Mathematics Materials

Mathematics materials require a different kind of reading than you're used to in other subjects because the text doesn't flow in the same way and much of the information you need is found in diagrams, tables, graphs, and examples. Much of the information is symbolic rather than textual. Some exercises may require you to use answers or other information from previous exercises. You need to pay careful attention to all the information provided to you, and this may require that you read a section more than once.

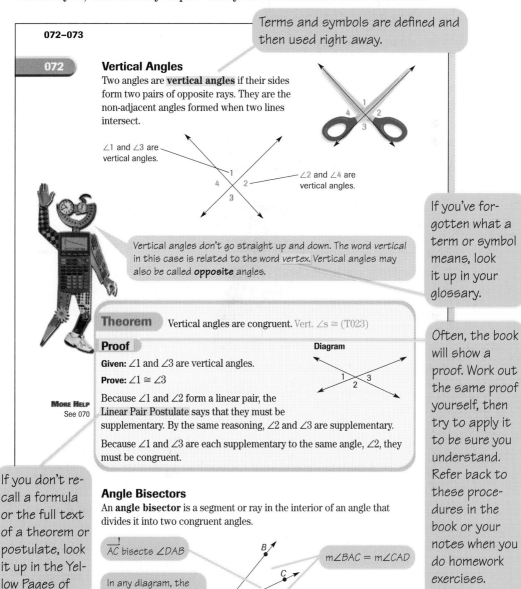

072–073

Terms and symbols are defined and then used right away.

072

Vertical Angles

Two angles are **vertical angles** if their sides form two pairs of opposite rays. They are the non-adjacent angles formed when two lines intersect.

∠1 and ∠3 are vertical angles.

∠2 and ∠4 are vertical angles.

Vertical angles don't go straight up and down. The word vertical in this case is related to the word vertex. Vertical angles may also be called **opposite** angles.

If you've forgotten what a term or symbol means, look it up in your glossary.

Theorem   Vertical angles are congruent. Vert. ∠s ≅ (T023)

Proof

Given: ∠1 and ∠3 are vertical angles.

Prove: ∠1 ≅ ∠3

MORE HELP
See 070

Because ∠1 and ∠2 form a linear pair, the Linear Pair Postulate says that they must be supplementary. By the same reasoning, ∠2 and ∠3 are supplementary.

Because ∠1 and ∠3 are each supplementary to the same angle, ∠2, they must be congruent.

Diagram

Often, the book will show a proof. Work out the same proof yourself, then try to apply it to be sure you understand. Refer back to these procedures in the book or your notes when you do homework exercises.

If you don't recall a formula or the full text of a theorem or postulate, look it up in the Yellow Pages of this handbook.

Angle Bisectors

An **angle bisector** is a segment or ray in the interior of an angle that divides it into two congruent angles.

$\overrightarrow{AC}$ bisects ∠DAB

m∠BAC = m∠CAD

In any diagram, the matching arcs identify congruent angles.

Managing Your Time

Do you have trouble getting things done on time (or at all)? The bad news is that you can't add more hours to the day. The good news is that you *can* get more things done in the hours you have. Time management will help you organize both your study time and your free time.

- **Keep a weekly schedule.** A weekly planner helps you organize your assignments and plan time to complete them. The planner makes it easier for you to prepare for tests and get projects and other homework done well and on time. Keep this schedule handy.

- **Make a daily list.** Write down things you need to do today and things you need to do tomorrow. Don't put off assignments (especially your least-favorite ones) until the last minute. Prioritize them in order of importance. Place the list someplace where you won't forget it. Check off items as you complete them.

- **Have a homework schedule.** Set aside a specific time for doing homework assignments. Allow yourself short breaks between each assignment, but don't make the breaks longer than five minutes.

- **Set goals.** Be realistic. Make sure the goals you set for yourself and the time you allow are reasonable. Reward yourself for completing tasks. Try to learn from goals or tasks that you don't quite achieve.

- **Get it done and turn it in on time.**

  - Go over any instructions your teacher has given for an assignment.

  - Pick an easy thing to do first, just to get started.

  - Carefully read the directions.

  - Check your notes and your textbook to make sure that you know how to do your homework as accurately as possible.

  - Be sure that proofs are logical and complete and that your diagrams are well-labeled and accurate.

  - Keep a list of things you don't understand to ask your teacher about.

  - After you're finished, check the directions again to make sure your homework is really complete.

  - Keep your completed assignments someplace safe!

Using a Rubric to Plan and Evaluate Your Writing   406

The nice thing about writing math ideas is that you can often use symbols and diagrams to save time and effort. A symbol is shorter than a word or phrase. A diagram, like any picture, can be worth a thousand words.

The slope of this line is 2. The diagram should help you understand the meaning of slope.

MORE HELP
See 098, 477

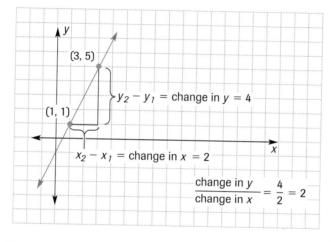

Using a Rubric to Plan and Evaluate Your Writing   406

You can use the outline below to help you organize your thoughts to write clearly in mathematics.

Statement of problem	
Solution	Detail: Step 1
	Detail: Step 2
	...
	...
	Detail: last step
Conclusion/Answer	

To improve your ability to write in mathematics, you can also use the following **rubric**, or explanation of scoring, to evaluate your own work. It tells you what you need to include in your writing to get a top grade. Check to see how much you understand from your own writing. Decide which level you think your solution would be. Then ask a parent, teacher, or friend to evaluate the solution. Discuss any differences. Keep in mind that it takes a lot of effort to reach the top level, but if you keep trying, you'll get there!

Rubric Level:

- **Excellent.** Solution is correct and correctly labeled. The writing shows a full understanding of the topic. It shows how you think through a problem. Each step is explained with both examples and words. The examples are worked out correctly and in detail. There may be sketches or diagrams. The problem is organized so that steps are in order. It is more than just calculations or lists of theorems.

- **Well done.** Solution is correct and correctly labeled. The writing is clear, the question is correctly understood, most procedures, calculations, and theorems are correct, and the flow of logical reasoning is evident.

- **Adequate.** Solution is correct. (Possible exceptions include copying errors or minor computation errors.) The writing shows a good understanding of the topic. You include examples, calculations, and maybe even diagrams. Steps are followed in order with each example or diagram explained. There may be some errors in computation, but your descriptions show that you can think through the details of the problem even though you may not have drawn a convincing conclusion.

- **Weak.** Solution is incorrect. The writing does not really explain what is going on in the problem. There are errors in understanding, logic, and calculation. There is nothing to explain what the examples mean or why the calculations were made, even though they may relate to the problem. Steps may not be in order.

- **Inadequate.** Solution is incorrect. The writing is unclear and it is not well organized. It appears that you did not understand the problem. Examples and calculations are not explained. There are many errors in logic, understanding, and computation.

EXAMPLE: What rubric level should be assigned to this exercise? Explain.

MORE HELP
See 152, 421

The ground, the wall, and the ladder form a right triangle. The ground and the wall are the legs of the triangle. The ladder is the hypotenuse of the triangle. I knew the lengths of two sides of the right triangle, so I used the Pythagorean Theorem: $c^2 = a^2 + b^2$.

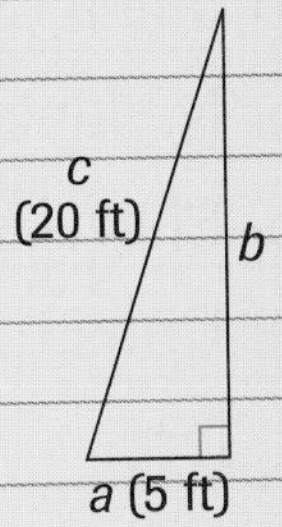

c (20 ft) b

a (5 ft)

$$c^2 = a^2 + b^2$$
$$20^2 = 5^2 + b^2$$ I used the Pythagorean Theorem and
$$400 = 25 + b^2$$ solved for b when $a = 5$ and $c = 20$.
$$375 = b^2$$
$$\sqrt{375} = b$$ I simplified under the radical by
$$\sqrt{25 \cdot 15} = b$$ finding a perfect square factor of 375.
$$5\sqrt{15} = b$$
$$5\sqrt{15} \approx 5 \cdot 3.873$$ To find the approximate value of b, I
$$\approx 19.365$$ used the Table of Powers and Roots
                         because I forgot my calculator.

If this is the standard form for answers in your class, stop here.

The ladder will reach about 19.4 feet up the wall.

★ Excellent. Good explanations. Correct answer. Well organized. Useful diagram.

407 Test-Taking Skills

Success on a test depends on how well you prepare along the way—how well you keep up with assignments, try practice problems, and ask questions when you don't understand something. To do well on a test, organize your approach to studying and give yourself ample time to develop confidence.

408 Reviewing Test Material

Even before you begin studying for a test, you should find out the rules and format of the test and what the test will cover.

- **What will be on the test?** Ask the teacher to be as specific as possible. Write a list of all the topics the test might cover.

- **What will the test questions be like?** Will there be short answer computation, word problems, graphs, multiple-choice or true/false questions, specific kinds of proofs, or a combination of these? Will it include vocabulary?

- **Make an outline of problem types.** List each kind of problem separately. Then you can focus on each type of problem one at a time. Find an example for each type of problem. Write your own sample questions.

- **Use index cards.** Use index cards to list and illustrate definitions, formulas, postulates, and theorems you need to memorize and/or use. Write the term or phrase on one side and a definition or explanation on the other side. Include an example or diagram. Ask someone to use the cards to quiz you.

- **Think about how things fit together.** The more you understand, the less you'll have to memorize. For example, if you understand why a formula works, you'll have an easier time remembering it.

- **Get any notes or assignments that you may have missed.** If you've missed any classes, you probably missed something important. Get copies of notes and do any homework that was assigned. Be sure it's correct before using it as a study tool. Your teacher or classmates will help if you ask ahead of time.

- **Start reviewing early.** Don't wait until the night before the test to study. Work out problems one at a time—don't rush through them. By studying a little each day for several days, you will gain confidence in your abilities, and you will remember more than if you try to study everything the night before the test.

- **Find a good place to study.** Find a quiet place. Make sure there's room to spread out your notes, open your textbook and your handbook, and try some sample problems.

- **Set up a specific time to study.** Don't let anything distract you from starting on time.

- **Review your notes, quizzes, and practice tests carefully.** Compare your class notes and examples with those in your textbook. Review your homework.

- **Make a list of questions.** If you are uncertain about anything, talk to your teacher several days before the test.

- **Practice, practice, practice.** Redo old homework problems or quiz problems. Try different examples to prepare for the test. You can even make yourself a practice test.

- **Use memory aids.** Silly sayings, called mnemonic devices, can help you remember complicated rules or procedures. See item 241 for an example.

  MORE HELP
  See 241

- **Make sure you get enough rest.** If you get tired, take a break or get some sleep. If you're tired on test day, you'll have trouble concentrating and that could hurt your grade.

- **Remember to eat well.** If you're hungry, it's hard to concentrate. If you've eaten too much, you may be sleepy.

- **Study in a group.** Have each group member review part of the test material and present a summary of the key concepts to the group. As you talk about how to solve problems, you will test your own understanding. After hearing the summaries and reviewing your notes and textbook, close your books. See how much you can recall as a group.

- **Study by yourself.** You will be taking the test alone, so you need to be able to do the problems on your own.

Taking the Test

- **Try to arrive early for the test.** Allow yourself time to get comfortable in your seat and get out the materials you need for the test.

- **Try to unwind before the test.** Breathe deeply and try to relax. Think of the problems as puzzles or mysteries that you want to solve.

- **Check that you have all the materials you need for the test.** You may need sharp pencils, paper, a ruler, compass, calculator, and so on.

- **Know the rules of the test.** How long is the test? Do all the questions count equally? Are your calculator, textbook, handbook, notes, a formula sheet, or a theorem list allowed? Is there partial credit for short-answer items? If it's a multiple-choice test, is a *guessing factor* used?

  > If a multiple-choice test uses a guessing factor, it's a good idea to guess only if you can eliminate one or two choices. On these tests, you earn a point for a correct guess and lose part of a point for an incorrect guess.

- **Look over the entire test quickly.** Try to get an idea of the length of the test and the points each type of problem is worth. Think about how much time you can allot for each problem. If you are not allowed a formula sheet, you may want to write down relevant ones at the beginning of the test while they're still fresh in your mind.

- **Read carefully.** Even if a problem seems easy, read it over a couple of times. Underline key words to help you stay on track.

- **Answer the questions you are sure of first.** If you are stuck, move on to the next question. Mark the questions you skip.

- **If time is running out, try not to panic.** Panicking only wastes time that could be used to finish a problem.

- **Never leave an answer blank.** Try to do some work on every question. You may receive partial credit. Take a fresh look at any problems you skipped the first time. An exception to this rule is when a guessing factor is used in scoring a multiple-choice test.

- **Double-check.** Make sure that you have answered all the questions that you can and that all of your answers make sense. Recheck your work carefully if you have time. Don't be in a rush to leave!

- **Only change your answers if you are sure they are wrong.** Do not rush through a problem a second time and quickly change your answer, but rethinking an answer you are uncertain about may help.

- **Check that all your answers are readable.** Be neat!

How to Use a Calculator on a Test _____

If a calculator is allowed during an exam, remember that it is only a tool. You are the problem solver and you must decide whether calculator answers are reasonable. Do not fail to study before a test or read carefully during a test just because you can use a calculator. If you are allowed to use a graphing calculator, your teacher may clear its memory before you begin the test. But your own memory should be clear on how to use your calculator effectively. Study the manual and practice.

In general, whether or not you use your calculator will depend on what type of answer you need. You should use your understanding of the material covered on the test to help you decide whether using the calculator will help you or whether it will slow you down.

■ Before you start pressing keys, ask yourself, *Can I do the problem in my head? Can I estimate?* These methods can be even faster and more reliable than using a calculator. Look at the numbers and think about the operations involved. Ask yourself questions such as, *Are these numbers part of a common Pythagorean Triple? Is this a special triangle (30°-60°-90° or 45°-45°-90°)?*

MORE HELP
See 153

■ When you do use the calculator, be sure to check all the calculator answers for reasonableness by estimating the answers.

■ For problems involving π, the choice may depend on the form required for the answer and the lengths involved. An answer in terms of π, in fraction form, or in decimal form may be required. The calculator may be quicker when the decimal form is required. If a length divisible by 7 is involved, using the approximation $\frac{22}{7}$ for π and pencil and paper may be quicker than using the calculator.

MORE HELP
See 174

■ Your calculator may be able to find roots. However, if you need an answer in radical form, it may be best not to use your calculator. Look at the numbers. You may be able to find the square root of a perfect square in your head.

■ If you are going to use your calculator for special operations, make sure you know how to use your calculator to produce correct answers. For example, to approximate right triangle trigonometric ratios, a graphing calculator must be in the degree mode.

MORE HELP
See 241, 389

■ Don't borrow a calculator you are unfamiliar with. Always use the type of calculator you have practiced with or you will waste time and risk making errors.

Tips for Multiple-Choice Tests

In a multiple-choice problem, there is usually one correct answer. If you read the problem carefully, think logically, and use your math sense, you can often eliminate one or two choices easily. Standardized college placement tests or tests required for state assessment contain two types of multiple-choice questions: standard multiple-choice questions and quantitative comparison questions.

The standard multiple-choice questions usually consist of a question and some choices. One choice may be *None of these* or *Cannot be determined*.

MORE HELP
See 190

EXAMPLE 1: What is the approximate length of the diameter of a circle that has an area of 28.26 square centimeters?

A. 3 cm   **B.** 6 cm
C. 9 cm   **D.** 9 cm^2
E. None of these

The answer is a length, so it can't be in square units; you can eliminate D. Now you can estimate using 3 for π in the formula for the area of a circle, $A = \pi r^2$.

$3 \times 3^2 = 27$, so choice A is the radius. Don't stop! The diameter is about 2×3, or 6 cm.

★ The answer is B.

The quantitative comparison questions consist of two quantities to be compared. Three of the choices are statements comparing the quantities. The fourth states that a comparison can't be made based on the given information.

MORE HELP
See 072,
075–080

EXAMPLE 2: Compare the sums of angles shown in the diagram.

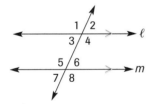

Column A	Column B
m∠1 + m∠2	m∠3 + m∠5

A. The quantity in Column A is greater.
B. The quantity in Column B is greater.
C. The two quantities are equal.
D. The relationship cannot be determined from the information given.

By the Linear Pair Postulate, ∠1 and ∠2 are supplementary. By the Same Side Interior Angles Theorem, ∠3 and ∠5 are also supplementary. This means m∠1 + m∠2 = 180°, and m∠3 + m∠5 = 180°.

★ The answer is C.

If you get stuck on a multiple-choice problem, skip it and go on to another problem. Make sure you mark it for later—use * for problems you think you can solve with a second look and ? for problems you're less sure of. When you go back, if you have time, go through each answer choice to see whether it could be correct.

Tips for Short Answer Tests

■ Answer the question that was asked. Show your solution.

■ Be very careful with your computation and include units of measure whenever needed.

■ Make sure your answer is in the form the directions ask for: simplest form, simplest radical form, in terms of π, rounded to the nearest tenth, rounded to the nearest degree, and so on.

■ Make sure you clearly label diagrams and constructions.

Problem	Solution/Check	Answer
A. Solve for x. $(2x + 4)°$ $(3x - 26)°$	$2x + 4 = 3x - 26$ $2x + 4 + 26 = 3x - 26 + 26$ $2x + 30 = 3x$ $2x - 2x + 30 = 3x - 2x$ $30 = x$ $2(30) + 4 \stackrel{?}{=} 3(30) - 26$ $64 = 64$	$x = 30°$
B. A 30°-60°-90° triangle has a hypotenuse of 8 centimeters. What is the area of this triangle? Write your answer in simplest radical form.	Find the base and height. $2x = 8$ cm $x = 4$ cm $\sqrt{3}x = 4\sqrt{3}$ Find the area. $A = \frac{1}{2}bh$ $= \frac{1}{2}(4)(4\sqrt{3})$ $= 8\sqrt{3}$	$8\sqrt{3}$ cm²
C. Copy figure *ABCD*. Draw its image after a clockwise rotation of 90° about *P*.	Use tracing paper to check.	

MORE HELP
See 072, 181, 239, 281

Tips for Constructed-Response Tests

If a problem asks you to explain your answer, include all the details needed to understand your thinking process. Grading is usually based on your answer *and* how you explain each step of the problem.

EXAMPLE: The vertices of a quadrilateral are $J(^-1, 2)$, $K(5, 5)$, $L(7, 1)$, and $M(1, ^-2)$. Without graphing the vertices, determine the most precise name for the quadrilateral. Explain your thinking.

MORE HELP
See 098, 156, 406

1. First determine whether any sides of *JKLM* are parallel. But don't stop here. Remember, you must determine the most precise name of the figure. If you stop here, you will only receive partial credit.

I can find the slope of each side of the quadrilateral to determine which sides, if any, are parallel.

Slope of $\overline{JK}$: $\dfrac{5 - 2}{5 - (^-1)} = \dfrac{3}{6} = \dfrac{1}{2}$

Slope of $\overline{KL}$: $\dfrac{1 - 5}{7 - 5} = \dfrac{^-4}{2} = ^-2$

Slope of $\overline{LM}$: $\dfrac{^-2 - 1}{1 - 7} = \dfrac{^-3}{^-6} = \dfrac{1}{2}$

Slope of $\overline{MJ}$: $\dfrac{2 - (^-2)}{^-1 - 1} = \dfrac{4}{^-2} = ^-2$

The slopes of parallel lines are equal, so $\overline{JK} \parallel \overline{LM}$ and $\overline{KL} \parallel \overline{MJ}$. Both pairs of opposite sides of JKLM are parallel, so JKLM is a parallelogram.

MORE HELP
See 162

2. A parallelogram with perpendicular sides is a rectangle. Is *JKLM* a rectangle?

The product of the slopes of perpendicular lines is $^-1$. $(\frac{1}{2})(^-2) = ^-1$, so $\overline{JK} \perp \overline{KL}$ and $\angle JKL$ is a right angle. Since parallelogram JKLM has a right angle, it is a rectangle.

MORE HELP
See 090, 164

3. A rectangle with sides of equal length is a square. Is *JKLM* a square?

I can use the Distance Formula to find the lengths of two adjacent sides.

$JK = \sqrt{[5 - (^-1)]^2 + (5 - 2)^2}$
$\quad = \sqrt{36 + 9}$
$\quad = \sqrt{45}$
$\quad = \sqrt{9 \cdot 5}$
$\quad = 3\sqrt{5}$

$KL = \sqrt{(7 - 5)^2 + (1 - 5)^2}$
$\quad = \sqrt{4 + 16}$
$\quad = \sqrt{20}$
$\quad = \sqrt{4 \cdot 5}$
$\quad = 2\sqrt{5}$

$\overline{JK}$ and $\overline{KL}$ are not congruent, so JKLM is not a square.

★The most precise name for *JKLM* is *rectangle*.

After a Test

- **Keep a record.** Record in your math journal how you study for tests. Compare how you prepared for the test with how the test turned out.

  - *Did you study all the topics for the test?*
  - *Did you cover each topic thoroughly?*
  - *Were you able to do different types of problems?*
  - *What types of practice exercises worked the best for you?*
  - *Did you learn all the theorems so you could use them in proofs?*

  Think about how you could improve your study habits, the way you study for a test, and how you actually take a test.

- **Correct the test and fill in the details.** If the teacher goes over the test in class, write the corrections with a different-color pencil or pen. Don't erase your original answers. Keep them there so you can figure out what went wrong. If you don't understand why an answer is wrong, ask your teacher after you've tried to figure it out yourself.

- **Evaluate the methods you used.** As you look through your test, consider whether you used appropriate strategies to solve problems. Think about whether alternate solution methods might have been easier or even possible.

  - *Did you use logical reasoning and math sense whenever you could?*
  - *Did you use a calculator and/or estimation when appropriate?*
  - *Were your mistakes computational or conceptual? Do you understand your error(s)?*
  - *Did you skip harder problems or only partially solve them when you studied?*

Use your test as a guide to how well you understand the topics tested. If you can identify what went wrong on your test and in your studying, you will be less likely to repeat the mistakes on future tests.

Handy Tables

416 **Degrees and Radians**

1 degree $= \dfrac{1}{360}$ of a circle

1 radian $= \dfrac{180°}{\pi} \approx 57.3°$

Degrees	30	45	60	90	120	180	270	360
Radians	$\dfrac{\pi}{6}$	$\dfrac{\pi}{4}$	$\dfrac{\pi}{3}$	$\dfrac{\pi}{2}$	$\dfrac{2\pi}{3}$	π	$\dfrac{3\pi}{2}$	2π

Plane Figures

Plane Figure	Number of Sides	Sum of Interior Angles $(n-2)180°$	Examples
triangle	3	180°	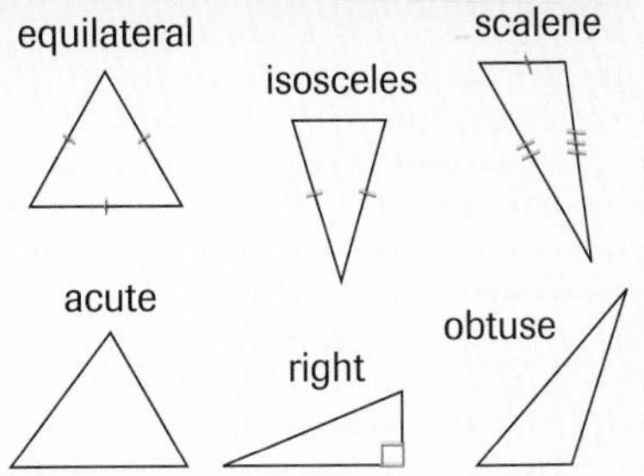 equilateral isosceles scalene acute right obtuse
quadrilateral	4	360°	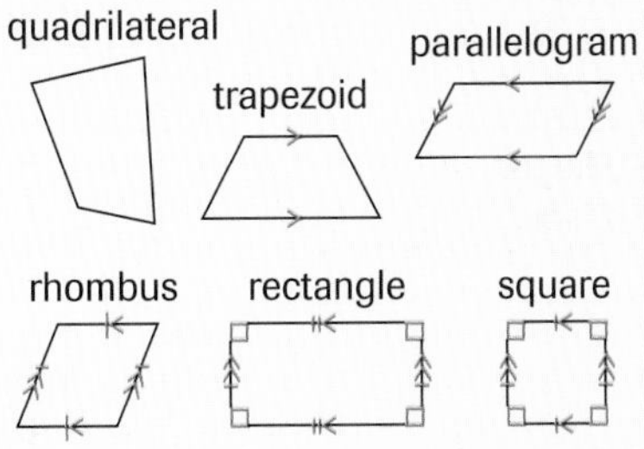 quadrilateral trapezoid parallelogram rhombus rectangle square
pentagon	5	540°	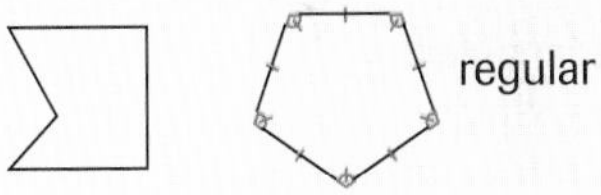 regular
hexagon	6	720°	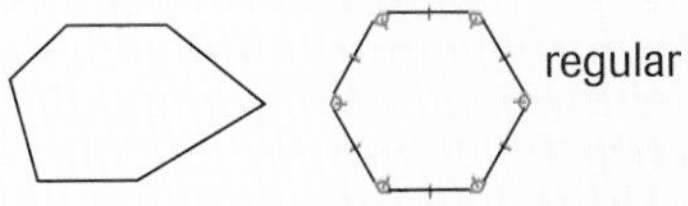 regular
heptagon or septagon	7	900°	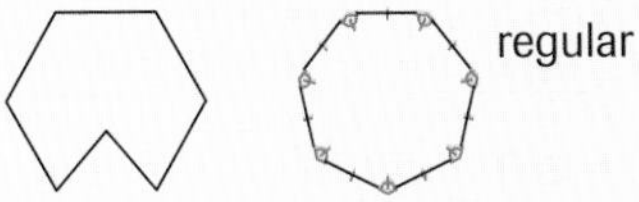 regular
octagon	8	1080°	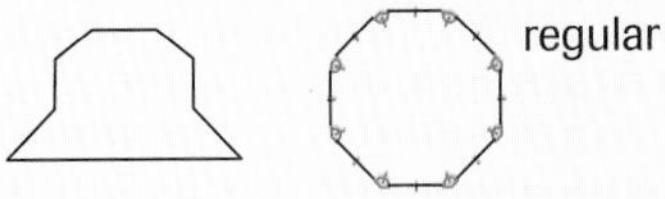 regular
nonagon	9	1260°	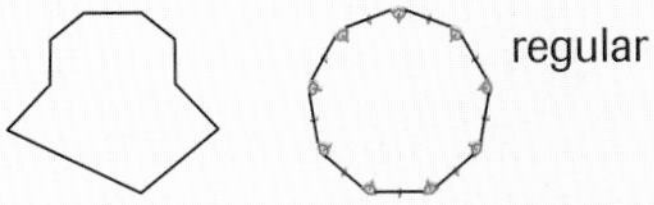 regular
decagon	10	1440°	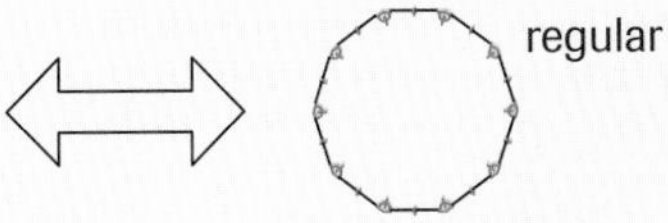 regular

MORE HELP
See 128

MORE HELP
See 133

MORE HELP
See 156

Geometric Solids

MORE HELP
See 322,
324–325

Polyhedron	Example	Net
cube (regular hexahedron)	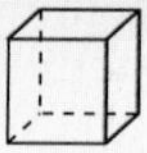	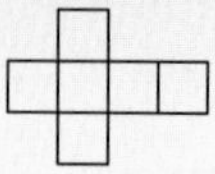
triangular prism	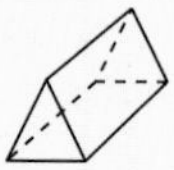	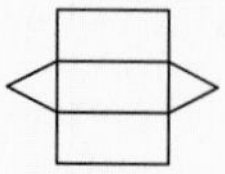
rectangular prism	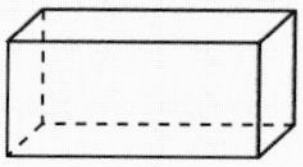	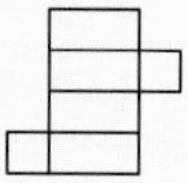
hexagonal prism	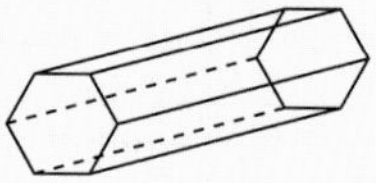	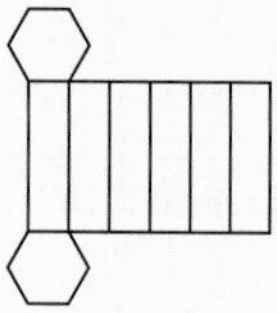
octagonal prism	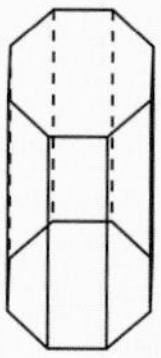	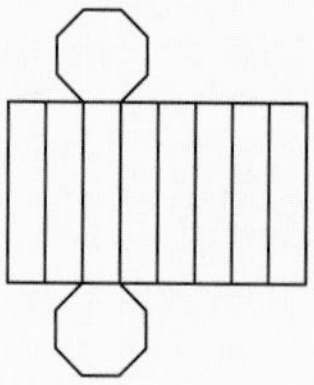
triangular pyramid (tetrahedron)	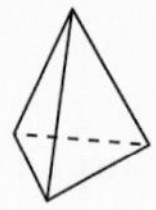	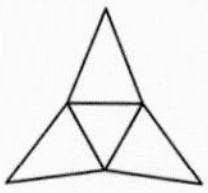
rectangular pyramid	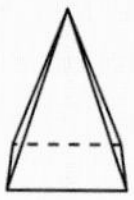	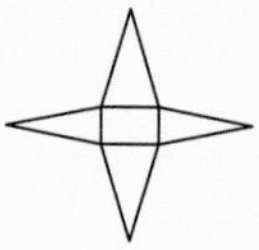

Polyhedron	Example	Net
pentagonal pyramid		
hexagonal pyramid		
octahedron		
dodecahedron		
cylinder		
cone		
sphere		

The Metric System

Linear Measure (length)		
1 centimeter	0.01 meter	0.3937 inch
1 decimeter	0.1 meter	3.937 inches
1 meter	1.0 meter	39.37 inches
1 dekameter	10 meters	32.8 feet
1 hectometer	100 meters	328 feet
1 kilometer	1000 meters	0.621 mile
1 myriameter	10,000 meters	6.21 miles

Capacity Measure		
1 centiliter	0.01 liter	0.338 fluid ounce
1 deciliter	0.1 liter	3.38 fluid ounces
1 liter	1.0 liter	1.0567 liquid quarts or 0.9081 dry quart
1 dekaliter	10 liters	2.642 gallons or 0.284 bushel
1 hectoliter	100 liters	26.42 gallons or 2.84 bushels
1 kiloliter	1000 liters	264.2 gallons or 35.315 cubic feet

Volume Measure		
1 cubic centimeter	1000 cubic millimeters	0.06102 cubic inch
1 cubic decimeter	1000 cubic centimeters	61.02 cubic inches
1 cubic meter	1000 cubic decimeters	35.315 cubic feet

Mass		
1 centigram	0.01 gram	0.0003527 ounce
1 decigram	0.1 gram	0.003527 ounce
1 gram	1.0 gram	0.03527 ounce
1 dekagram	10 grams	0.3527 ounce
1 hectogram	100 grams	3.527 ounces
1 kilogram	1000 grams	2.2046 pounds
1 myriagram	10,000 grams	22.046 pounds
1 quintal	100,000 grams	220.46 pounds
1 metric ton	1,000,000 grams	2204.6 pounds

Land Measure (area)		
1 centare	1 square meter	1.196 square yards
1 are	100 square meters	119.6 square yards
1 hectare	10,000 square meters	2.471 acres
1 square kilometer	1,000,000 square meters	0.386 square mile

The Customary System

Linear Measure (length)		
1 inch		2.54 centimeters
1 foot	12 inches	0.3048 meter
1 yard	3 feet	0.9144 meter
1 rod, (pole, or perch)	16.5 feet	5.029 meters
1 (statute) mile	5280 feet	1609.3 meters
1 (land) league	15,840 feet	4.83 kilometers

Square Measure (area)		
1 square foot	144 square inches	929.0304 square centimeters
1 square yard	9 square feet	0.8361 square meter
1 acre	43,560 square feet	4046.86 square meters

Cubic Measure		
1 cord foot	16 cubic feet	0.4531 cubic meter
1 cord	128 cord feet	3.625 cubic meters

Dry Measure (capacity, volume)			
1 pint		33.60 cubic inches	0.5505 liter
1 quart	2 pints	67.20 cubic inches	1.1012 liters
1 peck	16 pints	537.61 cubic inches	8.8096 liters
1 bushel	64 pints	2150.42 cubic inches	35.2383 liters

Liquid Measure			
1 fluid ounce	0.25 gill	1.8047 cubic inches	0.0296 liter
1 gill	4 fluid ounces	7.219 cubic inches	0.1183 liter
1 cup	8 fluid ounces	14.438 cubic inches	0.2366 liter
1 pint	16 fluid ounces	28.875 cubic inches	0.4732 liter
1 quart	32 fluid ounces	57.75 cubic inches	0.9463 liter
1 gallon	128 fluid ounces	231 cubic inches	3.7853 liters

Circular (or Angular) Measure			
60 seconds	1 minute	90 degrees	1 quadrant or 1 right angle
60 minutes	1 degree	4 quadrants or 360 degrees	1 complete rotation about a point

Weight (avoirdupois)		
1 grain	0.0001426 pound	0.0648 gram
1 dram	0.00390 pound	1.772 grams
1 ounce	0.0625 pound	28.3495 grams
1 pound	16 ounces	453.59 grams
1 hundredweight	100 pounds	45.359 kilograms
1 ton	2000 pounds	907.18 kilograms

Table of Powers and Roots

n	n^2	$\sqrt{n}$	n^3	$\sqrt[3]{n}$	n	n^2	$\sqrt{n}$	n^3	$\sqrt[3]{n}$
1	1	1.000	1	1.000	51	2601	7.141	132,651	3.708
2	4	1.414	8	1.260	52	2704	7.211	140,608	3.733
3	9	1.732	27	1.442	53	2809	7.280	148,877	3.756
4	16	2.000	64	1.587	54	2916	7.348	157,464	3.780
5	25	2.236	125	1.710	55	3025	7.416	166,375	3.803
6	36	2.449	216	1.817	56	3136	7.483	175,616	3.826
7	49	2.646	343	1.913	57	3249	7.550	185,193	3.849
8	64	2.828	512	2.000	58	3364	7.616	195,112	3.871
9	81	3.000	729	2.080	59	3481	7.681	205,379	3.893
10	100	3.162	1000	2.154	60	3600	7.746	216,000	3.915
11	121	3.317	1331	2.224	61	3721	7.810	226,981	3.936
12	144	3.464	1728	2.289	62	3844	7.874	238,328	3.958
13	169	3.606	2197	2.351	63	3969	7.937	250,047	3.979
14	196	3.742	2744	2.410	64	4096	8.000	262,144	4.000
15	225	3.873	3375	2.466	65	4225	8.062	274,625	4.021
16	256	4.000	4096	2.520	66	4356	8.124	287,496	4.041
17	289	4.123	4913	2.571	67	4489	8.185	300,763	4.062
18	324	4.243	5832	2.621	68	4624	8.246	314,432	4.082
19	361	4.359	6859	2.668	69	4761	8.307	328,509	4.102
20	400	4.472	8000	2.714	70	4900	8.367	343,000	4.121
21	441	4.583	9261	2.759	71	5041	8.426	357,911	4.141
22	484	4.690	10,648	2.802	72	5184	8.485	373,248	4.160
23	529	4.796	12,167	2.844	73	5329	8.544	389,017	4.179
24	576	4.899	13,824	2.884	74	5476	8.602	405,224	4.198
25	625	5.000	15,625	2.924	75	5625	8.660	421,875	4.217
26	676	5.099	17,576	2.962	76	5776	8.718	438,976	4.236
27	729	5.196	19,683	3.000	77	5929	8.775	456,533	4.254
28	784	5.292	21,952	3.037	78	6084	8.832	474,522	4.273
29	841	5.385	24,389	3.072	79	6241	8.888	493,039	4.291
30	900	5.477	27,000	3.107	80	6400	8.944	512,000	4.309
31	961	5.568	29,791	3.141	81	6561	9.000	531,441	4.327
32	1024	5.657	32,768	3.175	82	6724	9.055	551,368	4.344
33	1089	5.745	35,937	3.208	83	6889	9.110	571,787	4.362
34	1156	5.831	39,304	3.240	84	7056	9.165	592,704	4.380
35	1225	5.916	42,875	3.271	85	7225	9.220	614,125	4.397
36	1296	6.000	46,656	3.302	86	7396	9.274	636,056	4.414
37	1369	6.083	50,653	3.332	87	7569	9.327	658,503	4.431
38	1444	6.164	54,872	3.362	88	7744	9.381	681,472	4.448
39	1521	6.245	59,319	3.391	89	7921	9.434	704,969	4.465
40	1600	6.325	64,000	3.420	90	8100	9.487	729,000	4.481
41	1681	6.403	68,921	3.448	91	8281	9.539	753,571	4.498
42	1764	6.481	74,088	3.476	92	8464	9.592	778,688	4.514
43	1849	6.557	79,507	3.503	93	8649	9.644	804,357	4.531
44	1936	6.633	85,184	3.530	94	8836	9.695	830,584	4.547
45	2025	6.708	91,125	3.557	95	9025	9.747	857,375	4.563
46	2116	6.782	97,336	3.583	96	9216	9.798	884,736	4.579
47	2209	6.856	103,823	3.609	97	9409	9.849	912,673	4.595
48	2304	6.928	110,592	3.634	98	9604	9.899	941,192	4.610
49	2401	7.000	117,649	3.659	99	9801	9.950	970,299	4.626
50	2500	7.071	125,000	3.684	100	10,000	10.000	1,000,000	4.642

(Roots are rounded to the nearest thousandth.)

Trigonometric Functions

Angle	Sine	Cosine	Tangent	Angle	Sine	Cosine	Tangent
1°	.0175	.9998	.0175	46°	.7193	.6947	1.0355
2°	.0349	.9994	.0349	47°	.7314	.6820	1.0724
3°	.0523	.9986	.0524	48°	.7431	.6691	1.1106
4°	.0698	.9976	.0699	49°	.7547	.6561	1.1504
5°	.0872	.9962	.0875	50°	.7660	.6428	1.1918
6°	.1045	.9945	.1051	51°	.7771	.6293	1.2349
7°	.1219	.9925	.1228	52°	.7880	.6157	1.2799
8°	.1392	.9903	.1405	53°	.7986	.6018	1.3270
9°	.1564	.9877	.1584	54°	.8090	.5878	1.3764
10°	.1736	.9848	.1763	55°	.8192	.5736	1.4281
11°	.1908	.9816	.1944	56°	.8290	.5592	1.4826
12°	.2079	.9781	.2126	57°	.8387	.5446	1.5399
13°	.2250	.9744	.2309	58°	.8480	.5299	1.6003
14°	.2419	.9703	.2493	59°	.8572	.5150	1.6643
15°	.2588	.9659	.2679	60°	.8660	.5000	1.7321
16°	.2756	.9613	.2867	61°	.8746	.4848	1.8040
17°	.2924	.9563	.3057	62°	.8829	.4695	1.8807
18°	.3090	.9511	.3249	63°	.8910	.4540	1.9626
19°	.3256	.9455	.3443	64°	.8988	.4384	2.0503
20°	.3420	.9397	.3640	65°	.9063	.4226	2.1445
21°	.3584	.9336	.3839	66°	.9135	.4067	2.2460
22°	.3746	.9272	.4040	67°	.9205	.3907	2.3559
23°	.3907	.9205	.4245	68°	.9272	.3746	2.4751
24°	.4067	.9135	.4452	69°	.9336	.3584	2.6051
25°	.4226	.9063	.4663	70°	.9397	.3420	2.7475
26°	.4384	.8988	.4877	71°	.9455	.3256	2.9042
27°	.4540	.8910	.5095	72°	.9511	.3090	3.0777
28°	.4695	.8829	.5317	73°	.9563	.2924	3.2709
29°	.4848	.8746	.5543	74°	.9613	.2756	3.4874
30°	.5000	.8660	.5774	75°	.9659	.2588	3.7321
31°	.5150	.8572	.6009	76°	.9703	.2419	4.0108
32°	.5299	.8480	.6249	77°	.9744	.2250	4.3315
33°	.5446	.8387	.6494	78°	.9781	.2079	4.7046
34°	.5592	.8290	.6745	79°	.9816	.1908	5.1446
35°	.5736	.8192	.7002	80°	.9848	.1736	5.6713
36°	.5878	.8090	.7265	81°	.9877	.1564	6.3138
37°	.6018	.7986	.7536	82°	.9903	.1392	7.1154
38°	.6157	.7880	.7813	83°	.9925	.1219	8.1443
39°	.6293	.7771	.8098	84°	.9945	.1045	9.5144
40°	.6428	.7660	.8391	85°	.9962	.0872	11.4301
41°	.6561	.7547	.8693	86°	.9976	.0698	14.3007
42°	.6691	.7431	.9004	87°	.9986	.0523	19.0811
43°	.6820	.7314	.9325	88°	.9994	.0349	28.6363
44°	.6947	.7193	.9657	89°	.9998	.0175	57.2900
45°	.7071	.7071	1.000				

(Trigonometric values are rounded to the nearest ten-thousandth.)

Geometry Topics for Science Fairs _____

Explore Geometry in:
- Art
- Architecture
- Biology
- Design
- Engineering
- Games and Puzzles
- Nature
- Sculpture
- Space
- Sports

Try these Research Topics:
- Archimedes' Principle
- Astrolabes
- Boomerangs
- Carpenters' Tools and Technologies
- Conjectures
- Constructibility
- Computer Programs That Use If...Then... Form
- Egyptian Pyramids
- Gem Cutting
- Golden Rectangles
- Figurate Numbers
- Fractals
- Geodesic Domes
- Geometric Dissections
- Global Positioning Systems
- Indirect Measurement
- Islamic Art
- Isosceles Triangle Fallacy
- Isometrics
- Klein Bottle and Other Topological Curiosities
- Knot Design

- Latitude and Longitude
- Logic
- The Lune of Hippocrates
- Mandalas
- The Mandelbrot Set
- Maps and Map-making
- Mathematical Modeling
- The Nine Point Circle
- Non-Euclidean Geometries
- Optical Illusions
- Optimizing Area and Perimeter
- Orthocenters
- Parabolic Envelope
- Pi
- Pick's Theorem
- Sierpinski Triangle
- String Sculptures
- Surveying
- Tessellations
- Traveling Networks
- Transformations
- Vectors

Bibliography

Allinger, Glenn D., et al. *Mathematics Projects Handbook*, Fourth Edition. Reston, VA: National Council of Teachers of Mathematics.

Barr, S. *Experiments in Topology*. New York: Thomas Y. Crowell.

Blackwell, William. *Geometry in Architecture*. New York: John Wiley & Sons, Inc.

Boles, M., and Newman, R. *The Golden Relationship*. Bradford, MA: Pythagorean Press.

Downs, J. W. *Practical Conic Sections*. Palo Alto: Dale Seymour Publications.

Escher, M.C. *The Graphic Work of M.C. Escher*. New York: Hawthorne Publishing.

Garland, Trudi. *Fascinating Fibonnacci's: Magic and Mystery in Numbers*. Palo Alto: Dale Seymour Publications. **MORE ▶**

Jacobs, Harold. *Mathematics: A Human Endeavor*. San Francisco: W.H. Freeman and Co.

Johnson, Art. *Classic Math: History Topics for the Classroom*. Palo Alto: Dale Seymour Publications.

Lyng, Merwin J. *Dancing Curves: A Dynamic Demonstration of Geometric Principles*. Reston, VA: National Council of Teachers of Mathematics.

National Council of Teachers of Mathematics. *Historical Topics for the Mathematics Classroom*. Reston, VA: National Council of Teachers of Mathematics.

Seymour, Dale. *Introduction to Line Designs*. Palo Alto: Dale Seymour Publications.

Wenninger, Magnus J. *Polyhedron Models for the Classroom (Second edition)*. Reston, VA: National Council of Teachers of Mathematics.

Famous Geometricians To Read About

- Appolonius of Perga
- Archimedes of Syracuse *(see 303, 325, and 381)*
- Janos Bolyai *(see 368)*
- L. E. J. Brouwer
- Francesco Cavalieri *(see 206)*
- Arthur Cayley
- Leonardo da Vinci
- René Descartes *(see 087)*
- Eratosthenes *(see 176)*
- Maurits Escher *(see 296)*
- Euclid *(see 060 and 364)*
- Leonhard Euler *(084 and 323)*
- Pierre Fermat
- Buckminster Fuller
- Leonardo of Pisa (Fibonacci)
- Carl Friedrich Gauss *(see 368)*
- Hero of Alexandria *(see 182)*
- David Hilbert
- Hipparchos of Nicea

- Hypatia
- Felix Klein *(see 364)*
- Nicolai I. Lobachevsky *(see 368)*
- Benoit B. Mandelbrot *(see 254)*
- Augustus Ferdinand Möbius
- Blaise Pascal
- Plato *(see 324)*
- Henri Poincaré *(see 368)*
- Jean Victor Poncelet
- Ptolemy *(see 240)*
- Pythagoras *(see 152 and 251)*
- Georg Friedrich Bernhard Riemann *(see 364)*
- Ludwig Schläfi *(see 364)*
- Waclaw Sierpinski
- Thales *(see 227)*
- Pierre M. van Hiele

Yellow Pages

Glossary of Mathematical Formulas

Coordinate Plane

MORE HELP	Number	Formula	Variables and Symbols
089	F01	In the coordinate plane, the midpoint of a segment is $\left(\dfrac{x_1 + x_2}{2}, \dfrac{y_1 + y_2}{2}\right)$.	(x_1, y_1): one endpoint of the segment (x_2, y_2): other endpoint of the segment
090	F02	In the coordinate plane, the distance between two points is $d = \sqrt{(x_2 - x_1)^2 + (y_2 - y_1)^2}$.	d: distance (x_1, y_1): first point (x_2, y_2): second point
092	F03	The distance between a line and a point not on that line is $d = \dfrac{|ax_1 + by_1 + c|}{\sqrt{a^2 + b^2}}$.	d: distance $ax + by + c = 0$: equation of the line (x_1, y_1): point not on the line a, b, c: real numbers
099	F04	The slope of a line is $m = \dfrac{y_2 - y_1}{x_2 - x_1}$.	m: slope (x_1, y_1): one point on the line (x_2, y_2): a second point on the line
103–104	F05	The slope of a line, $ax + by + c = 0$, is $m = \dfrac{^-a}{b}$.	m: slope $ax + by + c = 0$: equation of the line a, b, c: real numbers
111	F06	On the graph of an equation in the form $y = ax^2 + bx + c$, the x-coordinate of the vertex is $\dfrac{^-b}{2a}$.	$y = ax^2 + bx + c$: equation of the curve a, b, c: real numbers
113	F07	A circle is the set of points satisfying the equation $(x - h)^2 + (y - k)^2 = r^2$.	(h, k): center of circle r: radius of circle (x, y): a point on the circle
123	F08	In a three-dimensional coordinate system, the distance between two points is $d = \sqrt{(x_2 - x_1)^2 + (y_2 - y_1)^2 + (z_2 - z_1)^2}$.	d: distance (x_1, y_1, z_1): first point (x_2, y_2, z_2): second point
124	F09	In a three-dimensional coordinate system, the midpoint of a line segment is $\left(\dfrac{x_1 + x_2}{2}, \dfrac{y_1 + y_2}{2}, \dfrac{z_1 + z_2}{2}\right)$.	(x_1, y_1, z_1): one endpoint of the segment (x_2, y_2, z_2): other endpoint of the segment
125	F10	In a three-dimensional coordinate system, a sphere is the set of points satisfying the equation $(x - h)^2 + (y - j)^2 + (z - k)^2 = r^2$.	(h, j, k): center of sphere r: radius of sphere (x, y, z): a point on the sphere

Angles in Polygons

Number	Formula	Variables and Symbols	MORE HELP
F11	The sum of the measures of the interior angles of a convex n-gon is $180°(n - 2)$.	n: number of sides of polygon	131
F12	The measure of each interior angle of a regular n-gon is $\dfrac{180°(n - 2)}{n}$.	n: number of sides of polygon	131
F13	The sum of the measures of the exterior angles of an n-gon is $360°$.	n: number of sides of polygon	132
F14	The measure of each exterior angle of a regular n-gon is $\dfrac{360°}{n}$.	n: number of sides of polygon	132

Perimeter and Circumference

Number	Formula	Variables and Symbols	MORE HELP
F15	The perimeter of an n-gon is $P = s_1 + s_2 + \ldots + s_n$.	P: perimeter n: number of sides of polygon $s_1, s_2, \ldots s_n$: lengths of sides of polygon	170
F16	The perimeter of a rectangle or parallelogram is $P = 2\ell + 2w$.	P: perimeter ℓ: length of one side w: length of adjacent side	170
F17	The perimeter of a square or rhombus is $P = 4s$.	P: perimeter s: length of each side	170
F18	The perimeter of a regular n-gon is $P = ns$.	P: perimeter n: number of sides of polygon s: length of each side	170
F19	The perimeter of a regular n-gon inscribed in a unit circle is $P = 2n \sin\left(\dfrac{180°}{n}\right)$.	P: perimeter n: number of sides of polygon	172
F20	The circumference of a circle is $C = \pi d$ and $C = 2\pi r$.	C: circumference d: diameter r: radius π: pi (about 3.14 or $\frac{22}{7}$)	176
F21	In a circle, the ratio of the length of a given arc to the circumference is equal to the ratio of the measure of the arc to $360°$: $\dfrac{a}{C} = \dfrac{m\widehat{AB}}{360°}$ or $a = \dfrac{m\widehat{AB}}{360°} \cdot 2\pi r$ or $a = \dfrac{m\widehat{AB}}{360°} \cdot \pi d$.	a: arc length C: circumference A and B: endpoints of arc r: radius d: diameter π: pi (about 3.14 or $\frac{22}{7}$)	177

Area of Plane Figures

MORE HELP	Number	Formula	Variables and Symbols
180	F22	The area of a square is the square of the length of its side: $A = s^2$.	A: area s: length of a side
180	F23	The area of a rectangle is the product of its length and width: $A = \ell w$.	A: area ℓ: length of one side w: length of an adjacent side
181	F24	The area of a triangle is half the product of a base and its corresponding height: $A = \frac{1}{2}bh$.	A: area b: length of base h: length of corresponding altitude
181	F25	The area of a triangle is equal to half the product of any two sides and the sine of the included angle: $A = \frac{1}{2}ab \sin C$.	A: area a: length of one side b: length of second side C: measure of included angle
182	F26	**Hero's Formula:** The area of a triangle is $A = \sqrt{s(s-a)(s-b)(s-c)}$.	A: area s: semiperimeter $\left(\frac{1}{2} \cdot \text{perimeter}\right)$ a, b, and c: lengths of sides
183	F27	The area of a parallelogram is the product of a base and its corresponding height: $A = bh$.	A: area b: length of base h: length of corresponding altitude
184	F28	The area of a regular polygon is half the product of the apothem and the perimeter: $A = \frac{1}{2}aP$.	A: area a: length of apothem P: perimeter
185	F29	The area of an equilateral triangle is one-fourth the square of the length of a side times $\sqrt{3}$: $A = \frac{s^2\sqrt{3}}{4}$.	A: area s: length of a side
187	F30	If the diagonals of a quadrilateral are perpendicular, then the area is half the product of the length of the diagonals: $A = \frac{1}{2}d_1 d_2$.	A: area d_1: length of one diagonal d_2: length of other diagonal
188	F31	The area of a trapezoid is half the product of the height and the sum of the bases: $A = \frac{1}{2}h(b_1 + b_2)$.	A: area h: length of perpendicular segment between bases b_1: length of one base b_2: length of other base
190	F32	The area of a circle is π times the square of the radius: $A = \pi r^2$.	A: area r: radius π: pi (about 3.14 or $\frac{22}{7}$)

Area of Plane Figures: (continued)

Number	Formula	Variables and Symbols	MORE HELP
F33	The ratio of the area of a sector to the area of its circle is equal to the ratio of the measure of the intercepted arc to 360°: $\dfrac{A}{\pi r^2} = \dfrac{m\overset{\frown}{RQ}}{360°}$.	A: area of sector r: radius of circle R and Q: endpoints of intercepted arc π: pi (about 3.14 or $\frac{22}{7}$)	191
F34	The area of a segment is: area of sector − area of triangle formed by the chord and its two radii.		192

Surface Area

Number	Formula	Variables and Symbols	MORE HELP
F35	The surface area of a right prism is $SA = 2B + Ph$.	SA: surface area B: area of a base P: perimeter of a base h: length of altitude of prism	196
F36	The surface area of a right cylinder is $SA = 2B + Ch$ and $SA = 2\pi r^2 + 2\pi rh$.	SA: surface area B: area of a base C: circumference of a base h: length of altitude of cylinder r: radius of a base π: pi (about 3.14 or $\frac{22}{7}$)	197
F37	The surface area of a right cone is $SA = \pi r^2 + \pi r\ell$.	SA: surface area r: radius of the base ℓ: slant height of cone π: pi (about 3.14 or $\frac{22}{7}$)	198
F38	The surface area of a regular pyramid is $SA = B + \frac{1}{2}P\ell$.	SA: surface area B: area of the base P: perimeter of the base ℓ: slant height of pyramid	199
F39	The surface area of a sphere is $SA = 4\pi r^2$.	SA: surface area r: radius π: pi (about 3.14 or $\frac{22}{7}$)	201

MORE HELP	Number	Formula	Variables and Symbols
207	F40	The volume of a cube is the cube of the length of its side: $V = s^3$.	V: volume s: length of a side
207	F41	The volume of a prism is $V = Bh$.	V: volume B: area of a base h: length of altitude of prism
207	F42	The volume of a rectangular solid is $V = \ell wh$.	V: volume ℓ: one dimension of solid w: second dimension of solid h: third dimension of solid
208	F43	The volume of a cylinder is $V = Bh$ and $V = \pi r^2 h$.	V: volume B: area of a base h: length of altitude of cylinder r: radius of a base π: pi (about 3.14 or $\frac{22}{7}$)
209	F44	The volume of a pyramid is $V = \frac{1}{3}Bh$.	V: volume B: area of a base h: length of altitude of pyramid
209	F45	The volume of a cone is $V = \frac{1}{3}Bh$ and $V = \frac{1}{3}\pi r^2 h$.	V: volume B: area of base h: length of altitude of cone r: radius of base π: pi (about 3.14 or $\frac{22}{7}$)
210	F46	The volume of a sphere is $V = \frac{4}{3}\pi r^3$.	V: volume r: radius π: pi (about 3.14 or $\frac{22}{7}$)

Diagonal of Rectangular Solid

MORE HELP	Number	Formula	Variables and Symbols
326	F47	In a rectangular solid the length of the diagonal is $d = \sqrt{\ell^2 + w^2 + h^2}$.	d: length of diagonal ℓ: one dimension of solid w: second dimension of solid h: third dimension of solid

Missing Measures in Right Triangles

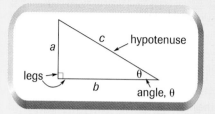

Formula	Variables and Symbols	MORE HELP
Pythagorean Theorem (T059): In a right triangle, the square of the length of the hypotenuse is equal to the sum of the squares of the lengths of the legs: $c^2 = a^2 + b^2$.	c: length of the hypotenuse a: length of one leg b: length of other leg	152
In a right triangle, the sine of an angle is the ratio of the length of the leg opposite the angle to the length of the hypotenuse: $\sin \theta = \frac{a}{c}$.	θ: measure of reference angle a: length of leg opposite θ c: length of hypotenuse	241
In a right triangle, the cosine of an angle is the ratio of the length of the leg adjacent to the angle to the length of the hypotenuse: $\cos \theta = \frac{b}{c}$.	θ: measure of reference angle b: length of leg adjacent to θ c: length of hypotenuse	241
In a right triangle, the tangent of an angle is the ratio of the length of the leg opposite the angle to the length of the leg adjacent to the angle: $\tan \theta = \frac{a}{b}$.	θ: measure of reference angle a: length of leg opposite θ b: length of leg adjacent to θ	241

Converting Coordinates

Formula	Variables and symbols	MORE HELP
When converting polar coordinates to rectangular coordinates, $x = r \cos \theta$ and $y = r \sin \theta$.	(r, θ): polar coordinates (x, y): rectangular coordinates	119
When converting rectangular coordinates to polar coordinates $r^2 = x^2 + y^2$ and $\tan \theta = \frac{y}{x}$.	(x, y): rectangular coordinates (r, θ): polar coordinates	120

MORE HELP	Number	Postulate
049	P01	A plane contains at least three noncollinear points.
049	P02	If two distinct points lie in a plane, then the line containing them lies in the plane.
049	P03	If two distinct planes intersect, then their intersection is a line.
051	P04	Three noncollinear points determine a plane.
054	P05	Through any two distinct points there exists exactly one line.
054	P06	A line contains at least two points.
054	P07	If two distinct lines intersect, then their intersection is exactly one point.
055	P08	**Ruler Postulate:** The points on a line can be matched, one-to-one, with the set of real numbers. The coordinate of a point is the real number that corresponds to it. The distance between two points, A and B, equals $\lvert a - b \rvert$. $AD = \lvert a - d \rvert$
057	P09	**Segment Addition Postulate:** Point B lies between points A and C if and only if $AB + BC = AC$.
060, 364	P10	**Parallel Postulate:** If there is a line and a point not on the line, then there is exactly one line through the point and parallel to the given line.
061	P11	**Perpendicular Postulate:** If there is a line and a point not on the line, then there is exactly one line through the point and perpendicular to the given line.
064	P12	**Protractor Postulate:** Rays from point O on $\overrightarrow{OA}$ to any point B can be matched one-to-one with the real numbers from 0 to 180. The measure of $\angle AOB$ is the absolute value of the difference between the numbers matched with $\overrightarrow{OA}$ and $\overrightarrow{OB}$. $m\angle AOB = \lvert 0 - 80 \rvert° = 80°$
065	P13	**Angle Addition Postulate:** If B is in the interior of $\angle AOC$, then $m\angle AOB + m\angle BOC = m\angle AOC$. $m\angle AOB + m\angle BOC = m\angle AOC$
070	P14	**Linear Pair Postulate:** If two angles form a linear pair, then they are supplementary; the sum of their measures is 180°. AC is a line $m\angle AOB + m\angle BOC = 180°$

Number	Postulate	
P15	**Corresponding Angles Postulate:** If two parallel lines are cut by a transversal, then the pairs of corresponding angles are congruent.	076
P16	**Converse of Corresponding Angles Postulate:** If two lines are cut by a transversal so that corresponding angles are congruent, then the lines are parallel.	076
P17	**Area Congruence Postulate:** If two polygons are congruent, then they have the same area.	178
P18	**Area Addition Postulate:** The area of a region is the sum of the areas of all of its non-overlapping parts. $A(ABCDEFGHI) = A(BCDE) + A(AFGI) + A(GHI)$	178
P19	**Volume Congruence Postulate:** If two polyhedrons are congruent, then they have the same volume.	205
P20	**Volume Addition Postulate:** The volume of a solid is the sum of the volumes of all of its non-overlapping parts.	205
P21	**AA Similarity Postulate:** If two angles of one triangle are congruent to two angles of another triangle, then the two triangles are similar.	227
P22	**SSS Congruence Postulate:** If three sides of one triangle are congruent to three sides of a second triangle, then the two triangles are congruent.	261
P23	**SAS Congruence Postulate:** If two sides and the included angle of one triangle are congruent to two sides and the included angle of a second triangle, then the two triangles are congruent.	262
P24	**Arc Addition Postulate:** The measure of an arc formed by two adjacent arcs is the sum of the measures of the two arcs. $m\widehat{AC} = m\widehat{AB} + m\widehat{BC}$	312
P25	In the same circle, or in congruent circles, two arcs are congruent if and only if their central angles are congruent. $m\widehat{AB} = m\widehat{CD}$ $\angle ACB \cong \angle COD$ $\widehat{AB} \cong \widehat{CD}$	313
P26	**Spherical Parallel Postulate:** Through a given point not on a given line there are no lines parallel to the given line.	364
P27	**Hyperbolic Parallel Postulate:** Through a given point not on a given line there is more than one line parallel to the given line.	368

Glossary of Theorems

Number	Theorem

T001 — On a number line, the coordinate of the midpoint of the segment with endpoints A and B is $\dfrac{a+b}{2}$.

T002 — **Perpendicular Bisector Theorem:** If a point is on the perpendicular bisector of a segment, then it is equidistant from the endpoints of the segment.

$AC = BC$

T003 — **Converse of Perpendicular Bisector Theorem:** If a point is equidistant from the endpoints of a segment, then it is on the perpendicular bisector of the segment.

T004 — The distance between two parallel lines is constant.

Don't forget, distance is always the length of a perpendicular segment!

T005 — If two parallel planes are cut by a third plane, then the lines of intersection are parallel.

T006 — If two or more lines are perpendicular to the same plane, then they are parallel.

T007 — If two planes are perpendicular to the same line, then they are parallel.

T008 — **Transitive Property of Parallel Lines:** If two lines are parallel to the same line, then they are parallel to each other.

T009 — If three parallel lines intersect two transversals, then they divide the transversals proportionally.

$\dfrac{AB}{BC} = \dfrac{DE}{EF}$

T010 — If two coplanar lines are perpendicular to the same line, then they are parallel to each other.

T011 — If two lines are perpendicular, then they intersect to form four right angles.

T012 — If two lines intersect to form adjacent, congruent angles, then the lines are perpendicular.

T013 — **Perpendicular Transversal Theorem:** If a transversal is perpendicular to one of two parallel lines, then it is perpendicular to the other.

T014 — Every segment has exactly two symmetry lines: (1) its perpendicular bisector, and (2) the line containing the segment.

Number	Theorem	MORE HELP
T015	If a line is perpendicular to each of two intersecting lines at their point of intersection, then the line is perpendicular to the plane determined by these two intersecting lines. ℓ is perpendicular to ℓ_1 and ℓ_2 at their intersection, so ℓ is also perpendicular to the plane determined by ℓ_1 and ℓ_2.	061
T016	There is one and only one line perpendicular to a plane at a point in the plane.	061
T017	There is one and only one line perpendicular to a plane from a point not in the plane.	061
T018	All the perpendiculars to a line, at a point on the line, lie in a plane that is perpendicular to the line at that point.	061
T019	If a line is perpendicular to a plane, then every plane that contains the line is perpendicular to that plane.	061
T020	All right angles are congruent.	064
T021	If two angles are complements of the same angle or congruent angles, then the angles are congruent.	068
T022	If two angles are supplements of the same angle or congruent angles, then the angles are congruent.	069
T023	Vertical angles are congruent.	072
T024	**Angle Bisector Theorem:** If a point is on the bisector of an angle, then it is equidistant from the sides of the angle.	073
T025	**Converse of Angle Bisector Theorem:** If a point in the interior of an angle is equidistant from the sides of the angle, then it lies on the bisector of the angle.	073
T026	**Angle Symmetry Theorem:** The line containing the bisector of an angle is a line of symmetry for the angle.	073
T027	**Alternate Interior Angles Theorem:** If two parallel lines are cut by a transversal, then the pairs of alternate interior angles are congruent.	077

	Number	Theorem
MORE HELP 077	T028	**Converse of Alternate Interior Angles Theorem:** If, when two lines are cut by a transversal, alternate interior angles are congruent, then the lines are parallel.
078	T029	**Alternate Exterior Angles Theorem:** If two parallel lines are cut by a transversal, then the pairs of alternate exterior angles are congruent.
078	T030	**Converse of Alternate Exterior Angles Theorem:** If, when two lines are cut by a transversal, alternate exterior angles are congruent, then the lines are parallel.
079	T031	**Same Side Interior Angles Theorem:** If two parallel lines are cut by a transversal, then the pairs of interior angles on the same side of the transversal are supplementary. $m\angle 1 + m\angle 2 = 180°$
079	T032	**Converse of Same Side Interior Angles Theorem:** If, when two lines are cut by a transversal, the interior angles on the same side of the transversal are supplementary, then the lines are parallel.
080	T033	**Same Side Exterior Angles Theorem:** If two parallel lines are cut by a transversal, then the pairs of exterior angles on the same side of the transversal are supplementary. $m\angle 1 + m\angle 2 = 180°$
080	T034	**Converse of Same Side Exterior Angles Theorem:** If, when two lines are cut by a transversal, exterior angles on the same side of the transversal are supplementary, then the lines are parallel.
085	T035	**Euler's Network Theorem:** A network is traceable if and only if it is connected and has at most two nodes of odd degree.
107	T036	Two nonvertical lines are parallel if and only if they have the same slope.
108	T037	Two nonvertical lines are perpendicular if and only if the product of their slopes is ⁻1.
129	T038	In any regular polygon, there is a point (its center) which is equidistant from all of its vertices.

Number	Theorem	MORE HELP
T039	Every regular *n*-gon contains: (1) *n* lines of symmetry, which are the perpendicular bisectors of each of its sides and the bisectors of each of its angles, and (2) *n*-fold rotational symmetry. An equilateral triangle has three lines of symmetry and three-fold rotational symmetry. A square has four lines of symmetry and four-fold rotational symmetry.	129
T040	The medians of a triangle are concurrent. Their common point, the centroid, is two thirds of the distance from each vertex to the midpoint of the opposite side.	136
T041	The lines containing the altitudes of a triangle are concurrent at the orthocenter.	137
T042	The lines containing the perpendicular bisectors of a triangle are concurrent. Their common point, the circumcenter, is equidistant from the three vertices of the triangle.	138
T043	The angle bisectors of a triangle are concurrent. Their common point, the incenter, is equidistant from the three sides of the triangle.	139
T044	In an isosceles triangle, the perpendicular bisector of the base, the bisector of the vertex angle, the altitude to the base, and the median to the base lie on the same line.	139
T045	**Midsegment Theorem:** The segment connecting the midpoints of two sides of a triangle is parallel to the third side and half its length. $\overline{DE} \parallel \overline{AC}$ $DE = \dfrac{AC}{2}$	141
T046	**Triangle Sum Theorem:** The sum of the measures of the interior angles of a triangle is 180°.	143
T047	**Third Angles Theorem:** If two angles of one triangle are congruent to two angles of a second triangle, then the third angles are also congruent.	143
T048	**Exterior Angle Theorem:** The measure of an exterior angle of a triangle is equal to the sum of the measures of the two nonadjacent interior angles. Nonadjacent angles are sometimes called remote angles.	144
T049	**Exterior Angle Inequality Theorem:** The measure of an exterior angle of a triangle is greater than the measure of either of the two nonadjacent interior angles.	144
T050	**Base Angles Theorem:** If two sides of a triangle are congruent, then the angles opposite them are congruent.	145

More Help	Number	Theorem
145	T051	**Converse of Base Angles Theorem:** If two angles of a triangle are congruent, then the sides opposite them are congruent.
146	T052	A triangle is equilateral if and only if it is also equiangular.
148	T053	If one side of a triangle is longer than another side, then the angle opposite the longer side is larger than the angle opposite the shorter side.
148	T054	If one angle of a triangle is larger than another angle, then the side opposite the larger angle is longer than the side opposite the smaller angle.
148	T055	**Triangle Inequality Theorem:** The sum of the lengths of any two sides of a triangle is greater than the length of the third side.
149	T056	**Hinge Theorem:** If two sides of one triangle are congruent to two sides of another triangle, and the included angle of the first is larger than the included angle of the second, then the third side of the first is longer than the third side of the second.
149	T057	**Converse of Hinge Theorem:** If two sides of one triangle are congruent to two sides of another triangle, and the third side of the first is longer than the third side of the second, then the included angle of the first is larger than the included angle of the second.
151	T058	The acute angles of a right triangle are complementary.
152, 236	T059	**Pythagorean Theorem:** In a right triangle, the square of the length of the hypotenuse is equal to the sum of the squares of the lengths of the legs.
154	T060	**Converse of Pythagorean Theorem:** If the square of the length of the longest side of a triangle is equal to the sum of the squares of the lengths of the two shorter sides, then the triangle is a right triangle.
154	T061	If the square of the length of the longest side of a triangle is less than the sum of the squares of the lengths of the two shorter sides, then the triangle is acute. 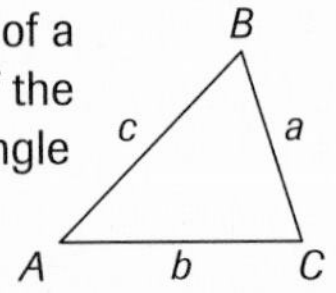 $c^2 < a^2 + b^2$ $\triangle ABC$ is acute
154	T062	If the square of the length of the longest side of a triangle is greater than the sum of the squares of the lengths of the two shorter sides, then the triangle is obtuse. 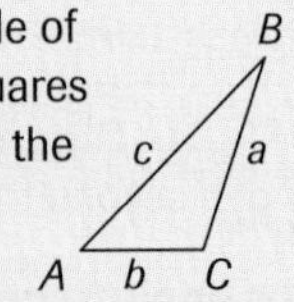 $c^2 > a^2 + b^2$ $\triangle ABC$ is obtuse
158	T063	If a quadrilateral is a parallelogram, then its opposite sides are congruent.
158	T064	If both pairs of opposite sides of a quadrilateral are congruent, then it is a parallelogram.
158	T065	If one pair of opposite sides of a quadrilateral is parallel and congruent, then it is a parallelogram.
159	T066	If a quadrilateral is a parallelogram, then its opposite angles are congruent.

Number	Theorem	MORE HELP
T067	If both pairs of opposite angles of a quadrilateral are congruent, then it is a parallelogram.	159
T068	If a quadrilateral is a parallelogram, then its consecutive angles are supplementary.	160
T069	If an angle of a quadrilateral is supplementary to both of its consecutive angles, then the quadrilateral is a parallelogram.	160
T070	If a quadrilateral is a parallelogram, then its diagonals bisect each other.	161
T071	If the diagonals of a quadrilateral bisect each other, then the quadrilateral is a parallelogram.	161
T072	If a parallelogram has one right angle, then it is a rectangle.	162
T073	A parallelogram is a rectangle if and only if its diagonals are congruent.	162
T074	A parallelogram is a rhombus if and only if its diagonals are perpendicular.	163
T075	A parallelogram is a rhombus if and only if each diagonal bisects a pair of opposite angles.	163
T076	**Trapezoid Base Angles Theorem:** If a trapezoid is isosceles, then each pair of base angles is congruent.	165
T077	**Trapezoid Diagonals Theorem:** If a trapezoid is isosceles, then its diagonals are congruent.	165
T078	**Converse of Trapezoid Diagonals Theorem:** If the diagonals of a trapezoid are congruent, then it is an isosceles trapezoid.	165
T079	If a trapezoid has one pair of congruent base angles, then the trapezoid is isosceles.	165
T080	**Midsegment Theorem for Trapezoids:** The midsegment of a trapezoid is parallel to each base and its length is half the sum of the lengths of the bases. $\overline{EF} \parallel \overline{AD} \parallel \overline{BC}$ $EF = \frac{1}{2}(AD + BC)$	165
T081	In a trapezoid, consecutive angles between a pair of parallel sides are supplementary. $m\angle A + m\angle B = 180°$ $m\angle C + m\angle D = 180°$	165
T082	If a quadrilateral is a kite, then its diagonals are perpendicular.	166
T083	If a quadrilateral is a kite, then exactly one pair of opposite angles is congruent.	166
T084	If two polygons are similar with corresponding sides in the ratio of $a{:}b$, then the ratio of their perimeters is $a{:}b$.	173

Number	Theorem
T085	If two polygons are similar with corresponding sides in the ratio of a:b, then the ratio of their areas is a^2:b^2.
T086	**Isoperimetric Theorem (2-d):** Of all plane figures with the same perimeter, the circle has maximum area.
T087	If two solids are similar with a scale factor of a:b, then corresponding surface areas have a ratio of a^2:b^2.
T088	**Isoperimetric Theorem (3-d):** Of all solids with the same surface area, the sphere has the largest volume.
T089	**Cavalieri's Principle:** If two solids have the same height and the same cross-sectional area at every level, then they have the same volume.
T090	If two solids are similar with a scale factor of a:b, then the corresponding volumes have a ratio of a^3:b^3.
T091	**Cross Product Property:** For positive numbers a, b, c, and d, $\dfrac{a}{b} = \dfrac{c}{d}$ if and only if $ad = bc$.
T092	**SAS Similarity Theorem:** If an angle of one triangle is congruent to an angle of a second triangle and the lengths of the sides including these angles are proportional, then the two triangles are similar.
T093	**SSS Similarity Theorem:** If corresponding sides of two triangles are proportional, then the two triangles are similar.
T094	**Triangle Proportionality Theorem:** If a line parallel to one side of a triangle intersects the other two sides, then it divides the two sides proportionally.
T095	**Converse of Triangle Proportionality Theorem:** If a line divides two sides of a triangle proportionally, then it is parallel to the third side.
T096	If a ray bisects an angle of a triangle, then it divides the opposite side into segments whose lengths are proportional to the lengths of the other two sides. $$\frac{a}{b} = \frac{d}{c}$$
T097	If the altitude is drawn to the hypotenuse of a right triangle, then the two triangles formed are similar to the original triangle and to each other.
T098	In a right triangle, the altitude divides the hypotenuse into two segments. The length of the altitude is the geometric mean of the lengths of the two segments.

189

202

204

206

211

220

228

230

232

232

233

235

236

Number	Theorem	MORE HELP
T099	In a right triangle, the altitude divides the hypotenuse into two segments. Each leg is the geometric mean of the hypotenuse and the segment of the hypotenuse that is adjacent to that leg.	236
T100	In a 45°-45°-90° triangle, the hypotenuse is $\sqrt{2}$ times as long as each leg.	238
T101	In a 30°-60°-90° triangle, the hypotenuse is twice as long as the shorter leg and the longer leg is $\sqrt{3}$ times as long as the shorter leg.	239
T102	**Law of Sines:** In any triangle ABC, $\frac{\sin A}{a} = \frac{\sin B}{b} = \frac{\sin C}{c}$. It's also true that $\frac{a}{\sin A} = \frac{b}{\sin B} = \frac{c}{\sin C}$.	248
T103	**Law of Cosines:** In any triangle ABC, $a^2 = b^2 + c^2 - 2bc \cos A$. It's also true that $c^2 = a^2 + b^2 - 2ab \cos C$.	249
T104	If a figure is symmetric, then any pair of corresponding parts under the symmetry is congruent.	256
T105	**Reflexive Property of Congruence:** Every figure is congruent to itself.	258
T106	**Symmetric Property of Congruence:** If figure A is congruent to figure D, then figure D is congruent to figure A.	258
T107	**Transitive Property of Congruence:** If figure A is congruent to figure D and figure D is congruent to figure G, then figure A is congruent to figure G.	258
T108	**ASA Congruence Theorem:** If two angles and the included side of one triangle are congruent to two angles and the included side of a second triangle, then the two triangles are congruent.	263
T109	**AAS Congruence Theorem:** If two angles and a nonincluded side of one triangle are congruent to two angles and the corresponding nonincluded side of a second triangle, then the triangles are congruent.	265
T110	**H-L Congruence Theorem:** If the hypotenuse and a leg of a right triangle are congruent to the hypotenuse and a leg of a second right triangle, then the triangles are congruent.	268
T111	**H-A Congruence Theorem:** If the hypotenuse and an acute angle of a right triangle are congruent to the hypotenuse and an acute angle of a second right triangle, then the triangles are congruent.	269
T112	**L-L Congruence Theorem:** If both legs of a right triangle are congruent to the corresponding legs of a second right triangle, then the triangles are congruent.	270

MORE
HELP
271

Number	Theorem
T113	**SASAS Congruence Theorem:** If three sides and the included angles of one quadrilateral are congruent to the corresponding three sides and included angles of another quadrilateral, then the quadrilaterals are congruent.
T114	**ASASA Congruence Theorem:** If three angles and the included sides of one quadrilateral are congruent to the corresponding three angles and included sides of another quadrilateral, then the quadrilaterals are congruent.
T115	**Properties of Isometries:** Every isometry preserves angle measure, betweenness, collinearity, and distance (length of segments).
T116	**Point Flip-Flop Theorem:** If A and B are points and A is the reflection of B over a line, then B is the reflection of A over the same line.
T117	**Figure Flip-Flop Theorem:** If A and B are figures and A is the reflection of B over a line, then B is the reflection of A over the same line.
T118	A reflection is an isometry.
T119	A rotation is an isometry.
T120	If two lines, ℓ and m, intersect at a point O, then a reflection in ℓ followed by a reflection in m is a rotation about point O. The angle of rotation is $2x°$; $x°$ is the measure of the acute or right angle between ℓ and m.
T121	If a figure has two lines of symmetry, intersecting at a point, then it is rotation symmetric with a center of rotation at that point.
T122	A translation is an isometry.
T123	If lines ℓ and m are parallel, then a reflection in ℓ followed by a reflection in m is a translation. If P'' is the image of P after the two reflections, then PP'' is perpendicular to ℓ; d is the distance between ℓ and m; and $PP'' = 2d$.
T124	The composition of two or more isometries is an isometry.
T125	A diameter is a line of reflection for a circle.
T126	If a line is tangent to a circle, then it is perpendicular to the radius drawn to the point of tangency.
T127	In a plane, if a line is perpendicular to a radius of a circle at its endpoint on the circle, then the line is tangent to the circle. ℓ is tangent to $\odot C$
T128	If two segments from the same exterior point are tangent to a circle, then the segments are congruent.

271
274
275
275
276
283
284
285
287
288
290
298
306
306
306

Number	Theorem	MORE HELP
T129	If a tangent and a chord intersect at a point on a circle, then the measure of each angle formed is half the measure of its intercepted arc.	307
T130	If two chords intersect in the interior of a circle, then the measure of each angle formed is half the sum of the measures of their intercepted arcs .	307
T131	If two secant segments are drawn to a circle from an exterior point, then the product of the lengths of one secant segment and its external secant segment is equal to the product of the lengths of the other secant segment and its external secant segment. $PB \cdot PA = PD \cdot PC$	308
T132	If a tangent segment and a secant segment are drawn to a circle from an exterior point, then the square of the length of the tangent segment is equal to the product of the lengths of the secant segment and its external secant segment. $(PA)^2 = PC \cdot PB$	308
T133	If a tangent and a secant, two tangents, or two secants intersect in the exterior of a circle, then the measure of the angle formed is half the difference of the measures of the intercepted arcs.	308
T134	In the same circle, or in congruent circles, two minor arcs are congruent if and only if their corresponding chords are congruent.	314
T135	If a diameter of a circle is perpendicular to a chord, then the diameter bisects the chord and its arc.	315
T136	If a chord is a perpendicular bisector of another chord, then it is a diameter.	315
T137	In the same circle, or in congruent circles, two chords are congruent if and only if they are equidistant from the center.	316
T138	If an angle is inscribed in a circle, then its measure is half the measure of its intercepted arc.	318
T139	If two inscribed angles of a circle intercept the same arc, then the angles are congruent.	318
T140	An angle that is inscribed in a circle is a right angle if and only if its corresponding arc is a semicircle.	318
T141	A quadrilateral can be inscribed in a circle if and only if its opposite angles are supplementary.	319
T142	**Euler's Theorem:** The numbers of faces, F, vertices, V, and edges, E, of a polyhedron are related by $F + V = E + 2$.	323

Glossary of Mathematical Terms

The numbers in black at the end of many entries refer you back to topic numbers, not page numbers. You will find topic numbers at the top of each page and next to each new piece of information in *Geometry to Go*.

Term   Abbreviation or Symbol   Definition

cosine (cos): In a right triangle, the ratio of the length of the leg adjacent to the reference angle to the length of the hypotenuse. $\cos A = \frac{4}{5} = 0.8$ Item Reference——**(241)**

Example

Illustration

hypotenuse

leg adjacent to $\angle A$

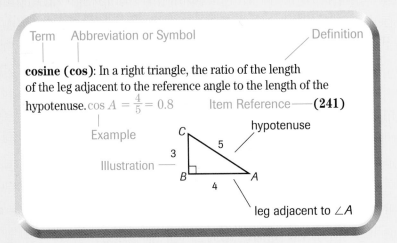

A

abscissa: *See x-coordinate*

absolute value (| |): The distance of a number from zero on the number line. For all real numbers, if $a \geq 0$, $|a| = a$; if $a < 0$, $|a| = {}^-a$.

acute: Having an angle measure greater than 0° and less than 90°. A triangle whose interior angles each measure less than 90° is an acute triangle. **(066)**

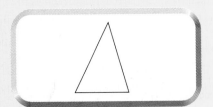

Addition Property of Equality: If you add equal amounts to equal amounts, the sums will be equal. For all real numbers a, b, and c, if $a = b$, then $a + c = b + c$. **(029)**

adjacent: Next to.

adjacent angles: Any two non-overlapping angles with a side in common. In both figures, $\angle 1$ and $\angle 2$ are adjacent angles. **(062)**

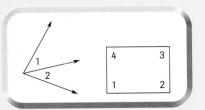

adjacent arcs: Two arcs of the same circle that intersect at exactly one point. $\overarc{PQ}$ and $\overarc{QR}$ are adjacent arcs; $\overarc{PR}$ and $\overarc{PQ}$ are not adjacent. **(312)**

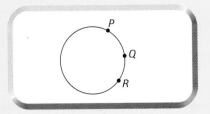

adjacent sides: Two sides of a polygon with a common vertex. *AB* and *BC* are adjacent sides.

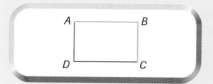

algorithm: A step-by-step method for computing or carrying out any mathematical procedure.

alternate exterior angles: When a transversal intersects two lines, alternate exterior angles are on opposite sides of the transversal and on the outside of the given lines. ∠1 and ∠7 are alternate exterior angles. So are ∠2 and ∠8. **(074)**

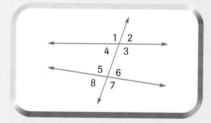

alternate interior angles: When a transversal intersects two lines, alternate interior angles are on opposite sides of the transversal and on the inside of the given lines. ∠4 and ∠6 are alternate interior angles. So are ∠3 and ∠5. **(074)**

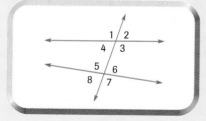

altitude of a cone or pyramid: A segment drawn from the vertex and perpendicular to the plane of the base. *See also height* **(327, 331)**

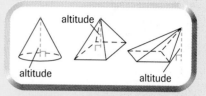

altitude of a cylinder or prism: A segment perpendicular to the planes of the bases and extending from a point on one base to a point on the other base or on the plane containing the other base. *See also height* **(326, 330)**

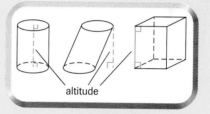

altitude of a triangle: A segment drawn from a vertex and perpendicular to the opposite side or to the line containing the opposite side. *See also height* **(137)**

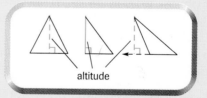

angle (∠): (1) The union of two rays that share a common endpoint. **(064)**

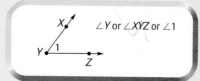

(2) The measure of a turn about a point. *See also angle of rotation* **(281)**

angle bisector: A ray in the interior of an angle that divides the angle into two congruent angles. $\overrightarrow{BD}$ bisects $\angle ABC$, so $\angle ABD \cong \angle DBC$. **(073)**

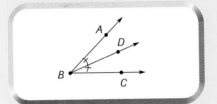

angle of depression or elevation: The angle between a horizontal line and the line of sight. If looking down, the angle is an angle of depression. If looking up, the angle is an angle of elevation. **(246)**

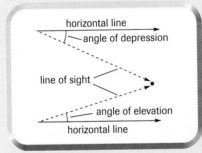

angle of rotation: The angle a figure is turned about a center of rotation. The angle of rotation of the triangle is 90°. **(281)**

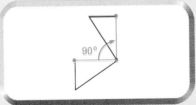

apex: *See vertex*

apothem: The perpendicular line segment (distance) from the center of a regular polygon to one of its sides. **(239)**

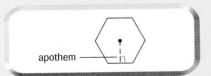

apothem

arc (⌒): A continuous part of a circle. The measure of an arc is the measure of the angle formed by two radii with endpoints at the endpoints of the arc. $\overarc{AB}$ is the shorter of the two curves connecting point A with point B. To name the longer curve, you need to use three letters. $\overarc{ACB}$ is the longer curve. **(309)**

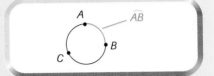

arc of the chord: An arc whose endpoints are the same as the endpoints of a chord. **(314)**

arc length: The length of an arc, or portion of a circle. **(177)**

area (A): The number of square units that a plane figure covers. **(178)**

Archimedean solid: A polyhedron composed of more than one type of regular polygon. The same number of faces meet in the same order at each vertex. **(325)**

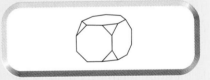

Associative Property of Addition: For all real numbers, a, b, and c, $(a + b) + c = a + (b + c)$. **(026)**

Associative Property of Multiplication: For all real numbers, a, b, and c, $(ab)c = a(bc)$. **(026)**

auxiliary line: An additional line or segment added to a diagram to complete a proof or visualize a problem. **(041)**

axes: Plural of *axis*

axiom: *See postulate*

axiomatic system: A set of statements consisting of postulates (axioms), and truths (theorems) that can be derived from the postulates. **(004)**

axis: (1) A reference line from which distances or angles are measured on a grid. **(087)**

(2) The vertical line through the vertex of each nap, or half, of a double-napped right cone. **(338)**

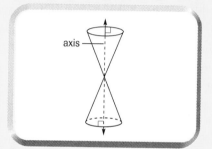

axis

axis of symmetry: *See line of symmetry*

B

balancing point: *See centroid*

base angles: (1) The two angles whose common side is the base of an isosceles triangle. $\overline{BC}$ is the base of the triangle, so $\angle B$ and $\angle C$ are the base angles. **(143)**

(2) A pair of angles whose common side is a base of a trapezoid. $\overline{EF}$ and $\overline{GH}$ are bases, so $\angle E$ and $\angle F$ are base angles and $\angle G$ and $\angle H$ are base angles. **(165)**

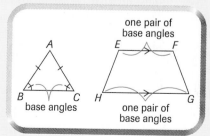

one pair of base angles

base angles

one pair of base angles

base edge: An edge formed by the intersection of the base and a lateral face of a solid. **(327)**

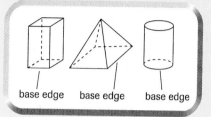

base edge   base edge   base edge

base of a polygon (b): (1) The side that contains one endpoint of the altitude. **(137)**

(2) The noncongruent side of a nonequilateral, isosceles triangle. **(135)**

(3) Either one of the two parallel sides of a trapezoid. **(165)**

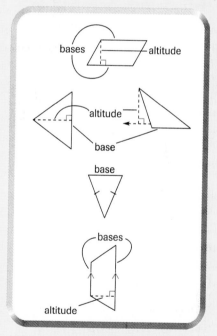

bases   altitude

altitude

base

base

bases

altitude

base of a power: The number used as the factor in exponential form. In 4^6, the base is 4 and the exponent is 6.

base of a solid (*B*): (1) Either of the two congruent parallel faces of a prism. **(326)**
(2) The face of a pyramid that does not have to be a triangle. **(327)**
(3) Either of the two circular faces of a cylinder. **(330)**
(4) The circular face of a cone. **(331)**

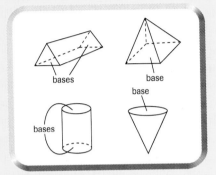
bases · base · base · bases

biconditional statement (⟷): A logical statement containing the phrase *if and only if*. Both the statement and its converse are true. *p* and *q* are statements; *p* if and only if *q*. **(011)**

bisect: Divide into two congruent halves. The midpoint of a line segment bisects the segment. **(056)**

border pattern: *See frieze pattern*

 C ─────────────

Cartesian plane: *See coordinate plane*

center: (1) The point that is equidistant from all points on a circle. **(298)**
(2) The common center of circles inscribed in and circumscribed about a regular polygon. A point equidistant from the vertices of a regular polygon. **(129)**
(3) The point that is equidistant from all points on a sphere. **(332)**

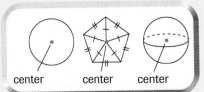
center · center · center

center of gravity: *See centroid*

center of rotation: The point about which a figure is rotated, or turned. **(281)**

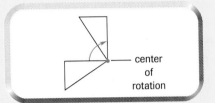
center of rotation

central angle: (1) An angle whose vertex is the center of a circle and whose sides are radii of the circle. **(310)**
(2) An angle whose vertex is the center of a regular polygon and whose sides intersect the polygon at adjacent vertices. ∠*ACB* is a central angle.

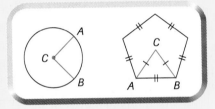

centroid: (1) The balance point of a plane figure. (2) The point where the medians of a triangle intersect. *See also point of concurrency* **(136)**

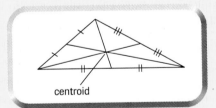
centroid

chord: (1) A segment whose endpoints are on a circle. **(305)**
(2) A segment whose endpoints are on a sphere. **(332)**

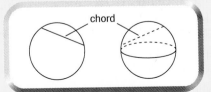
chord

circle: All points in a plane equidistant from a given point (the center). **(298)**

circular reasoning: Using as a reason in a proof the statement you are trying to prove. **(003)**

circumcenter: The point where the perpendicular bisectors of the sides of a triangle intersect. *See also point of concurrency* **(138)**

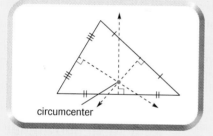

circumcenter

circumference (*C*): The distance around a circle. **(176)**

circumscribed: A circle containing a polygon whose vertices are on the circle is circumscribed about the polygon. The circle is circumscribed about the square. *See also inscribed* **(303)**

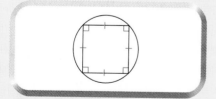

clockwise: In the same direction that the hands of a clock rotate.

closed figure: A figure that completely surrounds a region in a plane.

closed network: *See connected network*

coefficient: A (usually) numerical factor in a term of an algebraic expression. In $3x$, the coefficient of x is 3.

coincident: *See collinear*

collinear: On the same line. **(048)**

common tangent: A line or segment that is tangent to two coplanar circles. **(301)**

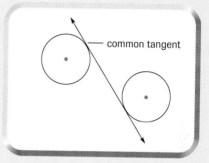

common tangent

Commutative Property of Addition: For all real numbers a and b, $a + b = b + a$. **(024)**

Commutative Property of Multiplication: For all real numbers a and b, $ab = ba$. **(024)**

compass: A tool used to draw circles and arcs. **(372)**

complement: An angle whose measure along with the measure of another angle has the sum of 90°. An angle whose measure is 30° is the complement of a 60° angle. **(068)**

complementary angles: Two angles with measures whose sum is 90°. **(068)**

complete axiomatic system: All theorems in an axiomatic system can be derived from the same set of postulates. **(019)**

component form (< >): A pair of numbers that describes a vector in the coordinate plane. The components of the vector are in the form <horizontal component, vertical component>. Vectors in a three-dimensional system have three components. **(289)**

composite figure: A figure that can be decomposed into two or more figures. This figure is made up of a triangle and a square.

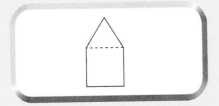

composition of transformations: The combination of two or more transformations resulting in the creation of a single image. A glide reflection is the result of a translation and a reflection. **(290)**

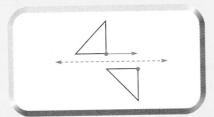

concave: (1) If a line that contains a side of a polygon also contains a point inside the polygon, the polygon is concave. **(129)**

(2) If a segment that connects two points on the surface of a polyhedron also contains a point outside the polyhedron, the polyhedron is concave or not convex. *See also convex* **(322)**

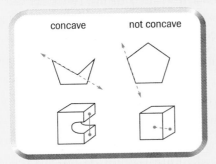

concave   not concave

concentric circles: Two or more coplanar circles that share the same center. **(300)**

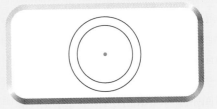

conclusion: The *then* part of a conditional statement. **(009)**

concurrent lines: Three or more lines that intersect at the same point. **(052)**

conditional statement ($\rightarrow$): A logical statement consisting of two parts, an hypothesis and a conclusion. p and q are statements. If p, then q ($p \rightarrow q$) is the conditional statement. **(009)**

cone: A solid bounded by a circular base and a curved surface with one vertex. **(331)**

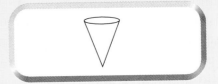

congruent ($\cong$): Having exactly the same size and shape. Congruent angles have the same measure. Congruent segments have the same length. **(256)**

conic section: Cross section of a double napped right cone. These may be circles, parabolas, or hyperbolas. **(338)**

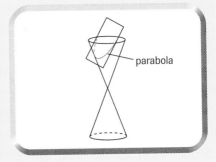

parabola

conjecture: An unproven statement based on observations. **(005)**

connected network: A network in which all nodes are joined by edges. **(085)**

consecutive angles: *See adjacent angles*

consecutive interior angles: *See same-side interior angles*

consistent axiomatic system: Proofs using the same postulates cannot contradict each other. **(019)**

constant: A quantity that always stays the same. In $2x - 3y + 4 = 0$, 4 and 0 are constants.

construction: An accurate image of a figure made using only a straightedge and a compass. **(372)**

contrapositive: In the contrapositive of a conditional statement, the hypothesis and conclusion are both reversed and negated. The contrapositive has the same truth value as the conditional statement. *If p, then q becomes If not q, then not p.* **(014)**

converse: In the converse of a conditional statement, the hypothesis and conclusion are reversed. *If p, then q becomes If q, then p.* **(010)**

convex: (1) If none of the lines that contain a side of a polygon also contain a point inside the polygon, the polygon is convex, or not concave. **(129)**
(2) If a segment that connects any two points on the surface of a polyhedron is completely inside or on the polyhedron, the polyhedron is convex, or not concave. *See also concave* **(332)**

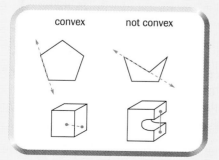

coordinate: (1) The real number that corresponds to a point on a number line. **(055)**
(2) The real number that corresponds to the x-, y-, or z-value of a point on a two- or three-dimensional grid. **(122)**
(3) The real number representing the distance of a point from the origin or the angle-measure of the angle between the polar axis and the ray from the origin through the given point. **(117)**

coordinate axes: The two or three perpendicular number lines that form a two- or three-dimensional coordinate system. **(087)**

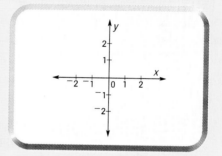

coordinate grid: *See coordinate plane*

coordinate plane: A plane determined by the intersection of two perpendicular number lines in which the coordinates of a point are its distances from the number lines. **(087)**

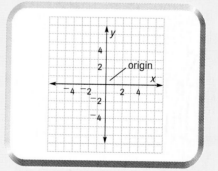

coordinate proof: A type of proof that involves a figure in the coordinate plane. **(043)**

coordinate system: A system for locating a point in a plane by its horizontal and vertical distance from each of two or three mutually perpendicular number lines. *See also coordinate plane*

coordinates: *See ordered pair and ordered triple*

coplanar: In the same plane.

corollary: A theorem that follows easily from another theorem that has already been proved. **(021)**

corresponding angles: (1) When a transversal intersects two lines, corresponding angles are on the same side of the transversal and on the same side of the given lines. $\angle 1$ and $\angle 5$ are a pair of corresponding angles. So are $\angle 2$ and $\angle 6$, $\angle 3$ and $\angle 7$, and $\angle 4$ and $\angle 8$. **(074)**

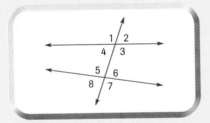

(2) Angles in the same relative position in similar or congruent figures. $\triangle MNO \cong \triangle PQR$, so $\angle M \cong \angle P$, $\angle N \cong \angle Q$, and $\angle O \cong \angle R$. **(222)**

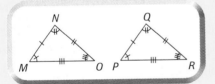

corresponding sides: Sides in the same relative position in similar or congruent figures. $\triangle MNO \cong \triangle PQR$, so $\overline{MN} \cong \overline{PQ}$, $\overline{NO} \cong \overline{QR}$, and $\overline{OM} \cong \overline{RP}$. **(222)**

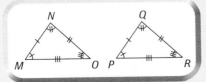

cosecant (csc): The inverse of the sine function. **(241)**

cosine (cos): In a right triangle, the ratio of the length of the leg adjacent to the reference angle to the length of the hypotenuse. $\cos A = \frac{4}{5} = 0.8$ **(241)**

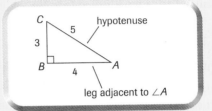

cotangent (cot): The inverse of the tangent function. **(241)**

counterclockwise: In a direction opposite to the direction that the hands of a clock rotate.

counterexample: An example that shows that a conjecture is not always true. **(005)**

cross multiplication: A method for finding a missing term in a proportion by setting the cross products equal to each other.

cross product: The product of one numerator and the opposite denominator in a pair of fractions or a proportion. *See also cross multiplication* **(220)**

cross section: The intersection of a plane and a solid. *See also conic section* **(337)**

cube: A prism whose faces are all congruent squares. **(334)**

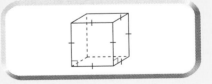

cubic unit: A unit, such as a cubic meter (m^3) or a cubic foot (ft^3), used to measure volume. **(205)**

curve: A smooth line, often one that is continuously not straight.

customary system: A system of measurement used in the United States. The system includes units for measuring length, capacity, weight, and temperature. Though no longer used in England, this system is also called English measure. **(420)**

cylinder: A solid bounded by two congruent and parallel circular regions joined by a curved surface whose cross section perpendicular to the axis is always a circle congruent to the bases. **(330)**

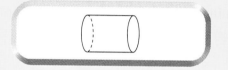

D

decagon: A polygon with ten sides.

deductive reasoning: Applying a general rule to a specific case. **(007)**

definition: Description of a new term using known words or terms. A definition is an acceptable reason for a statement in a deductive proof. **(017)**

degenerate conic section: A point, line, or pair of parallel or intersecting lines which can be formed by the intersection of a plane and a double napped cone. *See also conic sections* **(338)**

degree (angle measure) (°): A unit of angle measure. 1° is the measure of the central angle of a circle formed by rays that cut $\frac{1}{360}$ of its circumference. **(062)**

degree of a node: The number of edges that meet at a vertex in a network. **(085)**

degree of a polynomial: The highest power of any term of a polynomial.

determine: Provide sufficient information. We say *two points determine a line* because two points provide sufficient information to define a unique line. **(051)**

diagonal: (1) A segment that connects two vertices but is not a side of a polygon. $\overline{BE}$ and $\overline{CE}$ are diagonals. **(156)**

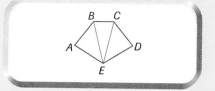

(2) A line segment that connects two vertices and contains points on the inside of the solid. $\overline{DF}$ is a diagonal of the prism. **(326)**

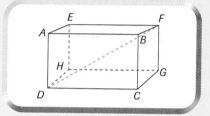

diagram: A drawing that represents a mathematical situation. **(298)**

diameter: (1) A chord that contains the center of a circle. **(298)**

(2) A chord that contains the center of a sphere. **(332)**

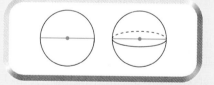

dihedral angle: The angle formed by two intersecting planes. The line of intersection serves as a vertex, called the edge. **(081)**

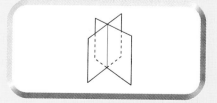

dilation: A transformation in which a similar image is formed by enlarging or reducing its preimage. The image and preimage are similar figures. $\triangle A'B'C'$ is a dilation of $\triangle ABC$. **(292)**

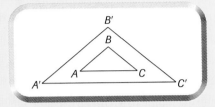

dimensional analysis: An algorithm used to convert a measurement into different units by using the product of unit fractions or conversion factors. Suppose you want to write 600 ft/min as mi/h. You can use the ratios $\frac{1\ mi}{5280\ ft}$ and $\frac{60\ min}{1\ hr}$.

$$\frac{600\ ft}{1\ min} \times \frac{1\ mi}{5280\ ft} \times \frac{60\ min}{1\ hr} = 6\frac{9}{11}\ mi/hr$$

directed line segment: *See vector*

direction of a vector: The angle a vector makes with a horizontal line. **(289)**

distance: (1) The absolute value of the difference of the coordinates of two points on a number line. $AB = |a - b|$. **(055)**

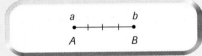

(2) The length of the perpendicular segment from a point to line. AB is the distance from A to ℓ. **(092)**

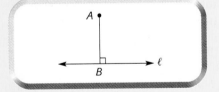

(3) The length of a perpendicular segment with endpoints on each of two parallel lines. ℓ is parallel to m. AB is the distance between ℓ and m. **(093)**

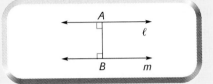

Distributive Property: For all real numbers a, b, and c, $a(b + c) = ab + ac$. **(027)**

Division Property of Equality: For all real numbers a, b, and c, $c \neq 0$, if $a = b$, then $\frac{a}{c} = \frac{b}{c}$. **(032)**

dodecagon: A polygon with twelve sides.

dodecahedron: A polyhedron with twelve faces.

double napped right cone: A solid composed of two right cones, with a common axis and a common vertex, whose lateral surfaces extend without end. **(338)**

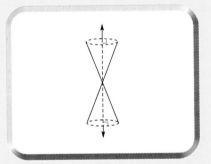

duality: A principle of projective geometry by which all the postulates and theorems have a counterpart in which the roles of *line* and *point* are interchanged.

E

edge: (1) A line segment where two faces of a polyhedron meet. **(322)**
(2) The line formed by two intersecting planes is the edge of a dihedral angle. **(081)**
(3) A segment or curve that connects two nodes in a network. **(083)**

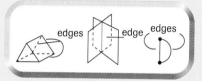

edges edge edges

element: Any line on a double-napped right cone that contains the vertex. **(338)**

ellipse: A closed curve shaped like an oval consisting of all points in a plane such that the sum of the distances $(d_1 + d_2)$ from each point to the two given points, called foci, is a constant. **(338)**

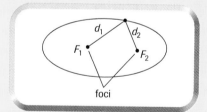

foci

elliptical geometry: *See spherical geometry*

endpoint: A point marking either end of a line segment or the end of a ray. **(054)**

English measure: *See customary system*

enlargement: A dilation in which the scale factor, or size change, is greater than one.

equal: Having the same numerical value.

equal ratios: *See proportion*

equation: A statement that two mathematical expressions are equivalent.

equiangular: All angles having the same measure. **(134)**

equidistant: Being the same distance from a given referent.

equilateral: All sides having the same length. **(134)**

equivalent: Having the same value. 0.4 and $\frac{2}{5}$ are equivalent.

even node: In a network, the point at which an even number of edges meet. **(085)**

exponent: The number that tells how many equal factors there are. In $8 \times 8 \times 8 \times 8 \times 8 = 8^5$, the exponent is 5.

exterior: Outside the boundaries of a figure.

exterior angle: (1) An angle formed by a side of a polygon and an extension of an adjacent side. At each vertex, there are two congruent exterior angles. **(132)**

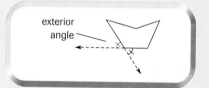

exterior
angle

(2) The angles that are not between two lines intersected by a transversal. *See also alternate exterior angles, same-side exterior angles*

external secant segment: The part of a secant segment that is outside the circle. *See also secant segment* **(308)**

externally tangent: Circles that intersect in one point and share no interior points are externally tangent. **(301)**

extremes of a proportion: The terms at either end of a proportion, when the proportion is written with colons. In the proportion $a{:}b = c{:}d$, a and d are the extremes. *See also means of a proportion* **(219)**

F

face: A plane figure that serves as one side of a solid figure. The six faces of a cube are squares. **(322)**

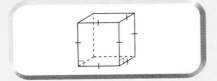

Fibonacci sequence: 1, 1, 2, 3, 5, 8, 13, ... **(252)**

flat angle: *See straight angle*

flip: *See reflection*

flow chart: A diagram using boxes and arrows to show a step-by-step process. **(045)**

flow proof: *See flow chart proof*

flow chart proof: A type of proof in which a flow chart is used to show the progression of a logical argument. **(045)**

foci: The plural of focus.

focus: The point at which the axis of a double napped right cone intersects a figure formed when a plane slices the double napped cone. *See also ellipse, hyperbola* **(338)**

formula: A general mathematical statement, equation, or rule. **(426)**

fractal: An object in which parts are similar to the whole. Fractals are said to have self-similarity. **(254)**

frieze pattern: A linear pattern that can be extended infinitely in opposite directions using reflections, rotations and/or translations. **(295)**

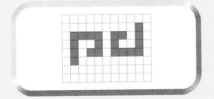

function ($f(x)$): A relation in which every value of x is associated with a unique value of y: the value of y depends on the value of x. If $y = x + 5$, then $f(x) = x + 5$. **(116)**

G

geometric mean: In the proportion $\frac{a}{m} = \frac{m}{b}$, m is the positive number called the geometric mean. **(236)**

geometric probability: A probability involving a measure such as length or area. **(203)**

geometric progression: A sequence of terms in which each term is created by multiplying the previous term by a constant. 1, 8, 64, 512, ...

geometry: The investigation of properties, relationships, and measurement of points, lines, angles, surfaces, and solids.

glide: *See translation*

glide reflection: A transformation that is a combination of a translation and a reflection. $\triangle K'L'M'$ is a glide reflection of $\triangle KLM$. **(290)**

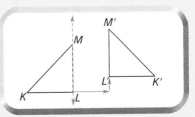

golden ratio: A ratio of $(1 + \sqrt{5}):2$, or approximately $1.618:1$. **(251)**

golden rectangle: A rectangle whose length and width are in the ratio of $(1 + \sqrt{5}):2$ or $1.618:1$. **(253)**

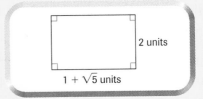

gradient: *See slope*

graph: A pictorial device that shows a relationship among variables or sets of data. *See also network*

graphing calculator: A calculator with the capacity to graph and display functions on a screen. Sometimes also called a graphics calculator **(389)**

great circle: A circle formed by the intersection of a sphere and a plane that includes the center of the sphere. **(337)**

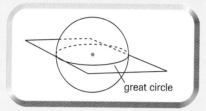
great circle

grid: A pattern of horizontal and vertical lines, usually forming squares.

 H ——————————

half line: *See ray*

half plane: The part of a plane that is on one side of a line in that plane but does not include the line. **(049)**

height (h): The length of an altitude. **(326)**

hemisphere: The points of a sphere on one side of a plane that passes through its center. **(332)**

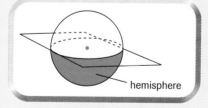
hemisphere

heptagon: A polygon with seven sides.

hexagon: A polygon with six sides.

hexahedron: A polyhedron with six faces.

horizontal: Parallel to or in the plane of the horizon. In a coordinate plane, the x-axis is a horizontal line.

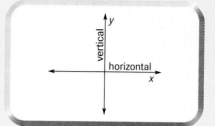

hyperbola: All points in a plane such that the difference between the distances, $|d_2 - d_1|$, from each point to two given points, called foci (F_1, F_2), is a constant.

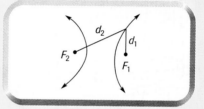

hyperbolic geometry: The geometry resulting from a parallel postulate that says more than one line is parallel to a given line through a point not on that line. **(368)**

hypotenuse: In a right triangle, the side opposite the right angle. **(150)**

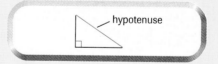
hypotenuse

hypotheses: The plural of *hypothesis*.

hypothesis: The *if* part of a conditional statement. **(009)**

 I ——————————

icosahedron: A polyhedron with twenty faces.

if-then statement: *See conditional statement*

image: The figure created when a figure undergoes a transformation. *See also preimage* **(274)**

incenter: The point where the angle bisectors of a triangle intersect. **(139)**

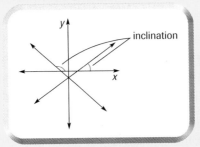

incenter

inclination: The measure, from the right, of the angle whose rays are 1) the part of a nonvertical line that is above the *x*-axis and 2) the *x*-axis. **(098)**

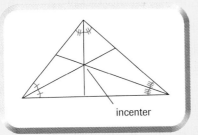

inclination

included angle: The angle formed by two adjacent sides of a polygon. In △WXY, ∠X is the included angle between $\overline{WX}$ and $\overline{XY}$. **(264)**

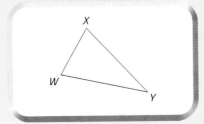

included side: The side between two angles. In △WXY, $\overline{XY}$ is the included side between ∠X and ∠Y. **(264)**

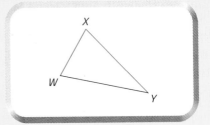

indirect proof: A type of proof in which you assume that what you are trying to prove is false and this assumption leads to a contradiction. **(046)**

indirect measurement: Using an easily found measurement and known relationships to compute a measurement that is more difficult to find directly. Using similar triangles is one method of indirect measurement. **(236)**

inductive reasoning: Making a generalization based on observation of specific cases and consideration of a pattern. **(005)**

inequality: A number sentence that contains one of the symbols ≠, <, >, ≤, or ≥.

initial point of a vector: The starting point of a vector. **(289)**

inscribed: A figure whose vertices are part of another figure is inscribed in that figure. A circle inscribed in a polygon touches each side of the polygon at exactly one point. An inscribed angle is an angle whose vertex is on a circle and whose sides are chords of the circle. *See also circumscribed* **(302)**

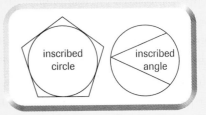

inscribed circle

inscribed angle

intercepted arc: The portion of a circle that is in the interior of an inscribed angle and whose endpoints are on the sides of the angle. **(310)**

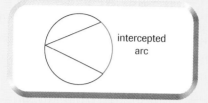

interior: Inside the boundaries of a figure.

interior angle: (1) An angle on the inside of a polygon, formed by the sides of the polygon. **(131)**

(2) The angles between two lines intersected by a transversal. *See also alternate interior angles, same-side interior angles* **(074)**

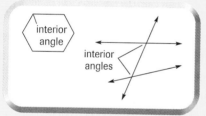

internally tangent: Circles that intersect in one point and share some internal points are internally tangent. **(301)**

intersect: To meet or cross. **(052)**

inverse: (1) In the inverse of a conditional statement, both the hypothesis and the conclusion are negated. *If p, then q becomes If not p, then not q.*
(013)

(2) An inverse operation is the opposite of another operation. Addition is the inverse of subtraction.

irrational number: A number that cannot be written as a ratio of two integers. In the decimal representation of an irrational number, the digits never terminate and never repeat. $\sqrt{2} = 1.41421356\ldots$

irregular polygon: A polygon in which at least one pair of sides or angles is not congruent. **(129)**

isometric drawing: A drawing that provides a corner view of an object, thus showing three dimensions. **(335)**

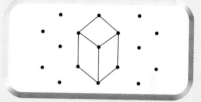

isometry: A transformation that creates an image that is congruent to the original figure. Rotations, reflections, and translations are isometries. **(274)**

isosceles: (1) A trapezoid with congruent legs.

(2) A triangle with two congruent sides. **(134)**

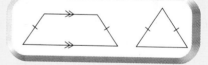

iteration: A repetition of a sequence of steps. **(254)**

 K

kite: A quadrilateral with two distinct pairs of adjacent congruent sides. **(166)**

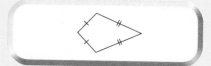

60

L

lateral edge: (1) An edge of a lateral face of a prism that joins the corresponding vertices of the bases. **(326)**
(2) An edge of a lateral face that joins the vertex of a pyramid to a vertex of the base. **(327)**

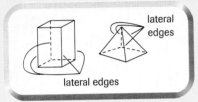

lateral edges

lateral edges

lateral edge of a cone or cylinder: *See base edge*

lateral face: A face of a prism or a pyramid that is not a base. **(326)**

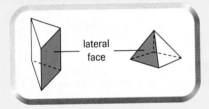

lateral face

lateral surface of a cone or cylinder: The curved surface of a cone or cylinder. **(330–331)**

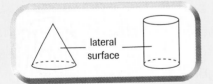

lateral surface

law of the contrapositive: A statement and its contrapositive are logically equivalent. **(014)**

law of cosines: In any triangle ABC,
$a^2 = b^2 + c^2 - 2bc \cos A$. **(249)**

law of detachment: If a statement is true and the hypothesis is true, then the conclusion must be true. If $p \to q$ is true and p is true, then q is true. **(016)**

law of sines: In any triangle ABC,
$$\frac{\sin A}{a} = \frac{\sin B}{b} = \frac{\sin C}{c}$$ **(248)**

law of syllogism: If $p \to q$ is true and $q \to r$ is true, then $p \to r$ is true. **(016)**

legs: (1) The two congruent sides of an isosceles triangle.
(2) The two sides of a right triangle that form the right angle. **(150)**

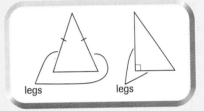

legs   legs

(3) The two sides of a trapezoid that are not parallel. **(165)**

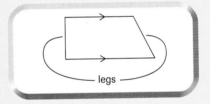

legs

length (ℓ): The distance along a line or figure from one point to another.

line (↔): Undefined. Loosely, an infinite set of points forming a straight path extending in opposite directions. **(052)**

line of reflection: The line over which two figures are mirror images of each other. **(275)**

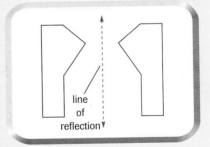

line of reflection

line segment (—): A part of a line that consists of two endpoints and all the points of the line between them. **(052)**

line symmetry: A figure has line symmetry if a line divides it into congruent halves, each of which is the reflection image of the other. **(279)**

line of symmetry: A line that divides a figure into congruent halves, each of which is the reflection image of the other. **(279)**

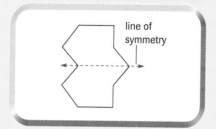

line of symmetry

linear equation: An equation in two variables whose graph in the coordinate plane is a straight line. **(095)**

linear inequality: An inequality in two variables whose boundary in the coordinate plane is a line.

linear pair: Two adjacent angles whose noncommon sides are opposite rays. ∠1 and ∠2 are a linear pair. **(070)**

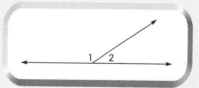

locus: The set of all points that satisfy a given condition or set of conditions. A circle is a locus of points on a plane equidistant from a given point. **(126)**

logic: A formal structure for reasoning.

logical argument: An argument tying together an hypothesis or set of hypotheses and a conclusion. **(007)**

logician: A mathematician that specializes in logical arguments. **(007)**

lower bound: In a set of numbers, a number less than or equal to every other number in the set. **(111)**

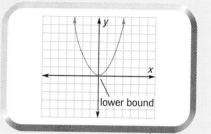

lower bound

lune: In spherical geometry, a closed figure with two sides. **(366)**

M

magnitude of a vector: The distance from the initial point to the terminal point of a vector. The magnitude of $\vec{AB}$ is three units. **(289)**

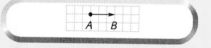

major arc: An arc greater than a semicircle (greater than 180°). $\overset{\frown}{ADB}$ is a major arc of circle C. **(310)**

map onto: Transform a preimage so that each image point lies on a preimage point. Equilateral triangle ABC is rotated about P 120° to map onto itself. **(274)**

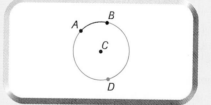

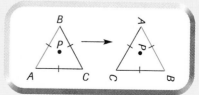

mass: The amount of matter in an object.

matrices: The plural of *matrix*.

matrix: A rectangular arrangement of data. **(290)**

means of a proportion: The terms in the middle of a proportion, when the proportion is written with colons. In the proportion $a:b = c:d$, b and c are the means. *See also extremes of a proportion* **(219)**

measure: (1) The dimensions, quantity, length, or capacity of something.
(2) To find the dimensions of something.

median of a trapezoid: *See midsegment*

median of a triangle: A segment from a vertex to the midpoint of the opposite side. **(136)**

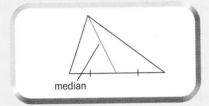
median

metric system: A system of measurement based on tens. The basic unit of capacity is the liter. The basic unit of length is the meter. The basic unit of mass is the gram. Temperature is measured in degrees Celsius. **(419)**

midpoint: (1) The point on a line segment that divides it into two congruent segments. **(056)**

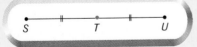

S T U

(2) The point on an arc that divides it into two congruent arcs. **(315)**
T and B are midpoints.

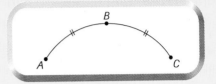

midsegment: (1) A segment that connects the midpoints of the legs of a trapezoid. **(165)**
(2) A segment that connects the midpoints of two sides of a triangle. **(141)**

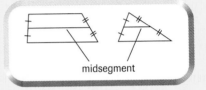
midsegment

minor arc: An arc that is less than a semicircle, or less than 180°. $\overset{\frown}{AB}$ is a minor arc of circle C. **(310)**

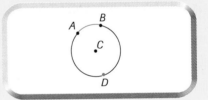

mirror image: *See reflection*

mixed measure: A measure that includes different units to specify the measure of one thing. 5 ft 3 in. is a mixed measure. **(171)**

Multiplication Property of Equality: For all real numbers a, b, and c, if $a = b$, then $ac = bc$. **(031)**

necessary condition: A condition that is required to be true in order for something else to be true. Being a quadrilateral is a necessary condition for a figure to be a square. **(008)**

negation (~): The negative of a statement. p is a statement. Not p (~p) is its negation. **(012)**

net: A two-dimensional pattern that can be folded to form a solid. This net can be folded to form a cube. **(336)**

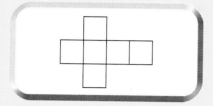

network: A collection of points which may or may not be connected by edges. **(083)**

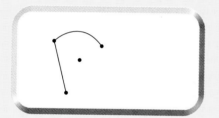

n-gon: A polygon with n sides.

node: A point in a network that may be connected to other points in the network by edges. **(083)**

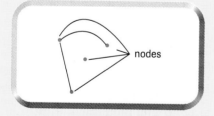

nodes

nonagon: A polygon with nine sides.

non-convex: *See concave*

non-Euclidean geometry: Any geometry using postulates different from those in Euclidean geometry. **(363)**

non-rigid transformation: A transformation that creates an image that is not congruent to the original figure. A dilation is a non-rigid transformation. **(291)**

oblique: (1) Lines that are not horizontal or vertical.
(2) A relationship between lines and/or plane figures that is not perpendicular or parallel. In an oblique cone, the segment joining the vertex and the center of the base is not perpendicular to the base. In an oblique cylinder, the segment joining the centers of the bases is not perpendicular to the bases. In an oblique prism, the lateral edges are not perpendicular to the bases. **(326)**

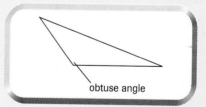

obtuse: Having an angle measure greater than 90° and less than 180°. A triangle with exactly one interior angle that measures more than 90° is obtuse. **(066)**

obtuse angle

octagon: A polygon with eight sides.

octahedron: A polyhedron with eight faces.

octant: One of the eight sections into which space is divided by the three coordinate planes of a three-dimensional coordinate system. The box is in the first octant. **(121)**

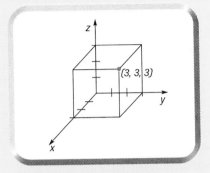

odd node: In a network, the point at which an odd number of edges meets. **(085)**

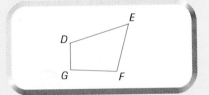

open network: A network in which not all nodes are connected. **(083)**

opposite: Symmetrically opposed in position or direction. (1) The opposite angles of a quadrilateral are pairs of interior angles with no common sides. $\angle D$ and $\angle F$ are a pair of opposite angles. So are $\angle E$ and $\angle G$. **(156)**

(2) The opposite sides of a quadrilateral are pairs of nonadjacent sides. $\overline{DE}$ and $\overline{FG}$ are a pair of opposite sides. So are $\overline{EF}$ and $\overline{DG}$. **(156)**

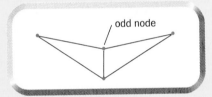

(3) Opposite rays are a pair of rays with a common endpoint that form a line. If B is between A and C on $\overleftrightarrow{AC}$, then $\overrightarrow{BA}$ and $\overrightarrow{BC}$ are opposite rays.

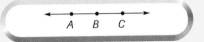

See also vertical angles

ordered pair: In a rectangular coordinate system, a pair of numbers that describes the location of a point on a coordinate plane. The coordinates of the point are given in the order (horizontal coordinate, vertical coordinate). $(3, {}^-2)$ describes the point located 3 units to the right of the y-axis and 2 units below the x-axis. **(087)**

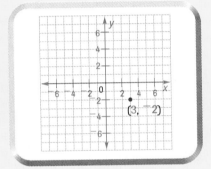

(2) In a polar coordinate system, a pair of numbers (r, θ) that locate a point. The distance of the point from the origin is r, the measure of the angle between the polar axis and a ray from the origin through the point is θ. **(117)**

ordered triple: Three numbers that describe the location of a point in a three-dimensional coordinate system. The coordinates of the point are given in the order (x-coordinate, y-coordinate, z-coordinate). **(121)**

ordinate: *See y-coordinate*

origin: The intersection of the x- and y-axes on the coordinate plane or the x-, y-, and z- axes in a three-dimensional co-ordinate system. It is usually described by the ordered pair (0, 0) or ordered triple (0,0,0) and may be labeled O. *See also quadrant, octant* **(087)**

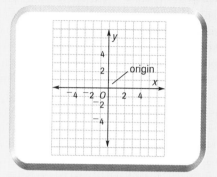

orthocenter of a triangle: The point where the altitudes of a triangle meet. **(137)**

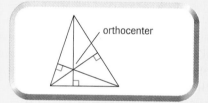

orthographic drawing or projection: Three separate two-dimensional views of an object: top view, front view, and side view. **(336)**

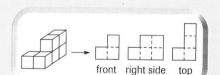

front   right side   top

P

parabola: A curve with a line of symmetry that is the graph of a quadratic equation in the form $y = ax^2 + bx + c$. **(110)**

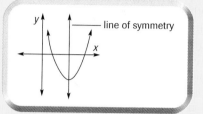

line of symmetry

paragraph proof: A type of proof written in paragraph form. **(044)**

parallel (∥): In Euclidean geometry, always the same distance apart. Parallel lines lie in the same plane and do not intersect. Parallel planes never intersect. **(052)**

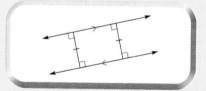

parallelepiped: A polyhedron with faces and bases that are parallelograms. **(326)**

parallelogram: A quadrilateral in which both pairs of opposite sides are parallel. **(157)**

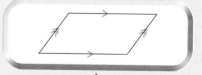

pattern: A design or sequence that is predictable because some aspect of it repeats.

pentagon: A polygon with five sides.

perimeter: (P): The distance around a figure. **(170)**

perpendicular: (⊥): Intersecting to form right angles. **(056)**

perpendicular bisector: A line, line segment, ray, or plane that is perpendicular to a segment at its midpoint. A perpendicular bisector of a triangle is perpendicular to and bisects one side. **(056)**

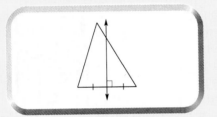

pi (π): A constant representing the ratio of the circumference of a circle to its diameter. The number π is irrational. The Greek letter π is lowercase. The upper case form is Π. Common approximations for π are $\frac{22}{7}$, 3.14, and 3.1416. **(174)**

plane: A flat surface with infinite length and width but no thickness. **(049)**

plane angle: An angle formed by slicing a dihedral angle perpendicular to the line of intersection of the two planes. **(081)**

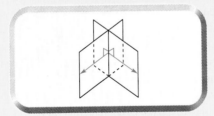

plane divider: A line that divides a plane.

plane figure: Any figure completely contained in a plane. Angles, polygons, circles, and arcs are plane figures.

Platonic solid: A polyhedron whose faces are regular congruent polygons with the same number of edges meeting at each vertex. There are five Platonic solids. *See also regular* **(324)**

plot a point: Locate a point on the coordinate plane or three-dimensional system using an ordered pair or ordered triple. **(088)**

point: An exact location in space. **(048)**

point of concurrency: The point of intersection of three or more lines. **(135)**

point of tangency: The point at which a tangent intersects a circle or the intersection of two circles. A radius to this point is perpendicular to the tangent. **(301)**

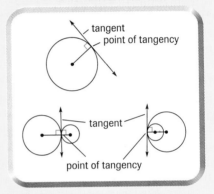

point-slope form: A form of a linear equation, $y - y_1 = m(x - x_1)$, where m is the slope of the line and (x_1, y_1) is a point on the line. **(105)**

point symmetry: *See rotational symmetry*

polar axis: In a polar coordinate system, the fixed ray. *See also polar coordinate system* **(117)**

polar coordinates: A pair of values that describes the location of a point in a polar coordinate system. The coordinates are (r, θ), where r is the distance of the point from the origin and θ is the measure of the angle between the polar axis and the ray extending from the origin through the given point. *See also polar coordinate system* **(117)**

polar coordinate system: A system for locating a point in a plane by its distance from the origin and the measure of the angle between the polar axis and the ray extending from the origin through the given point. **(118)**

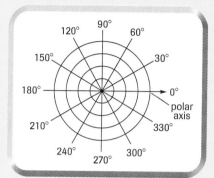

polar points: In spherical geometry, the endpoints of the diameter of a sphere. **(365)**

pole: In a polar coordinate system, the endpoint of the polar axis. Analogous to the origin in a coordinate plane. **(117)**

polygon: A closed, plane figure formed by line segments that meet only at their endpoints. **(128)**

polyhedra: One way to write the plural of *polyhedron*.

polyhedron: A solid bounded by polygons that enclose a single region of space. **(322)**

polynomial: The sum of numbers, variables, products, and quotients. $18r^4 + 9r^2 + \frac{r}{3} + 6$ is a polynomial.

postulate: A statement that is accepted as true. **(019)**

power: A number expressed as a repeated factor using a base and an exponent. The exponent tells the number of times the base is used as a factor. 3^4 is read *the fourth power of three* or *three to the fourth power*.

precision: An indication of how finely a measurement was made. When you calculate with measured values, you may need to round to the smallest place in the roughest actual measurements. Suppose you ride 62.5 miles in 6.0 hours. Divide to find the hourly rate. A calculator will show the result, 10.41666667. Since the original measurements were in tenths of an hour and tenths of a mile, the hourly rate is precise only to the tenths place, 10.4 miles per hour.

preimage: The original figure in a transformation. $\triangle ABC$ is the preimage of $\triangle A'B'C'$. *See also image* **(274)**

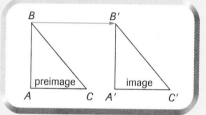

prism: A polyhedron that has two congruent and parallel faces called bases joined by faces that are parallelograms. **(326)**

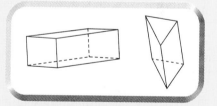

prismoid: A polyhedron that has two parallel bases that are not necessarily congruent. **(329)**

probability: The measure of the likelihood of an event occurring.

projective geometry: The study of the properties of a three-dimensional figure that remain unchanged when it is projected onto a plane.

proof: A logical argument that shows why a statement must be true. **(001)**

proof by contradiction: *See indirect proof*

properties: Attributes.

proportion: An equation showing that two ratios are equivalent. **(213)**

proportional: Having equivalent ratios. **(220)**

protractor: A tool used to measure angles. **(064)**

pyramid: A polyhedron with three or more triangular faces that meet at a point and one other face, a polygon, that is called the base. **(327)**

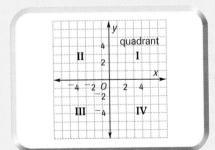

Pythagorean triple: A set of three positive integers that make the statement $a^2 + b^2 = c^2$ true. 3, 4, 5 is an example of a Pythagorean triple. **(153)**

Q

quadrant: One of the four sections into which the coordinate plane is divided by the x- and y-axes. The quadrants are numbered I, II, III, and IV counterclockwise starting in the upper right quadrant. **(087)**

quadratic equation: A polynomial equation of degree two. **(110)**

quadrilateral: A polygon with four sides. **(156)**

R

radian: A unit of angle-measure. $180° = \pi$ radians; one radian is about $57°$. **(242)**

radical ($\sqrt{\ }$): The symbol used to indicate a root.

radii: The plural of *radius*.

radius (r): (1) A segment or distance from the center of a circle to a point on the circle. **(305)**
(2) The segment or distance from the center to the edge of each base of a cylinder. **(330)**
(3) A segment or distance from the center of a sphere to a point on the sphere. **(332)**

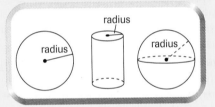

(4) The segment or distance from the center of a regular polygon to a vertex.

rate: A ratio that compares two quantities that have different units. Miles per hour is a rate. **(217)**

ratio: A comparison of two or more numbers using division. **(214)**

ray ($\rightarrow$): A part of a line that has one endpoint and goes on infinitely in one direction. **(052)**

rationalizing the denominator: Rewriting an expression so that there is no radical in the denominator.

$$10\sqrt{2} = \frac{10}{\sqrt{2}} \cdot \frac{\sqrt{2}}{\sqrt{2}}$$
$$= \frac{10\sqrt{2}}{2}$$
$$= 5\sqrt{2}$$ **(238)**

rectangle: A parallelogram with four right angles. **(162)**

rectangular prism: A prism whose bases are rectangles. **(326)**

rectangular pyramid: A pyramid whose base is a rectangle.

reduction: A dilation in which the scale factor, or size change, is greater than 0 but less than 1. **(292)**

reference angle: The acute angle being referred to in a trigonometric ratio. In $\sin A = 0.5$, A is the reference angle.

reflection: A transformation in which a figure is flipped over a line called the line of reflection. All corresponding points in the image and preimage are equidistant from the line of reflection. $\triangle K'L'M'$ is a reflection of $\triangle KLM$ over line ℓ. **(275)**

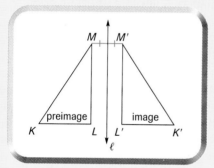

Reflexive Property: (1) A value is equal to itself, $a = a$. (2) An object is congruent to itself, $A \cong A$. **(034)**

region: A part of a plane or space.

regular: Having all examples of each attribute equal or congruent. A regular polygon has all sides congruent and all angles congruent. In a regular prism, all faces are regular congruent polygons, and the same number of edges meet at each vertex. The base of a regular prism or pyramid is a regular polygon. **(129)**

regular tessellation: A tessellation composed of congruent images of one regular polygon. *See also tessellation* **(296)**

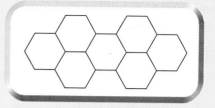

relation: A set of ordered pairs (x, y). The set of ordered pairs for a relation between age and grade in school may be $(15, 10)$, $(15, 11)$, $(16, 11)$, and $(14, 10)$. **(116)**

remote: Nonadjacent.

revolution: A 360° turn about a point.

rhombi: The plural of *rhombus*.

rhombus: A parallelogram with four congruent sides. **(063)**

right (⌐): Relating to 90°. (1) A right angle has a measure of 90°. **(066)** (2) A right triangle has one interior angle that measures exactly 90°. **(134)** (3) In a right cone or pyramid, the altitude (a perpendicular segment) intersects the base at its center. **(327)**

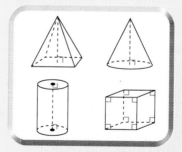

(4) In a right cylinder, a segment joining the centers of the bases is perpendicular to each base. **(330)** (5) The lateral edges of a right prism are perpendicular to its bases. **(326)**

right-angle method: A technique for locating the center of a circle. **(318)**

rigid transformation: *See isometry*

rise: The change in y-values between two points in the graph of a line. The rise is $1 - {}^-2$, or 3. *See also run* **(099)**

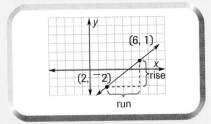

root: The inverse of a power. For $3^2 = 9$ or $\sqrt{9} = 3$, 3 is the second root, or square root of 9. **(421)**

rotation: A transformation. The image is formed by turning its preimage about a point. $\triangle K'L'M'$ is the result of rotating $\triangle KLM$ 90° about point P. **(281)**

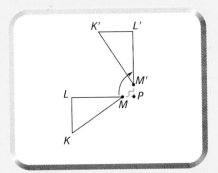

rotation-symmetric: A figure that maps onto itself after a rotation. *See also rotational symmetry* **(285)**

rotational symmetry: A property of a figure that is mapped onto itself by a rotation of 180° or less. A parallelogram has rotational symmetry. **(285)**

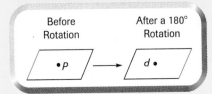

Before Rotation — After a 180° Rotation

rubric: A detailed explanation of how a piece of work will be evaluated or scored. **(406)**

run: The change in x-values between two points in the graph of a line. The run is $6 - 2$, or 4. *See also rise* **(099)**

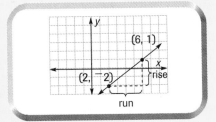

S

same-side exterior angles: When a transversal intersects two lines, same-side exterior angles are on the same side of the transversal and on the outside of the given lines. $\angle 1$ and $\angle 8$ are same-side exterior angles. So are $\angle 2$ and $\angle 7$. **(074)**

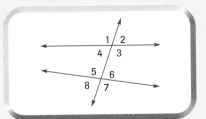

same-side interior angles: When a transversal intersects two lines, same-side interior angles are on the same side of the transversal and on the inside of the given lines. $\angle 4$ and $\angle 5$ are same-side interior angles. So are $\angle 3$ and $\angle 6$. **(074)**

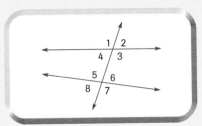

scale: The ratio of length in a model or drawing to the corresponding length in the actual object or region. **(221)**

scale factor (k): In a dilation, the ratio of the length of a segment in the preimage to the length of the corresponding segment in the image. **(222)**

scalene triangle: A triangle that has no congruent sides. **(134)**

secant: (1) The inverse of the cosine function. **(241)**
(2) A line that intersects a circle in two points. **(305)**

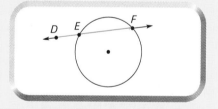

secant segment: A segment that is on a secant. DF is a secant segment. DE is outside of the circle, so it is an external secant segment. **(308)**

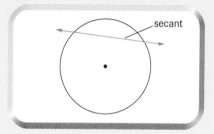

sector of a circle: The region bounded by two radii of the circle and the arc they intercept. **(191)**

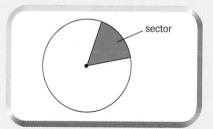

segment of a circle: The region bounded by a chord and the minor arc it intercepts. **(191)**

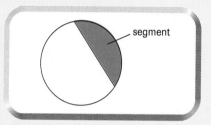

self-similarity: The property of an object, like a fractal, which makes a part of the object similar to other parts and to the whole object. **(254)**

semicircle: An arc whose endpoints are the endpoints of the diameter of the circle. $\widehat{PQR}$ is a semicircle. So is $\widehat{PSR}$. **(310)**

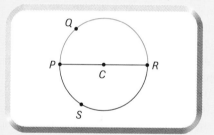

semiperimeter: One half the perimeter of a polygon. **(182)**

semiregular polyhedron: *See Archimedean solid*

semiregular tessellation: A tessellation composed of congruent images of more than one regular polygon which meet in the same order at each vertex. **(296)**

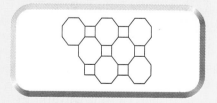

short radius: See *apothem*

side: (1) One of the line segments that form a polygon. **(128)**
(2) One of the rays that form an angle.
(3) Sometimes, a face of a polyhedron.

similar (~): Having exactly the same shape, but not necessarily the same size.
(1) Similar plane figures have proportional corresponding sides and congruent corresponding angles. **(212)**

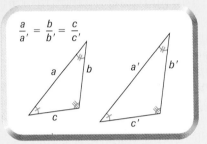

$$\frac{a}{a'} = \frac{b}{b'} = \frac{c}{c'}$$

(2) Similar solids have proportional corresponding linear measures, such as length and height.

similarity ratio: The ratio of the lengths of corresponding sides of similar polygons or polyhedrons. **(222)**

sine (sin): In a right triangle, the ratio of the length of the leg opposite the reference angle to the length of the hypotenuse. $\sin A = \frac{3}{5} = 0.6$. **(241)**

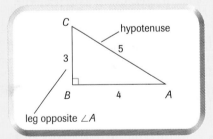

leg opposite ∠A

size change: *See scale factor*

skew lines: Non-coplanar lines that do not intersect. **(052)**

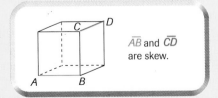

$\overline{AB}$ and $\overline{CD}$ are skew.

slant height: (1) The length of a segment from the vertex to the lateral edge of a right cone. (2) The length of a lateral edge of an oblique prism. (3) The height of any lateral face of a regular pyramid. **(327)**

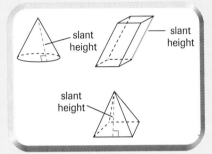

slant height

slant height

slant height

slide: *See translation*

slide arrow: A vector that shows the distance and direction of a translation. **(286)**

slope (m): The ratio of the rate of change in y with respect to a change in x. Slope measures the steepness of a line as you look at it from left to right. The slope is $\frac{1 - -2}{6 - 3} = \frac{3}{3} = 1$. *See also rise, run* **(098)**

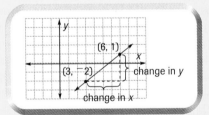

slope-intercept form: A form of a linear equation, $y = mx + b$, where m is the slope of the line and b is the y-intercept. **(103)**

snub: Having a rounded shape. **(325)**

solid: A figure that encloses a region of space. **(321)**

solid figure: *See solid*

solution: Any value for a variable that makes an equation or inequality true.

space figure: *See solid figure*

sphere: All points in space equidistant from a given point. **(332)**

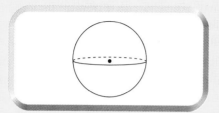

spherical coordinates: The real numbers used to identify the location of a point in three-dimensional space. **(367)**

spherical geometry: The geometric system generated when the parallel postulate says *through a given point there are no lines parallel to a given line.* **(365)**

square: A parallelogram with four congruent sides and four right angles. **(164)**

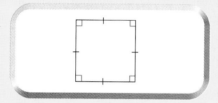

square unit: A unit, such as a square meter (m^2) or a square foot (ft^2), used to measure area. **(178)**

straight angle: An angle with a measure of 180°. **(066)**

straightedge: A tool used to draw straight lines. **(372)**

strip pattern: *See frieze pattern*

Substitution Property of Equality: For all real numbers a and b, if $a = b$, then a can be replaced by b in any equation or expression. **(037)**

Subtraction Property of Equality: For all real numbers a, b, and c, if $a = b$, then $a - c = b - c$. **(030)**

sufficient condition: A condition whose truth is enough to be sure a statement is true. Being a square is a sufficient condition for a figure to be a quadrilateral. **(008)**

supplement: An angle whose measure along with the measure of another angle has the sum of 180°. An angle whose measure is 110° is the supplement of a 70° angle. **(069)**

supplementary angles: Two angles with measures whose sum is 180°. **(069)**

surface area: The sum of the areas of the faces and any curved surfaces of a solid. **(195)**

symbol: A sign used to represent something, such as an operation, quantity, or relation. **(477)**

symmetric: Having symmetry. *See also line symmetry and rotational symmetry*

Symmetric Property: If $a = b$, then $b = a$. If $A \cong B$, then $B \cong A$. **(035)**

symmetry: A figure has symmetry if a reflection or rotation maps it onto itself. *See also line symmetry and rotational symmetry*

system of equations: Two or more equations related to the same situation. **(097)**

tangent (tan): (1) In a right triangle, the ratio of the length of the leg opposite the reference angle to the length of the leg adjacent to the given angle. $\tan A = \frac{3}{4} = 0.75$. **(241)**

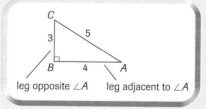

leg opposite $\angle A$ leg adjacent to $\angle A$

(2) A line in the plane of a circle that intersects the circle in exactly one point. **(305)**

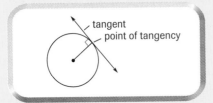

tangent
point of tangency

tangent circles: Coplanar circles that intersect in exactly one point. **(301)**

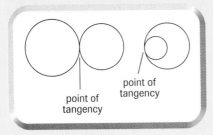

point of tangency
point of tangency

tangent line: *See tangent*

tangent segment: A segment drawn from a point external to a circle, tangent to the circle at its other endpoint. $\overline{AB}$ is tangent to circle C at point B. **(308)**

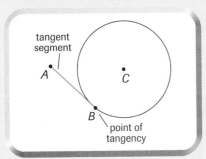

tangent segment
A
C
B
point of tangency

terminal point of a vector: The ending point of a vector, signified by an arrowhead. **(289)**

terms of a proportion: Each element of a proportion is a term. In $3:7 = 15:35$, 3, 7, 15, and 35 are terms. *See also means of a proportion and extremes of a proportion* **(219)**

tessellation: The complete covering of a plane with a repeating pattern of figures so that no gaps or overlaps occur. *See also regular tessellation, semiregular tesselation* **(296)**

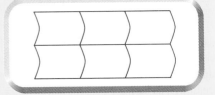

tetrahedron: A polyhedron with four faces.

theorem: A mathematical statement that can be shown to be true based on postulates, definitions, or other proven theorems. **(020)**

three-dimensional coordinate system: A system of locating a point in space by its distance from the origin along three mutually perpendicular lines called the x-, y-, and z-axes. **(121)**

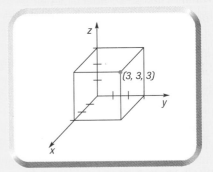

z
$(3, 3, 3)$
y
x

tiling: *See tessellation*

topologically equivalent: If a figure can be bent, stretched, or compressed without cutting to form another figure, the figures are topologically equivalent. **(083)**

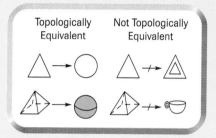

Topologically Equivalent Not Topologically Equivalent

topology: The branch of geometry that studies the properties of a figure that remain unchanged when the figure is distorted. **(083)**

torus: A donut-shaped three-dimensional figure.

traceable network: A network in which you can begin at one node and move along to all other nodes by tracing each edge exactly once. **(084)**

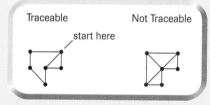

Traceable Not Traceable

start here

transformation: An operation that creates an image from an original figure, or preimage. Reflections, rotations, translations, and dilations are transformations. **(274)**

transformation image: *See image*

Transitive Property: (1) If $a = b$ and $b = c$, then $a = c$. **(036)**
(2) If $A \cong B$ and $B \cong C$, then $A \cong C$. **(258)**
(3) In the same plane, if $\ell_1 \parallel \ell_2$, and $\ell_2 \parallel \ell_3$, then $\ell_1 \parallel \ell_3$. **(060)**

translation: A transformation in which an image is formed by moving every point on a figure the same distance in the same direction. $\triangle K'L'M'$ is the translation image of $\triangle KLM$. **(286)**

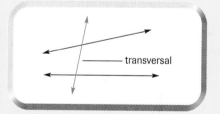

transversal: A line that intersects two or more other lines at different points. **(074)**

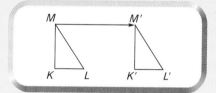

transversal

trapezium: A quadrilateral with no parallel sides. **(156)**

trapezoid: (1) A quadrilateral with exactly one pair of parallel sides. **(165)**
(2) Alternate definition: A quadrilateral with at least one pair of parallel sides.

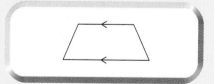

triangle: A polygon with three sides. **(134)**

triangular prism: A prism whose bases are congruent triangles.

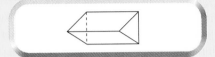

triangular pyramid: A pyramid whose base is a triangle.

trigonometric functions: *See trigonometric ratios*

trigonometric ratios: Ratios that compare the lengths of two sides of a right triangle. *See also sine, cosine, tangent* **(241)**

trigonometry: The branch of mathematics based on properties of right triangles. **(240)**

truncate: (1) To cut off part of a geometric figure. **(325)**

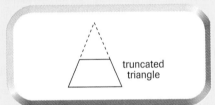

truncated triangle

(2) To ignore (as opposed to round) decimal digits. 0.777 rounds to 0.78 but truncates to 0.77.

truth table: A table in which the truth values of each part of a statement and of the whole statement is recorded. **(015)**

truth value: The truth or falseness of a statement. **(015)**

turn: *See rotation*

turn center: *See center of rotation*

turn symmetry: *See rotational symmetry*

two-column proof: A type of proof consisting of ordered statements in one column and the corresponding reasons in the other column. **(041)**

U

unit: A precisely fixed quantity used to count or measure.

unit cube: A cube whose edges are all one unit long. **(205)**

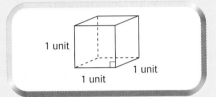

unit circle: A circle whose radius is one unit and whose center is at the origin of a coordinate plane. **(115)**

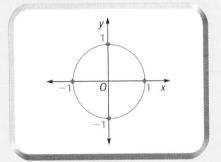

unit rate: A rate in which the second part is one unit. 60 miles per hour, or 60 miles:1 hour, is a unit rate. **(217)**

upper bound: In a set of numbers, a number greater than or equal to every other number in the set. **(111)**

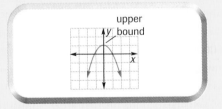

V

vector (→): A quantity that has direction and distance. **(289)**

vertex: (1) The common endpoint of the two rays that form an angle. **(062)**

(2) The point where two sides of a polygon intersect. **(128)**

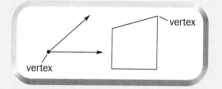

(3) The point opposite the base of a cone or pyramid. **(327)**

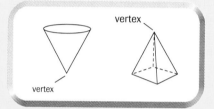

(4) A point where three or more edges of a polyhedron meet. **(322)**

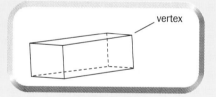

(5) The point where the line of symmetry intersects a parabola. **(111)**

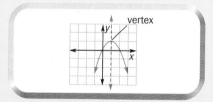

vertex angle of an isosceles triangle: The angle opposite the base of an isosceles triangle.

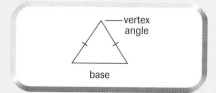

vertical: Perpendicular to the horizon. In a coordinate plane, the y-axis is a vertical line.

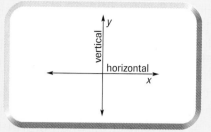

vertical angles: The non-adjacent angles formed by intersecting lines. Sometimes called opposite angles. Vertical angles are congruent. $\angle 1$ and $\angle 3$ are a pair of vertical angles. $\angle 2$ and $\angle 4$ are another pair. **(072)**

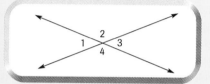

vertices: The plural of *vertex*.

volume (V): The amount of space occupied by a solid; measured in cubic units (units^3). **(205)**

 W

weight: A measure of the heaviness of, or the force of gravity on, an object.

 X

***x*-axis:** (1) The horizontal number line in the coordinate plane. **(088)**

(2) One of three mutually perpendicular number lines in a three-dimensional coordinate system. **(121)**

***x*-coordinate:** The value in an ordered pair or ordered triple that tells the distance from the origin in a direction parallel to the x-axis. In (6, ⁻3), 6 is the x-coordinate. **(087)**

x-intercept: The value of x in an ordered pair or ordered triple describing the point at which a line or graph of an equation intersects the x-axis. If a line intersects the x-axis at $(6, 0)$, the x-intercept is 6. **(106)**

xy-plane: The coordinate plane determined by the x- and y-axes in a three-dimensional coordinate system. **(121)**

xz-plane: The coordinate plane determined by the x- and z-axes in a three-dimensional coordinate system. **(121)**

y-axis: (1) The vertical number line on the coordinate plane. **(088)** (2) One of three mutually perpendicular number lines in a three-dimensional coordinate system. **(121)**

y-coordinate: The value in an ordered pair or ordered triple that tells the distance from the origin in direction parallel to the y-axis. In $(6, {}^-3)$, ${}^-3$ is the y-coordinate of a point. **(087)**

y-intercept: The value of y in an ordered pair or ordered triple describing the point at which a line or graph of an equation intersects the y-axis. If a line intersects the y-axis at $(0, 3\frac{1}{2})$, the y-intercept is $3\frac{1}{2}$. **(106)**

yz-plane: The coordinate plane determined by the y- and z-axes in a three-dimensional coordinate system. **(121)**

z-axis: One of three mutually perpendicular number lines in a three-dimensional coordinate system. **(121)**

z-coordinate: The value in an ordered triple that tells the distance from the origin in a direction parallel to the z-axis. In $(3, {}^-2, 4)$, 4 is the z-coordinate. **(121)**

z-intercept: The value of z in an ordered triple describing the point at which a line or graph of an equation intersects the z-axis. If a line intersects the z-axis at $(0, 0, 0.5)$, the z-intercept is 0.5. **(121)**

Glossary of Mathematical Symbols

Symbol	Meaning	Example
$=$	is equal to	$45 + 37 = 82$
$\neq$	is not equal to	$40 - 5 \neq 30$
$\approx$	is approximately	$\pi \approx 3.14$
$\cong$	is congruent to	$\overline{AB} \cong \overline{BC}$
$\sim$	is similar to *See also negation*	$ABCDE \sim FGHIJ$
$<$	is less than	$58 + 16 < 100$
$\leq$	is less than or equal to	$8.79 \leq 9$
$>$	is greater than	$5.24 > 5.1$
$\geq$	is greater than or equal to	$7.2 \geq 7.2$
$+$	plus (addition)	$5.9 + 8.4 = 14.3$
$^+$	positive	$^+24$ is the integer 24 units to the right of zero on a number line.
$-$	minus (subtraction)	$60.3 - 12.8 = 47.5$
$^-$	negative	$^-24$ is the integer 24 units to the left of zero on a number line.
$\times$, $\cdot$, $a(b)$, $*$	times (multiplied by)	$1.2 \times 7.5 = 9$; $6 \cdot 18 = 108$; $51(3) = 153$; $2 * 7 = 14$
$\div$, $\dfrac{a}{b}$	division	$8.1 \div 9 = 0.9$, $\dfrac{8.1}{9} = 0.9$
$\pm$	plus or minus	$a^2 = 4$ $a = \pm 2$
$()$	parentheses: used as grouping symbols	$(5 + 7) - 2 = 12 - 2$ $= 10$

Symbol	Meaning	Example
( )	parentheses: used to write an ordered pair or ordered triple	(2, ⁻5) is the point on the coordinate plane 2 units to the right of the y-axis and 5 units below the x-axis.
[ ]	brackets: used as grouping symbols	$3[(5 + 7) - 2] = 3[12 - 2]$ $= 3 \cdot 10$ $= 30$
$\begin{bmatrix} \\ \end{bmatrix}$	brackets: used to write a matrix	$\begin{bmatrix} 0 & 2 & 4 \\ 3 & 4 & 5 \end{bmatrix}$
{ }	braces: used as grouping symbols	$0.1\{[(5 + 7) - 2] \cdot 3\}$ $= 0.1\{[12 - 2] \cdot 3\}$ $= 0.1\{10 \cdot 3\}$ $= 0.1 \cdot 30$ $= 3$
{ }	braces: used to list elements of a set	{0, 1, 2, 3, 4, 5, 6, 7, 8, 9}
< >	brackets: used to write the component form of a vector	$\overrightarrow{AB} = <4, 2>$
%	percent	75%; 75 percent
:	to (ratio)	$9{:}11 = \frac{9}{11} = 9$ to 11
| |	absolute value	$\left\|⁻123\right\| = 123$ and $\left\|123\right\| = 123$
$5.\overline{12}$	repeating decimal	$5.\overline{12} = 5.121212\ldots$
a^n	using the number a as a factor n times	$2^6 = 2 \cdot 2 \cdot 2 \cdot 2 \cdot 2 \cdot 2$ $= 64$
$\sqrt{}$	principal square root	$\sqrt{144} = 12$
$\sqrt[3]{}$	cube root	$\sqrt[3]{64} = 4$
$\longleftrightarrow$	line	$\overleftrightarrow{CD}$
—	line segment	$\overline{ST}$
$\longrightarrow$	ray	$\overrightarrow{AB}$
$\longrightarrow$	vector AB Some books may use $\overline{AB}$ for $\overrightarrow{AB}$.	$\overrightarrow{AB}$

Symbol	Meaning	Example
⊥	is perpendicular to	$\overline{CD} \perp \overline{EF}$
‖	is parallel to	$\overline{QR} \parallel \overline{ST}$
⫽	lines with the same number of symbols are parallel	$\overline{QR} \parallel \overline{TS}$ $\overline{QR} \parallel \overline{RS}$
∠	angle	$\angle PQR$ or $\angle Q$ or $\angle 1$
∟	right angle	$\angle WXY$ is a right angle.
°	degree	The measure of a right angle is 90°.
ρ	rho: the first spherical coordinate; represents the distance from the origin to a given point	
ϕ	phi: the second spherical coordinate; represents the angle between the positive z-axis and a ray from the origin through a given point	

Symbol	Meaning	Example
θ	theta: The third spherical coordinate represents the angle formed by a projection of a given point onto the *xy*-plane.	
θ	theta: the angle measure in a pair of polar coordinates	For (3, 60°), θ = 60°.
△	triangle	△*LMN*
⊙	circle	⊙*A*
⌒	arc	$\overparen{JK}$
π	the ratio of the circumference of a circle to its diameter is π	The irrational number π ≈ 3.14159.
'	read *prime;* used to indicate an image.	*A'* is the image of point *A*.
∴	therefore	m∠*ABC* is 30° ∴ ∠*ABC* is an acute angle
→	conditional statement	*p* → *q* means *If p, then q.*
↔	biconditional statement	*p* ↔ *q* means *p if and only if q.*
~	negation *See also is similar to*	~*p* means *not p.*

This index contains topic numbers, not page numbers. You will find topic numbers at the top of each page and next to each new piece of information.

494

Illustration Credits

Part opener illustrations by Joe Spooner: pp. 001, 047, 086, 127, 168, 212, 255, 273, 297, 320, 339, 363

All remaining creative illustration: Rob Dunlavy: pp 004, 005, 049, 061, 073, 081, 084, 108, 110, 126, top and bottom, 133 top, 149, 152 156, 176, 178, 186, 191, 204, 208, 210, 215, 236, 239, 246, 253, 261 bottom, 277, 282, 286, 296, 300, 306, 322, 343, 345, 346, 348, 349, 350, 352, 358, 359, 360 top, 388, 399, 404, 406, 413, 415. **Bryan Thompson:** pp. 051, 058, 061, 067, 069, 075, 098, 113, 126 center, 133 bottom, 136, 164, 176, 177, 193, 197, 201, 203, 206, 209, 221, 238, 245, 246, 254, 258, 261 top, 276, 281, 292, 295, 301, 337, 343, 344, 347, 351, 354, 357, 360 bottom left; top and center right, 403.

Technical Art: Nesbitt Graphics, Inc.

Robot Characters: Bill SMITH STUDIO with Jon Conrad

Map Art: Joe Lemonnier: pp. 086, 117, 193, 306, 359, 364